EASTER ISLAND

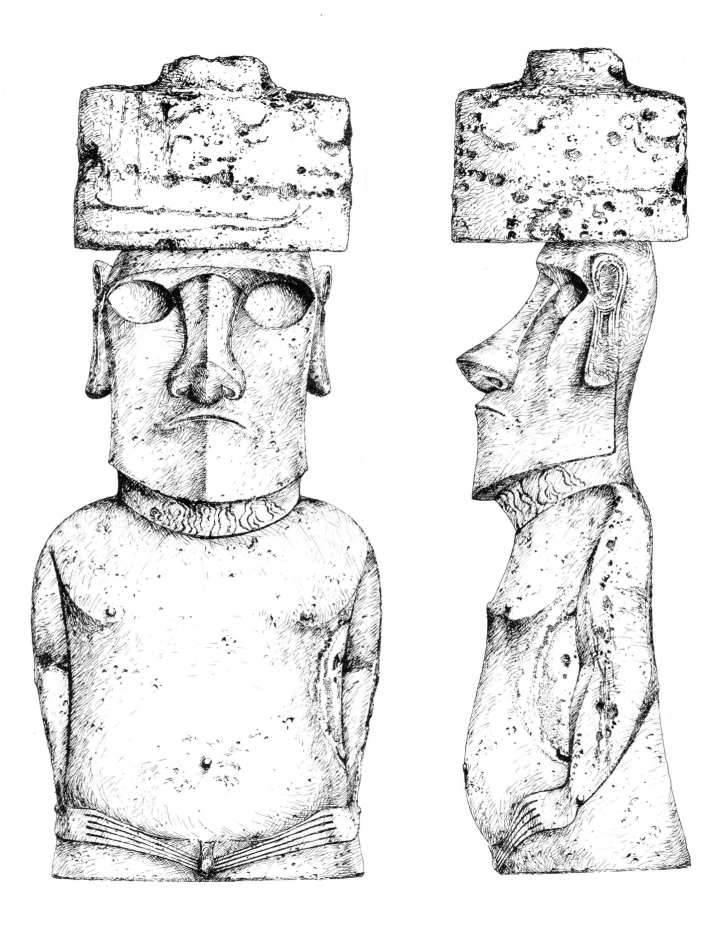

EASTER ISLAND

ARCHAEOLOGY, ECOLOGY AND CULTURE

Jo Anne Van Tilburg

BRITISH MUSEUM PRESS

This work is meant to mark the eightieth anniversary of the Mana *expedition to Easter Island, 1914–15, and to honour the memory of Katherine Scoresby Routledge, who, with her Rapa Nui collaborators, brought an educated, dedicated, creative and insightful intelligence to bear on 'the mystery of Easter Island'.*

The author and publishers gratefully acknowledge the support of the Foundation for Archaeology and Rock Art and the following sponsors:

Mr. James L. Amos
James L. Amos Photography, Inc.

Dr. and Mrs. Julius Bendat

Mr. Mark Benjamin
Benchmark Construction Company

Mr. and Mrs. Robert Ezrin

Mr. Abe Fassberg

Ms. Marty Gonzalez

Mr. and Mrs. Sheldon S. Gordon
The Gordon Company

Mr. Paul Keller
Keller Construction Company, Ltd

Mr. Russell Kord
Kord Photographics

Mr. and Mrs. Raymond J. Rutter
Caymen Development

Mr. Patrick Stewart

Rev. Lloyd Tupper
in memorium Robert A. Chapek

Mr. Johannes Van Tilburg
Johannes Van Tilburg and Partners
Architects, AIA, Inc.

Mr. and Mrs. Scott Watt
The Watt Companies

Front jacket: *Moai* of Rano Raraku glow in the warm rays of the setting sun.
Back jacket: The author placing photogrammetric grid on the Ahu Akivi statue which represents the statistically average *moai* on Rapa Nui.
Frontispiece: Conjectural reconstruction of *moai* from Ahu Vinapu (see fig. 92)

Published by British Museum Press
A division of British Museum Publications
46 Bloomsbury Street, London, WC1B 3QQ

British Library Cataloguing in Publication Data
A catalogue record for this book is available from the British Library

ISBN 0 7141 2504 0

Designed by Behram Kapadia
Typeset by Create Publishing Services Ltd, Bath
Printed by Bath Press Ltd

Contents

Foreword

The history of Easter Island (Rapa Nui) has often seemed the ultimate in entangled problems: as isolated a location as can be found, yet settled at some distant time by peoples whose achievements in terms of architecture and technology, not least monumental stone carving, have been startling. It has attracted intrepid modern voyagers seeking to recreate the original circumstances of supposed settlement. Technical experiment has tried to show how the famous massive stone figures produced there might originally have been moved and installed; and theoreticians have tackled an imagined scenario by which a once complex society of monument builders purportedly 'degenerated'. Presumptions about the original settlers of the island have intermingled with presumptions about the character of their descendants in ways which have only enhanced the apparent 'mystery'. The history of Easter Island has at times seemed as enigmatic as the riddles that once surrounded Great Zimbabwe or the monuments of Ancient Egypt.

Yet, as with other such mysteries, the process of enlightenment is often more cathartic than it is forensic. Demystification can come as much from purging inquiry of unwarranted assumption, as from the solution of a previously impenetrable problem by the brilliance of new insight. The process can be stimulated in part by giving, often for the first time, appropriate weight and authority to local indigenous perceptions. This book presents in an accessible and balanced way the results of more recent re-evaluation of this kind. And the realities that emerge are every bit as arresting as the 'mysteries' they succeed.

The author, Dr Van Tilburg, is a leading archaeologist with long experience of Easter Island. She has already published an authoritative study centred on the figure of Hoa Hakananai'a in the British Museum, discussing it in the context of museum examples elsewhere and their associated archaeological context (British Museum Occasional Papers No 73, 1992). She has also taken groups from the Museum to the island and explained its culture at first hand. That the Museum should publish this further, more general, review is additionally appropriate since it is now eighty years since the arrival of Mr. and Mrs. Scoresby Routledge in Easter Island, which they visited shortly before the First World War at the suggestion of British Museum curators. Mrs. Scoresby Routledge's book *The Mystery of Easter Island* appeared in 1919 and remains a much quoted and perceptive early source. We are pleased to be associated with a worthy successor.

JOHN MACK
Keeper of Ethnography
British Museum

Acknowledgements

My ability to compile these data and write this book is due to the people and institutions who have found value in it and supported it, and I am grateful to them all. Permission to conduct field work on Rapa Nui was first granted in 1982 by the Consejo de Monumentos and Claudio Cristino F., then director of the Centro de Estudios, Universidad de Chile, and as an Associate Investigator of the Moai Documentation Project begun by Patricia Vargas C. (now director of the Instituto de Estudios, Universidad de Chile) and Lilian González N. These scholars and the support staff of the Instituto de Estudios have been unfailingly gracious and helpful with statue site numbers and descriptions. Numerous of the island's various institutions and agencies graciously provided assistance in many ways, and I especially wish to thank Sr. Sergio Rapu H., former governor of the island; Sr. Javier Labra V., former provincial head of Corporación Nacional Forestal (CONAF) for permission to camp and work at Rano Raraku and Anakena and for staff support; Sr. José Miguel Ramírez A., current provincial head of CONAF for Rapa Nui; Sr. Claudio Gomez P. and Sra. Fermina Zamorano and staff of the Museo Antropológico R.P. Sebastián Englert, Rapa Nui who facilitated documentation of selected artefacts in the museum's collection.

Among my Rapa Nui colleagues and island friends I am indebted beyond measure to Felipe Teao A. and the late José Fati; special thanks to Raúl Paoa I. for field work in 1982 and follow-up work in 1983; to Cristián Arévalo Pakarati for field work almost continuously since 1989 and museum research in Santiago in 1991; to the late Amelia Tepano I. and Kiko Paté for information on the Poike sites; to Jacobo Riroroko T. for ethnographic information on domestic architecture; to Graciela Hucke Atan, Felicita Hucke de Mazuela, Maria Eugenia Hucke A., Nelson Mazuela, Elena Mazuela Hucke for logistic and moral support since 1983; to Rosita Cardinali, Nico Haoa and their family for steadfast friendship and expertise in nearly everything; to Oscar Tepano and Ana Tepano and her many lovely sisters, always but especially in 1983; to Upertina Pakarati and Ricardo Tuki for the use of their house in 1983; to the late father Dave Reddy, parish priest on Rapa Nui who provided me with his jeep in 1982 and radio contact with my family in Los Angeles; to Noemi Pakarati for help on the north coast survey in 1989; to Greg Sablic and Steven Pakarati Sablic at Hanga Tee and environs in 1982; to Luis Haoa P. at Vai Mata; to Alberto Ika A. at Rano Raraku, Anakena and Vai Tara Kai Ua; to Keremo Ika at Ahu Akivi; to the Hereveri family at Vai Atare in 1989; to the Robert Weber family and the children of Hanga Roa for enriching my daughter's (and our family's) life immensely; to Kenny Roloff for logistical assistance at Ahu Akivi in 1990.

The field work has been variously funded by University Research Expeditions Program (UREP), University of California, Berkeley (1983); UCLA Institute of Archaeology, Rock Art Archive and the National Geographic Society. For funding which allowed comparative research in the Republic of Belau (Palau), Micronesia in 1987 I wish to thank the School of the Pacific Islands, Inc. All of the UREP volunteers are greatly appreciated. Special thanks for field assistance are owed to Johannes Van Tilburg, Marty González, Ann Lockie, Lynn Lockie, Steve Williams, Valerie De Gier, Jim Heaton, Frank Bock, A.J. Bock and Jim Amos.

My thanks to UCLA Professor Emeritus Clement W.

Meighan for his unfailingly good guidance and support always. At UCLA Peter Christiansen accomplished statistical analyses required for statue type classifications and Robert Gregor advised on human work capacity for the transport study. Harrison Eiteljorg, II patiently taught me about photogrammetry. I am grateful to my colleagues in Rapa Nui archaeology and anthropology for discussions and input over the years on a variety of topics, especially Bill Ayres, Pat McCoy, Chris Stevenson, Georgia Lee and Joan T. Seaver Kurze. Various chapters or preliminary versions of this work were kindly read, critiqued or commented on by Dave Steadman, Adrienne Kaeppler, Roger Green, Ben Finney, Pat McCoy, Doug Owsley, Will Kyselka, Matt Spriggs, Zvi Shiller and Evan Haddingham. Their comments were noted or incorporated where appropriate, but none of the individuals mentioned here are in any way responsible or accountable for either content included, interpretations or errors made in this volume.

In the extensive museum work I have undertaken over the years I wish to thank, most especially, Dorota Starzecka and her staff and colleagues at the Museum of Mankind, British Museum; Dr. Adrienne Kaeppler and staff at the National Museum of Natural History, Smithsonian Institution, Washington, D.C.; Dr. Francina Forment at the Musées Royaux d'Art et d'Histoire, Brussels; Dr Dirk Smidt, Rijksmuseum voor Volkenkunde, Leiden; Mevr van Hof at the Koninklyke Biblioteek in The Hague, The Netherlands; Dña Eliana Duran Serrano at the Museo Nacional de Historia Natural, Santiago; Ms Linda Mowat, the late Bryan Cranstone and student volunteers at the Pitt Rivers Museum, Oxford; Martin Beckett at the Mitchell Library, Sydney; Gillian Scott at the Pacific Manuscripts Bureau, Canberra; Bryan Young at the Provincial Library, Victoria, British Columbia; Tony Han in the Anthropology Department, Marge Kemp and the photographic archives staff at the Bernice P. Bishop Museum, Honolulu; Martha Labell and Kathleen Skelly at Peabody Museum of Archaeology and Ethnology, Cambridge; Susan L. Meyn at the Cincinnati Museum of Natural History; Mrs Christine Kelly and Ms Rachel Duncan at the Royal Geographical Society, London; Gilles Artur at the Musée Gauguin in Papeete, Tahiti and H.P.S.M. van den Donk of the Zeeuws Museum, Middleburg, The Netherlands.

Some illustrations used in this volume and others solicited were kindly provided by the National Geographic Society, Ben Finney, Francisco Mellén-Blanco, Adrienne Kaeppler, Robert Fisher, Gonzalo Figueroa G-H, W.S. Ayres, Stanley D. Stevens, Patrick C. McCoy, E.N. Ferdon, Jr., Joan T. Seaver Kurze, Zvi Shiller, Jim Amos, the family of the late Lorenzo Dominguez, Ana Tepano, Graciela Hucke A., Juan Grau V., Corson Hirschfeld, David Steadman, Dick Murphy of the Cousteau Society, Pat Kirch, Matt Spriggs and Roger Green. Computer drafting of site maps and plans was accomplished by Gordon Hull and Curtiss H. Johnson with the assistance of Lucia Chang and Mike Ohara of Johannes Van Tilburg and Partners, AIA. Photographic filing and curation of field photos and negatives was organised by David C. Ochsner. Three-dimensional graphics used in the statue transport study were created by Satish Sundar and Mike Ohara. The scale model of the Ahu Akivi statue used in the same study was sculpted by Gary Lloyd with Bruce Yanomoto and Norman Yanomoto. Craig Cronenburg advised on computer modeling from the scale model.

I am grateful to Elizabeth King and Lucy Turner at British Museum Tours for the pleasure of collaboration with them over the past four years on organised journeys to Rapa Nui. These allowed me to follow-up on various details of field work but also introduced me to groups of wonderful and adventurous travellers. Finally and most especially, I wish to extend my deepest gratitude to Celia Clear of the British Museum Press, editor Carolyn Jones and book designer Behram Kapadia for their professional expertise, patience, fortitude, good ideas and sound advice.

A Note on Orthography

Variant spellings of the Polynesian name of Easter Island (which dates to *c.*1863) are common in the literature. Following Krupa, who reviews the problem of what constitutes a morpheme and defines word classes in Polynesian languages, I consider that capitalisation of the proper name Rapa and the adjective Nui forms the place name Rapa Nui.[1] This usage conforms with that of the University of Chile archaeological survey, most recent scientific literature in Spanish, and the majority of Chilean official maps and documents. It is widespread and current usage in both Spanish and English, and is the form preferred by the Rapa Nui people themselves.[2] When dealing specifically with the name of the language spoken by the Rapa Nui people, the form Rapanui is used. This is in accordance with the convention observed by most linguists. A precedent of sorts for allowing the two variant spellings exists in Hawaii (Hawai'i).[3]

Whenever possible, usage of Rapanui terms as place names follows the University of Chile maps. Some other names were provided to me by Rapa Nui colleagues, or are found in the existing literature, and there is an inconsistency of spelling and capitalisation in many cases. I have tried to resolve this as much as possible by writing these names to conform to my reading of the style used in the maps. Some archaeological sites have Rapanui names, while others are designated by the number of the quadrant first and then the number of the site. Statues are assigned figure numbers which are unique to each respective site except in Quadrants 3 and 13, where they are numbered consecutively. Museum statues are designated by a code defining their present location.

All Rapanui words are written exactly as they are encountered in the sources. This means that there is an inconsistent use of the glottal stop (') and hyphens. It was standard practice during much of the period when Polynesian ethnographies were being collected to insert hyphens between Polynesian words, but it is also now common to remove them. Unless, therefore, hyphenated words are included within a direct quote, I have removed the hyphens. Terms which are formed of repeated words, such as *rongorongo* or *kaikai*, are often written as *rongo rongo* or *kai kai* in the literature. My practice here has been to write each as a single word. Similarly, the Rapanui nasal *ng* is sometimes encountered or is more often written as simply *g*. I have not tried to seek conformity in this convention. The plural of Rapanui words is not formed by adding the letter 's'. The plurality of a noun is understood in the context of the English sentence. Spanish and Rapanui surnames include the father's last name followed by the mother's last name or initial.

Prologue

We never seem to leave early enough. It is September, and we are nearing the equinox, here where the Southern Hemisphere seasons are reversed for us. The weather has become steadily warmer, the days longer and less rainy than in July, when we began this season's field work. Still, out of habit, we stand on the front veranda of our rented Hanga Roa house and watch the constantly changing sky for a while before embarking on our day's work.

We load our gear into the Land Rover as it stands in front of the house, stacking camera and tripod cases, day packs, metre sticks, clip boards and recording forms in a routinely workable way. The vehicle is filthy, covered inside and out with the red dust of Easter Island's unpaved roads. The dust gets into everything. By the end of the day it will lie on our skin and in our hair, and sometimes the deepest pockets of our field jackets are filled with the annoying stuff. The tyres are bald and dangerous, and the radiator cap has long since been lost. Jan, my husband, cleverly cut the metal top of his Dutch tobacco tin into a new cap and fastened it on with wire. Each morning we check the radiator, always finding the brightly coloured and steadfast Dutch burghers still painted on the cap and the cap still in place. This invention of his has become something of a novelty over the past weeks, coveted by the Rapa Nui mechanics who service our vehicle.

David turns the car into the road and we drive slowly through the village, trying not to raise the dust in front of the open windows of our neighbours' houses. Stopping in front of Felipe Teao Arancibia's gate we find him ready and waiting, cheerful and talkative, even at this early hour. Felipe (called Hanihani) is well into his late sixties, bronzed skin stretched tight over the bones of his slender frame.

We've worked together for several field seasons, and know each other well. The first thing he does is ask David for a cigarette or some pipe tobacco. He sits back and draws deeply, launching into a long and apparently amusing story in Rapanui to Raúl.

The road from Hanga Roa to the *campo* (countryside) is always empty this early in the morning, and it's impossible to talk over the sound of the engine and the rush of wind through the open windows. As we turn to run east along the coast we can see the soundless, breaking waves rolling against the distant shore line. The long, blond grass is profusely dotted with sunshine yellow dandelion flowers, and David reminds us again of what fine wine we could make if only we would all just turn to and gather zillions of the plants. Falcons sit on fence posts and wrens flit amidst the grass. Suddenly, David stops the car and we all gaze in silence at two lanky, graceful, pure white cattle egrets as they gingerly pick their way through the stones at the side of the dusty road. They're oblivious to us, and we sit for many minutes as they stroll along and then, finally, take graceful wing. These egrets are new to the island, blown here by some distant storm, and the Rapa Nui always quietly catch their breaths when they first see them.

Today we're working inland, walking many kilometres in search of *moai* (statues) lying abandoned 'in transport'. Felipe knows where some of them are, as well as the shortest route to reach them. Suddenly, he reaches forward and taps David on the shoulder, telling him to stop, *aquí, ahora*. David pulls the car off the road and we all pile out, stretching, to load up our gear. We check the map and then look up to see Felipe already ahead of us, moving through the long grass. It's easiest to follow in his footsteps over the rough terrain, so we hurry to catch up with him. We each have our own packs, and Jan carries some of David's equipment. I have his tripod on my shoulder.

Raúl and Felipe always prefer to work the coast, with the fresh sea breeze blowing. Inland, the ground is rough and rock strewn, and sometimes the air is heavy with flies. I have been here in February when the sun is beastly hot and there isn't a breath of air. Today it's still comfortable, and we follow Felipe at a good pace. Occasionally we startle nesting partridges which then spin angrily and noisily into the air in a whirl of wings and feathers, causing us to jump in the morning silence. Just as we come up over a small rise we see the *moai*, lying on its back in front of us. It's about 9 m long and very dark brown.

We have been doing this work together for so long that we have a system of approaching it, a manner of working which suits us all very well. First we all have a good look at the statue and the environs, walking around and observing everything. David sets up his cameras and takes out his recording forms. Jan, Felipe and I take all of the statue's measurements in sequence, being careful to note anomalies in the form. Raúl begins to sketch the statue, and Jan and I map the site and its associations. We crawl around, pushing the grass back and brushing the nests of black widow spiders out of the statue's eyes and ears. I fill pages in my field book with observations and comparative references to other, similar sites.

Our afternoon unfolds in much the same way as the morning. It is satisfyingly productive, and I like the feel of the field book in my hand as it fills up with notes and numbers. Today we've hiked miles, and I've 'collected' five more of these incredible *moai*. They dangle in my mind like charms on the bracelet of an ancient giantess. All of their 'vital statistics' are now neatly recorded on my forms and in our photos, maps and drawings, safely tucked in our packs. There is more to learn from them, but the sun is low in the sky. We decide it's time to head back to the road and load up our gear, walking again behind Felipe and trusting to his unerring sense of direction. We stop occasionally along the way to pick some guava. If it were my choice, I would head off slightly more to the west, but Felipe is adamant and, in the end, quite right. His way turns out, to no one's surprise, to be the shorter route.

And so ends our day in the field. Some seasons we camped in Rano Raraku quarry, and at other times at Anakena, returning to the village on the weekends. Graciela Hucke [Huki] Atan, or sometimes her sister Felicita Hucke de Mazuela, cooked for us when we were in the *campo*, and we always enjoyed freshly caught fish. I loved camping and being away from the distractions of the village, and we always got a lot of work done at those times.

Often we have worked in unfavourable weather, fighting rain and wind. Instead of using our vehicle we have sometimes had to depend upon Rapa Nui's recalcitrant horses to get us to where we have to go.

Over the years, new people have joined our effort. In Felipe's absence, the late José Fati P. occasionally joined us.[1] Raúl Paoa Ika left the island to travel first to California and then to Kansas City, Missouri, where he studied at the Kansas City Art Institute. In his place, a remarkable young Rapa Nui man named Cristián Arévalo Pakarati joined us. Cristián is a gifted artist, sensitive to the changing currents of his island culture and vitally interested in learning about its past. He is the nephew of Leonardo Pakarati R. and the grandson of the late Amelia Tepano Ika. Cristián's mother's maternal grandfather was Juan Tepano Huki. Her paternal grandfather was Nicholás Pakarati Urepotahi, one of the first Rapa Nui catechists. Cristián's skill and dedication are a major contribution to my work and this project, and he carries on the venerable Rapa Nui tradition of scholarship exemplified by generations of his family and the ancient institutions of an especially artistic culture.

The architectural talents of my husband, Johannes (Jan) Van Tilburg FAIA, who participated in the field work at the very inception of the project and continues always as critic and steadfast ally, have been invaluable, and he has had an influence on my understanding of architectural design and construction procedures. He and his colleagues and staff at Johannes Van Tilburg and Partners, AIA are a valuable source of expertise in graphics, computer modelling and a host of other areas. When he is not able to be with us, another talented architect, Curtiss H. Johnson, has ably contributed his skill. The computer analyses of statistical data which Gordon Hull has tirelessly worked to achieve have been equally helpful, and he has taught me a great deal about a subject that still seems like *rongorongo* sometimes. David Ochsner is more than a photographer, he is a philosopher and a good companion, a man of endless patience and good humour. His work in the field and in creating photographic files has been invaluable.

Much of the success of my work is due to the unfailing devotion of the intrepid Graciela Hucke A. Since 1982 she has seen me through every crisis, organised every household, cooked every meal and, in every way, extended herself to make me and my crew feel at home. When we wanted to do aerial reconnaissance, it was Graciela who used her contacts with the Chilean Air Force to arrange it. When we needed a vehicle repaired, it was Graciela who found the proper mechanic. She worked all day every day, well into the night, and then raised her powerful voice in song at Sunday mass. Through her, the entire Hucke family has become a major support system for me when I'm on the island.

Like so many other working mothers, I struggle to combine my family and my work. Our daughter, Marieka, beginning at the age of eight, has been with me in the field during several seasons, and it was not always easy for her. Through her own strength and the help of other mothers on the island her sojourns there are now, in large part, happy memories. Over the course of five years, Felicita's daughter Elena lived with us in California, where she attended and graduated from Santa Monica High School. I like to think that through the familial support we Van Tilburgs have extended to Elena as her *matua hangai* (adoptive parents) I have, in some small way, expressed my gratitude to the Hucke women for their friendship.

John Terrell reports that a famous quote by the great physicist William Thomson (Lord Kelvin) is usually paraphrased as: 'Unless you have measured it, you don't know what you are talking about'.[2] While such an idea was obviously not originally applied to Easter Island, I find it expressive of how I feel about the many generalities and simplistic characterisations which are often stated about the statues. What I have learned from taking the measure of the *moai* in the field is that each statue is unique, each varies from the others in some way which speaks aloud of the individuality of the human creative hand. Words such as 'standardised' or 'mass produced' are often used in connection with the statues and the statue 'industry', but our work seeks the human dimension and detail evident in each object. That dimension, as this work reveals, is assuredly present.

These pages hold as many questions as they do answers, and there is no pretence to 'solving' the 'mystery' of Easter Island, however that 'mystery' is defined. As the great scholar Sir J.G. Frazer stated in the preface to his anthropological classic *The Golden Bough*, I am aware of, and familiar with, the 'hydra of error' which may spring from, or be inherent in, a work such as this.[3] I can only say that I am reasonably certain, given my own limitations, of my data. Whether the interpretations I offer of those data are correct or not remains to be determined by time, further research, and the informed evaluation of my colleagues in Polynesian studies. The essence of science is the question, not the answer, and I expect that my thinking on the subject of the *moai* as the significant shaping force of Rapa Nui history will continue to evolve over time and through fresh insight.

Most importantly, I mean this work to acknowledge the Rapa Nui people, past and present, who have participated so fully in recording and interpreting their own culture. I wish to put names to the faces, living and dead, who, too often, are anonymous in the pages written by Western scientists and historians. In the process, my hope is to share with my readers the sheer joy I have experienced through this work and these people on Rapa Nui, one of the world's most special islands.

In the Wake of the Mana

It is not a beautiful country nor even a striking one, but it has a fascination of its own . . . from every part are seen marvellous views of rolling country; everywhere is the wind of heaven; around and above all are boundless sea and sky, infinite space and a great silence.

KATHERINE SCORESBY ROUTLEDGE Ethnographer

The Routledge Expedition

The *Mana*, a custom designed schooner of 90 feet (30 m) overall length and 126 yacht tonnage, was about the size of Sir Francis Drake's famous *Golden Hinde* (fig. 1). The keel was laid in the autumn of 1911, at Whitstable, and in 1912 she was christened by Katherine Scoresby Routledge (née Pease) with the words, 'I name this ship *Mana*, and may the blessing of God go with her and all who sail with her'.[1] She sailed from Falmouth Harbour on 25 March, 1913, beginning the first leg of an historic journey to the Pacific and Rapa Nui. Aboard the vessel was a complement of ten, including the scientific party and members of the ship's crew. William Scoresby Routledge, Katherine's husband, was official master, while H.J. Gillam was sailing master.

In the tense atmosphere which preceded World War I, the Routledges sought an adventure. The decision to mount an expedition to Easter Island, a territory of Chile, was made at the suggestion of British Museum scholars, who responded to William's inquiries about what work remained to be done in the Pacific.[2] Initially, Katherine and her husband had wanted to sail tranquil, tropical seas, and were unsure about their ability to undertake investigations on what was, even then, one of the most famous islands in the world. In addition, the logistics of the voyage were daunting. Letters and other Routledge papers in the archives of the Royal Geographical Society, London, reveal a deep vein of self-doubt embedded in Katherine's extensive consideration of and preparation for the project.

In reality, however, the Routledges were surprisingly well-qualified to undertake the adventure of Easter Island exploration. Theirs was a unique partnership, a symbiotic and complex relationship about which little of a personal nature is known. William Scoresby Routledge, while not anonymous in the paper trail which documents his career in Easter Island studies, makes his presence felt mostly through the work he did as draughtsman, surveyor and collector of ethnographica. It is Katherine's voice, in her journals, field books and letters, which speaks to us through time with the most resonant timbre. It is her perception of Easter Island, its people and its past, which we recognize and identify by its unique and distinctive character, rising above the cacophony of sound which has swirled and eddied around Easter Island since its 'discovery' by the Dutch in 1722.

Both Katherine and her husband were well-educated and well-to-do products of the Victorian and Edwardian eras. William Scoresby Routledge was born in 1883 and named after a family friend, one Dr. Scoresby, who was an Arctic explorer. William held an MA degree from Christ Church, Oxford, and then took a degree in medicine, but also had a keen interest in the out-of-doors, faraway places and the sea. He was restless and inquisitive, travelling to India and Labrador, sailing extensively and then yielding to the 'magnetic attraction of Africa', settling in Nyeri, East Africa, in 1902.[3] In 1904 he was again in England, studying geodetic surveying at Oxford. In that year, he married Katherine Pease.

Katherine Maria Fell Pease was born to Mr. and Mrs. Gurney Pease, a well-known Quaker family in the north of England, in 1880. She was a student at Somerville College, Oxford, from 1891 to 1895, 'at which time women were not members of the University and could not take the degrees for which they qualified'.[4] Her field of study was history, in

1 Katherine and William Scoresby Routledge's yacht *Mana* off an unknown coast. *Courtesy of the Museum of Mankind, British Museum.*

which she achieved honours, and in 1906 she availed herself of the opportunity to claim an *ad eundem* M.A. degree from Trinity College, Dublin.

Colleagues and mentors who were significant throughout Katherine's academic and scientific career included some of the era's most accomplished scholars in Polynesian and Oceanic studies, and she corresponded frequently on academic and other matters with A.C. Haddon, W.H.R. Rivers and B.G. Corney.[5] Each of these individuals lent their names or provided contacts to the Routledges during their initial efforts to finance the construction of the *Mana* and fund the Easter Island expedition. R.R. Marett of Exeter College, Oxford, was exceedingly supportive of Katherine, counselling her on excavation techniques, arranging introductions with Chilean government officials

and suggesting scholars who might be appropriate members of the Expedition team.

While Katherine's Oxford education was in history, she matriculated in an era and at an institution which saw the increased maturation of archaeology as a scientific discipline.[6] The antiquity of man and the existence of 'prehistory' had been established as early as 1833, and the division of time into 'ages' of stone, bronze and iron was widely accepted. Charles Lyell had published his *Principles of Geology* in 1830–33, greatly influencing Charles Darwin's *On The Origin of Species*, published in 1859. William Matthew Flinders Petrie, the greatest of theoreticians in archaeological goals and practices, had introduced scientific methods of documentation into the field of Egyptology, publishing *Ten Years Digging* in 1892, the year after Katherine Pease entered Sommerville College.

The Royal Geographical Society (RGS), which holds the corpus of original Routledge papers and notes, is housed today in Lowther Lodge, Kensington Gore, as it was in Routledge's time.[7] The Reading Room is reached by ascending a gracefully sweeping central staircase to the second floor, passing in front of glass cases filled with mementos of Arctic and African explorers from another time.[8] The Reading Room itself is lined with bookcases and filled with strategically-placed polished wood tables. During the weeks I worked there, the sunlight of a London summer found its way through the tall windows, warming the room, and the noise of the tourist-filled streets outside was stilled. As box after box of papers, letters, field books and drawings was opened and placed before me, the work of Katherine and William Scoresby Routledge came alive.

As the hours passed, I read about Katherine's many visits to the Royal Geographical Society Reading Room, sometimes to meet and talk with friends in Oceanic scholarship, especially B.G. Corney.[9] I tried to imagine at which table she had pulled up her chair to read, or which book she had taken from the shelves. I listened for her voice in a room filled with the low murmur of dusty whispers, and came to recognize it in all of its many moods. She was patient and tactful when answering the many, sometimes bizarre questions addressed to her by a public fascinated with the 'mystery' of Easter Island. She was supportive of friends and colleagues, and generous with her information. Sometimes she was critical and judgemental of the work of others, sometimes very territorial about Easter Island and her research there. Occasionally, frustration with the sexism of her era, as it manifested itself in her life and work, surfaced.[10]

In her journal I found the names of Easter Island men and women, great-grandparents of some of my own friends and collaborators, who were her trusted informants. She learned some Rapanui, but had no command of it. Her notes, in a frustratingly poor hand, are peppered with Rapanui words and phrases, usually rendered in a singularly creative fashion. I read the endless lists of equipment and supplies required to mount the expedition, as well as the letters written by Katherine but sent out over her husband's signature to raise funds for the construction of the Mana. I leafed through dozens of handwritten letters mailed to Katherine at the Royal Geographical Society, a convenient address she used because she and her husband seemed to move around a great deal. Some of these were from admirers in the general public, while others were from concerned church goers who wondered, for example, if she had considered the Biblical story of the Deluge as a possible explanation for what they saw as Easter Island's peculiar history.[11]

The Routledges, both singly and together, excavated a number of sites on Easter Island, including many of the stone houses at Orongo, caves on the southeast coast, and

between twenty and thirty statues in Rano Raraku, the volcanic crater and quarry (fig. 2). As far as can be ascertained, no records of stratigraphic controls exist. In September of 1914, when the excavations at Rano Raraku were being undertaken, Katherine left her Rapa Nui crew alone to dig unsupervised while she rode off on horseback with Juan Tepano, her chief informant, along the southeast coast to map several sites. She paid the men their wages on a piece work basis after arguing with them about 'stolen' artefacts (prehistoric stone adzes called *toki*), some of which were ultimately returned.[12]

Katherine and William Scoresby Routledge were explorers, excavators and collectors in the waning tradition of the Antiquarians. They were gentry whose 'curiosity was the chrysalis of cultivated opinion from which, in the fullness of time, modern archaeology was to emerge and take wing'.[13] At the same time, they were educated and had been exposed to some of the best minds and latest methods in Oceanic scholarship. Katherine, seemingly more than William, had the habits and interests of a scholar. While both were clearly exceptional people, living unconventional lives, their work in archaeology and ethnography also certainly reflects the social and intellectual context of their time.

The *Mana* arrived on Easter Island on 29 March 1914, one whole year after it had sailed from England and just one week earlier than Easter week of 1722, when the island had been 'discovered' by the Dutchman Jacob Roggeveen. It was a hot, Southern Hemisphere day, and *Mana* anchored in Cook's Bay, in front of the island's only village, called Hanga Roa. Only 250 people lived on the island, and the land outside the village was leased for sheep ranching to the Williamson, Balfour Company. Percy Edmunds, resident company manager, provided hospitality for the expedition at his Mataveri residence and logistical support when they were in the field. The Mana Expedition was to remain on the island nearly seventeen months, until 18 August 1915.

In *The Mystery of Easter Island*, Katherine Scoresby Routledge spends nearly half of the book's length spinning colourful traveller's tales about refined adventures *en route* before arriving on Easter Island and, following the departure of *Mana* from the island, describes the long voyage home. Some of her most evocative writing deals with the vessel, the seascape, and the reflective time spent aboard the ship of which she was so clearly fond.[14] Her musings reveal one of the interests she shared with her husband, a man who had always loved sailing and the sea.

Work began in the general environs of the village of Hanga Roa, where Routledge confirmed the original loca-

2 Excavations of two standing statues (*moai*) on the interior slope of Rano Raraku by members of the Mana Expedition to Easter Island, 1914–15. *Courtesy of the Museum of Mankind, British Museum.*

tion of Moai Hava, one of two basalt statues in the collection of the British Museum. Orongo, the famous 'village' of stone houses at the rim of the magnificent crater Rano Kau, held the attention of the expedition for three and a half months, from April to mid-July. Katherine and Lt. Ritchie mapped Orongo, and the party excavated several of the houses, including the one from which, in 1868, the crew of HMS *Topaze* had removed Hoa Hakananai'a, the world famous basalt statue now in the collection of the British Museum.[15]

Beginning in mid-July, and until Lt. Ritchie departed in mid-August aboard the Chilean warship *General Baquedano* and W.S. Routledge sailed for Chile on 5 December, Katherine, William and Lt. Ritchie turned their attention more towards the ceremonial sites (*ahu*) which had once supported erect statues (*moai*), and the Rano Raraku statue quarry.[16] Katherine was intrigued by the curious patterns of breakage on some of the statues lying along the 'trans-

port roads'. The maps of the interior and exterior quarries and slopes were produced by the Routledges and Lt. Ritchie, drawn in the field and then redrawn or supplemented later with the aid of photos and additional field data. The Routledge crew counted 150 statues in the various quarries, forty on the exterior slopes and another twenty on the interior slopes, and were aware that they had probably missed some. The Rano Raraku survey was an enormous task which Katherine found to be lengthy but enjoyable.[17]

After William departed for Chile and during most of the ensuing three months until his return aboard the *Mana* on 15 March, Katherine moved her base of operations again to Mataveri, where she and Bailey the cook were the only two expedition members to remain on the island. At Mataveri she devoted most of her time to collecting ethnographic information from trusted informants. Her work on delineating the beliefs and practices of the birdman cult of Orongo is of immeasurable value. Her descriptive data on political organisation relative to land boundaries and population distribution give us precious insight into rank and status relationships among the Rapa Nui. Virtually no contemporary research on a wide variety of archaeological and socio-historical questions can be undertaken without consulting the data collected by Routledge.

The objects and artefacts collected by the Mana Expedition were donated, in large measure, to the British Museum, and photographic documentation is curated by the Royal Geographical Society and the Museum of Mankind. Some objects were given to the Pitt Rivers Museum, Oxford. All are catalogued under the name of William Scoresby Routledge, who was responsible for their collection. Unfortunately, the documentation provided to the museums for some of the objects is less thorough or specific than one would like, and William's interest in the task of cataloguing and describing seems to have been somewhat less than enthusiastic. Certainly, he made no attempt at orderly classification.

Katherine Routledge's papers were deposited in the Royal Geographical Society by her husband in 1929, when the record shows she was suffering from 'mental illness'. Six years later, in 1935, and a mere four years before her husband, she died aged fifty-five, never having written her promised 'more scientific' account of the Mana expedition. This is, of course, a great loss. But science is fortunate that a researcher of such intuition, common sense and intellect journeyed to Rapa Nui at a critical time in the history of the island, and Katherine Scoresby Routledge acquitted herself honourably as the first woman to work on Easter Island and one of the first in Pacific archaeology.

Archaeological Survey and the Statue Project

'In the wake of the Mana', the Easter Island Statue Project began as a component of archaeological survey, something which Routledge understood to be the very basic first step necessary to any investigation of the meaning and function of the moai. Many of Katherine Routledge's observations of the statues, the quarries and stone as a sculptural material, the carving process and the tools employed are straightforward and as valid today as when she first made them. She held the opinion that not all of the statues in the quarry were originally intended to be removed to ahu sites, and pointed out that not all work was done concurrently. She was an astute and careful observer of the similarities and differences in statue style, and had a healthy respect for the complexities and nuances of form.[18]

Modern archaeological survey is the method used to locate, identify and describe the total number of sites and features, including statues, which exist on the island. There are essentially two kinds of survey strategies, one which is problem-oriented and another which is aimed at cataloguing and counting. A non-problem-oriented survey may be fast and superficial or intensive and thorough. On Easter Island it has been, since its inception, systematic, detailed and very thorough. Whether problem-oriented or inventory, any good survey is begun by establishing arbitrary but logical boundaries of manageable size. Field workers then walk the terrain within these boundaries, metre by metre and in an orderly way, mapping the topography or employing existing topographical maps. When a site or feature is encountered, it must be assigned a number according to an established system, mapped in place and fully described through detailed field notes, drawings, measurements and photographs. As the list of sites and features grows, the archaeologist is logically required to establish a system of site classification. This is the first level of data analysis.

The first phase of the survey lasted less than a year, from February to December 1968, but accomplished a great deal.[19] Conceptualised by American archaeologist William Mulloy of the University of Wyoming, the field work was accomplished by Patrick C. McCoy, then of Washington State University. The entire island was first arbitrarily divided into forty-five quadrangles, although this format has subsequently been trimmed to thirty-five overlapping quadrangles. Each quadrangle is now numbered consecutively in a horizontal pattern beginning with 1 at Rano Kau and ending with 35 at Anakena. McCoy surveyed Rano Kau and environs to the vicinity of Hanga Tee (Quadrangles 1,2,4,5 or 19 km^2), recording 1,738 sites over the course of eight and a half months. Assisting him was Mario Arévalo P. as surveyor, William S. Ayres and others, as well as Rapa Nui field workers Felipe Teao A., Rafael Rapu, Juan Haoa and Jacobo Riroroko. Final mapping was accomplished with the assistance of Chilean cartographer Roberto Izaurieta S. During this same period, ahu were restored at the ceremonial site of Tahai in Quadrangle 8 by W. Mulloy and W.S. Ayres, who also surveyed a portion of the immediate vicinity.

From 1969 to 1976 work on the survey halted, replaced by various ahu excavation and restoration projects accomplished by W.S. Ayres, W. Mulloy and Chilean archaeologist Gonzalo Figueroa G-H. Beginning in 1976, the University of Chile archaeological field team undertook the continuation of the survey. Claudio Cristino F., Patricia Vargas C., Lilian González N. and Roberto Izaurieta S. formed the nucleus of the investigating team, with the assistance of Reginald Budd P. and Felipe Teao A. These investigators were based primarily at the Centro de Estudios, the research station then established on the island (now called Instituto de Estudios and based in Santiago). Between 1976 and 1979, 195 statues were identified in eight

3 View of Rano Raraku from Poike toward Rano Kau. *Photo by David C. Ochsner, 1989.*

survey quadrants of the south coast. An additional eighty-three were subsequently inventoried in Quadrants 14, 18 and 28.

Rano Raraku is a satellite cone of Maunga Terevaka, one of three volcanoes which produced Easter Island (fig. 3).[20] Its distinctive outer configuration was partially created by ancient wave action thousands of years before the Rapa Nui arrived on the island. The crater is awkwardly shaped, with steeply rising cliffs on its southeast side and much lower, softer, eroded slopes on the northwestern side. Rano Raraku is formed of consolidated *lapilli* tuff, the most sig-

nificant geological resource on Rapa Nui. The term *lapilli* refers to the nodules of dark, dense, metamorphic rock which are naturally randomly embedded in the hardened volcanic ash. The tuff is arrayed in distinctly visible, horizontal bands at the upper levels of the interior and exterior of the quarry, and varies in quality and hue. The presence of natural fissures or visible nodules of large or nonuniform size tends to affect the quality of the tuff as a sculptural material, and areas of superior stone were more frequently chosen and more heavily utilised.

Among its distinctive qualities, Rano Raraku tuff is a pleasing reddish orange when freshly cut. This colour weathers over time and at different rates, changing to shades of grey, brown and even black. The stone varies in quality, but is relatively easy to work. It can also take a

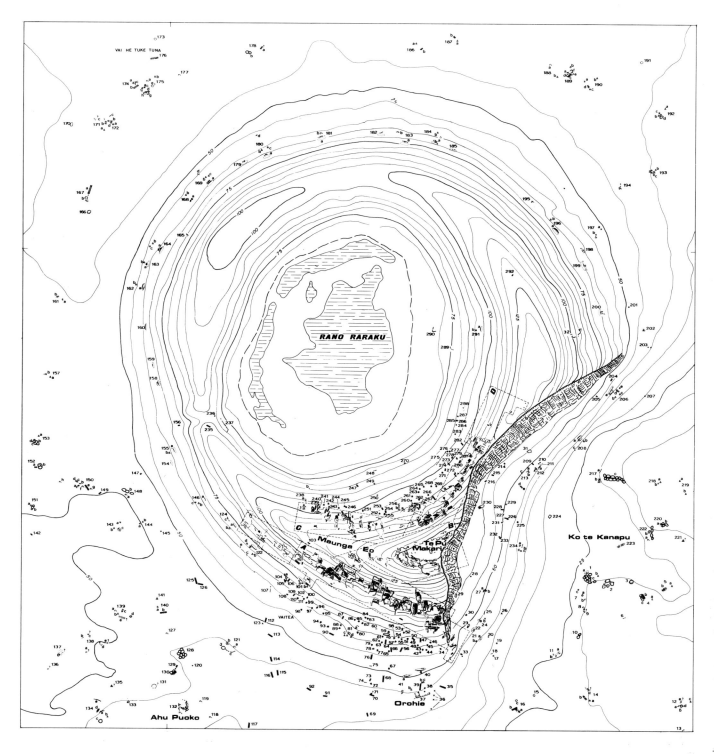

4 Plan of Rano Raraku quarry zone (1978). *Courtesy of Instituto de Estudios de Isla de Pascua, Universidad de Chile.*

polish quite well, and many of the sculptures in the quarries and even some on *ahu* still bear traces of their original, smoothly polished surfaces. The polish was achieved by scouring the stone surface with rounded chunks of coral, said by Routledge to be called *punga* but known in Spanish as *piedra del mar* by contemporary Rapa Nui, and found in

quantities on many *ahu* sites. Another quality of Rano Raraku stone is that it tends to absorb rainwater and saltspray. This affects the weight of the sculpture and its resistance to

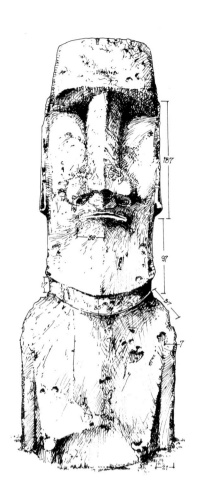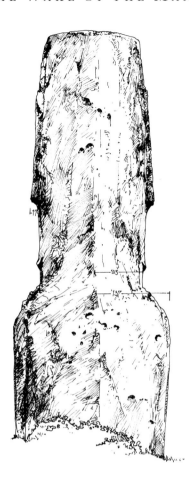

5 Monolithic statue (*moai*) on the exterior slope of Rano Raraku. *Drawing by Cristián Arévalo Pakarati.*

breakage. As the water moves through the stone, it leaves unsightly black and white deposits of salts on the surface, creating special problems for conservationists in their effort to preserve the statues.

Rano Raraku crater is divided into five discrete survey zones and a total of 397 statues are still *in situ* (figs 4, 5).[21] The tallest statue of all is lying supine in one of Rano Raraku's exterior quarries and measures 21 m (71 feet) total length. All of the statues were quarried in rectangular blocks, then undercut and braced in place prior to removal. This procedure is the same as that used to cut coral (beach rock) in Tonga (West Polynesia) or stone on Rota (Micronesia). The heads and faces were usually roughed out before other details were added. Through the evidence gained in mapping Rano Raraku, a list of fifty-five discrete measurements describing statue attributes was developed, and a preliminary strategy for typological classification on the basis of body and head shapes emerged.

In 1981, I joined the Centro de Estudios as an Associate Investigator and began my own field work as Director of the Easter Island Statue Project in 1982. By that time, Chilean and American archaeologists had surveyed fifteen of the island's quadrants and located 278 statues. This number was exclusive, of course, of the 397 statues found within the quarry survey zone. A great deal of work had been accomplished, but much more still remained to be done.

My goal was to begin at the beginning, measuring and describing each located statue fully, and then to carry on into the unsurveyed areas, working parallel with the survey as much as possible. Using the Centro attribute list as a base, I created two recording forms.[22] The first allowed preliminary ordering of the data in the field by identifying and noting statue location, position and material. The second was to transfer the measurements from the frequently rain-spotted, torn or dirtied field diagrams on which they were first recorded to a more coherent format. This enabled me to check the data right away while still fresh, noting any gaps or errors if there were any, and to make copies for my Chilean colleagues. Most importantly,

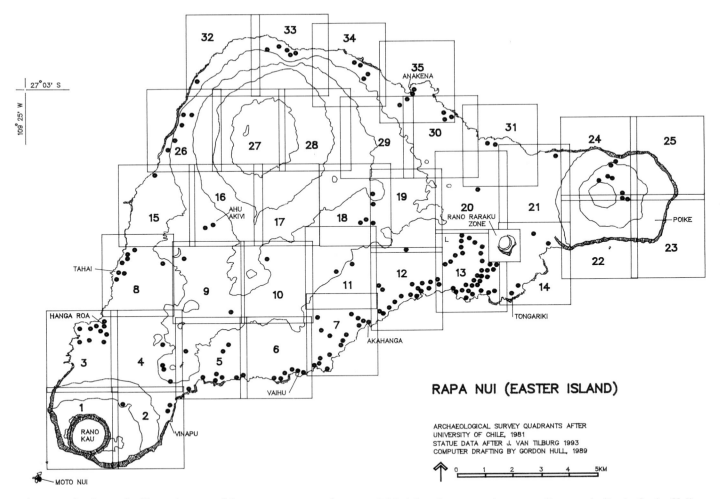

RAPA NUI (EASTER ISLAND)

ARCHAEOLOGICAL SURVEY QUADRANTS AFTER
UNIVERSITY OF CHILE, 1981
STATUE DATA AFTER J. VAN TILBURG 1993
COMPUTER DRAFTING BY GORDON HULL, 1989

6 *Moai* sites documented to 1993. *Computer drafting by Gordon Hull.*

the transfer forms facilitated entry of the measurement data into a computer filing system. Subsequently, the University of Chile developed similar forms for their own record-keeping.[23]

In my first full season of field work I documented 150 statues on forty-eight sites in Hanga Roa and between Vinapu and Akahanga, making important revisions in the data recording system and categories of data. Over the course of subsequent field work, conducted independently under my direction and parallel to the larger survey, we added a great deal of archaeological and conservation information to the data base. We have amassed thousands of field sketches, maps, photographs and slides which serve to amplify the metric descriptions of the statues. A preliminary description of sites and an ordering of the statues into artefact type categories was the subject of my 1986 doctoral dissertation. Including the 397 statues in Rano Raraku quarry sector, a collective total of 887 *moai* has been inventoried to date (figs 6, 7, plates 1, 2).

There are 383 statues sufficiently intact to be entered in a computerised data base. Of these, 134 have ten crucial

measurements which define body and head shape. Morphometric analysis has defined size, shape, weight and proportionate relationships of head to body, producing a classification of statues which is a revision of my 1986 typology. Essentially, there are four groups of statues (fig. 8). The first consists of statues which tend to be small and squat. The second and third groups are equally-proportioned but different in size. They range from medium-sized to large and have moderate proportions. Their body shapes are vertically rectangular and inverted trapezial. The fourth group is the large, vertically rectangular statues found standing on the slopes of Rano Raraku. They are distinguished by their slender proportions (plate 3).

The numerically preferred form for *ahu* statues was the vertically rectangular, oval cylinder, while the majority of those still in Rano Raraku tend more toward rectangular

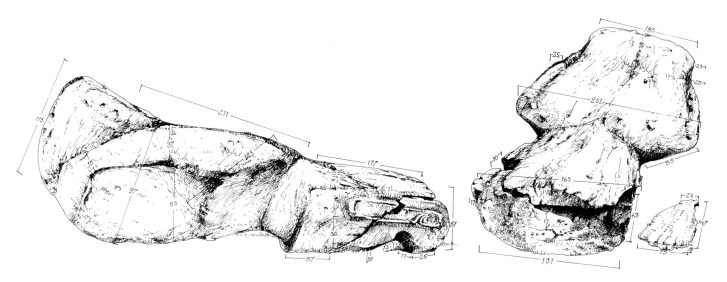

7 Monolithic statue lying prone on *ahu* site, with some attribute measurements indicated. *Drawing by Cristián Arévalo Pakarati.*

slabs. Most of these slablike forms are among the largest and latest in the quarry, and many stand erect on exterior slopes. It is these statues which are most frequently photographed, and have come to be symbolic of Rapa Nui prehistory. The disproportionate size emphasis on the hands, head, eyes and nose illustrates the iconic significance of these features. Cluster analysis and other statistical operations have isolated the statue which is the average, or norm. This average statue, examples of which were moved to virtually every part of the island, is 4.05 m tall and weighs 12.5 m tons (fig. 9).[24]

There are fifty-four statues which were not carved in Rano Raraku quarry, but instead were created in small,

regional quarries out of locally available materials over a long period of time (table 1). Eighteen are carved of red scoria from a quarry in Puna Pau or a denser, darker red scoriaceous material which occurs near the island's coastline and is a result of oxidation of iron compounds in the stone due to weathering.[25] Puna Pau is a small cinder cone of friable and brittle scoria of a distinctive rusty red colour, and was extensively quarried to provide material for *pukao*, the cylindrical 'topknots' or 'headdresses' worn by between fifty-five to seventy-five statues on *ahu* (figs 10, 11). The total number of *pukao* produced is not known since some were cut up for use in prehistoric or protohistoric burials or to be recycled in construction. Some *pukao* have

8 Variation of *moai* head and body shapes on Ahu Vai Uri illustrates statue type categories. *Drawing by Cristián Arévalo Pakarati.*

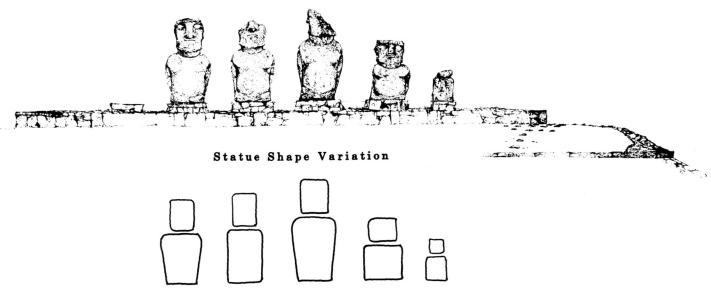

Statue Shape Variation

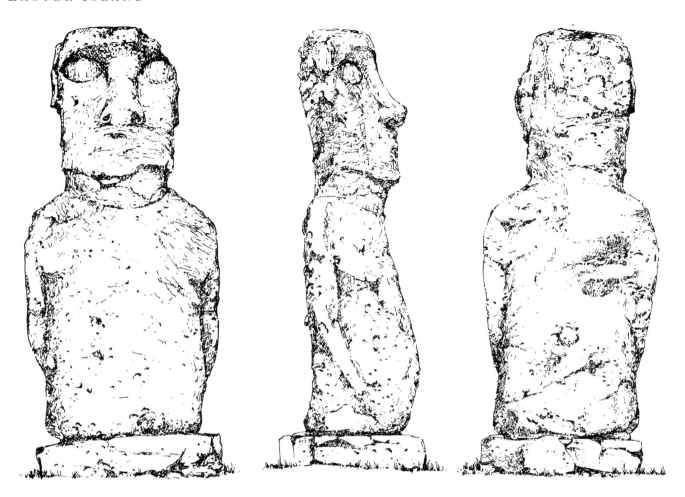

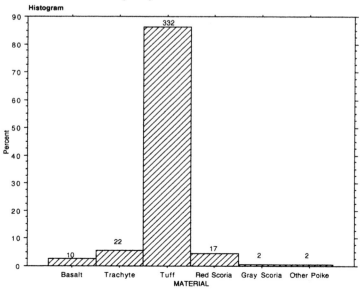

9 Statistically average *moai* (4.05m tall, 12.5 m tons) derived from a sample of 134 statues. *Drawing by Cristian Arévalo Pakarati.*

Table 1 Percentage distribution of statue material for 53 or 54 known statues. *Histogram by Gordon Hull.*

petroglyphs and cupules applied as a secondary reuse somewhat late in time.[26] In addition to *pukao*, red scoria was used to carve some portable sculpture, decorative fascia for some of the coastal *ahu* and a variety of features called *taheta*, or basins. Red scoria was also used in crematoria and in many tombs, scattered profusely over human remains.

Statues of red scoria or red scoriaceous materials are considerably smaller than the average statue of Rano Raraku tuff, with the tallest intact figure being 2.38 m (fig. 12). One round head with rounded eye sockets and naturalistic ears is of red scoriaceous material and tentatively presumed to be associated with Ahu Tahai I. This statue head, if the assumption that it was part of the *ahu* fill of Tahai I is correct, may be the earliest sculpture on Easter Island (plate 4).

There are two statues still *in situ* in one grey scoria quarry. Some 117 small, sometimes bas-relief and generally quite sketchy or incomplete human figures of the *moai* type have been recorded as petroglyphs at various sites on the island (fig. 13).[27] These may be late, and some of them appear to relate in style and position (but not in scale or

material) to two in a grey scoria quarry which, in turn, relate to forms and positions of statues in Rano Raraku quarries. Some of these clusters of small figures, therefore, may have been meant to replicate symbolically statues in Rano Raraku quarries for unknown reasons.

Another twenty-three statues (twenty-two of which are included in the data base) are of an equally distinctive rock called trachyte which comes from lava domes on Poike, in the eastern sector of the island (fig. 14). Poike, at about 2.5

10 Two *pukao* on the exterior slope of Puna Pau. *Photo by David C. Ochsner, 1989.*

11 Map of Puna Pau drafted by the Mana Expedition to Easter Island, 1914–15. *Courtesy of the Museum of Mankind, British Museum.*

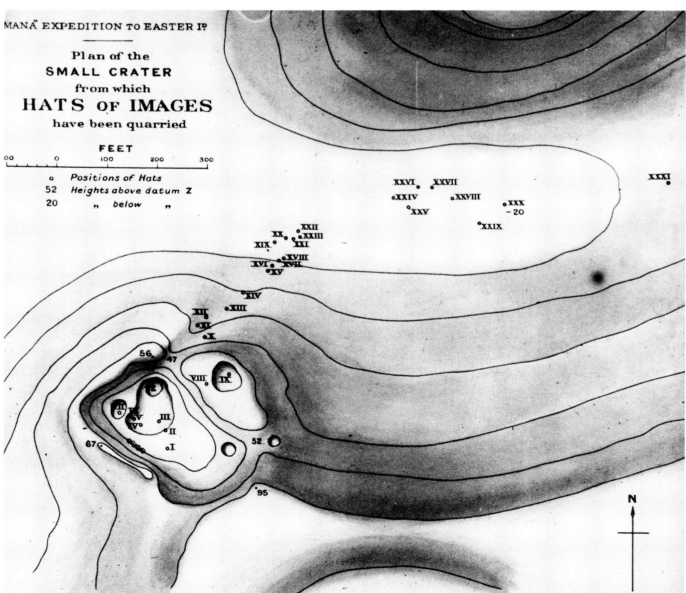

MANĀ EXPEDITION TO EASTER I?

Plan of the
SMALL CRATER
from which
HATS OF IMAGES
have been quarried

FEET

00   0   100   200   300

o   Positions of Hats
52   Heights above datum Z
20   „   below   „

N

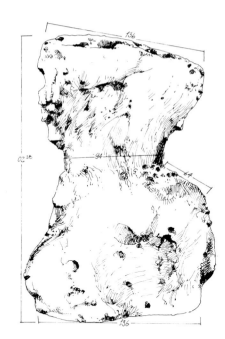
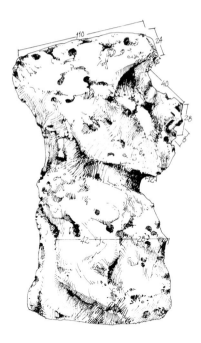

12 Red scoria *moai* (8–137–02) at Tahai, 2.38m tall. *Drawing by Cristián Arévalo Pakarati.*

13 Overhead view of basalt rock (12–14a) carved with *moai* type petroglyphs. *Drawing by Cristián Arévalo Pakarati.*

million years old, is the oldest of the three volcanoes which created Easter Island, and is 370 m tall with a shallow, dry crater called Puakatiki (Pua Katiki) at its summit. Poike is composed largely of porphyritic and aphyric basaltic lava flows, and hawaiites. Its soil cover is generally quite deep and relatively fertile, although there is no evidence of extensive prehistoric cultivation. Cliffside erosion is pronounced, and a total of only 586 archaeological sites/features has been documented on Poike.[28]

The lava domes which provided the stone for the trachyte statues are the same which were utilized by the Spanish when they raised three Christian crosses amid pomp and ceremony in 1770, claiming the island for the King of Spain. As a partial consequence of this impressive event it is possible that some statues carved of this material may postdate 1770, representing a revival of a previously important practice. Trachyte is a stone which is dense, heavy and whitish in colour, and very difficult to carve. All of the trachyte statues are now, or were originally, associated with *ahu*, and one small statue is standing erect on the slope of the central volcano which formed Poike (plate 5).[29] Trachyte statues average less than two metres tall, with the tallest being 2.50 m.

There are only thirteen known basalt statues, ten of which are included in this study (figs. 15, 16). This small number is very surprising, since basalt of varying quality is widely available on the island and was quarried extensively for building material and tools. As a sculptural material, basalt is similar to trachyte in that it is dense and difficult to carve. Statues carved of either material may have been ritually less desirable for *ahu* sculpture than the red and reddish colours of tuff or scoria. The common availability of the material might also have mitigated against its use in

14 ABOVE Statue carved of trachyte on Poike (25–60A–01) is 1.86m tall. *Photo by David C. Ochsner, 1989.*

15 BELOW LEFT Basalt statue numbered 84 by S. Englert is 1.72m tall. *Photo by David C. Ochsner, 1989.*

16 BELOW RIGHT Basalt statue 84 showing unique hand form and unusual facial details. *Drawing by Cristián Arévalo Pakarati.*

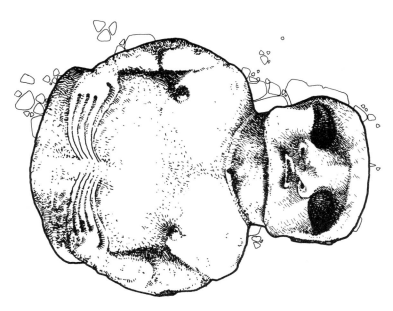

sacred sculpture. On the other hand, the association of trachyte with the ceremonies of the Spanish and basalt with the sacred site of Orongo may have been factors in choosing either material. Six statues in museum collections, including Hoa Hakananai'a and Moai Hava in the British Museum, are carved of basalt.

Rano Kau is about one million years old, rising 324 m above sea level. It was formed by a series of basaltic lava flows. The enormous caldera of the volcano is over 115 m in diameter and between 200 and 250 m deep, filled at the bottom by a fresh water lake (*rano*). The complexity of stone types which make up Rano Kau include aphyric and porphyritic basalt, hawaiite and benmoreite, with a type of pumice and obsidian also present. Basalt outcroppings at Orongo on the very brink of Rano Kau were carved into an extraordinary series of petroglyphs associated with the cult of the creator god Makemake and the incarnation of that god in the form of a birdman (*tangata manu*).

The fifty-four statues contained within this small subset of sculpture quarried from non-Rano Raraku stone demonstrate a number of stylistic innovations within an established attribute norm which we find fully articulated in the Rano Raraku images. These design innovations appear to be largely accomplished within the western sector of the island. Further, it is very clear that the scoria, trachyte and basalt images were quarried and carved individually in various sectors of the island over a long period of time, and cannot be lumped together as either all early or 'prototypical', as has been suggested.[30] On the contrary, some

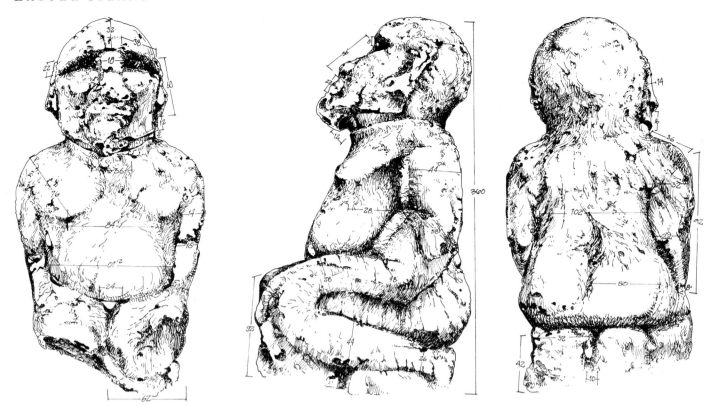

17 Tukuturi, the kneeling, bearded *moai* with petroglyph type eyes is 3.6m tall. *Drawing by Cristián Arévalo Pakarati.*

may be quite late in time. The statue showing the greatest evolution in design, form and posture is the kneeling statue of Rano Raraku, called Tukuturi (fig. 17). This statue may be, in fact, one of the last statues carved on the island.

Fragments of red scoria and Rano Raraku tuff statues or intact statues of basalt or red scoria are occasionally incorporated into *ahu* construction, and some have been used in habitation and other types of sites. Sometimes they are hidden in caves or partially buried in the ground. They are found in prone, supine, vertical and lateral positions, with the largest number lying prone, especially if they are on *ahu* sites. Distributional patterns demonstrate that there are

more statues in the coastal zone than in the interior, and that the majority of statues are found in the eastern sector of the island and the southeast coastal zone.

The overwhelming majority of statues in all materials found outside the Rano Raraku sector are on *ahu* sites (70.2%) (table 2). The largest statue successfully raised on *ahu* is called Paro and is 9.8 m tall. It is located on Ahu Te Pito Kura on the northeast coast. Another statue only 1 cm taller (9.9 m) was transported to Ahu Hanga Te Tenga on the southeast coast, but it appears to have fallen very soon after it was raised or while it was being raised. In spite of these impressive accomplishments, the mean height of all statues successfully raised upon *ahu* is only 3.78 m. Statues which we have documented along roads between Rano Raraku and the coasts average 2.01 m taller than *ahu* statues. This illustrates a generalised, island-wide trend toward larger statues over time.

TABLE 2 Easter Island monolithic statue count and percentages by location category.

	Location	Frequency	Percent	Cumulative frequency	Cumulative percent
0	Other	3	0.8	3	0.8
6	In transport	46	12.0	49	12.8
7	Intermediate	56	14.6	105	27.4
8	Ahu	269	70.2	374	97.7
9	Incorporated in ahu	9	2.3	383	100.0

Easter Island monolithic statue count and percentages by location, exclusive of Rano Raraku sector

Making History on Easter Island

If we are to continue to do ethnography at all, I cannot see that we have any other option than to listen carefully to what people say, watch what they do, and keep our voices down.

ROBERT J. SMITH Anthropologist

The modern era of scientific investigation on Rapa Nui was preceded by nearly 150 years of exploration, observation and collection. The general flow of this effort is best understood by considering the data collected in terms of the methods used. For example, the early record is comprised largely of observations and impressions gleaned by explorers, ships' officers and crewmen, and begins with the 'discovery' of the island by the Dutchman Jacob Roggeveen in 1722. This information is, by definition, anecdotal and is found in ships' logs and seamen's journals, cargo records and diaries. These sources must be considered within the context of the relatively short time spent by most of these people on the island (some actually observed from shipboard), and with the awareness that those making the observations were also, at the same time, usually experiencing exciting and sometimes even trying circumstances. In addition to the time and circumstance factors, the reliability of the observers varied substantially.

Another important consideration when using the data of all early explorers in the Pacific is that, after first contact, each subsequent ship and ship's crew became a part of each island's history, affecting and in some cases altering the way the individual island populations acted and interacted with outsiders. This is especially true if violence was involved, as it often was on Rapa Nui. The history of Rapa Nui, as that of nearly all Pacific islands, reflects and refracts through the crystal of interactive behaviour. As Greg Denning wrote in 1980 about the Marquesas Islands: 'We are concerned to write the anthropology and the history of those moments when native and intruding cultures are conjoined. Neither can be known independently of that moment.'[1]

The entry of the Western world into the lives of Pacific islanders was one of the forces responsible for what has been frequently referred to as the 'transformation' of island societies. European incursion into the Pacific produced a 'context of drastically changing times when the Polynesian systems had to take account of political and religious powers originating from outside themselves.'[2] This 'taking account' in the non-literate societies of Polynesia produced different ways of knowing the past on individual islands and differing accounts of the past on the same island. Enduring traditions, passed down from generation to generation were often disrupted, frequently altered and occasionally destroyed in their entirety.

The End and the Beginning

From the time of first contact with Europeans, Rapa Nui society began to evolve in new and, as yet, not fully understood ways. Each of the first two known contacts was especially memorable and must have astounded the populace. Jacob Roggeveen's 1722 'discovery' of the island, by the very fact of being the first contact, obviously made a huge impact.[3] The events immediately surrounding this first contact carried with them potentially profound consequences for Rapa Nui history, society and ritual. Three Dutch ships mounted with cannon appeared on the Rapa Nui horizon on Easter Sunday, and when the 114 Dutchmen set foot ashore the next day they were arrayed in armed military ranks. Within moments of their landing, at least thirty muskets were fired and between ten and twelve Rapa Nui people, some of whom were certainly chiefs or priests, fell instantly dead before the eyes of their startled kin. An unknown number were wounded.

Precontact Rapa Nui was a traditional, hierarchical

society which perceived history as 'heroic', the natural extension of the sacred chief's life. In such societies, history 'shows an unusual capacity for sudden change or rupture: a mutation of the cultural course'.[4] European intrusions into several island societies caused just such ruptures and mutations, producing some startlingly rapid social changes of direction. Other tribal societies outside the Pacific sphere, such as in the Americas and Africa, when faced with the death, conversion or other loss of sacred, hereditary leadership, were often plunged into internal crises of genuinely cosmic proportions, causing old gods and images to be violently cast aside and bringing social disequilibrium, disarray and collapse.

There is little doubt that the course of Rapa Nui history was altered forever that April day in 1722. While the European 'discovery' of the island may not have achieved the tragic, mythic proportions of Cook's arrival in Hawaii as described by anthropologist Marshall Sahlins, there was assuredly, in the words of historian Alan Moorehead, a 'fatal impact' of unknown proportions. The landing (and killing) site itself may have taken on some special, even if temporary, ritual significance. The Rapa Nui ceremonial calendar may have been altered by this April thunderclap

of discovery. The status of the chiefly landholder on which these events took place may have been influenced. If an important chief died in the rain of Dutch powder and shot, as he well may have, the sacred forces which centred upon his being would afterwards have been regarded in a new way.

The memory of the Dutch 'discovery', and the terrifying events associated with it, must still have been strong when a Spanish expedition, led by Don Felipe González de Haedo, arrived only forty-eight years later (in 1770). The Spanish expedition vastly outdid the Dutch in military and religious pomp and ceremony. Priests and soldiers in full regalia marched in procession with colourful banners and flags flying, accompanied by drums and the singing of litanies, raising three wooden crosses on each of three very prominent Poike hillocks. Voices were raised harmoniously in prayer and song. Seven rousing cheers were followed by a 'triple volley of musketry from the whole party, and, lastly,

18 Map of 'Isla San Carlos' (Rapa Nui), 1770. Note the three crosses erected on Poike. *Biblioteca Central de la Diputacion de Barcelona. Courtesy Francisco Mellén-Blanco.*

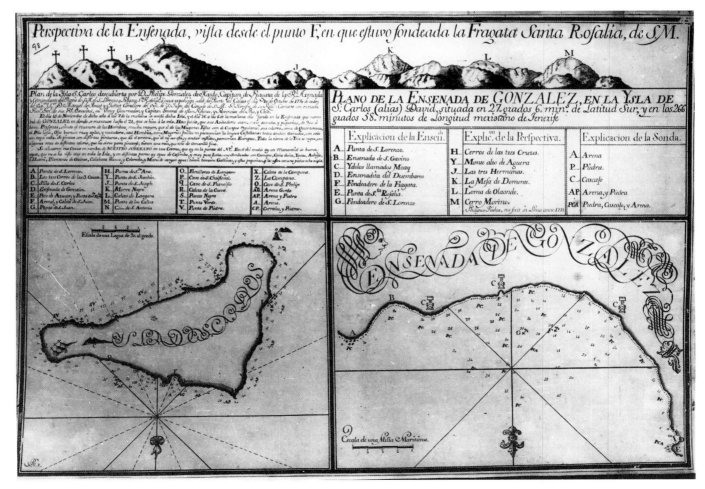

our ships [lying in the nearby bay] saluted with 21 guns'.[5] All of this magnificent show of power and presence was meant to claim the island for Don Carlos of Spain (fig. 18). It also most assuredly made a profound impression on the deeply ritualistic Rapa Nui culture.

The Rapa Nui would have understood immediately the Spanish need to create a sacred place upon landing on this new island. Such an undertaking is very much a part of the Polynesian way. So, too, is the desecration or removal of symbols associated with such sites. The Spanish crosses were no longer in place when Captain Cook arrived, just four years later. How or when they were removed is not known. Elsewhere in Polynesia, such symbols of foreign domination did not long remain in place. In New Zealand for example, the flagstaff flying the British colours above Kororareka in the Bay of Islands was cut down four separate times by Maori warriors. The flagpole itself, as a symbol, was the root cause and strategic objective of Maori warfare.[6] The erect or upright pole, whether cross or flagstaff, would have been immediately recognised, by East Polynesians in particular, as a sacred sign of domination.

Captain Cook arrived in 1774, sailing the *Resolution* into Hanga Roa Otai, now called Cook's Bay on some maps (fig. 19). He was recovering from an illness, and spent most of his limited time ashore in the vicinity of Hanga Roa.

19 Rapa Nui as mapped on Cook's second voyage, 1774. *Courtesy Bernice P. Bishop Museum.*

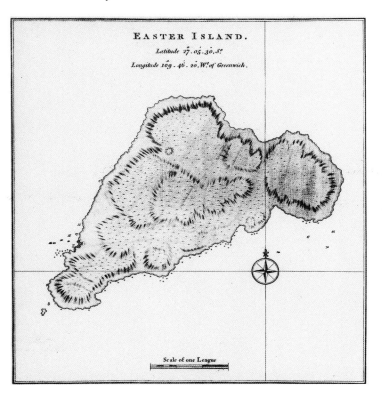

Cook and several of the individuals who sailed with him, unlike the Dutch and the Spanish, had experience in the Pacific and could make comparative judgements about what they were seeing and experiencing. They had a Tahitian from Bora Bora with them named Mahine, and he spent most if not all of his time while on the island in the company of the Rapa Nui, talking and trading.[7] Cook's men explored a portion of the island by walking in single file along a well-established coastal trail which ran eastward from Vinapu. At a point near Hanga Tee, they were joined by an important Rapa Nui man, a chief or priest, who made a ceremonial gesture of greeting and then led them in procession behind an upraised staff with a white banner. Rapa Nui people lined both sides of the trail and offered cooked food. It is at least possible that Cook's men had thus fallen inadvertently into a ceremonial pattern which was already well established on the island.[8]

When Cook arrived, only four years had elapsed since the Spanish pageantry and fifty-two since the Dutch murders. It is likely that some of the Rapa Nui whom Cook met that day had been alive to meet both the Dutch and the Spanish, and one wonders just what they thought about the behaviour and habits of these three very different groups of Europeans. Seeing things from the Rapa Nui point of view, they must have been perplexed and intrigued, probably also suspicious, cautious and perhaps somewhat awestruck or frightened. Others with shorter memories or more calculating minds may have had other reactions. Their interactions with Cook were peaceful and largely gracious. They offered to trade and barter and gave generously of their provisions.[9]

The first on-shore contact of the new century was in 1804, and the Pacific slave trade, commonly called 'blackbirding', was visited upon Rapa Nui occasionally until 1862. In that year, it struck Rapa Nui in full and terrible fury. During the short span of one year, a level of injury, death and loss was inflicted upon the Rapa Nui population which was savage, leaving the demoralised remnants largely bereft of cultural leadership. This bleak and tragic period produced what anthropologists call 'broken traditions', a general loss of continuity with the communal past.

At this vulnerable time in their history, the Rapa Nui were introduced to Christianity and intensified commerce, the two most effective forces for change the western world has created. Catholic missionary activity began the year after the slave raids ceased, and in 1866 the island's priestly staff was augmented by native assistants from Mangareva and the Tuamotus. Without their informed consent, Rapa Nui people were removed from their ancestral lands and required to live in the vicinities of Hanga Roa and Mataveri. Records indicate that the total Rapa Nui populace had been baptised by the year 1868.[10] The effect of the missionaries extended beyond the spiritual realm, reaching into and profoundly altering certain aspects of ordinary Rapa Nui life. The missionaries 'introduced the islanders to crafts such as large-scale woodworking and home-building skills', playing a 'major role in the conversion of the islanders to a more European mode of living and thinking'.[11] Conversion to Christianity was accomplished in an horrific atmosphere of introduced diseases, malnutrition and death.

Throughout the Pacific, Catholic and Protestant missionaries were ubiquitous and persistent.[12] Within a generation of the arrival of Christianity in the Pacific, more than a hundred mission stations of various faiths had been established. Conversion of island populations to the Christian faith was breathtakingly swift and without major incident in most places, although there is some evidence that it was often a matter of convenience rather than conviction.[13] The writings and lectures of missionaries during fundraising and educational efforts in London and elsewhere served to aid in the creation of a stereotypical impression of Pacific islanders which amounted to a profound cliché by the end of the 1800s. In the eyes of the missionaries, the most grievous cultural sins of the Polynesians were homosexuality and general eroticism. Cannibalism, human sacrifice, infanticide and abortion were also, of course, soundly condemned social practices.

The Christian attitude toward sexuality made an impact first and most visibly on Pacific material culture. For example, the modes of island dress (really undress) were changed almost immediately, and tattooing and the use of body paint and oil were curtailed or ended. The missionaries' selective collection of ethnographic material influenced the islanders' perception of its worth, beginning the long and close association between the types of objects Polynesian craftspeople produced (then and now) and non-Polynesian tastes. Destruction or transformation of art styles, particularly the sculptural representation of the nude human form, began everywhere with contact and was intensified by missionary influence and trade.[14]

Commerce on Rapa Nui began with trade and barter between islanders and ships' crews. The Spanish traded metal objects for sexual favours, and the Dutch may have as well. In an engraving of a drawing made by Duché de Vancy, who was with La Pérouse on Rapa Nui in 1786, Rapa Nui women are shown admiring themselves in mirrors and enveloped in striped fabric (fig. 112).[15] Since the Rapa Nui barkcloth was said by all early Europeans to be either white or red-orange, the fabric illustrated may either have been presented by the La Pérouse party or is the 'striped linen' which Roggeveen's party had traded some sixty-four years earlier for 'fowls, some yams and bananas'. Nine years later, in 1795, Captain Charles Bishop sketched a Rapa Nui woman, said to be named 'Te'ree', with what appears to be a mirror in her hand as well (fig. 20). A Rapa Nui man, sketched at the same time, holds what appears to be a metal hatchet. Cloth, mirrors, beads and hatchets were all common European trade items.[16]

20 Tattooed or painted Rapa Nui man and woman (called 'Te'ree') with trade items. *Drawing by Captain Charles Bishop, 1795. Courtesy of the British Columbia Archives and Records Service.*

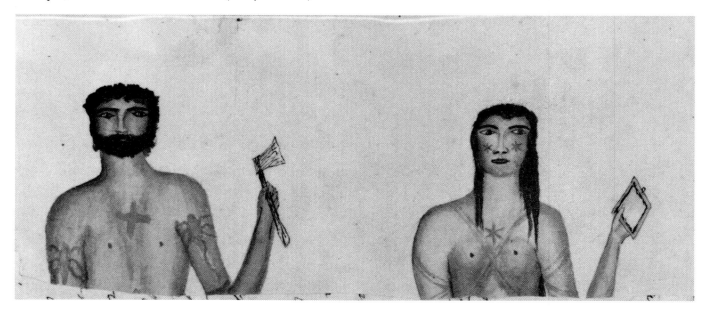

Rapa Nui Informants and Leaders

Out of the multiple tragedies of the slave trade, introduced diseases, evangelism and conversion, commercial exploitation, enforced poverty and relocation a few Rapa Nui leaders arose to facilitate the entrance of their island culture into the western dominated 'real world', providing a remarkable demonstration of cultural resiliency and individual survival skills. Some of these individuals interacted with Europeans who later published relatively detailed accounts of their experiences. Others were associated with the earliest efforts at collecting material objects, as well as with the ethnographers who recorded the most useful and widely cited ethnohistoric information.

Among the earliest mentioned Rapa Nui leaders was Torometi, a man of traditional status who was a member of the Haumoana Miru (fig. 21).[17] Torometi had cannily secured a position of personal leadership through first tormenting, exploiting and then dominating the Catholic missionaries. He was a fearsome and militaristic individual who led a group of at least eighty Rapa Nui men and women in stone-throwing attacks on the Hanga Roa mission station. He acted as liaison between the island community and various ships' crews which called at the island during his lifetime, very probably gaining increased

21 Rapa Nui man named Torometi. *Watercolour by J. Linton Palmer, 1868. Courtesy Royal Geographical Society.*

social stature as a result. It was Torometi who aided the crew of HMS *Topaze* in their removal of the basalt statue Hoa Hakananai'a in 1868.[18] Land purchase records indicate that Torometi sold nine hectares of land in Hanga Piko for 100 francs in 1869, the year following the visit of the *Topaze*.[19] He then departed Rapa Nui for Tahiti with others who were to work on commercial and Catholic mission plantations. Within a year, Torometi and many other Rapa Nui in Tahiti were dead, victims of diseases exacerbated by the unfamiliar climate and poor living conditions. Only 111 Rapa Nui remained on Easter Island in 1872.[20]

Three fascinating people, Juan Tepano Huki, the 'prophetess' Angata and Catechist Nicholás Pakarati Urepotahi, lived lives which were intertwined and influential, greatly influencing Rapa Nui history as well as the preservation of data. One of these remarkable individuals, Juan Tepano, deserves a great deal of credit for the salvage and preservation of Rapa Nui cultural information, and every ethnographer and archaeologist who has ever worked on the island owes him a debt of gratitude (fig. 22). To this day, some of the information the old Rapa Nui men are able to share is recognised by them to have originated with or been communicated by Tepano. A more direct impact may be seen in the woodcarving tradition, where Tepano functioned both as carver and teacher.[21]

Born *c.*1876 in the territory which lies between Tongariki and Rano Raraku, Juan Tepano Huki was the son of Veriamo Huki a Puhi a Kau and a man recorded simply as Rano (fig. 23). The name Tepano (the Tahitian version of Steven or Stephanus) was given to Rano at his baptism, recorded in the 1886 census.[22] Juan Tepano's status in the community, plus his own intellect and curiosity, placed him in the position of conduit of information not only from his culture to ethnographers (K. Routledge, A. Métraux, H. Lavachery and S. Englert) but also and equally important, from science to the Rapa Nui people. In his youth he spent some seven years on the Chilean mainland, during which time he served in the military and learned to speak, read and write Spanish.[23]

When the famous Rapa Nui 'rising' witnessed by Routledge in 1914 took place, Tepano was living in Mataveri, working for Percy Edmunds. The majority of the Rapa Nui were living in greatly impoverished circumstances, building stone walls, working in the gardens and sheering sheep for incredibly low wages (about 20–40 centavos per day). There was a sharp and very visible contrast between quantity and quality of food and clothing available to the Rapa Nui who were on the regular staff at Mataveri, including Juan Tepano, and that of the rest of

22 Juan Tepano Huki, Rapa Nui informant, artisan and community leader. *Photo by A. Métraux. Courtesy Ana Tepano and family.*

23 Viriamo Huki a Puhi a Kau, Juan Tepano Huki's mother and source of some of his information. *Courtesy Bernice P. Bishop Museum.*

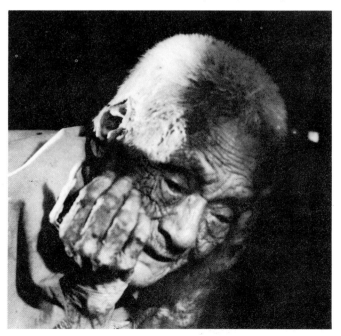

the Rapa Nui in Hanga Roa. The few lepers confined to their isolated and filthy quarters on the outskirts of Hanga Roa were in even more dire circumstances.[24] The coming of the Mana Expedition, with its ample stores so carefully planned and organised by Katherine Routledge, seems to have exacerbated that situation somewhat.

The 'rising' was instigated by Angata, actually Maria Angata Veri Tahi a Pengo Hare Kohou, a Mangareva trained catechist and relative of Simeon Riroroko, the last Rapa Nui 'king' (fig. 24). Angata was a 'frail old woman with grey hair and expressive eyes, a distinctly attractive and magnetic personality. She wore suspended round her neck some sort of religious medallion, a red cross'.[25] She was apparently a woman of great spirituality and hardened resolve, determined to intercede with her idea of the Christian god on behalf of the Rapa Nui. She reportedly had visions in which God spoke to her. These visions were mediated by her son-in-law Daniel Maria Teave Haukena, a respected spiritual leader whom Routledge somewhat disparagingly referred to as 'priest'. Angata said that God told her to encourage the Rapa Nui to steal stock animals and material goods from the foreigners headquartered at Mataveri.

Angata promised that no harm would befall the Rapa Nui when they took what she felt rightfully belonged to

24 Maria Angata Veri Tahi a Pengo Hare Kohou, Rapa Nui prophetess and influential leader. *Photo by the Routledge Expedition to Easter Island, 1914–15. Courtesy of the Museum of Mankind, British Museum.*

them, and convinced those involved that they were protected from death or injury at the hands of Edmunds and others, in spite of the fact that Edmunds, W.S. Routledge and Juan Tepano were then going about visibly and threateningly armed. Angata, nevertheless, inspired decisive action in the Rapa Nui, instigating 'crimes' for which they were later held accountable by Chilean officials when the warship *General Baquedano* arrived and lifted the siege. The acts consisted primarily of robbing stores at Mataveri (including some of those belonging to the Mana Expedition) and butchering animals. The food and clothing thus secured were distributed among the Rapa Nui, including the lepers. An unknown number of men participated in these events, although between eight and a dozen were ultimately identified. Several strong-minded women apparently formed a core group around Angata, encouraging the men to take the action she advocated.

Angata died just six months after the abrupt end of the 'rising'. Routledge attended her funeral service at the church where 'she used to take part in the assemblies and address her adherents.'[26] The coffin was removed to the cemetery where Routledge 'stood at a little distance watching gleams of sunshine on the great stones of the terrace of Hanga Roa and on the grey sea beyond, and musing on the strange life now closed, whose early days had been spent in a native hut beneath the standing images of Raraku'. The coffin was lowered into the ground and Angata interred to the sound of three rousing 'English cheers – hip, hip, hooray'!

Another Rapa Nui individual who had considerable influence upon the selective preservation of island culture, and whose memory is revered to this day, was Catechist Nicholás Pakarati Urepotahi (Ure Potahi a Te Pihi) (fig. 25). His father, Te Pihi, was Tupahotu, and his mother, Ko Te Oho a Neru, was Marama (fig. 26). Pakarati married Elisabet Rangitaki, from Fagatau in the Tuamotus, and fathered eleven children, three of whom were informants for Thomas Barthel in his ethnographic researches into

25 Catechist Nicolás Pakarati Urepotahi, his wife Elizabet Rangitaki Temaki Urepotahi and their three children. *Courtesy of the Bernice P. Bishop Museum.*

26 Ko Te Oho a Neru, mother of Nicolás Pakarati Urepotahi, in front of thatched shelter. *Photo by Percy Edmunds. Courtesy of the Bernice P. Bishop Museum.*

kohau rongorongo (fig. 27). His oldest son, Timoteo Pakarati R., worked with Englert to compile his Rapa Nui grammar. Nicholás Pakarati Urepotahi was one of Routledge's informants, especially about the Orongo ceremonies. He was one of those who provided leadership to the priestless Rapa Nui congregation after the departure of the missionaries. During the time of the 'rising' led by Angata, Pakarati remained out of the fray.[27] Angata's use of the church building to address the congregation, however, took advantage of the religious realm to present a political message, a time-honoured method for creating a power base. The political and economic goals of the 'rising' were

legitimated through the ideological rationale she created, and to which the Rapa Nui responded.

These remarkable Rapa Nui people, along with others still alive today who have worked with investigators Thomas Barthel, Grant McCall and the scientists of the Norwegian Archaeological Expedition, have preserved the history and culture of their island as it is transmitted from the past to the present (fig. 28). The work which they have accomplished with Western investigators provides the very core of ethnographic studies on Rapa Nui. The information secured from them, of course, was all post-1860, and the data which they provided must all be considered within

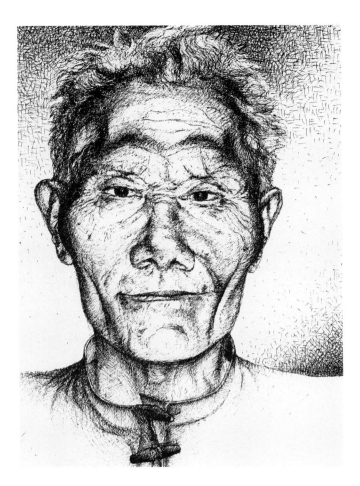

27 Leonardo Pakarati, respected Rapa Nui elder. *Drawing by Cristián Arévalo Pakarati.*

Traditional Knowledge of History

Early scholars in Polynesian studies regarded mythology as ethnohistory, correct in the largest sense of main events or central characters, but frequently incorrect in specific detail. Myths were seen as narratives of actual events including real people, but because of the passage of time some of these events and people were overlain with or obscured by rhetoric. Recent scholarship suggests that some Oceanic mythology can and should be seen as a window on the past which is different from but complementary to the insight gained through archaeological investigation. Traditions encompassing several generations prior to European contact often represent actual events and affairs of real people, although factual distortion, metaphor and allegory are usually present. The literal truth of the traditions is not the most important issue in such cases. Traditions are valuable because they give an 'alternative view of historical *process*'. Thus, myth may be regarded as 'an important means of *organising* and *interpreting* history rather than *chronicling* it.[28]

In order to understand the complexity of research which must be undertaken to elucidate specific traditions as history, a single example of two interrelated Rapa Nui traditions will be examined here.[29] The first tradition deals with the 'story of the Long Ears'. Thomson was the first to mention it, and he got it from Alexander Salmon. Two versions of the story were recorded by Routledge, one from someone called 'Kilimuti' and the other from 'three old men in conclave'. Métraux apparently took down his information of the tale from Tepano. Englert probably got some of his two post-Métraux versions from Tepano, but there are other possible sources as well. The name of a specific informant for this tale is not given by Englert. The 'story of the Long Ears' was widely publicised by Englert, who included it in a series of radio programmes about the island's history which was subsequently published. Since then, it has become a significant part of the oft-repeated folklore of the island.

Briefly, the 'story of the Long Ears' suggests that an altercation began in the Orongo and/or Vinapu area between two groups 'who lived together mixed up all over the land'.[30] The source of the conflict was the deaths of seven sons in a single family, murdered by someone named Ko Ita who lived at Orongo. The motivation for the murders was cannibalism. The conflict spread to Poike, where the Long Ears (Hanau Eepe) took refuge. There, the epic battle of the Long Ears and the Short Ears (Hanau Momoko) took place. The Long Ears constructed a ditch and plotted to drive their enemies into the trench, where a

the context of the time in which it was collected. Juan Tepano was assuredly the most indefatigable and worldly source. Pakarati's data may have been affected by both Catholic teaching and Tuamotuan custom. In general, men were more frequently sought after as informants than were women, giving a certain gender bias to the data collected. Clearly, the information which all of the Rapa Nui informants imparted was not only from their own memories, but was synthesised from a variety of known and unknown familial and other sources, including impressions, opinions and values communicated to them, knowingly or not, by ethnographers, visitors, traders and various other outsiders.

28 Felipe Teao Arancibia, Rapa Nui elder and indefatigable scientific resource. *Photo by David C. Ochsner, 1989.*

massive fire would consume them. One of the Short Ears women, married to a Long Ears man, betrayed the plan to her kinfolk, who then succeeded in fatally diverting the Long Ears into their own trap.

This story has been frequently told and retold in various books about the island, and has been argued by some to suggest that two separate 'races' of people, one with Polynesian and the other with South American origins, once inhabited the island at the same time.[31] This hypothesis had its origin in Thomson's report, who describes a 'long-eared race' with no justification at all for the use of the word 'race'. The Rapanui word *hanau* actually means 'to be born' and implies child or progeny. Englert's redefinition of *eepe* as corpulent and *momoko* as thin suggests not a racial difference but, instead, physical characteristics which may metaphorically represent economic and social conditions.[32] That is, a distinction was being drawn between the 'haves' and the 'have nots', those of high status and others of lower status.

Archaeological evidence, the ultimate test of historic analysis, reveals that the Poike 'ditch' is really a series of related trench-like features which run north/south between Mahatua and Te Haka Rava at the base of Poike, delineating the peninsula from the island's main mass (plate 6).[33] The purpose of the trench construction is not known, but it has little or no value as a defensive structure to protect the whole of the peninsula. Evidence of fire in a part of the ditch dated to cal. AD 240–660 is not directly associated with any evidence of human activity.[34] Massive human remains required to substantiate the story of confrontation between the Hanau Eepe and Hanau Momoko are definitely not present.

Routledge's assessment of her informants' recall of salient points in the story of the Long Ears agreed with that of one of the men's wives, who said that 'they don't know anything about it'.[35] Métraux reached the conclusion that 'this tale presents no definite evidence of the existence of two different races on the island. It has been inspired partially by the native desire to explain local geographical characteristics; very likely the fight between the Long-ears and the Short-ears is a recent theme'.[36] If Routledge and Métraux are correct in discounting the tale, how then can we account for it in the oral history of Rapa Nui? Obviously, status differentiation is of great antiquity in Polynesia, so its presence in a Rapa Nui legend of this sort is not surprising. Outside of that, where might this story come from and what does it mean?

One myth of unknown antiquity in the rich East Polynesian corpus is the only place, to my knowledge, where Poike, a non-generic Rapa Nui place name, is known. On Pukapuka in the Cook Islands, Poike is a place on their mythical island of Yayake.[37] Poike is described as a 'copulating place', and it is here that a huge battle was waged between two brothers from Tonga called Manawune and Tangaloa and the people of Poike. The brothers 'struck down all the people' and 'ravaged the entire island' to avenge the deaths of two Tongan women. Thus, we may be faced with a situation wherein the remnants of an earlier myth were retained in Rapa Nui oral history, elaborated and personalised. Geographical characteristics of Poike relative to the rest of the island, as Métraux suggested, may account, in part, for this retention. On a metaphorical level, it is very likely that the story relates tensions, aggressions and conflict between two separate groups of Rapa Nui, probably over concerns of status and resources (women and food) and probably over a very long period of time.

The second tradition to be considered here is related to the story of the Long Ears and was recorded only by

Englert. He was told that a Rapa Nui man named Ororoina was the only Long Ears survivor of the Poike battle, and a descendant of his, who was in his approximate fifties, was the first man to go aboard Roggeveen's ships in 1722, making contact the day before they actually landed on Rapa Nui.[38] The exact words of the Rapa Nui tradition are that the Dutch 'gave him liquid and food but he did not eat or drink. He took the liquid and washed himself with it by pouring it over his head.' At the end of the visit, the Rapa Nui man was given some presents and two strings of blue beads, and then he returned to the island.[39] Tragically, he was among the dozen or more individuals mortally wounded by the Dutch when they fired upon the excited Rapa Nui crowd the following day.

Comparison of the tradition with the literature reveals that Roggeveen does, indeed, mention a Rapa Nui man coming aboard but not this specific incident. Bouman, a ship's officer, says that 'we gave him a glass of brandywine, which he poured over his face, and when he felt the strength of it he began to open his eyes wide. We gave a second glass of brandywine with a biscuit, none of which he used'. Behrens, a German who was with the Dutch, says that 'we gave this South Lander or foreign visitor a glass of wine to drink but he only took it and tossed it into his eyes'. Englert did not mention Roggeveen or Bouman, but thinks that the tradition matches Behrens' account, thereby illustrating its veracity.

There is a possibility that this rather colourful event may have been described to some Rapa Nui by one of the earlier ethnographers, and that the 'tradition' told to Englert may have been subsequently created, modified or otherwise affected.[40] If this did not happen, it is possible that the Rapa Nui man would have had time to tell of his adventures before he was murdered by the Dutch. Englert offers genealogical data to support the tradition, tracing eight generations (of what he believes is a probable nine) from Ororoina to the modern era, but these data are clearly incomplete. On present evidence, it cannot be certain that this story is a legitimate retention of Rapa Nui traditional history.

One of the most interesting analyses of the invention of tradition was conducted on Pukapuka, in the Cook Islands, giving detailed insight into the ways in which Pukapukans reformulated their traditions to allow aspects of the past to meet the needs of the present. This time-honoured and socially valued Polynesian tradition of 'making history' inevitably affects anthropological data collecting. The effect of anthropologists on the shape, form and content of informant data must also inevitably lead to some distortion

and bias. Such biases need not negate the value of anthropological accounts, but it is folly not to recognise them or to ignore them. The interactive threads strung like a sticky, tenuous web between investigator and investigated, observed and observer catch and hold the myths, legends and traditions as they are being remembered, repeated, altered and invented. When one understands this, one understands the inherent problems in trying to interpret *literally* any Polynesian oral history, most of which is, by definition, metaphorical and allegorical.

We may assume, as archaeologist P.V. Kirch suggests, that Rapa Nui oral traditions, fragments of which were recorded and re-recorded between approximately the mid-1800s and into the 1950s, may once have reflected actual events and real people during the preceding several generations, perhaps but not certainly reaching back to 1722 and the advent of Europeans. The enormous drop in the Rapa Nui population level in 1877 is logically assumed to have affected the oral history data base, just as it obviously must have affected the community in a hundred other ways. It is extraordinarily difficult to determine the veracity of some aspects or details of even the most recent, postcontact traditions. The fragments of myths, stories, legends and events available to scholarship are here used, with care and caution, to reconstruct aspects of Rapa Nui history, but it should be understood that these are living traditions distilled, condensed, altered and restructured to an unknown degree, and reflect only a very late and imperfect remnant of a rich and varied oral literature. They are the product of a remarkable effort on the part of researchers and informants alike, but do not represent a fully literal description of Rapa Nui history of any period.

The Rapa Nui culture is a complex and rich amalgam of artistic expression, myth and reality, encouraging and challenging scholars in a wide variety of fields to investigate, catalogue, sort out, compare and analyse. The traditions so valiantly preserved by Rapa Nui informants and collected by scholars are the basis upon which contemporary Rapa Nui society is rediscovering itself. These traditions deserve to be treated as a dynamic and living source which includes elements of diversity, ambiguity, uncertainty, creativity and occasional lack of clarity in detail. Today, Rapa Nui ethnographic sources are being used to explore and integrate aspects of the past into today's life on the island, and pride of place and culture is intensely felt. Rapa Nui elders continue to preserve, interpret and share the past with today's interested youngsters, and they communicate their knowledge unselfishly, as they always have, to a wide circle of international scholarship.

3

The Country for the King
(I te Kona mo te ariki)

We shall not cease from exploration
And the end of all our exploring
Will be to arrive where we started
And know the place for the first time.

T.S. ELIOT, 'FOUR QUARTETS'

Ku tomo takoa ana te vaka o Hotu-matua. He tomo ana, he poreko ana ko Tuu-ma-heke te poki, i poreko a Hotu-matua i te kainga nei ko te Pito-o-to-henua.[1]

RAPA NUI LEGEND

Polynesian societies, while diverse and varied in many ways, all stem from a common root which has been designated Ancestral Polynesian Society. All of the known evidence of ethnobotany, linguistics and archaeology suggests that individual island societies initially developed slowly and conservatively for as long as 1,000 years before marked changes in food production, technology and sociopolitical organisation occurred. Ancient structural principles of economics and social order formed the framework within which this pioneering people met the challenges of island environments.[2] The staging area for the development of Ancestral Polynesian Society appears to be in the Fiji-Tonga-Samoa area of West Polynesia from about *c.*1500 BC. The population which gave rise to Ancestral Polynesia was Austronesian-speaking and had, originally, been part of what archaeologists call the Eastern subgroup of the Lapita Cultural Complex.[3] On many Polynesian islands there is direct historical continuity between the ethnographic present and the historic past, allowing investigators to examine data from one island society to illuminate similar developments on another. On islands like Rapa Nui, where there was a serious break in traditional historic continuity due to outside influence, this Pacific context is an especially important research advantage.

The Lapita Cultural Complex and Ancestral Polynesia

Lapita is reasonably suggested to be the basic archaeological horizon of Oceanic anthropology and prehistory, representing the first human exploration of the remote Pacific. It is the founding cultural complex from which the various Neolithic societies of Polynesia, eastern Micronesia and island Melanesia were produced.[4] The name Lapita is drawn from a single site in Melanesian New Caledonia, and the distinctive and well-documented archaeological assemblages which represent the Lapita Cultural Complex are found in a series of excavated and dated sites which indicate over-water trade and travel contact between and among island sites and over distances of up to 3,400 km (fig. 29). Lapita sites are distributed from the Bismarck Archipelago of Melanesia out into the Pacific in a wide arc of islands increasingly more distant from one another.

There are two principal language groups in Southeast Asia. The older is Austroasiatic and the other Austronesian (sometimes called Malayo-Polynesian). Either or both of these groups are thought to have been the originators of cultural ideas which produced megalithic remains. Megaliths of several types are widespread in island Southeast Asia, as are forked wooden posts. Celebrations involving

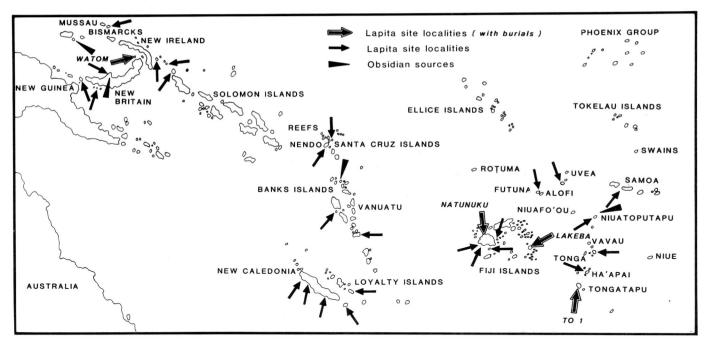

29 Lapita site localities and obsidian sources, West Pacific. *Courtesy of Roger C. Green.*

these monuments are characterised as Feasts of Merit, and an associated belief is that a powerful, supernatural force is situated in the human head.

Lapita people are believed to have spoken some branch of Austronesian, possibly Proto-Oceanic. Pacific Island languages, including Rapanui, are part of the Austronesian family of languages. All archaeological and linguistic evidence to date indicates that a common Austronesian protoculture existed in Southeast Asia and Near Oceania. The prehistoric expansion of Austronesian speakers is suggested to have originated with Proto-Austronesian speaking peoples that migrated out of mainland southern China into Taiwan by *c.* 4000 BC.[5] From there, some 1,000 years later, their descendants moved first into the Philippines and then spread rapidly throughout the Indonesian Archipelago. A critical focus of current research is to determine whether or not Lapita people were actually members of the early Austronesian speaking population which expanded from the Southeast Asian mainland or, instead, developed their distinctive culture in the Bismarck Archipelago.[6]

Lapita people, in addition to developing the marine technology required to support their movement into the Pacific, appear to have raised roots and tubers (yams and taro) using ancient methods of swidden (slash and burn) agriculture. There is some indication that simple methods of agricultural intensification, such as irrigation, may have

been known, although the evidence on this point is, as yet, somewhat equivocal.[7] There is a strong tradition of cropping fruits and nuts in Melanesia, but the relative uses of root and tuber plants and arboriculture are not clear. Arboriculture thus may be an earlier innovation incorporated into Lapita. Bone remains extracted from Lapita site excavations illustrate that pigs, dogs and chickens were

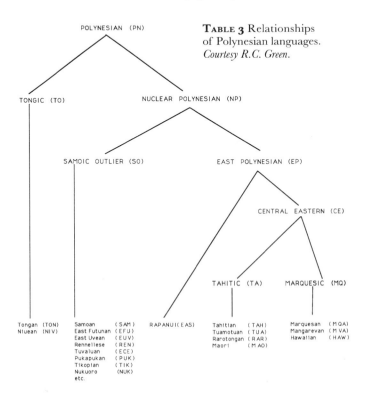

TABLE 3 Relationships of Polynesian languages. *Courtesy R.C. Green.*

raised for food. Food preparation methods included the earth oven (which may have occurred earlier in the Bismarcks) and underground storage pits. The cumulative archaeological and linguistic evidence illustrates that Lapita people were responsible for the introduction into Western Polynesia of domestic animals and crops, as well as methods of land clearance and cultivation.[8] These ancient economic strategies had a major impact upon the preservation of soil quality and other interrelated ecological variables.

Ancestral Polynesia is a term coined to define the reconstructed baseline of Polynesian culture.[9] It describes a society which grew and developed out of Lapita in West Polynesia from *c.* 1000 BC. Analysis of Ancestral Polynesian settlement patterns is only beginning, but the preliminary evidence suggests the existence of small, dispersed, generally coastal villages made up of discrete household units, and it is likely that a communal assembly ground (*malae*) was related to the settlements, although no large-scale public architecture (as on Rapa Nui and some other East Polynesian islands) is known. Ancestral Polynesian society was organised on the principle of the conical clan, and the ramage or cognatic descent group held ancestral land in common. A system of hereditary rank calculated upon the genealogical distance from a founding ancestor determined status. Clan deities were created from apotheosised chiefly ancestors, and chiefs were both sacred and secular rulers whose power (*mana*) emanated from the gods. The concept of sacred prohibition (*tapu*) was known, as was the notion of a spirit or soul separate from the body. Sacred ritual probably incorporated the use of the shrub *Piper methysticum* to produce a ceremonial drink called *kava*. Red or yellow-red pigments and paint were used.

Polynesian culture developed from its Ancestral Polynesian foundation in Fiji-Tonga-Samoa in relative isolation and over an as yet not fully clarified period of time. Dispersal from there into increasingly remote Oceania is believed to have been accomplished by voyaging parties of exploration and settlement which sailed westward into the wind, using developed skills of navigation and marine technology. This 'into the wind' strategy was a conservative and prudent method for maximising the opportunity of return voyaging. Experimental efforts with replicas of Polynesian voyaging canoes have been accomplished by Ben Finney and his colleagues in Hawaii, leaving no doubt about the feasibility of this settlement strategy.[10]

Genetic research supports the linguistic data, clearly illustrating two branches of the human family in the Pacific.[11] One includes the native peoples of Australia and New Guinea, who are genetically variable and differ greatly from place to place, suggesting their antiquity as a group. The second branch is more genetically uniform, definitely related to east Asians, and includes all Polynesians. Recent genetic research has shed new light on Pacific colonisation. A unique genetic mutation, developed about 5,000 years ago in a single individual on the tiny island of Tongariki in the Melanesian archipelago of Vanuatu, resulted in that individual becoming a carrier for an inherited condition known as alpha-thalassaemia. Linked to the environmental presence of mosquitoes and malaria, alpha-thalassaemia is certain to have arisen in Melanesia, where it was amplified as a protection against local malaria, and then was transported by colonisers eastward into the Pacific, where malaria was unknown. For example, a relatively high frequency of alpha-thalassaemia is present in Tahiti, central Polynesia, even though there is no malaria there and never has been. Further, the Tahitian alpha-thalassaemia is of the very same sub-type as that found in Vanuatu. There is now conclusive proof that the Pacific was colonised from west to east 'in spite of Thor Heyerdahl's daring crossing of the Pacific on a balsa raft'.[12]

East Polynesian Prehistory

The settlement of the Pacific is a population movement or original peopling of a previously uninhabited area. It was an areal advancement which variously resulted in expanded and changed languages and culture. As the overwater distances between islands and island groups increased so interaction, intercommunication and interbreeding decreased. Any population which settles a previously vacant environment tends to develop a culture more sharply different from its parent culture than does an immigrant group arriving at already-settled islands. According to Irving Rouse population movement tends to produce divergence and immigration tends to produce convergence.

Previous research into the settlement sequence for East Polynesia had integrated available archaeological and linguistic data to produce a settlement model which has come to be known as the 'orthodox scenario'.[13] In brief, the orthodox scenario states that, following the settlement of the Fiji-Tonga-Samoa region and the development there of Ancestral Polynesian Society over some 1,500 years, the Marquesas Islands became the first island group in East Polynesia to be colonised by people who still made and used pottery, in about AD 300–600. Subsequently, the Marquesas developed into a major dispersal centre from which colonising parties reached Hawaii in *c.* AD 600–700, the Society Islands in AD 800 and New Zealand between

AD 800–1000. Since linguistic evidence suggests that Rapa Nui could have been settled as early as AD 300–400, voyagers to its shores would, therefore, have been among the earliest to depart the Marquesas, almost immediately upon initial settlement. More recent evidence now argues for considering alternative hypotheses of East Polynesian settlement. This natural course of science has great import for understanding Rapa Nui prehistory.

Archaeologist Roger Green suggests that investigators might now usefully abandon the search for a specific island or island group as the East Polynesian homeland, and believes that pinpointing a regional locale is a more reasonable approach. In his opinion, the Southern Cook Islands through the Australs and Society Islands to the Marquesas should be considered as a single, regional source of East Polynesian culture.[14] There is a paucity of excavated sites and dated materials from the earliest phases of prehistory on many islands and island groups, and founder period sites in most of tropical Polynesia are as yet unknown. This naturally results in what archaeologists call sampling error. Little has been accomplished in Polynesian sequence-oriented archaeology beyond a definition of so-called Classic or Protohistoric periods in the Australs and a few late site reports for the Tuamotus. In the Society Islands, assemblages of portable artefacts dating only from AD 800 to 1200 are known, and the Cook Islands sequence extends only to AD 800. Even in the Marquesas, where the evidence is strongest, it is doubtful that actual colonisation sites have been excavated. Because the early phases on so many islands remain 'wholly enigmatic', and partially because of an academic debate over radiocarbon dating results, the sequence of East Polynesian settlement is still not fully known.[15] A quite specific reassessment of Marquesan archaeological evidence has been undertaken by P.V. Kirch, who suggests that the originally postulated initial settlement date of AD 300 is too late.[16]

Settlement of Rapa Nui: Polynesia or Peru?

If the 'orthodox scenario' of East Polynesian settlement is no longer acceptable to many researchers, what can usefully take its place and where does that leave Rapa Nui? It is now 'extremely doubtful that Easter Island was settled from the Marquesas; a more southerly origin in the Austral, Mangareva, Pitcairn region is far more likely both culturally and in terms of known voyaging possibilities'.[17] Linguistic evidence remains firmly indicative of a relatively early Rapa Nui settlement in the first few centuries AD, but certainly before AD 800.[18] Anthropologist Ben Finney suggests three possible settlement routes based on his ex-

perience with and understanding of seasonal patterns of winds, currents, weather and Polynesian marine technology and traditions (fig. 30). Settlement Route 1 from the Marquesas would have required a period of major El Niño westerly winds. Pitcairn, which was settled and then abandoned by East Polynesians, may have been an interim destination along Settlement Route 2 from the Tuamotus/Mangareva during a period of 'winter westerlies'. Voyagers leaving the Southern Cooks or the Australs might also have used these winter westerlies to sail east toward Rapa Nui, either directly or via intervening islands including Mangareva and Pitcairn. Finally, especially adventurous voyagers from any of these islands along the southern fringe of East Polynesia might have braved the cold seas and higher latitudes to catch the westerlies which became increasingly prevalent below 30°S latitude. The extant statue data do not rule out any of Finney's possibilities, but the direct Marquesas route is least indicated. I tend to favour a route from the Cooks or the Australs via Rapa. Some Rapa Nui traditions suggest two arrivals of settlers over an unspecified time. If this indeed did happen, the secondary settlement was very likely from the Tuamotus/Mangareva.

Rapa Nui traditions of settlement vary in detail and order of detail, depending upon the source consulted. The first version of the settlement tale was collected by Thomson, and Métraux regarded it as 'the more ancient as well as the more consistent, [but] not entirely reliable and many things seem to have been misinterpreted'.[19] Both Routledge's and Métraux's versions of the tale came largely from Juan Tepano, and Métraux regarded Routledge's version as incomplete. Considering that the time depth of oral traditions in the Pacific is generally thought to be from four to six generations, and remembering our analysis above of Rapa Nui post-1860 oral history, it is unreasonable to assume that the legend of Rapa Nui settlement is able to transmit very much solid information. Further, if the original Rapa Nui voyage of settlement was later succeeded by a voyage of immigration, then the traditions may be actually associated with this more recent event.

Nevertheless, let us examine the Rapa Nui tradition of settlement, seeking insight into both the event and the central characters whose names have been retained or otherwise included in the traditions. Barthel utilises written and oral data collected from the Pakarati, Hereveri, Atan and other families in 1958 to analyse the settlement story in which Rapa Nui was discovered and settled by voyagers sailing one or perhaps two canoes. There is said to be the possibility of an earlier, exploratory party of six men sailing a canoe called *Te Oraora-miro* (The Living Wood).

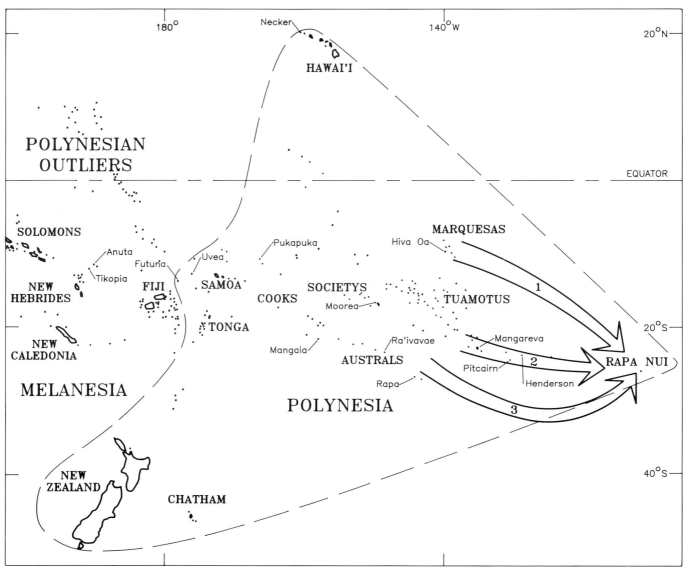

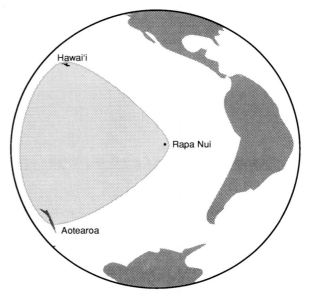

30 ABOVE Three possible Rapa Nui settlement routes suggested by Ben Finney. BELOW Rapa Nui's location. *Map drafted by Curtiss H. Johnson.*

These explorers, when they saw the pink sand beach of Ovahe, said 'here is the country for the king'.[20]

The mythic leader of the settlement expedition is said to have been Hotu Matu'a, the Great Parent. He sailed from *hiva* (literally, a foreign place), described as either Marae-renga or Marae-toe-hau in a great canoe, each hull of which was 30 m (90 ft) long and 3 m (6 ft) deep, or two canoes of the same dimensions. With him was his wife, called Ava Rei Pua, his family and extended family. 'Tuu-ko-ihu' (Tu'u Ko Ihu), said to have been in the second canoe, performed the ritual of cutting the navel cord of Hotu Matuʻa's newborn son after landing on Rapa Nui. In Rapa Nui legend Tuʻu Ko Ihu is variously regarded as a priestly/sacred figure or a culture hero (similar to Maui elsewhere). He was said to be an expert canoe maker but he may also have been a god. The settlers came ashore at Hiramoko in the vicinity of Anakena, the island's most hospitable landing place, and Hotu Matuʻa established his residence there (plate 7).[21] Within a short time, the settlers had explored, divided and settled the island, beginning immediately to establish the plants brought from their homeland.

Who was Hotu Matuʻa? Where did he come from, and why did he leave his homeland, risking his own life and that of his family on a long and dangerous journey? The more reliable versions of the traditions agree that Hotu Matuʻa was a chief, and that he sailed at the urging of his tattooer, Haumaka, who had a vision of a new land, or that he gathered up his family and left after a quarrel.[22] The Haumaka fragment of mythic history suggests that the roles of chief and priest were fulfilled by two individuals, rather than concentrated in the person of the sacred chief. Such social differentiation is characteristic of East Polynesia and partially related to the development there of monumental ceremonial architecture. Haumaka (and perhaps Tuʻu Ko Ihu) were visionary and expert artisans who claimed special advisory relationships to Hotu Matuʻa.

The Polynesian term *marae* (found in Marae-renga and Marae-toe-hau) is applied in the Society Islands, Tuamotus, Cook Islands and Austral Islands to a sacred, ceremonial place which usually contains an *ahu* (raised, rectangular stone platform). In Rapanui usage, *ahu* refers to the entire structure and the word *marae* is not used. Consequently, either the place Marae Renga is a postcontact introduction into Rapa Nui oral history, which is quite possible, or it is a legitimate place name retained only as a proper noun (i.e. Marae and not *marae*). Where is Marae Renga? Is it a real place, an introduced idea or a mythic memory?

When we look elsewhere in Polynesia for Marae Renga, we find the vaguely similar Arerenga in Rarotonga, a high island and the largest of the Cook Islands. Arerenga is the name of a traditional land section in the exact coastal midpoint of the west sector of the island. Two late sites (RAR 97 and RAR 98) at Arerenga consist only of basalt and coral curbing.[23] On Pukapuka in the Cook Islands, as we have seen, myths speak of Poike, a 'copulating place' where a huge battle was fought by rival factions over the death of two valued women. There are many generic place names scattered widely in the Pacific, but Poike is not one of them.

If Poike is indeed a legitimate name in Pukapukan mythology which was not introduced postcontact, then a connection with Rapa Nui is implied that, in turn, strengthens the Arerenga/Marae Renga relationship somewhat.

The settlement party may have consisted of twenty-five to one hundred people per vessel. Adult males and females of several age levels were included, and probably some children. A variety of gender-specific expertise in fishing, building, farming, cloth and mat-making, healing and many other traditional skills would have been represented. The party, which was probably formed of related individuals, would have been led by a respected male whose power aboard the vessel was absolute. That man was assuredly of chiefly rank. Whether he was also navigator of the vessel is not known, but is quite possible. Navigation was a highly specialised science, taught to high-ranking and/or highly gifted men in organised and secret schools of learning. The power of the navigator was derived from the gods and was made visible in profound and striking ways, time and again, throughout the journey. The voyage may have lasted a month or more, during which time strong leadership was required to maintain order, dispense supplies, secure food as those supplies were depleted, determine course, direct the repair of damage to the vessel and its sails, predict and control the weather. In short, the leader in whom group confidence was placed was expected to assure the success of the voyage and protect the very lives of all aboard the vessel.

One of several signs of land sought by the navigator would have been the movements of birds. If it is true that the voyagers arrived on Rapa Nui during the month called Anakena (July), as some traditions relate, then the island at that time would have been the target of huge flocks of birds. As many as twenty-five bird species, ranging from sub-Arctic to tropical, have been identified by David Steadman and his colleagues in archaeological contexts at Anakena on the north coast of Rapa Nui. Included among those remains are many birds now extinct on Rapa Nui, such as rails, owls, parrots and herons. Sooty Terns are sparse but present throughout the Anakena sequence. Thousands of these birds would have been migrating to Rapa Nui, in varying but probably nearly continuous waves, from about the end of June to the end of August, and their visual and audible presence would have been discernible from some distance, indeed quite impossible to ignore.

The value of birds as a sign of land to Polynesian navigators varied in several ways. During the middle of the day seabirds are very active, diving, swooping, flying great distances and changing direction frequently. At the end of the day they align in formations and head directly home. At that time they are highly dependable directional indicators of land. When canoes are within striking distance of land the numbers of adult birds foraging to feed their young visibly increases. All of these behaviours were known to Polynesians. Navigators could have taken a bearing off either migrating flocks or fishing birds returning to their island base, and Ben Finney suggests such a bearing, when converted to a star compass heading, would have led directly to Rapa Nui.

The significant presence of birds in Rapa Nui ideology might well have been a part of the belief system brought from the Polynesian homeland. The iconographic merging of bird and human male attributes to produce the sacred Rapa Nui birdman (*tangata manu*) image might stem, in part, from the legendary interactive role of birds with the male leader in actually finding the island on the settlement journey. Belief in the sacred nature and esoteric power of the leader who initiated and led the journey may have been threatened en route and then reaffirmed, established and enhanced once landfall was achieved. The magnitude of his leadership accomplishment, growing out of his hereditary ability to influence the supernatural, was a direct reflection of his intimate contact with nature witnessed by all on the life-threatening journey of settlement.

Some of the Rapa Nui traditions say that one of Hotu Matu'a's sons left Rapa Nui to return to the homeland. Certainly it would have been possible, from a resource point of view, to construct an adequate voyaging canoe or raft of palm wood sometime within *c.*300 to 500 years after settlement, although the motivation for doing so is obscure. The monolithic stone sculptures of the Marquesas, for example, were carved and erected a good deal later than those on Rapa Nui. Could the tradition of the *moai* have been exported with returning voyagers? There is no direct archaeological evidence of such an event. Neither does the temporal or stylistic evidence of the statues which stood upon *ahu* suggest that they inspired direct replication elsewhere in East Polynesia. The use of other monolithic sculpture on Rapa Nui sacred sites, such as a few of the red scoria examples which were not directly placed upon *ahu*, however, is another matter. Much more work needs to be done on the development of the monolithic stone sculpture tradition in the Pacific before such a question can be addressed.

Since the nineteenth century a prehistoric connection between Rapa Nui and South America has occasionally been suggested but never demonstrated. Some forty years ago, this idea found a dramatic and outspoken advocate in Thor Heyerdahl. The movement of pre-Columbian people from the coast of South America into the Polynesian geographic sphere is extremely plausible when one considers, as Heyerdahl did, the east to west trade wind pattern. As of this writing however, no reliable archaeological, linguistic or biological data on the mainland, in East Polynesia or on Rapa Nui support such an east to west population movement. In the absence of such evidence, is it then reasonable to postulate a single immigration event from South America to Rapa Nui? Again, no data have emerged from the extensive archaeological investigations undertaken on the island to make such a proposition acceptable. How, when and by whom the sweet potato, a New World cultigen, was transferred to the Pacific is one of the great mysteries of archaeology. Its presence there (discussed below) suggests either a trading event or an immigration event between South America and Polynesia. Neither of these possibilities however, requires the prehistoric geographic or cultural involvement of Rapa Nui.

The Challenge of Place: 'Land's End'

Lying isolated in the East Pacific, in an extreme windward position, Rapa Nui is the easternmost of 287 islands contained within the cultural entity called Polynesia.[24] The island is roughly triangular in shape and is approximately 160 km² in area.[25] It is located in the Southern Hemisphere at 27°9' south latitude and 109°26' west longitude. The coast of Chile is a full 2,300 km away to the east, and its nearest island neighbour is uninhabited Sala y Gomez, which lies about 415 km to the east/northeast. Both Rapa Nui and Sala y Gomez are Chilean territory. Pitcairn, some 1,400 km westward of Rapa Nui, was inhabited prehistorically by Polynesians who left stone remains, including sculpture carved of red tuff. Another 1,600 km beyond Pitcairn lies Rapa, inhabited prehistorically by Polynesians who were accomplished builders and engineers of massive earthworks. Mangareva lies approximately 2,000 km to the east of Rapa Nui.

Polynesians have many legends about how various islands came to be. In some of them Maui, the trickster and maker of miracles, fishes up the islands from the bottom of the sea. We have no record of what the Rapa Nui believed about the origin of their island, nor do we know for certain that they ever called it anything but *te kainga*, the land. In their creation chant they account for the origin of many plants, animals and other attributes of the natural world in the typical Polynesian way of male procreation with natural objects, but the island itself is not included. Over the years it was given several names, with Rapa Nui being the one that stuck. Thomson was told by Alexander

Salmon that the name 'Te-Pito-te-Henua' was given to the island by Hotu Matuʻa, but it may have been only applied to the volcanic craters Rano Raraku and Rano Kau. This name, frequently translated as 'navel of the world', has caught the imagination of many writers. The actual meaning of the phrase may be, as linguist W. Churchill has pointed out, 'end of the land' or 'land's end'.

The limited native flora present at settlement included a tree (*Sophora toromiro*) and relatively vast palm groves (plate 8).[26] While pollen identification made by John Flenley and his colleagues is not absolutely firm, these scientists reasonably speculate that the Rapa Nui palm is the same as or similar to the incredible *Jubaea chilensis* (fig. 31). Root moulds or traces of the soil channels cut by the roots of a growing tree which appear to be appropriate to *Jubaea chilensis* have long been known. If the Rapa Nui palm was indeed *Jubaea chilensis*, then we would be dealing with palm forests which, when mature, may have reached some ten to twenty metres in height. The trees have smooth, cylindrical trunks which may bulge slightly in the middle range of their height but are also frequently quite straight, depending on the age of the tree. The *Jubaea chilensis* has large fronds, similar to those of the Canary Islands palm. On a mature tree, the fronds may reach four metres in length and are thus useful in thatch construction. The tree is probably the hardiest of the feather-leafed palms, able to withstand dry summers as well as occasional, very low temperatures. *Jubaea chilensis* grows from seed, and can take from six months to three years to germinate, depending

primarily upon available moisture. After germination, growth is very slow. Natural replacement or regeneration of *Jubaea chilensis* forests requires a great deal of time, even under the very best of conditions. This palm grows in California gardens and sporadically along the coastal zone in mainland Chile, where it was once somewhat more abundant than it is today.

Fossil palm nuts have been found by various people in several parts of the island, all in undated contexts (i.e. in surface contexts of caves or in accessible caches). These palm nuts are small to tiny, and appear when cut to look like miniature coconuts. The fruit of *Jubaea chilensis* is a fleshy yellow when fresh, and drops once a year in autumn for easy harvesting. Inside the hard, outer shell or husk are marble-sized edible nuts with a strong coconut flavour. It is probable that the nuts were stored and used as famine food at various times on Rapa Nui, just as *Pandanus* kernels were on most other Pacific islands. Towards the end of the Rapa Nui prehistoric cultural sequence, the nuts may have become an even more important element in the Rapa Nui diet. Roggeveen remarked upon an 'old and hoary' Rapa Nui person cracking 'a large and hard nut, whose shell was thicker and more resisting than our peach stones' with his or her teeth.[27]

The interior of Rano Raraku contains what was once a freshwater lake but is now more of a swamp. Quantities of soil have eroded into the lake, probably as a result of quarrying activity. The lake is fringed with the green spikes of *Scripus californicus*, commonly called the *totora* reed. This

31 *Jubaea chilensis* palm grove, mainland Chile. *Courtesy Juan Grau V.*

reed, because of its inherent physical qualities, is very useful and was widely used by prehistoric people wherever it occurred for various sorts of boats. For example, in Southern California the reed is widely known by the name of tule or bullrush, and was tied in bundles by the coastal Chumash, Yokuts and Pomo peoples to build small fresh-water or sea-going balsa craft.[28] There is no evidence that the reed was used on Rapa Nui to construct boats, but it was used to build floats called *pora*, which were used as a kind of surfboard during historic times (fig. 32).

The *totora* reed was speculated by Thor Heyerdahl to have been brought to the island by hypothetical settlers from South America, and he frequently illustrated his argu-ment with photos of historic Peruvian balsa craft which are nearly identical in form to those of the Native Californians. When peoples of culturally unrelated and geographically widely separated areas (such as California, Peru and Rapa Nui) each create similar artefacts of the same unique materials, archaeologists describe this as independent in-vention. Most significantly, the *totora* reed has been grow-ing on Rapa Nui for more than 30,000 years and, therefore, colonised the island by natural means.

32 Tattooed Rapa Nui man with reed *pora* by an unknown artist, HMS *Portland*, 1853. *Courtesy of the Royal Geographical Society.*

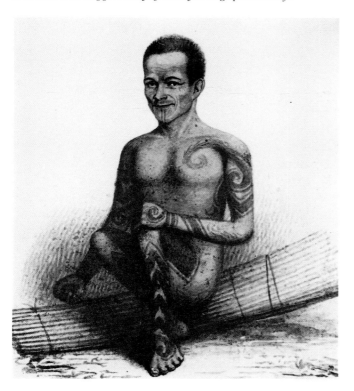

The plant which has plagued Pacific and New World researchers for some time is *Ipomoea batatas*, or sweet potato. Botanists all agree that the sweet potato is of New World origin, and that it is ideally suited to be transferred by humans. Speculation on just how the sweet potato was carried into the Pacific has been extensive and reasoned, but the discussion became rather heated whenever it centred on Rapa Nui. Douglas Yen, whose work on the question of the sweet potato in the Pacific is the definitive effort to date, advanced the hypothesis that the plant was introduced into central Polynesia from tropical South America before *c.*AD 700.[29] He suggested a three stage model for transfer of the sweet potato from Central Poly-nesia.

Recent archaeological investigations on Mangaia in the Cook Islands provide evidence of sweet potato presence at the Tangatatau rock shelter site (MAN-44).[30] The date of colonisation of Mangaia is not fully clear, although early dates from Pukapuka, Aitutaki and Rakahanga suggest occupation by at least AD 600 and probably earlier. How-ever, the establishment of the sweet potato in securely dated contexts on Mangaia by at least *c.*AD 1000 does lend archaeological support to Yen's hypothesis of sweet potato distribution. The only evidence to date of sweet potatoes in an archaeological context on Easter Island is AD 1600, although it is hypothesised by all researchers that the plant was introduced by the Polynesians at settlement. How did the sweet potato get to Polynesia? It is generally thought that the transfer was made by Polynesians, after a voyage of exploration to the South American coast. Ben Finney suggests that such an event might have taken place from Hawaii, the Marquesas during a major El Niño event or from Rapa Nui early in prehistory by exploiting an extended spell of winter westerlies.

The endemic terrestrial fauna of Rapa Nui, even by Pacific island standards, was limited, with insects com-prising by far the largest category.[31] Only one possibly in-digenous lizard species (*Cryptoblepharus boutonii*) is known and there were no indigenous mammals. The Polynesian rat (*Rattus exulans*), widely introduced to Pacific islands by Polynesians as a source of protein food, is known from Rapa Nui archaeological contexts. The introduction of rats had both a positive and a negative side, as these rodents did significant damage to both plants and birds wherever they were known. It is apparent that, in late prehistory, the rat was a significant item in the Rapa Nui diet, while chicken was a more preferred feast food. The Polynesian rat is now extinct on the island, although the European rat is, unhap-pily, abundant.[32]

The marine ecosystem in the clear and cold waters off

33 Calibrated ages for Rapa Nui radiocarbon dates. Open bar defines upper and lower values at 2 s.d., cross line defines mean, multiple cross lines define multiple mean values from curve intersect. *Courtesy W.S. Ayres.*

Rapa Nui, while not barren, is certainly sparse (plates 9, 10).[33] The island lacks a fringing reef, although coral definitely grows offshore and is occasionally thrown up along the coast. The waves which frequently thunder against the rocky coastline also batter the tidepools in which the Rapa Nui have traditionally scavenged for urchins, eels and sea creatures of several varieties. Submarine microhabitats exist and are increasingly well studied.[34] Between 111–140 species of fish are thought to be present, depending upon the source consulted, and the Rapa Nui today favour herbivorous fishes such as the *nanue* (*Kiphosus bigibbus*) and the *maito* (*Acanthurus leucopareius*). The remains of large pelagic fish such as tunas (*kahi*) are known from archaeological contexts, and Yellowfin (*Thunnus albacares*; *kahi aveave*) and three other varieties of tuna are regularly taken today. Remains of whale, seal or sea lion, shark and turtle are also archaeologically present, although all but the shark are rarely sighted today. The Rapa Nui lobster (*Panulirus pascuencis*; *ura*) is sought seasonally by divers. The porpoise appears to have been an important source of protein in the vicinity of Anakena.[35]

The endemic biota of Rapa Nui was unique to this island in terms of the specific numbers, types and interrelationships of plants, birds, insects and marine life. But Rapa Nui was not unique among islands in being highly vulnerable to introduced change. This vulnerability to environmental change or disturbance encourages botanists and other researchers to study islands and is, for example, one of the reasons Darwin contemplated the Galapagos. Ecological vulnerability led to visible and sometimes drastic change whenever humans, in the form of prehistoric Polynesian settlers, arrived on any island. Through landscape modification, plant and animal introductions and other sorts of direct and indirect impacts, island environments and whole ecosystems were altered, sometimes irrevocably. On Rapa Nui, the effect of human impact is visible today to even the most casual visitor, and one can see for oneself the degraded landscape, the loss of palm forest and expanse of grasslands which replaced those forests. While known in broad outline, the full extent of environmental change and the subtleties of effect which that change had on Rapa Nui culture are not yet fully understood.

Rapa Nui Cultural Sequence

Developing a time frame for cultural change is one of the most important goals of archaeology. In 1961, the scientists of the Norwegian Archaeological Expedition first suggested a three-period cultural sequence for Rapa Nui. This sequence was helpful but somewhat limited. While it drew

attention to perceived architectural changes in *ahu* wall construction, it allowed little flexibility in describing regional or site-specific variation and was less than useful in understanding statue design change over time. In 1973, archaeologist W.S. Ayres suggested that Rapa Nui history was best understood as four defined and discrete but process-related cultural phases, although not all archaeologists agree. My own interpretation is close to that of Ayres except that I have redefined his Decadent Phase as the Decadent/Restructure Phase and take a more narrative approach.[36] The calendric dates used to quantify the chronological scheme I propose are based on radiocarbon analysis. All radiocarbon dates are estimates, and not all Rapa Nui dates are regarded as equally reliable. The corrected radiocarbon dates I give are drawn from the work of W.S. Ayres (fig. 33). As is the case with all such explanatory schemes in archaeology, the one presented here is imperfect. The reader is encouraged to regard it as a general, organising framework while also keeping in mind that not all changes happened at the same time on the island as a geographic whole. Rapa Nui life was not lived as a series of static or discrete phases but as a continual ebb and flow of human and natural events.

Phase I of Rapa Nui prehistory thus begins, according to linguistic data alone, in the first few centuries AD, probably *c.*AD 300–400. East Polynesian settlers brought with them certain traditions of both wood carving and stone carving as part of their repertoire of skills. They also brought intricate esoteric ideas and principles wrapped skillfully in a fabric of social and economic organisation. Their communal ways, while tradition-bound, were flexible enough to enable successful adaptation to the new but limited island world which had so miraculously appeared on the horizon.

Following ancient traditions that reached back across the waves to Ancestral Polynesia and beyond, the settlers explored the land, identifying familiar marine resources and wild plants. The food value of the palm nut was probably recognised right away. Initial settlements were established in the coastal zone, near the water but away from the seaspray, and the able-bodied began to clear the land by the ancient 'slash and burn' method of swidden agriculture. The crop plants which had successfully survived the voyage, including taro, yam, sweet potato, banana and sugar cane were planted by men and women together in the newly cleared soil, although as time passed the work of weeding and mulching the growing fields was probably more in the hands of women. The important paper mulberry tree (*Broussonetia papyrifera*) was nurtured to produce the Rapa Nui version of Polynesian barkcloth (*mahute*) and

34 Two Rapa Nui men paddling a plank canoe drawn over an unfinished sketch of the island, Cook's second voyage, 1774. *Courtesy Staatsbibliothek Zu Berlin Preussischer Kulturbesitz.*

the coastal tree *Thespesia populnea* (*mako'i*) may have been introduced.

Palm wood was probably the main source of new vessel construction. These vessels, built by experts and used in seeking the large, pelagic fish and porpoises plying the deep water zones lying at least a kilometre or more offshore were seaworthy and strong, completely unlike the small, fragile and oft-repaired outriggers which greeted European explorers (fig. 34). In addition to marine life, birds and birds' eggs were extremely plentiful, readily and easily available.[37] Some birds nested in ground burrows, others in the shrubs and brush. Unused to the presence of humans, the birds simply waited to be snatched from their nests. Within the first few generations after settlement, the Rapa Nui people made a marked to severe impact on the bird population through direct harvesting as well as habitat destruction. The chickens brought on the canoes established themselves immediately with little trouble. As far as we know, no dogs or pigs were introduced.[38]

At Ahu Tahai I, on the west coast near the village of Hanga Roa, a corrected radiocarbon date gives a range of AD 600–1050 for the *ahu*, which is composed of vertical, carved or shaped stone slabs. At two standard deviations a reading of AD 600–800 is reasonable and consistent for this site. A single statue head, carved of red scoriaceous material and broken from its body, was found in the bay during reconstruction of this site. If this head was part of the *ahu* platform fill, as archaeologist W.S. Ayres, the original excavator of the site, speculated it may have been, then the intact statue would likely have been associated with Ahu Tahai I.[39] Although this is by no means certain, as there are other red scoria statues and heads in the near vicinity of Tahai II, it is possible. In any case, it is highly likely that one of the first acts of the settlers upon reaching the island was the construction of a sacred site.

The establishment of the Rapa Nui on their new island home required an adaptive transformation in social behaviour, technology and resource utilisation. A series of cultural selections took place in which aspects of their definition as a people were abandoned while others were preserved and possibly redefined or emphasised in new ways. Choices were made by individuals on every level of the society which were prompted by the actual environment but also by their *perception* of that environment. When specific choices were acceptable to the community as a whole, they became group-adaptive responses. The island environment didn't cause the Rapa Nui people to change, but the people and the environment, enmeshed in a positive-feedback cycle, began to change each other.

The monolithic statue cult, a profoundly and uniquely Rapa Nui innovation on an ancient, established theme, grew and developed out of this human/culture/nature interaction. Strong control by a recognised authority such as the navigator or chief and unquestioning adherence to shipboard requirements has been suggested as one of the prerequisites for the success of Polynesian settlement of the Pacific. Is this a long- or short-term social characteristic? Is it transferred intact along with plants and animals at settlement? Does it then grow and develop into a social norm expressed in an ideology? If so, how does that ideology choose a stone image as its symbolic vehicle? How do social norms combine with technology and available resources (particularly stone resources) to produce a social structure like that of Rapa Nui? There are many questions to be framed about how and why the statue cult emerged and took the unique form it did on this small island.

Phase II is called the Ahu Moai Expansion Phase, and begins from *c.* AD 1000 to 1680. It is a time largely of adaptive modifications and adjustments in response to the changing island environment, increasing population size and agricultural intensification. We presume that this scenario was enacted in isolation from outside contact, either with other Polynesian cultures or with South America. Such isolation would naturally affect cultural development, just as later European contact obviously did. The defining element of this time span is the growing intensification of scale, size, complexity and architectural variety of ceremonial platforms (ahu) and cleared ceremonial spaces which, as we will explore in more detail below, are derived in form and function from the East Polynesian marae concept.

The ritually important sites of Rano Raraku and Rano Kau were largely deforested during this time. Deforestation, whether it occurs on Rapa Nui or in the Amazon rain forest, is the first in a linked chain of environmental events which can include, among other problems, soil depletion and erosion, water contamination and loss of bird habitat. That chain, however, is not inevitably forged, but can be broken or bent at any time by people with foresight and ingenuity. Thus, while some Rapa Nui were cutting all or nearly all of the trees on the lands where they had use rights, elsewhere socially acceptable methods such as interdiction may have been enacted to slow or stem the deforestation process. On the basis of an agricultural carrying capacity estimate and present archaeological indications, a peak population of between 7,000 and 9,000 is conjectured to have been reached by c. AD 1550, and the number of people on the south coast is thought to have doubled.[40] Significantly, archaeologist Chris Stevenson has found indications that trees may have been still growing on the island in the AD 1400s–1500s, forcing us to rethink the currently popular, but simplistic scenario that the demise of the statue cult was due only to the lack of wood caused by overexploitation of palm trees.

Throughout this phase, Rano Raraku was actively quarried for stone to produce monolithic statues for placement upon ahu. Rano Kau, in use from at least the mid-AD 1300s as a ceremonial site, was elaborated and used more intensively. Both of these sacred centres had a pan-island significance, and each was spatially and symbolically related to the other in a complex ideological matrix.

The Rapa Nui social structure emphatically encouraged the production of more and larger statues, and food resources initially increased in response to the community's need of them to fuel this task. At the same time, political integration, especially on the south coast, increased. Ceremonies of which the statues were the central focus were held on lineage or combined-lineage lands, and the most elaborate rituals took place on the most architecturally complex sites. The design attributes and proportions of the ahu images were carefully controlled and executed by a professional carvers' 'guild', and ahu image production grew more 'standardised'. Ritual renovation of sacred sites to accommodate larger statues sometimes required the destruction of earlier, smaller statues. Variation in statue body shape, the defining characteristic of statue type differences, is evident in the statue corpus. At Ahu Akivi, an ahu originally built in the fifteenth century and possibly earlier was remodeled and seven moai of statistically average size, shape and weight were erected on the second construction phase after the AD 1400s and before the mid-1600s.

The unique Rapa Nui house form called hare paenga is associated with this phase, distributed primarily in the coastal zone and usually in proximity to ceremonial sites. If the Rapa Nui traditions of a secondary voyage are taken at face value, then it is during the early part of this phase that such a voyage of immigration, possibly from the Manga-reva-Tuamotu region, may have occurred, introducing the hare paenga form. More likely, it is a Rapa Nui innovation partially in response to resource scarcity. In any case, the elaboration of many attributes of Rapa Nui culture which took place during Ahu Moai Phase II has rightfully been called a florescence.

Phase III of Rapa Nui prehistory is the Decadent/Restructure Phase, suggested to reach from c. 1680 to 1722, when the Dutch 'discovered' the island. From about the fifteenth century until 1868 (nearly 150 years beyond contact with Europeans) the statue cult was variously in a complex process of change, termination, revival and sporadic renewal, with the hallmark of the time being a reconsideration of long-held beliefs. Limited aspects of the cult as a world view were retained, but the continued development of the birdman cult was more successful in seasonally restructuring the social order to accommodate a frightening evolution of natural reality. Significant environmental stress, created largely through increased population, meant that Rapa Nui food shortages were frequently created or exacerbated. Intensified land use, continued deforestation and probable soil depletion interacted to produce increasing events of crop failure. Short-term environmental crises such as drought would have significantly aggravated a precarious situation. Varying degrees of inter-clan and/or inter-class conflict erupted, although the types and extent of these conflicts are not well understood.

At an unknown point during this phase, or late in the preceding, the Rapa Nui arranged themselves into two opposing confederacies of related lineage groups (mata).[41] This division had very ancient roots, and may have been

35 'East end of the Winipoo [Vinapu] crypt' showing fallen *moai* with incised lines on the neck, red crescent and white anthropomorph painted on left side of the torso. *Watercolour by J. Linton Palmer, 1868. Courtesy Royal Geographical Society.*

36 BELOW *Moai* (13–486–07) lying 'in-transport' with pecked crescent shapes on its right side is 8.51m tall. *Drawing by Cristián Arévalo Pakarati.*

known and acknowledged for many generations. Indeed, it is probable that it was inherent from settlement. The highest ranked kin group (ramage) on the island throughout its history was the Miru. The Honga lineage of the larger Miru kin group claimed direct descent from Hotu Matu'a, and through him to the gods Tangaroa and Rongo. The Miru held the highest status within the western confederacy, collectively known as Ko Tu'u Aro Ko Te Mata Nui. The Ko Tu'u represented power through hereditary status. The far more populous, lower-ranked eastern confederacy was designated Hotu Iti Ko Te Mata Iti. It has been suggested that the confederacies grew out of war alliances, but the genesis and evolution of the groups could also have been a result of the increasing political integration once required to support both agricultural intensification and statue production. In either case, the development of the confederacies is probably a somewhat

long-term and complex social response to a number of interactive factors.

Rano Raraku quarry continued in use, and it is probable that the revival of some aspects of the cult produced some limited statue carving even during Phase IV, the historic. The reuse of *ahu* and *moai* sites through the application of petroglyphs and paint, recarving of *pukao* and modification of structures for burials and other purposes is evidence of continuity in ideological precepts and practice which extends into postcontact time (figs 35, 36). The ceremonial centre at Orongo continued to be the site of seasonal, pan-island rituals which were evolving in form. The integral relationship of the birdman cult to the statue cult accounted for the limited evolution of statue form at this time, producing Tukuturi, the kneeling statue. When the Dutch arrived, the evolution of Rapa Nui culture was *interrupted and redirected* for all time.

4

The Birdman Cult: Ideology, Ecology and Adaptation

He loaded his tuna fish [and] he went up crying, I [bring it] for the god, for Toitoi of Motu-nui, for Makemake.

RAPA NUI CHANT

Centred upon a universal creator god and provider called Makemake, who became incarnate in the *tangata manu*, or birdman, the rituals which grew out of the statue cult and moved from lineage *ahu* sites to the pan-island location of Orongo on Rano Kau are among the most astonishing in Pacific prehistory (plate 11). Early investigators saw the statue and birdman cults as discrete entities, unrelated to one another, while Routledge suspected their integral relationship.[1] This was, on the surface, logical. The evidence of the fallen statues and ostensibly unused *ahu* seemed mute testimony to an ideology rejected violently, out of hand. In contrast, some aspects of the birdman cult rituals continued until 1866–67, especially those of initiation. While not actually witnessed by ethnographers, these remnant practices were described to Routledge and others. It is my opinion that both the statue cult and the later birdman cult have similar structural qualities, the same principal actors, shared basic goals and related iconography.

The cultural content of birdman rituals cannot be projected, in its entirety, on the unknown practices of the statue cult. The birdman cult may well have been a sub-tradition of the statue cult, existing within or alongside of it for generations before emerging from subordinate status to that of dominant practice. Reasons for its emergence include (but are not limited to) power shifts between priestly and chiefly classes and/or fluctuating political relationships among hereditary lineages, but the overall ecological and resource situation on the island was certainly a major factor in creating and shaping change.

Just as we have, for too long, assumed that Rapa Nui is a single natural environment without area or region-specific nuances, we have also assumed that the statue cult ideology fully dominated all aspects of cosmological thinking. The widespread proliferation of the *moai* as a symbol is good evidence for considering the cult to have been a dominant force in the culture, but the emergence of the birdman cult is equally clear evidence that ideological thinking had some flexibility and creativity available to it. In short, the evolution in ideological practice which we see in the statue cult/ birdman cult (Rano Raraku/Rano Kau) historical juxtaposition on Rapa Nui, reveals the cultural possibilities inherent in the island's social, political and religious framework. The birdman cult is not merely a substitution or variant form of the statue cult. It is the profoundly graphic essence of Rapa Nui cultural adaptability.

Culture, as anthropologist Fredrik Barth has pointed out, is always 'in the making'. Because societies which depend upon oral means to ensure continuity of tradition employ metaphorical meanings in ritual, the performance of those rituals often changes over time. Cosmological notions evolve and expand in an effort to contain and transmit changing social, political and other realities of life. Thus we must assume a varying pace of change among peoples who organise their society, as the Rapa Nui did, along lineage lines. In short, we must work to respect the notion of local variation, seeking signs of that variation in the archaeological record and assuming that it exists even in cases where there is strong evidence, as there is on Rapa Nui, for dominant, society-wide ideological practices.

Birdman Cult Ideology: Pacific Genesis

The antiquity of the creator god Makemake in the Rapa Nui belief system can be traced with certainty to 1770 and the Spanish expedition, led by Felipe González de Haedo. The birdman cult is inferred to have been in existence at the same time, when Rapa Nui chiefs signed a treaty which ostensibly annexed the island to Spain, using characters which appear to be symbolic of the sacred bird concept. These characters were extremely roughly drawn, and also include the *komari* or vulva form and a very prominent bird figure similar to one recorded on *pukao* at Akahanga. It has been speculated that the characters are related to *rongorongo* symbols, but they might also be tattoo designs. In New Zealand, for example, Maori chiefs signed European documents with their distinctive tattoo marks. In Tikopia, tattoo marks were used to distinguish ownership of sago vats.

Makemake or Ko Makemake was born in the sea from a skull belonging to an old woman priestess of Ahu Tongariki.[2] According to the understanding of Catholic missionaries, Makemake rewarded the good and punished the bad, and spoke through both male and female priests. The priests were 'very able ventriloquists', demanding contributions of food from the Rapa Nui. Warriors associated with these priests appear to have formed a secret society, occasionally making off with small children as sacrificial offerings. These priestly/godly demands, at a period late in ethnographic time, often approached the terrifying level of extortion, and are similar in their actions and emblems to other secret societies in both Polynesia and Micronesia.

Haua, a little-known spirit mentioned first by Geiseler and only in conjunction with Makemake, was thought to be the male companion of the god. He fished to provide food for the priestess and, together with Makemake, drove clouds of birds from place to place, finally bringing them to Motu Nui. The priestess was responsible for teaching the people incantations and rituals designed to give thanks to Makemake and Haua for the food they provided. Alfred Métraux quite reasonably suggested that Makemake (the Great God or Etua) was a creator god cognate with either or both Tane or Tiki of central and East Polynesia. This idea is based upon Makemake as creator of humankind through multiple copulations with elements of the natural world. He also thought that Makemake's origin from a skull explained the profusion of skull or mask-like petroglyphs as probable representations of Makemake.

In addition to Makemake and Haua, Hina-kauhara, the daughter and first woman born of Tiki and Hina-popoia (Hina-the-heaped-up), are mentioned in an 'obscure and garbled myth' told to Métraux.[3] Hina-the-heaped-up was first created by Tiki from a heap of sand ('ahu-one'), with which he copulated. In the story, Hina-kauhara or Hina, who is 'undoubtedly a woman, becomes a man who wants to be mistaken for Makemake'. This sexual transformation and/or ambiguity attributed to Hina-kauhara is a recognisable element of Rapa Nui art style in the presentation of some anthropomorphic figures, and will be discussed in more detail in a following chapter.

The birdman cult is a unique creation of the Rapa Nui mind and culture, but it also contains within it retained Polynesian beliefs or references. Although we need not look outside of Rapa Nui for a direct parallel or inspiration for the birdman cult, it is instructive to seek comparative references.[4] Birds are widely regarded in Oceania as omens, signs, spirit helpers and spirit messengers. Various species were considered to be animate representatives (messengers) of gods. Terrance Barrow maintains that the combination of human and bird elements is consistent in Oceanic art. Occasionally, a god was thought to be truly present in the bird or other living representative, just as a god was believed to take possession of an inspirational priest or inhabit an image. In the Marquesas, a legend which mentions Makemake is known.

On Pukapuka in the Cook Islands we find direct evidence of an approach to the supernatural which contains some of the same natural and mythological elements inherent in the Rapa Nui birdman concept. There, just as on Rapa Nui, the people possessed a great god in the same sense that they possessed a chief of one dominant lineage as supreme chief of the island. This god was called Mataliki or Mataaliki and was the god of the i Tua lineage.[5] Mata[a]liki was a 'man inside the stone' of the island who, with his wife, lived on the west side of the island in opposition to another godly couple on the east side of the island. He was believed to be the supreme god of all male activities and the supreme protector of all men. Men were called 'te manu o Mata[a]liki (the birds of Mata[a]liki)'. The female counterpart of Mata[a]liki was Taua, and women were called 'te manu o Taua (the birds of Taua)'. Although Taua had considerable power, she was never elevated to the status of supreme goddess of the island, but remained chief goddess of the dominant lineage.

In one of the Pukapukan migration tales accounting for settlement of their island and including references both to Tonga and the mythical island of Yayake (wherein Poike is located), a child called Te Vave-na-to-i-Te-Aumaloa (The Warrior Born at Te Aumaloa) grew into a man who was capable of flying on high like a bird, although he had no wings. He flew above the sea to catch turtles and whole schools of bonito and albacore, which he brought back to the island for the people to eat. Te Vave's emblem was the Ghost Tern or White Tern (*Gygis alba*). In spite of his ability to produce huge quantities of fish and other seafood for the island people to eat, Te Vave was betrayed to two warriors by an old woman who was angry over her meagre share of food. The warriors plotted, and with the help of the goddess Taua, struck down Te Vave with their spears. Upon cutting him open, the people found that Te Vave had eight hearts in his chest cavity, thus explaining his ability to fly.

There are obvious variations in the Pukapukan and Rapa Nui concepts, and Pukapukan is a Samoic (West Polynesian) language in contrast to the East Polynesian origin of Rapanui. Nonetheless, there is also the implication of continuity and adaptation in the central and comparative mythological themes. Mata[a]liki, Taua and the man/bird on Pukapuka, Cook Islands and Makemake, Haua and the birdman on Rapa Nui appear to be variations on the same ideological and iconic themes. If we extend the inference, we find that the most important gods of both Pukapuka and Rapa Nui are Tongaroa and Rongo, ancestors of the highest ranking chief of the dominant lineage in both societies. These gods, however, are remote in time and space, and the lineage gods, Mata[a]liki on Pukapuka and, perhaps, Makemake on Rapa Nui, assume the more intimate relationship with life and the living. Tongaroa and Rongo, however, remain the legitimisers of hereditary chiefly rule.

In my view, the apparent goals of the seasonal Rapa Nui birdman rituals were both secular and spiritual. The spiritual goals centred upon a concern with fertility and fecundity. The secular purpose varied over time. In the beginning, the major purpose for developing a pan-island site for birdman ritual rather than using *ahu* on lands belonging to competing lineages was to concentrate, consolidate and maintain power in the hands of the Miru, the traditional ruling elite. As time passed, the rites also served to signal a structural change in society, acknowledging the separation of sacred and secular power and legitimising the achievement of that power through competition. Not until the final, postcontact unraveling of intertwined ritual beliefs and social structure, however, did the birdman rituals at Rano Kau fail to serve the purposes of the Miru.

Katherine Routledge reasonably suggested that the birdman symbols carved as petroglyphs and painted in house interiors at Orongo on Rano Kau represented victorious birdmen in much the same way that *moai* represented deceased, deified ancestors (fig. 37). Depicted primarily in rock carvings and woodcarvings, the birdman is composed of avian/human characteristics combined in

37 Removal of painted slabs from the interior of an Orongo house, Rano Kau, by crew of USS *Mohican*, 1886. *Courtesy of the Department of Anthropology, NMNH, Smithsonian Institution.*

several ways, and three distinct types have been identified in the petroglyphic corpus (fig. 38, plate 12).[6] A total of 481 birdman petroglyphs are known island-wide, and of these 86% are located at or near Orongo. Fifteen identifiable, realistic frigatebird (*Fregata minor; makohe*) motifs are known, thirteen of these at Orongo and Motu Nui (fig. 39). The frigatebird is said to be associated with the Miru, although the distribution of frigatebird petroglyph motifs alone does

38 Bas-relief petroglyph of a highly stylised birdman carved in Rano Kau basalt at Orongo. *Drawing by Cristián Arévalo Pakarati.*

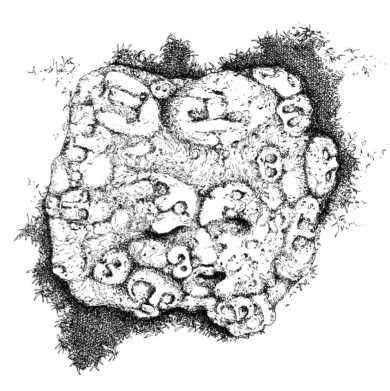

39 Naturalistic Frigatebird petroglyphs are distinctly rare in the island's rock art corpus. *After Lavachery 1939, Lee, 1986.*

40 Carvings of the type said to represent the god Makemake on a small boulder near two in-transport statues (12–14A). *Drawing by Cristián Arévalo Pakarati.*

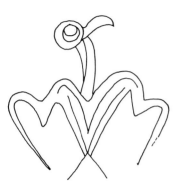

Frigatebird petroglyph,
Mata Ngarau, Rano Kau

Frigatebird petroglyph with
red pigment, Moto Nui

substantiate that notion. In addition, a total of twenty-four bird petroglyphs identifiable as the Sooty Tern (*Sterna fuscata; manutara*) and seventy-nine generic bird petroglyphs are known.

Three distinct types of human heads/faces are carved on the rocks of Orongo, and these are variously said to depict individuals or the creator god Makemake. Today, all head/face petroglyph images are automatically said by Rapa Nui to represent Makemake (fig. 40). Although the antiquity of this association is not known Métraux accepted it based upon the connection of Makemake and the human

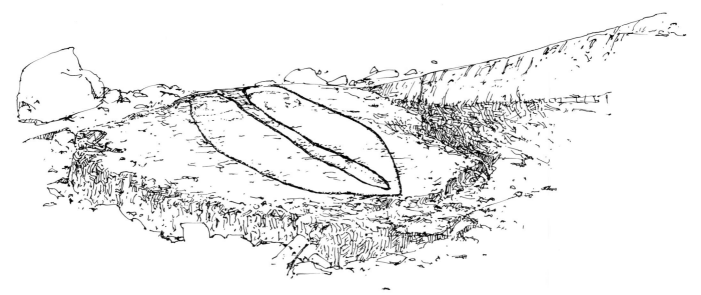

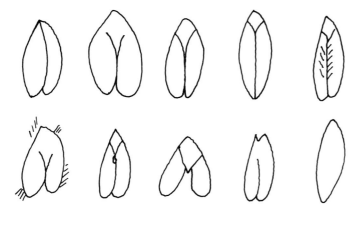

41 *Komari* (vulva) incised into a *paenga* in the vicinity of Ahu Tongariki measures 130cm in length. *Drawing by Cristián Arévalo Pakarati.*

42 Range of design variation in *komari* (vulva). *After Lee, 1986.*

skull in legends, but did not test it further. The basic facial features used to depict the face as a petroglyph are the eyes/nose, although eyes alone are also carved. A total of 517 of these types of human heads/faces have been documented, with the vast majority associated with either Orongo or territories said to belong to the ranking Miru. It is clear that, if we are to make judgements based upon numbers alone, it is the human head/face image rather than the frigatebird which is most closely related to the Miru.

By far the most numerically significant iconic symbol associated with Orongo, however, is the *komari* or vulva (figs 41, 42). A total of 564 of these motifs has been recorded, with 334 (66%) of them occurring in the Orongo/Rano Kau area. The ethnographies associate the *komari* with rites of adolescent initiation, and the integration of these ceremonies with those of the birdman cult is suggested by the juxtaposition of symbols at Orongo. Thus we see that, from the standpoint of sheer repetition of symbols, the *komari*, the human head/face, the *tangata manu* and a few realistic bird images are the symbols most frequently used to give a sense of place and purpose to the ritual site of Orongo. It is these forms which must be regarded, therefore, as expressive of the principles and practices of Orongo ritual.

The birdman cult and the designs associated with it offer a compelling vision of charismatic innovation wherein the accepted esoteric idiom was greatly expanded to accommodate a range of diverse, dynamic, parallel and convergent imagery. Orongo birdman rituals were held yearly, but there is significant disagreement between Routledge and Métraux about the exact time frame and order of the events as well as in specific details. Métraux concedes that his reconstruction is somewhat less supportable than hers, but also feels that she confused the order of events significantly. In any case, Routledge's version is the earlier and Métraux's is based largely on reinterviews with her informants.

Ecological Impetus of the Cult

Birdman ritual was predicated upon the seasonal arrival (variously from June to August and encompassing the traditional arrival of Hotu Matu'a in July) and nesting (September or October) of the Sooty Tern on Motu Nui (fig. 43). The arrival of huge numbers of these birds was said by Routledge to have marked the lifting of an apparent *tapu* on

43 Sooty Tern (*Sterna fuscata*) nesting on Motu Nui is intimately associated with the seasonal arrivals of tuna and other pelagic fish schools to Rapa Nui waters, and was the major focus of the *tangata manu* cult. *Photo by David C. Ochsner, 1989.*

some large, deep-sea fish and the beginning of the season in which these fish could legitimately be taken by lineages other than the highest-ranked. Métraux also says that the deep-sea fishing season opened with the coming of the *manutara*, although the various *tapu* surrounding the taking of tuna are somewhat confused. Tuna were originally the province of the Miru paramount chief, but were later claimed as spoils by warriors. The arrival of the birds was predicted by the highest status priests (*ivi atua*), and Routledge says that 'the approach of the manu-tara can be heard for miles, for their cry is their marked peculiarity, and the noise during nesting is said to be deafening'.[7] The principal actors in this melodramatic event appear to be depicted in the carvings on the back of Hoa Hakananai'a, a central and somewhat transitional symbol of cult activity.

A competition was organised wherein four (and, at various times, more) important men, members of the Ao or 'ascendent clan' in current residence at the feast centre of Mataveri were nominated by *ivi atua* to participate in the birdman rites. Mataveri, at the base of Rano Kau, means 'place of the centipede' and is associated with cannibalistic feasts by high-ranked warriors. It is also, unfortunately, poorly documented archaeologically because of commercial use of the area over a very long time. Members of *matakio*, inferior or defeated groups, were not allowed to participate in the rituals. Thus, a built-in mechanism for retaining power within the politically dominant group was established.

After many months in residence and at an appointed time in July, participants at Mataveri ascended the crater via a ceremonial path designated the 'road of the Ao'. The sign which was taken by the priests as an indicator for the start of these seasonal activities is not known, but may have been the rising of the Pleiades in conjunction with the Austral solstice. Each of those chosen acted in the name of one of four gods associated with the cult. In addition to Makemake and his companion Haua ('Hawa-tuu-take-take'), the other two gods were their wives Vie Kenatea and Vie Hoa, respectively. Thus, there were two godly couples represented by four men, two of whom obviously represented female entities. Those chosen chanted the name of the appropriate god before the competitive ordeal began.

The ordeal consisted of each man descending the outer wall of Rano Kau, entering the sea and swimming its treacherous (and occasionally shark-infested) waters to Motu Nui. Once there, they remained sheltered in caves until the first one of their number found an egg of the nesting Sooty Tern, and during this time the *ivi atua* gathered at Orongo predicted who would be successful at this task. The successful individual then shouted (or otherwise signalled) the news to those assembled at Orongo, and a *tangata rongorongo* announced the winner to the multitude. The final task was for all participants to return safely to the island, the winner of the ordeal being allowed to remain on Motu Nui until he felt spiritually prepared to return.

During the time the egg was in his possession, he was obligated to fast. In some instances, the actual physical act of swimming to and from Motu Nui was undertaken by *hopu* or *hopu manu*, a term Routledge understood as servant.[8]

The termination of this part of the ritual was the consecration of the birdman and the attainment (or, more often, retention) of secular power. Routledge says that, when the *hopu* arrived on the mainland, he handed over the egg to the man whom he represented, who had already shaved his head and painted it either white or red. A *tangata rongorongo*, ceremoniously and with chanting, tied a fragment of red barkcloth and a piece of wood from the sandalwood tree (*Santalum*; *naunau*) around the *hopu*'s arm which had held the egg. A signal fire was lit on the summit of Rano Kao, on either the west or the east side, announcing the confederacy to which the victorious Ao belonged. It is possible that human sacrifices were offered.

The newly decreed *tangata manu* took the egg in his own extended palm, held it above his head and led the multitude in a procession along the southeastern shore (including part of the route traversed by Captain Cook's men) to Rano Raraku if he was of the eastern confederacy. If he was of the western confederacy, he went to Anakena (and, presumably, Ahu Naunau). Once in residence at either of these sites, his person was *tapu* for five of the twelve months he was *tangata manu*. An *ivi atua* shared his house but never his food. The *tangata manu* allowed his nails to grow and wore a special headdress of human hair. The *hopu* also remained in seclusion at his own home, and various *tapu* were placed upon his behaviour for the subsequent year. The sacred egg was hung from the rafters of the *tangata manu*'s house for three days, and then the contents were blown from the shell and a fragment of red barkcloth was inserted.

The secular power acquired through the enactment of the *tangata manu* ritual was now in the hands of the victorious *mata* and, by extension, the confederacy to which the newly designated birdman belonged. The birdman required tribute in the form of food (Routledge notes sugar cane as of special interest), and this tribute concept was increasingly extended to benefit those within his *mata* and/or confederacy. The demand for tribute was usually enforced by the *matatoa* (or other classes of warriors), and those who did not comply were in danger of retribution, including having their houses and fields burned. The level of extortion apparently varied with time and resources, and with the character, needs and power of the victorious *mata*.

After the election of each new *tangata manu*, a period of ritual inactivity was decreed until the eggs on Motu Nui were hatched. At that time, the second phase of rites began

and men of the victorious Ao, who had been living since the initial rites at Mataveri and on Motu Nui, collected the eggs and hatchlings (*piu*) of the *manutara*. Oddly, Routledge says that both the eggs and the baby birds were consumed only by the subservient clans, not by the Ao. The first two or three eggs were 'given to God' in a kind of first fruits ceremony. Some of the *manutara* were confined till grown, after which pieces of red barkcloth were tied on their wings and legs, and they were released with priestly admonishments to return to Hiva, the ancestral homeland. Aspects of the cult's focus on the *piu* may be reflected or paralleled in the associated adolescent initiation rites.

The power which the *tangata manu* and, by extension, his kin group acquired was spiritually sanctioned and carried certain privileges, although it was also circumscribed by *tapu*. The cult was a dynamic adaptation of traditional beliefs and practices. Primary foci were 'first fruits' offerings, initiation and fertility, as they very likely were in the statue cult as well. The birdman cult was associated with or gave birth to many other, related Rapa Nui religious practices which are late in time and ethnographically documented. While the general outline and many of the details of the birdman cult are known and have been described above, what was the impetus for its creation? What was its function? How did such a seemingly unusual practice have its beginnings?

While a connection between the Orongo ceremonies and deep-sea fish is documented, important details are lacking or confused. Perhaps this is a partial explanation for why the ethnographic emphasis has always been on the more obvious birds and birds' eggs rather than on fish as a resource impetus for the cult. Assuredly, the importance of birds and eggs as food resources was always present on Rapa Nui. It is also clear that the reliance on migratory birds as protein food grew more emphatic over time, just as it did on the rat and domestic chicken as staple and ritual foods. This could have been due to any number of factors, including the decreased availability of fish protein.

In my judgement, the symbolic and actual relationship of the seasonal arrival of birds with the presence of porpoise and large fish such as tuna was, in the early stages of the cult, equally or perhaps even more important (fig. 44). This relationship became less central as the ability of the Rapa Nui to actually procure the fish decreased with either the lack of wood to build seaworthy canoes, some natural fish shortage as yet not documented by biologists or archaeologists or a combination of factors. Some clues to understanding the idea of bird/fish interaction can be found if we look at the feeding ecology of seabirds in the marine ecosystem of the East Pacific.

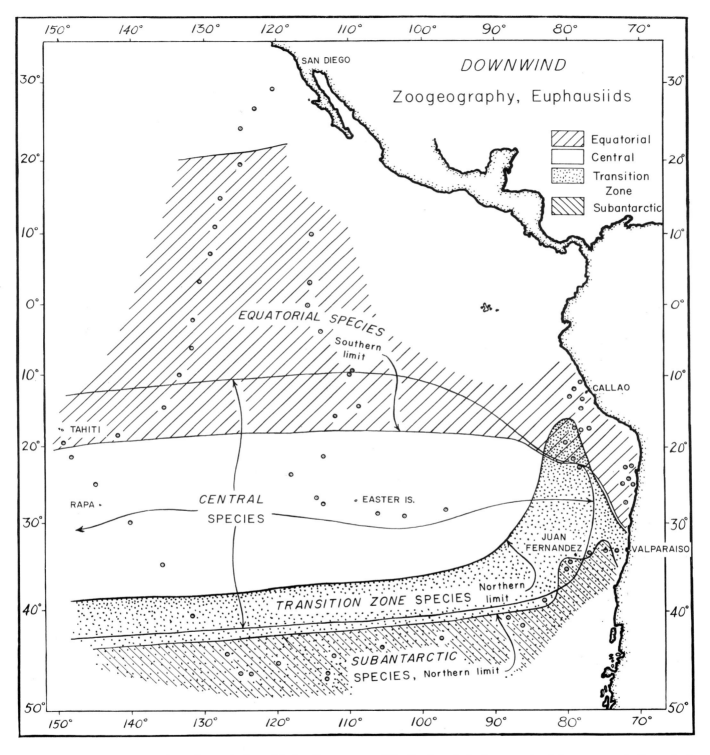

Among the many species of tropical seabirds, Sooty Terns, White Terns, the Brown and Black Noddy and shearwaters comprise a guild of the most common tropical seabirds. All of these species feed primarily in association with porpoise schools and large predatory fishes, especially the tunas such as Skipjack (*Katsuwonus pelamis*) and

44 Distribution of plankton species defines tuna and other pelagic fish zones, with Rapa Nui in the zone of Central South Pacific euphausiids, a group adapted to relatively barren waters. Seabird flocks, including the Sooty Tern, follow fish schools. *Courtesy Robert L. Fisher, Expedition Downwind.*

Yellowfin (*Thunnus albacares*). Recent observations in the eastern tropical Pacific indicate that these birds rarely feed in the absence of fish schools, a characteristic of which the Polynesians were well aware.[9] This strong relationship between birds and tunas results from the fact that a large proportion of the foods taken by the birds (primarily squid in the case of Sooty Terns) is made available at the surface only by the feeding activities of the tunas. It appears that this relationship is especially marked in the case of Sooty Terns, shearwaters and Skipjack Tuna. Skipjack Tuna and seabirds are generally surface feeders, whereas Yellowfin tend to forage at greater sea depths. Recent studies clearly illustrate that the movements of birds such as Sooty Terns can be used by fishermen to locate tuna schools efficiently.[10]

Frigatebirds are large, commanding creatures with black plumage and a brilliant red gular pouch which inflates during mating. Their size, colouration and interesting behavioural characteristics no doubt account for their importance in Rapa Nui and larger Oceanic iconography (plate 13). Their main food is flying fish and jumping squid, which they snatch just above the water's surface since they are structurally unable to land on the water. Their other main feeding method is kleptoparasitism of such birds as boobies, terns and tropicbirds. Frigatebirds forage close to their nests and feed their young at least once per day, so their aggressive kleptoparasitic behaviour on Rapa Nui was an observable phenomenon. The red gular pouch of the bird is indicated on the bas-relief birdman petroglyphs, and the configuration of the wings during 'sunning' behaviour was incorporated into a few other petroglyphic representations of the birds.[11]

The currently circumscribed number of seabirds which nest on Rapa Nui and the offshore islets does not reflect an accurate picture of what the Polynesians actually found there at settlement. The complete loss (extinction) of some bird species once present such as the rail, Scrappy Owl, parrot and heron was largely if not entirely a function of human predation. This situation is not unique, of course, to Rapa Nui. The emerging data describe a magnitude level of bird extinction throughout the Pacific.[12] The current research clearly demonstrates that Rapa Nui was *the* seabird nesting island in the entire East Pacific, the southernmost locality for bird species that ranged from the equator to the sub-Arctic. The impact of the Rapa Nui on the bird population through habitat destruction and pred-

ation was enormous and, in too many cases, fatal. As archaeologist Patrick McCoy has suggested, the choice of Rapa Nui's offshore islets as breeding territory by the Sooty Tern in late prehistoric and historic times was probably dictated by the increasing population of humans on the island, decreasing bird populations and the comparative immunity these sites provided the birds from disturbance by humans of sexual and reproductive functions.[13]

Management of an incredibly valuable food resource such as the birds and their eggs provided, when they were present on lineage lands, would have been in the hands of chiefs, and the traditional means include interdictions called *rahui*. The depletion and then virtual extinction of some species demonstrates, in part, either the nonuse or failure of these management methods. Preservation by the Rapa Nui of the Sooty Tern and, to a lesser degree, the frigatebird (two widely known and extremely common birds throughout the Pacific) may have been related to their status as symbolic figures. Conversely, the adaptation these birds made to the human threat by moving to Motu Nui could also have been an initiating factor of the cult. I doubt, however, that the central role of the elected birds in this complex cult was just a process of elimination. The ancient, symbolic value of the frigatebird and the ecological connection of the Sooty Tern with the arrival of valued porpoise and Yellowfin Tuna were, in my opinion, central to the rationale upon which the birdman cult was built. The Miru, as manipulators of symbols and managers and controllers of resources, are the central characters in this drama.

One of the incomparably sad notes echoing from the carved rocks of Orongo is the fact that the Rapa Nui knew full well that the arrival of the birds meant the arrival of the fish. The cult activity they created allowed them controlled, ritual and real access to the birds and birds' eggs, but the highly desirable, large pelagic fish were unavailable to them without adequate vessels. From the mid-to late-AD 1600s on, those vessels were nonexistent without palm wood. It must have been incredibly frustrating, both physically and spiritually, to gather seasonally on the cliffs of Orongo, far above the sea, knowing that the churning depths below were probably filled with the elusive, thrashing bodies of delectable and life-sustaining tuna. A palpable yearning for the unobtainable, and the resilient hope of its existence, is deeply cut into the dense, black rock of Orongo.

5

The Built Environment

People organise their projects and give significance to their objects from existing understandings of the cultural order.
MARSHALL SAHLINS Anthropologist

The patterns of Rapa Nui prehistoric life are familiar and recognisable, composed of innovations and adaptations on the Ancestral Polynesian and East Polynesian themes. The original settlers lived on the island in clusters of related groups, called cognatic descent groups by anthropologists.[1] They divided the land in the traditional Polynesian fashion of the *kainga*, a wedge-shaped piece of land which extended, in clearly demarcated parcels, both inland toward the island's centre and outward from the shoreline into the seascape. All of the resources within the boundaries of the *kainga* were reserved to the lineage head and his kin. As the land was increasingly needed by a growing population, it was cleared for agriculture and other uses by cutting and burning the native vegetation and fertilising the soil with the resultant ash. A limited range of traditional agricultural products was planted and tended by family groups.

Vernacular Architecture

In neolithic, agrarian chiefdoms such as Rapa Nui, the land is utilised in distinctive, patterned ways. These patterns are usually determined by the way in which society organises its members and the spatial and symbolic requirements of the dominant ideological construct. The houses, fields and religious monuments of Rapa Nui constitute a settlement system rooted in the concept of territoriality. Lineage members who jointly utilised the land lived within its boundaries, in patterns of structures and associated features which are variously revealed in the archaeological record (fig. 45).[2]

The usual Polynesian distinction between coastal and inland habitation types exists, and the coast was settled first. The major natural variables for clustering and growth of settlements appear to be altitude, the availability of fresh water and marine resources. Social constraints of spatial order would also have existed. The greatest number of people, quite logically, was clustered in the vicinity of the largest ceremonial sites. Habitations and settlements were, in general, not constructed within the first 100–200 m from the shoreline. This land segment was reserved for the construction of *ahu* and settlements reached directly inland for 1 km or more. A distinction between interior and coastal settlement patterns has been drawn by University of Chile researchers within a study area encompassing eight survey quadrants. Patricia Vargas C. and her colleagues describe a clear differentiation between coastal site and feature types and those found within the interior. Interior is defined as terrain which lies at or rises above 160 m high, and the coastal zone throughout the island varies from a wide and relatively flat zone on the south, southeast and west coasts to a narrow strip on the north and northwest coasts.

Throughout the evolution of community living patterns, the single most important economic and political variable was the management and control of marine resources, water and arable land. No walls or fences were built to separate lands owned by discrete kin groups. Small piles of stone called *pipi horeko* are suggested to have been property line markers but they may have been *tapu* or other markers (fig. 47). Since nearly all appear to be in the coastal zone they may also have been fishing markers of some sort. In the Polynesian manner boundaries would have been changed fairly often as land and sea use rights were redistributed with changing population patterns, socio-economic power shifts and the vacillating fortunes of individual kin groups. Structures of every type were periodically renovated, abandoned, reoccupied and recycled.

A coastal living unit would have included one or more of the documented Rapa Nui forms of habitation as well as a rectangular structure called a *hare moa* and a circular stone

45 Thatched house forms, Rapa Nui, 1886. *Courtesy of the Department of Anthropology, NMNH, Smithsonian Institution.*

structure called a *manavai* (fig. 46). Juan Tepano told Routledge that a *hare moa* was meant to house and safeguard chickens. There is a formal and structural variation of *hare moa*. They appear to have evolved from simple thatched coops, and some may not have functioned as 'chicken houses' at all but as either burial structures or storage facilities for tuberous food sources.[3] Further, some may have been built for one purpose and then adapted at a later date to another, with the 'chicken house' function being protohistoric. Greater archaeological clarification is required before clear functional purposes are understood. Intensified chicken husbandry has been suggested to be a Rapa Nui substitute for the generalised Polynesian practice of pig raising. To date, 1,233 *hare moa* have been recorded by the survey and nearly all are in the coastal zone.[4]

Manavai are walled surface enclosures or pits designed to trap rainwater and protect plants from the wind, especially banana and the paper mulberry, used to make the Rapa Nui barkcloth (*mahute*). Some *manavai*, when covered, may have served as storage facilities for tubers. Douglas Yen has suggested that the *manavai*, of which 1,450 are recorded, are a 'technological miniaturisation' of the crater of Rano Kau which, in his opinion, provided a sheltered and safe repository for most cultigens, indigenous and introduced. In fact, La Pérouse's party saw cultivated gardens within the crater. While the generalised forms of *manavai* are documented, there are important variations in structural qualities, and these require further investigation. Both *hare moa* and *manavai* are, on present evidence, technological innovations of late date in the Rapa Nui sequence, probably protohistoric. Smaller circular stone lined pits called *pu* were apparently used for growing taro.

Like all Polynesian islands, Rapa Nui has a windward side and a leeward side, although the wind patterns are somewhat complex. In the summer, the southeast trade winds blow almost constantly, and in the winter the northwest and southwest winds can sometimes be quite fierce.

46 OPPOSITE ABOVE Stone 'boundary marker' (*pipi horeko*), Rapa Nui. *Photo by A. Métraux. Courtesy of the Bernice P. Bishop Museum.*

47 OPPOSITE BELOW Stone walled garden enclosure (*manavai*), Rapa Nui. *Photo by A. Métraux. Courtesy of the Bernice P. Bishop Museum.*

While the overall climate is generally mild or temperate and fairly uniform, and rainfall averages about 1270 mm (50 inches) per year, the water is rarely held for long by the porous soil and periods of drought are known. Drought on Rapa Nui is brought about by extended periods of low precipitation compounded by winds which cause increased evapotranspiration. The most dependable sources of water are the crater lakes (*rano*), but reservoirs (*puna*) were dug by the Rapa Nui along some parts of the coast. Several European observers commented upon the lack of drinking water on the island, and on the Rapa Nui ability to tolerate brackish water which they found distasteful. Many Polynesians living on atolls routinely drink extremely salty water.

Fresh rainwater is said by contemporary Rapa Nui to have been caught in archaeological features which are square or round catchment basins pecked into bedrock, rock outcroppings or even fallen statues. These features, along with stone bowls of either basalt or red scoria, are today known as *taheta* (fig. 48).[5] More shallow 'slicks' are usually described in the literature as 'grinding stones' or 'grinding surfaces'. Several red scoria bowls are carved with bas-relief symbols from the petroglyph corpus, including those described as Makemake.

The Rapa Nui version of the typical Polynesian earth oven (*umu*) was used.[6] Earth ovens are usually stone-lined pits in which wrapped food was placed after the stones had been heated in a wood fire built in the pit. Earth was then mounded over and the food was steamed for two or more hours, the length of time required depending upon the type of food being cooked. Some Rapa Nui ovens, called *umu pae*, are delineated above ground by placing five to seven stones in pentagonal, circular or rectangular shapes, with the pentagonal shape frequently the result of the use of foundation stones removed from domestic structures. *Umu pae* and traces of *umu* are found most often in association with habitation sites, but are also sometimes related to ceremonial centres. Very few earth ovens are found in the interior zone.

The types of shelters in which the Rapa Nui people lived during protohistoric time include modified and unmodified caves (*ana*; *ana kionga* were refuge caves), rock shelters (*karava*), lava tubes and thatch houses in elliptical, rectangular or round forms, some with attached pavements (*paepae*) at the entrance. Round houses (*hare oka*) are believed to have been temporary shelters constructed for special events or specialised purposes. Interior zone houses are largely rectangular or circular, and earth ovens are rarely associated. Instead, other features are present. It is currently hypothesised by P. Vargas that interior and coastal habitation sites may have been occupied contemporaneously, and that ac-

48 Rapa Nui children and prehistoric red scoria stone bowls (*taheta*). *Photo by Percy Edmunds, c.1911. Courtesy of the Bernice P. Bishop Museum.*

tivity specialisation was a factor in the coastal and interior settlement pattern differences. Such a possibility obviously has implications for estimating population and understanding the degree of social stratification in late prehistory.

Some type of sigmoid or logistic population curve is suggested by Patrick Kirch to have been operative on Polynesian islands during precontact time, although not all experts agree. Roger Green tends to support a growth rate of 1% or less as reasonable, and believes that an oscillating population model is applicable in some cases to Western Polynesia. Some demographic models suggest that island populations settling in pristine or open environments seek to increase their numbers and maximise reproduction, while others question that premise. In order to double every generation a population must be growing at a rate of from 2.7% to 3.0% each twenty-four to twenty-six years. Projections for Rapa Nui are not yet fully clear but an oscillating model may be appropriate. At a 1% rate of increase seventy years would be required for the population to double in size.

Archaeologists usually estimate population numbers by counting the number of house foundations and then multiplying by five, the average size of the nuclear family in many societies. Métraux recorded nine members per Rapa Nui family. If we multiply the 3,244 house foundations known to date by nine we arrive at the extraordinary population estimate of 29,196. At five family members, we still have a very high figure of 16,220. Many Rapa Nui shelters were recycled and reused, and it is not yet certain how many houses were contemporaneous, specialised or temporary. A good rule of thumb is to reduce the population estimate by two-thirds. This gives us a figure of 9,732 people (at nine per family) or 5,406 at five per family. Considering the bulk of the survey evidence and the previous 7,000 estimate of McCoy's research, a total population of between 7,000 and 9,000 people, or a gross density of between 44 and 56 people per square kilometer, is quite reasonable and in fact, somewhat low by Polynesian standards.[7]

Habitation patterns and house forms are well described by McCoy in the area of Rano Kau (figs 49, 50). In the interior of the crater, specialised stone habitation terraces are fairly large and well built, constructed primarily of locally available thin, flat slabs of basalt (keho) laid horizontally upon large, unworked stones. Basalt slabs of the same sort were used to build the forty-seven stone houses of Orongo 'village', the ceremonial centre located on the southwestern rim of Rano Kau. Built over the course of some 300 years and frequently remodeled or elaborated, the stone houses of Orongo were used seasonally and did not really constitute a village in the ordinary sense.

The Orongo houses have floor plans which are either basically oval or rectangular, and the roofs were constructed by a technique known as corbelling. This technique produced a house with maximum ceiling height at the centre and decreasing height at the room ends. End walls were oval and the houses were very similar in form to that of the elliptical, thatched structures called *hare paenga*. In Rapanui, *hare* means house and *paenga* means both stone or stone foundation and family/family life. There is, no doubt, a symbolic connection between these concepts, and the Orongo houses are thought to be a site-specific adaptation of the *hare paenga* form.

49 Distribution and spatial relationship of *hare paenga* relative to *ahu* in portions of Quadrants 1 to 6, Rapa Nui. *Courtesy of P.C. McCoy.*

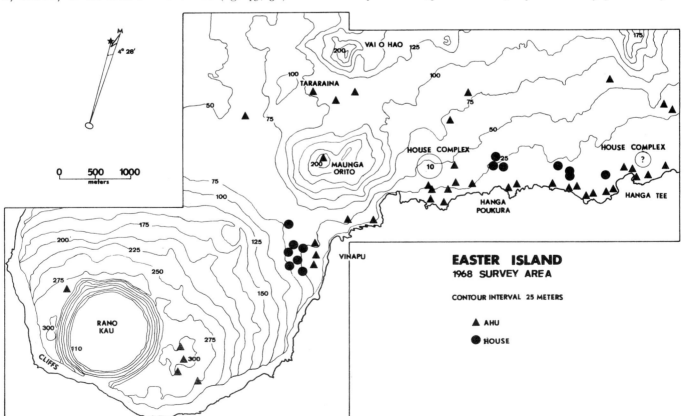

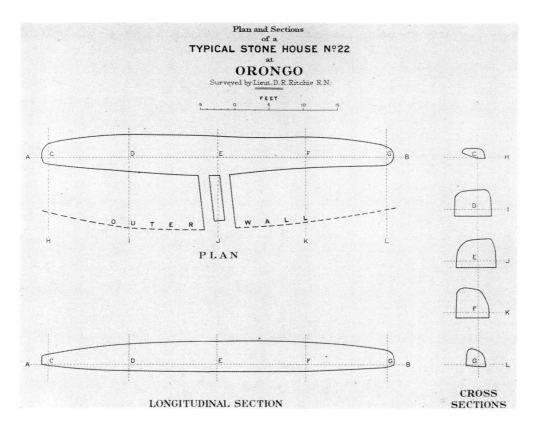

Plan and Sections
of a
TYPICAL STONE HOUSE N.º 22
at
ORONGO

Surveyed by Lieut. D. R. Ritchie R.N.

FEET

PLAN

LONGITUDINAL SECTION

CROSS SECTIONS

50 Plan and sections of a typical Orongo stone house (Routledge's no. 22) showing its elliptical shape and extended, covered entry. *Drafted by Lt. Ritchie, Mana Expedition to Easter Island, 1914–15. Courtesy of the Museum of Mankind, British Museum.*

Domestic Architecture: Style and Symbolism

The antiquity of *hare paenga* on the island is not known beyond doubt, but they were assuredly associated with Ahu Moai Phase II. Rapa Nui traditions recorded only by Englert hold that a master builder of *hare paenga* named Nuku Kehu arrived with Hotu Matu'a.[8] The first known drawing of this unique structure was made by the Spanish expedition in 1770.[9] Another sketch dates to Cook's voyage (fig. 51). Nearly all early descriptions compare the structure to an overturned boat. Foundations are most often called 'boat-shaped'. *Hare paenga* are usually but not always found, singly or in clusters, within 50–100 m inland of the largest image *ahu*, but they are also related to smaller *ahu* of different types. M. de Langle, who travelled with La Pérouse, reported seeing intact and occupied *hare paenga* as well as their stone foundations in proximity to one another on the southeast coast. One partial foundation is found at Orongo.

The largest *hare paenga* are believed to have served specialised or ceremonial community purposes, and are called *hare nui*. These houses were built by wealthy families, for example to shelter invited guests at feasts (*koro*), although rectangular thatch houses are also known to have served the same purpose during ethnographic time. There is some scant, late ethnographic evidence that stone images

decorated the doorways and wooden images the interiors of *hare nui* at *koro*. Because of the Polynesian penchant for storing objects by hanging them from interior rafters and walls however, we are not sure if wooden images were 'decorative' as suggested or were simply being kept out of harm's way.

Stone pillars which may have been torsos of monolithic sculptures (*moai*) are reported to have stood one on each side of the entrance to a *hare paenga* at Ahu Tepeu.[10] The largest elliptical structure of which we have a record measures more than 100 m in length and is at Ahu Tepeu. The drawing of this structure, produced by the La Pérouse expedition, illustrates one door on each of the two sides of the building, each door slightly offset from centre and measuring less than 1 m in height. The houses at Orongo had painted and carved symbols on the interior walls. Some foundation stones of *hare paenga* bear petroglyphs.

The foundations of *hare paenga* were constructed of cut and dressed basalt blocks which were placed in elliptical configurations in trenches (*hao*) excavated to a depth of between 30 cm and 1 m into the ground (fig. 52). According to what Juan Tepano and others told Englert, the foundations themselves, once in place, were referred to as *vaka ure* (literally, canoe/penis [lineage]), and were cut and dressed under the direction of expert craftsmen called *maori hare*. An arched superstructure of pole and thatch construction

51 Sketch of thatched house, Rapa Nui, Cook's second voyage, 1774. Note raised midpoint of the roof. *Courtesy Staatsbibliothek Zu Berlin Preussischer Kulturbesitz.*

was erected by placing each pole in a drilled hole (*ko rapu*) in the *paenga*. These holes are not always aligned directly opposite one another on either side of the house, which means that the poles didn't always arch across in perfect formation. The *paenga* were frequently scavenged and reused from one site to another, and using the existing holes must have sometimes been preferred over drilling new, symmetrically placed ones. The *paenga* which were specially shaped to make up the curved end portions of the foundation were called *pini hare paenga* or *paenga vari pini*. In front of the door (*papare*), which was a low, tunnel-like thatched extension of the structure's side wall, a semicircular terrace or pavement of rounded beach cobbles (*poro*, but also today referred to as *tau pea*) was often present. The 'terrace' itself was called *hiritoke*.[11]

Neither Felipe Teao Arancibia nor Jacobo Riroroko Tuki ever lived in a *hare paenga*, but both are well informed about the buildings and their methods of construction, and

some of their information came to them personally from Juan Tepano. They recently described an idealised example of a *hare paenga*, telling us that the parts of the frame are the main and end rafters (*oka*), ridgepoles (*ivi tika*, which literally means spine, or *hahanga*) and purlins (*kaukau*, also applied to rafter) (figs 53, 54). Juan Tepano told Métraux and Englert that ridgepoles were called *pou* or *tuu*, but this term is not used today. Métraux was told that the central ridgepole 'had magic in it.'[12] The huge structure included in the La Pérouse report was said to have been supported by a 'pillar of hewn stone, eighteen inches thick', but Tepano never mentioned such a pillar and contemporary Rapa Nui never heard of their use.[13] The preferred wood for *hare paenga* construction is said to have been *toromiro*, but *hau* (*Triumfetta semitriloba*), *marikuru* (*Sapindus saponaria*) or *mako'i* (*Thespesia populnea*) were variously used.

Three layers of thatch (*hatunga*) were secured to the wooden framework in a horizontal manner somewhat similar to methods once used in Hawaii. The inner layer was of mats (*moenga*) made of reeds (*Scirpus californicus*) and sewn together with *hau* cords. The middle layer was composed of sugar cane leaves (*toa* or *rau toa*) which were also probably sewn together to form matwork. The topmost layer was of bundled grass (*mauku*), laid horizontally and held in place by purlins (*kaukau miro*). Felipe and Jacobo said that the *hau* cords which secured the purlins to the rafters and the rafters to the ridge pole were always to be knotted towards the right and in three revolutions, 'like [tying off] the umbilical cord of a baby'.[14] A similar practice was once utilised (and occasionally still is) to fasten the lines on a boat. Hotu Matu'a, they said, had promised that if this triplicate practice were followed, fishermen would not lose their lives when their boats capsized at sea and *hare paenga* would not be torn from their foundations by the wind. Felipe said that this information came originally from Juan Tepano.

The interior of the *hare paenga* was said, by the Westerners who entered one, to be dark and bare but dry.[15] Its form and the low entry way protected the inhabitants from wind and blowing rain, but also prevented fresh air circulation. Household possessions such as calabashes, used for holding water but also to protect valuable relics, feathers and ornaments, baskets for food and other objects were hung from the rafters. Since cooking was always done outdoors, the structures were primarily used for sleeping, and individuals arranged themselves on either side of the central doorway. Older people apparently slept nearer the door with children placed at the more cramped ends of the building. Mats or layers of grass were laid upon the dirt floors, and Behrens noted coverlets (presumably barkcloth)

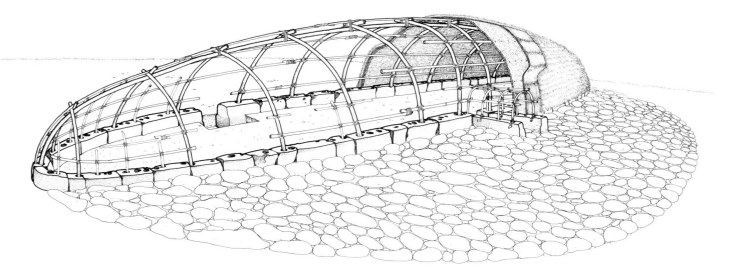

52 OPPOSITE Katherine Routledge (right) and assistant measuring the length of an elliptical *hare paenga* foundation near Poike. *Courtesy of the Museum of Mankind, British Museum.*

53 ABOVE Conjectural reconstruction of *a hare paenga* based on data by contemporary Rapa Nui informants. *Drawing by Cristián Arévalo Pakarati.*

of red and white. Stone 'pillows' (*ngarua*) or fetishes, one with incised designs of birds, vulva forms (*komari*) and a Y-shaped design, are documented.[16]

The form of the *hare paenga* is unique to Rapa Nui, but some important comparisons may be made between it and structures in other parts of Polynesia. Many temporary and even permanent shelters on several islands were very simply constructed of easily available materials, generally resembling the form of a roof set directly on the ground,

with entrances at one or both ends. Round-ended houses are known in Samoa, Mo'orea, the Tuamotus and Hawaii. At the Halawa Dune site on Molokai a conjectural reconstruction of an early round-ended house with a crawl entrance is very similar to the Rapa Nui *hare paenga*.[17]

Métraux noted the similarities in plan and general aspect between Rapa Nui and Tuamotuan structures, and E.N. Ferdon Jr. postulated that Tuamotuan canoe cabins were the source of *hare paenga*.[18] These cabins were meant to

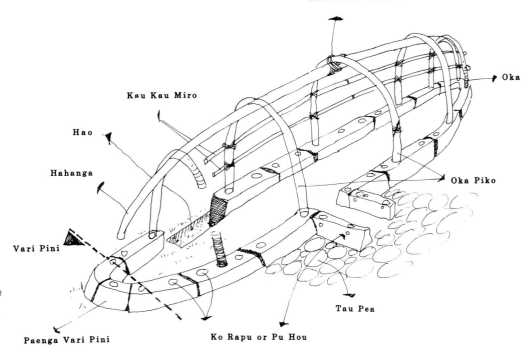

Hau Kaka Maika - Hau Mahute

Kau Kau Miro

Hao

Hahanga

Vari Pini

Oka

Oka Piko

Tau Pea

54 Labelled parts of a *hare paenga* as described by contemporary Rapa Nui informants. *Drawing by Cristián Arévalo Pakarati.*

Paenga Vari Pini

Ko Rapu or Pu Hou

provide shelter for crew members while aboard the large double canoes in which the highly adventurous and very capable Tuamotuan voyagers sailed long distances. The structures were cleverly designed to be carried ashore after landing, thus providing ready-made, temporary shelter. We have few construction details for the Tuamotuan deck cabins, but the distinctive, boat-shaped exterior form of one on a double-canoe model from Fagatau (Fangatau) is precisely that of a *hare paenga*. Its rectangular door is set in the side wall of the structure, just as are the doors of all the *hare paenga* archaeologically known. Contemporary sources say that the actual space for the door in the sidewall of a *hare paenga* was rectangular, although it was sheltered by the extension of a porch which was either oval or rounded in section. The late K.P. Emory, a noted authority on Polynesian archaeology and material culture, believed that the Fagatau canoe model was a faithful representation of a truly ancient Tuamotuan form.

The very close resemblance between the Tuamotuan, Hawaiian and Rapa Nui structures, of course, could be merely independent invention, with the foundation and porch being discrete Rapa Nui and Hawaiian innovations. The round-ended house form may have been abandoned in Hawaii but retained on Rapa Nui. Could the *hare paenga* form have been brought to Rapa Nui aboard a Tuamotuan vessel, carried ashore and, because it housed a high status family, been modified over time to become a permanent feature of the culture, as Ferdon has suggested?

Possibly, although the Tuamotus could not have been the single source of Rapa Nui settlement. To accommodate the Tuamotuan influence on house form, we are forced to accept the notion of two successful voyages to Rapa Nui. As described above, the first, early settlement could have been from the Cook-Australs-Pitcairn region, establishing the Rapa Nui plant and fowl economy. A second settlement from the Tuamotus-Mangareva region could then have brought the *hare paenga* idea and created the associated legends of Hotu Matu'a. This second voyage, considering the range of oral tradition retention and the archaeological context of the *hare paenga*, would have taken place somewhat late in Rapa Nui prehistory and after the linguistic and architectural concept of the *ahu* had been established. While the original settlement was a peopling of an uninhabited island, any hypothetical second voyage would have been an immigrant incursion of minor scale relative to the population present at the time. Such events in Polynesia, especially if they are rare or unique, are often retained to some degree in the oral history. Occasionally they contribute items of material

culture. Clearly, more work is required before the history of the *hare paenga* in the Rapa Nui built environment is fully understood.

The structural forms of all important houses in Polynesia, especially those which were used for communal or large group purposes such as meetings, or housing significant objects or valuables such as canoes, were complex renderings of social and cosmological relationships wherein foundation forms, entrances, upright supports, interior spatial divisions, lashings and all decorative enhancement such as paintings or carvings had interwoven, mythic value. House posts, in particular, often represented storied and honoured ancestors, and some were carved in anthropomorphic form, serving to mark the places where individual chiefs sat during meetings. The communal house was not only the shelter for political and religious events, it was the living record of those events, and of the people and gods who participated in them. In a Maori meeting house, which is conceptualised in its entirety as a model of and metaphor for the cosmos, 'the house can be seen as the sky father enclosing his progeny as he embraces the earth.' A similar concept in Tahiti explains the first godhouse as the body of the creator god Ta'aroa (Tangaroa). The god's 'backbone was the ridgepole [and] the ribs were the supporters' of the superstructure.[19]

Important Polynesian houses were commissioned at great cost, designed and built by expert craftsmen, some of whom were members of 'guilds' with defined ritual and emblems of identity. In Samoa the carpentry guild was an especially honoured and powerful group with its own insignia, a Y-shaped emblem. This emblem, in the form of a Y-shaped stick, was cleverly inserted into the interior, overhead thatch of an especially artful structure. It was a sign of the guild's pride of workmanship as well as an emblem of satisfaction with the manner in which the business between craftsmen and client had been conducted. Some *moai* bear bas-relief, Y-shaped symbols carved on their chins, and a variation of it is found on the backs of others. It is possible that one function of these symbols is to signify special rank or status in a similar way.

Though a cursory comparison of Maori, Hawaiian, Samoan and Rapa Nui house forms reveals the utter simplicity and paucity of materials utilised by the Rapa Nui, there is no reason to assume that the Rapa Nui *hare paenga* (or other house forms, for that matter) were bereft of similar symbolic meanings. In fact, the evidence is quite opposite. It is reasonable to assume that those who understood how to build *hare paenga* were considered to be master craftsmen, and that commissioning the houses was a procedure not unlike that known elsewhere in Polynesia. Further, because the houses were reserved for the highest ranking lineage chiefs and priests, and some of the materials (such as the reeds) came from the sacred sites of Rano Raraku and Rano Kau, we may presume a web of associated esoteric meanings attached to the house components as well as rituals involved with construction. In my opinion, the sheer simplicity of *hare paenga* design may reveal an especially graphic representation of aspects of Polynesian dualistic philosophy.

Polynesians visualised their natural and material world in terms of the spiritual and physical relationships of gods, ancestors and living people. They ordered their lives, their arts and even their languages in response to the ways in which the gods and sacred ancestors ordered the universe. The existence of humans and the natural world was believed to be the result of either the power of a single creator god (Tangaroa, Io or variants thereof) or the unity of male (upper world; light; sky, *rangi*) and female (lower world; dark; earth, *papa*) sacred forces. These forces are called by differing names on different islands, personified by gods with slightly differing attributes, and the details of their creative powers vary, but their male and female associations and their respective places in the upper and lower realms of the world are not in doubt. Combined male and female procreative force is both the generative heat of family and lineage as well as the metaphorical basis for the very existence of the cosmos.

It is certainly true that the exterior form of the *hare paenga*, when the superstructure and thatch are intact, resembles an overturned boat, with the form established by the foundation. However, it is equally true (and perhaps equally important) that the configuration of the foundation is otherwise most like the Rapa Nui vulva design called *komari*. The *komari* is the quintessential female symbol which is everywhere prominent in Rapa Nui art, often carved in rock and wood, incised on human crania, and painted on the human body. In the *hare paenga* foundation form, the *komari* is cut in stone and embedded in the earth, the cosmologically female realm. Spanning above, over and virtually into this *komari* foundation is the ridgepole 'backbone' and curved rafter 'ribs' of what I surmise to be a symbolically male form. In short, we have a shelter which may be metaphorically understood as 'the sky father enclosing his progeny as he embraces the earth'. Those progeny entered and departed this male/female, earth/sky form through a low, dark tunnel which may be logically compared to the birth canal.

This postulated symbolism does not, of course, negate the 'overturned boat' comparison, since Polynesian canoes

were often likened to the bodies of great ancestors or to Tane as First Man. The canoe which transported the first, exploratory voyage to Rapa Nui was said to have been called *The Living Wood*, a reference to Tane. Indeed, it is likely that the 'overturned boat' concept and its relationship to home, hearth and lineage, which is so graphically visible, was commonly understood (hence its retention in the oral literature), while the more esoteric godly connections, perhaps along the lines of those explored here, were known only by spiritual leaders. The loss of many of these individuals after European contact naturally caused the loss of more esoteric values and meanings, leaving visible only the broadly accessible symbolism of such features of Rapa Nui daily life as the *hare paenga*.

Semantic Architecture

Non-domestic buildings which mark or otherwise distinguish territorial and social units are classified as semantic in anthropology.[20] Neolithic, agrarian societies have produced a wide range of semantic architecture, clearly anchoring spiritual concepts and ideological notions to territoriality. Grandiose scale does not have to be a distinguishing characteristic of semantic architecture, and godhouses of a very humble sort, for example, are considered semantic. Semantic architecture is always related to spatial, social and symbolic contexts which differ between discrete societies. In the case of Polynesia, the *marae* as a sacred site is functionally analogous in important ways to the sacred, fenced enclosures of Austronesian tribal societies.[21]

Polynesian semantic architecture encompasses the magnificent tombs of Tonga, the enormous 'stepped pyramid' platforms of Tahiti, the *me'ae*, *ahu* and *tiki* of the Marquesas Islands and the complex *heiau* of Hawaii. It also includes more modest structures such as the small shrines and whimsical, anthropomorphic 'slab' sculptures of isolated Necker Island, the *marae*, *ahu* and stone uprights or pillars, called *pou*, of the Tuamotus and the shrines and portable anthropomorphic sculpture (*ti'i*) of Mo'orea. Polynesians carved and built a wide range of sculpture/architecture complexes on *marae* and shrine sites on virtually every prehistorically inhabited Pacific island, employing a recognisably Polynesian semantic vocabulary to articulate a range of related ideological beliefs (fig. 55). The monumental *ahu* of Rapa Nui are among the more impressive of these structures (plate 15).[22]

In the Southern Marquesas Islands, Society and Austral Islands and in the Tuamotuan Archipelago *ahu* refers only to a raised, rectangular platform which dominates the sacred, ceremonial court. On Rapa Nui and the northern

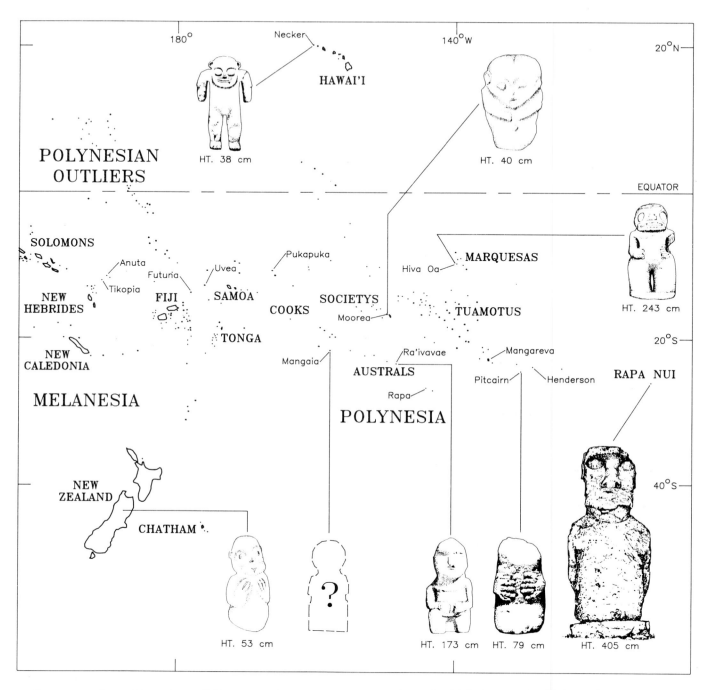

55 Occurrence of portable and monolithic stone sculpture related to stone semantic architecture in Polynesia. Not to scale, heights of statues given. *Drawing by Curtiss H. Johnson.*

Marquesas Islands of Nuku Hiva and Ua Pou, *ahu* is the term used to define the entire ceremonial structure. Some scholars have argued that this means that these areas were not affected by the diffusion of the term *marae* from Tahiti. The term *ahu* is a cognate of the more ancient *afu*, the meaning of which is complex.[23] Essentially, *afu* in Polynesian languages is based on 'the notion of piling up or heaping together, as a shoal or reef islet is built up by the action of natural forces, or as a raised platform is made (usually of rocks) for a house site or for religious purposes'. In the Polynesian outlier of Tikopia, a link has been suggested and debated between the concept of heaping up, procreation and a female deity.[24]

The magnitude of the Rapa Nui architectural/ sculptural complex is so impressive that many observers

56 Monolithic stone
sculpture, Taiohae,
Marquesas Islands. *Photo
courtesy of the Bernice P.
Bishop Museum.*

have focused upon its perceived uniqueness, failing to see the many ways in which it expresses its Polynesian genesis. Some scholars however, such as K.P. Emory, W.S. Ayres and others, suggested very early some ways in which the *ahu* and *moai* related to other forms of Polynesian semantic architecture. One of the first suggestions was that the statues were related to erect stone slabs which stood upon *marae*.

In general, the erect stone slabs of most Polynesian *marae* appear to have served to mark the traditional and ceremonial place or position during ritual of respected and powerful chiefs and priests. In addition, some (especially those erect upon *ahu* platforms) seem to have been memorial stones erected to deceased chiefs and priests. The stones themselves were not regarded as gods but were thought capable of absorbing or otherwise containing the *mana* of the chiefs and priests who leaned against them, sat on them or were memorialised by them, and various *tapu* were associated. In contrast, cylindrical stone or wood forms (portable or monolithic) were thought to represent gods (usually but not always deified ancestors), most had a decidedly phallic connotation, and nearly all were associated with fertility and procreation. The erect pillar, post or pole embedded in the earth (sometimes with an associated pavement) was a metaphorical reference to the virility of the chiefly 'pillar', responsible for the society's procreative and fertility potential, but also had a symbolic relationship to the mast (*tira*) of the double canoe. The mast, in turn, referred to the gods of creation and fertility, such as Tongaroa and Rongo.[25]

'Pole' images are differentiated from 'slab' images in Polynesia by their forms, whether these images are carved in wood or in stone (fig. 56). The relative antiquity of material use or preference of material is not known. However, in island Southeast Asia (on the island of Timor), all sacrificial posts of both wood and stone are called *ai tos* or wood/hard, indicating that the original preferred material may have been wood.[26] It has been suggested that the original impetus for the post with human features is the sacred meeting house of tribal Austronesian societies, with the direct, metaphorical reference being to the sacred chiefly leader/god as 'post' around whom the community is ordered.[27]

In New Zealand the first act of the Maori, Polynesian immigrants who settled the land they call Aotearoa, was to create their sacred site (*'tuahu*). Also known as a *pouahu* or post-mound, it was a post or tree set in a low mound and was said to symbolise First Man (Tane) in the act of 'fructification of the Earth Mother, from which issued mankind', or else 'Tane's primordial separation of Heaven and Earth'.[28] The central post of the shrine could also be an erect canoe-end, again representing Tane. Tane is the god associated with trees (and birds which live in the trees), carpentry and building. Other Maori rituals, practised both within and without the sacred site, involve poles set in mounds which represent the negative, female power of death (*toko mate*). The *toko mate* pole is called 'Great mound (or Mons Veneris) of Papa (Earth) [and] is overthrown, leaving erect a *'tuahu* of the Heavens or male pole of life (*toko ora*)'.

On Ra'ivavae in the Australs Islands, *marae* lack raised platforms but possess upright slabs, and one site has a stone pillar positioned in the very centre of the court with a flat stone laid at its base. This is believed to be the place where the investiture of the chief occurred. Stone slabs up to 4 m tall and monolithic, anthropomorphic statues (some of which are female or asexual) in red scoria are known to have been associated with *marae*.[29] Gods invoked on *marae* are of several different classes and had varying functions, with an emphasis on the creation of humans and the natural world. In the Cook Islands, 'the religious structures of Pukapuka are generally considered to be intermediate between the god houses of western Polynesia and the *marae* structures of eastern Polynesia'.[30] On Mangaia, also in the Cook Islands, Rongo was the god of warfare, and was invoked on *marae*. Ceremonies there included those associated with the declaration of both war and peace, and human sacrifice was practised. On both Raratonga and Atiu in the Cook Islands we find sacred sites called Orongo.

Functional differentiation of ceremonial architecture in the Cook Islands includes an assembly court called *koutu ariki*. A raised stone platform (*ta'au*) was adjoined by a massive basalt pillar used in the investiture of chiefs. These pillars were sometimes associated with horizontal basalt slabs called *papa*, and are known to have reached upwards of 3 m in height. They were frequently transported over considerable distances at relatively great labour. The ceremony itself required that the *ariki* be invested with a headdress, feather girdle and chiefly staff of authority. It is claimed that on one site, seven lower grade chiefs recited the appropriate chants and then actually lifted the newly invested *ariki* onto the pillar.

On Rapa Nui, semantic architecture takes several forms. Approximately 600 religious and ceremonial structures of several types have been recorded. Others, such as the interesting tower structure called *tupa* found in the coastal zone, had unknown functions but may have also been semantic, perhaps associated with a minor East Polynesian god called Tupa (fig. 57). The inventory of *ahu* includes a few rather small, rectangular, thick-walled structures, some of which

57 Stone structure (*tupa*) of unclarified function near La Pérouse, Rapa Nui, by A. Métraux. *Courtesy of the Bernice P. Bishop Museum.*

58 BELOW Diagram of a composite coastal image *ahu* by the Mana Expedition to Easter Island, 1914–15. *Courtesy of the Museum of Mankind, British Museum.*

held burials but no statues, and a few boat-shaped or wedge-shaped burial structures called *ahu poepoe*, also lacking sculpture. Those *ahu* which held *moai* are classified as image *ahu*, and are the most impressive architectural accomplishments of the prehistoric Rapa Nui culture (fig. 58).[31]

Image *ahu* are defined by the presence or absence of a finite number of structural and design attributes which are combined to produce varying forms and sizes of stone terraces, earth mounds and cleared grounds in the tradition of the East Polynesian *marae* concept. Image *ahu* vary from a simple alignment of stones on the slightly mounded or otherwise flat ground, to the highly elaborate, multiple phase megalithic coastal structures. In our study, image *ahu* are first classified, as are *marae* on most Polynesian islands, in either coastal or interior divisions (fig. 59). Within these divisions, platforms are distinguished as being elevated

(raised on a mound of earth or built on a naturally elevated stone outcrop) or non-elevated.

On both elevated and non-elevated platforms we find that a clearly observable architectural methodology was widely implemented, with important variations. First, a horizontal footing to support the image *ahu* rear wall was usually set down, often in a prepared trench just like the *hare paenga* foundations. In the absence of an actual footing, a first course of stone was laid horizontally. Usually the footing extended the whole length of the wall, sometimes it didn't. Upon that footing, worked blocks or vertical unworked slabs of locally available stone were placed to form a rear retaining wall for the interior core of the platform (fig. 60). That core was a heaped mound of soil, rubble and vegetable matter. The upright slabs or worked blocks of the walls were propped and chinked to maintain their positions of stability in the wall and to assure a tighter and more

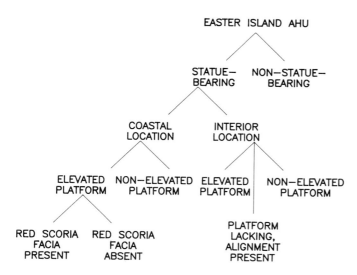

EASTER ISLAND AHU

STATUE–BEARING · NON–STATUE–BEARING

COASTAL LOCATION · INTERIOR LOCATION

ELEVATED PLATFORM · NON–ELEVATED PLATFORM · ELEVATED PLATFORM · NON–ELEVATED PLATFORM

RED SCORIA FACIA PRESENT · RED SCORIA FACIA ABSENT · PLATFORM LACKING, ALIGNMENT PRESENT

59 Classification of Rapa Nui image *ahu*. *Drafted by Curtiss H. Johnson.*

balanced fit. Occasionally, the props and chinks were carefully shaped and fashioned to fit, as at Vinapu and a few other sites. Oddly, at an occasional site we have found one of these chinks cut in a triangle shape, echoing the form of the island itself, and prominently placed. If the spaces between the stones of the walls are somewhat large, the propping and chinking takes on the visual form of rubble. The blocks or uprights are then frequently capped by a third course of stone which is laid horizontally. In many cases, this third course is formed of *paenga* which have been recycled from other construction. The visual purpose of this final course is to provide a nearly horizontal, finished line to the wall.

Stylistic or design attributes of the largest, coastal image *ahu* include a raised central platform formed of rubble contained within front and rear stone walls, sometimes with lateral extensions called wings, a sloping front ramp paved with beach cobbles (*poro*) and a levelled, occasionally paved, rectangular front court. Additionally, on some but not all of these image *ahu* a fascia of shaped red scoria is cleverly cut to hang on the face of the front wall. This fascia is usually present where the statues have been given red scoria *pukao* or headdresses, and is probably contemporaneous with that practice. Basalt oxidised to a deep purple-red was sometimes incorporated into rear walls, but whether this was a deliberate practice or not is still unclear. At such sites as Ahu Ko Te Riku and Ahu Akahanga elaborate terracing at the rear of each *ahu* is associated with crematoria. At Ahu Tahai and Ahu Hanga Te Tenga paved ramps descend to the sea. Statues once stood on *ahu* which possess all of the defined attributes of image *ahu*, but are also found on some

which are merely a perfunctory alignment of stones set upon the slightly raised ground. All of these forms, because of the presence of statuary, deserve to be called image *ahu*, although they obviously vary greatly in architectural complexity and, therefore, in the sizes of the groups which built them and the types of ceremonies conducted.

On several coastal sites, the image *ahu* front or rear walls do not run in a completely straight line, but are slightly bowed outward. This slight curve is not caused by the weight of the statues on the *ahu* but is a part of the design of the structures. At Ahu Vaihu in the southeast coastal zone, this curve is very visible when the *ahu* is viewed in plan form (fig. 61). It appears that a modified boat or *komari* shape, which is clearly used in the ceremonial houses of Orongo, in *hare paenga* and in some *ahu poepoe* or burial cairns made or used in the historic period, was also sought in some of the larger image *ahu*. Routledge said that Rapa Nui people told her that 'poe-poe' described 'a big canoe, such as their ancestors came in to the island'.[32]

60 Rear wall of Ahu Tongariki with standing fragment of diagonally broken statue, still on its base stone prior to a 1960 *tsunami* which levelled the site. *Photo by Lorenzo Dominguez, 1960. Courtesy of Sra. Clara Dominguez.*

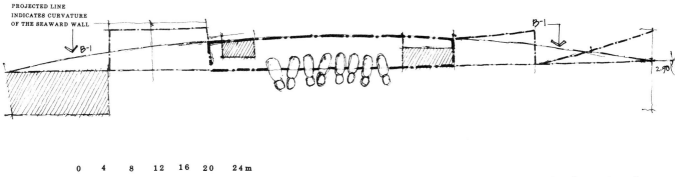

PROJECTED LINE
INDICATES CURVATURE
OF THE SEAWARD WALL

0 4 8 12 16 20 24m

61 Plan diagram of Ahu Vaihu (6–255) showing projected curve of the seaward retaining wall. *Drawing by Raúl Paoa Ika, 1983.*

Planning of image *ahu* sites varies within a well established norm, demonstrating consistent patterns. Perhaps the most important variables that the Rapa Nui builders had to take account of in their *ahu* construction methods were terrain configuration and the reality of previous structures. Frequently, the front and/or rear walls take advantage of terrain height, utilising lava flows or natural rock outcroppings to provide elevation. Some sites on flat terrain are given height by first heaping or mounding the soil and then constructing the *ahu* in place on the mound. All of the final stages of image *ahu* are constructed to relate to existing, surface patterns of human habitation and site use. The massive rear walls of some of the later stages of coastal image *ahu* served a very real support function as the height and weight of the statues erected upon them was extended and increased over time. The front walls of these same *ahu*, in contrast, are usually a single course of well-shaped basalt placed on edge.

The impressive rear walls of many image *ahu* have long interested observers and investigators of Easter Island prehistory. This interest was originally sparked by the magnificently constructed walls of the impressive Vinapu site of Ahu Tahiri (plate 14). Beginning in the mid-1800s, these walls, formed of carefully fashioned and fitted basalt blocks, were frequently compared to those constructed by the Inca in far-off (and archaeologically unrelated) Peru. This comparison, at first glance, is understandable. We now know however, that the walls of Ahu Tahiri are really a local expression in excellence of a defined Rapa Nui building tradition, and have nothing other than a very limited and superficial similarity in common with Peruvian structures.[33]

It is evident that a linear temporal development of *ahu* masonry style is not present on an island-wide basis. Each individual site of more than one construction phase possesses an individualised history of masonry development

which responds directly to terrain, previous building episodes, statue size and weight, locally available material and a host of other variables. Further, post-Ahu Moai Phase II reuse of sites frequently resulted in construction changes. For example, paved approaches were built on at least two sites, shelters on others and *manavai* on quite a few. This site history is sometimes hard for the visitor to Rapa Nui to comprehend when he or she views the reconstructed image *ahu*, all of which are restored to the final and more complex of their several incarnations.[34]

At Ahu Akahanga on the southeast coast, we find an instructive example of a complex *ahu* containing multiple phases of development that can provide a clearer picture of architectural evolution (fig. 62). Known as the 'platform of the King', Akahanga is said in legend to be the place where Hotu Matu'a was laid to rest after his death at Orongo. It is an especially beautiful site located in a small bay with excellent marine resources. There is, as yet, no evidence of *ahu* construction in the region of Akahanga before *c.*AD 1300.[35] Over time, and by at least AD 1500, increased population levels, successful resource management and a movement towards political integration along the southeast coast from Hanga Hahave to Akahanga resulted in the creation there of multilineage units. At Akahanga, elite living complexes, marked by *hare paenga*, were built inland from the *ahu*. Ahu Akahanga itself, elaborated over time to hold larger and heavier statues, contains within it solid evidence of island-wide building trends and a history of use and reuse which is typical of this part of the island.

Platform 1 had at least two phases of construction, both of which possessed statues. Fragments of the statues from the first phase, which stood between 1.84 m and 2.57 m tall, are incorporated into this platform's second phase construction, a common Rapa Nui practice.[36] Platform 2, which was built slightly above Platform 1, supported six statues in the 3 m height range. It is unclear whether this

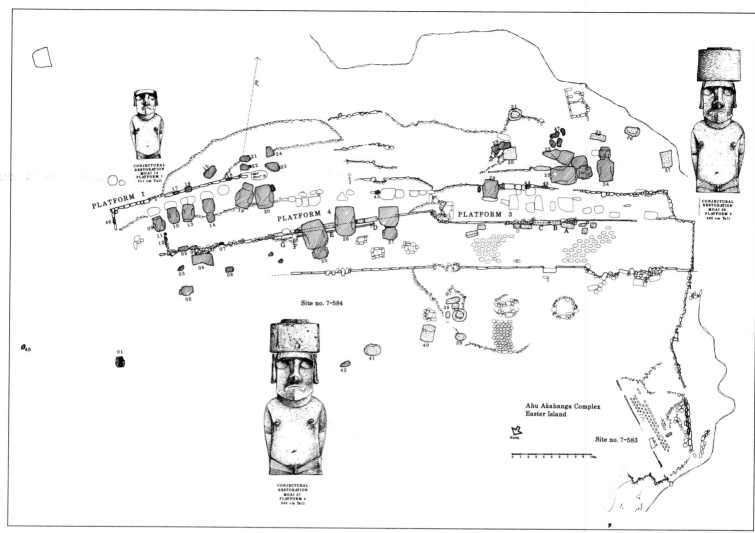

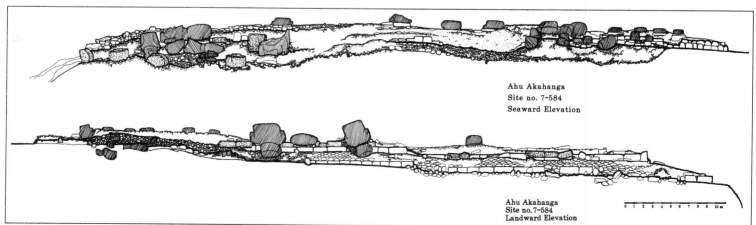

62 ABOVE Plan view of Ahu Akahanga (7–584) with conjectural restoration of three *moai*, each associated with a different *ahu* construction phase. *Plan drawn by Johannes Van Tilburg, 1983. Reconstructed statues drawn by Cristián Arévalo Pakarati.* BELOW Seaward (top) and landward elevations of Ahu Akahanga. *Drawings by Johannes Van Tilburg.*

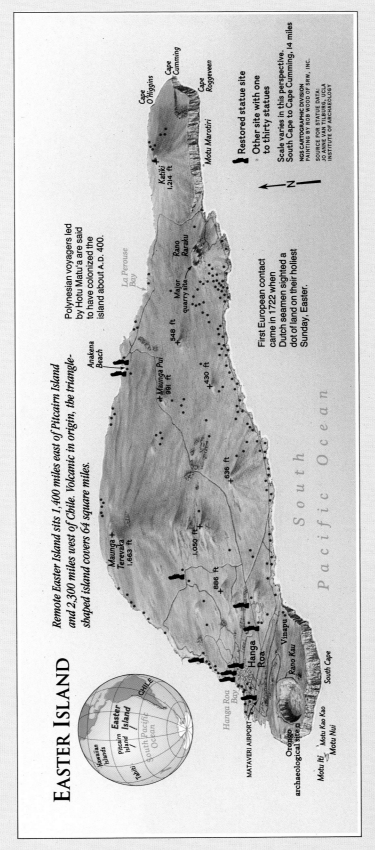

EASTER ISLAND

Remote Easter Island sits 1,400 miles east of Pitcairn Island and 2,300 miles west of Chile. Volcanic in origin, the triangle-shaped island covers 64 square miles.

Polynesian voyagers led by Hotu Matu'a are said to have colonized the island about A.D. 400.

First European contact came in 1722 when Dutch seamen sighted a dot of land on their holiest Sunday, Easter.

Hawaiian Islands
Pitcairn Island
Easter Island
Tahiti
CHILE
South Pacific Ocean

Hanga Roa Bay

MATAVERI AIRPORT
Orongo
archaeological site
Motu Iti
Motu Kao Kao
Motu Nui
Rano Kau
South Cape
Vinapu
Hanga Roa

Maunga Terevaka
1,663 ft

886 ft
1,050 ft
636 ft
430 ft

Maunga Pui
991 ft

Anakena Beach

548 ft

La Perouse Bay

Major quarry site
Rano Raraku

Katiki
1,214 ft

Cape O'Higgins
Cape Cumming
Cape Roggeveen
Motu Marotiri

South Pacific Ocean

■ Restored statue site

▬ Other site with one to thirty statues

Scale varies in this perspective. South Cape to Cape Cumming, 14 miles.

N

SOURCE FOR STATUE DATA:
NGS CARTOGRAPHIC DIVISION
PAINTING BY ROB WOOD OF SRW, INC.
JO ANNE VAN TILBURG, UCLA
INSTITUTE OF ARCHAEOLOGY

Plate 1 Relief map of Rapa Nui where sites having from one to thirty statues each are indicated. Map courtesy National Geographic Magazine Cartographic Division. Statue and site data, J. Van Tilburg.

Plate 3 ABOVE Two of the most magnificent of the 397 statues in the quarries of Rano Raraku stand amidst grass charred by wildfire. *Photo by David C. Ochsner, 1989.*

Plate 2 LEFT Archaeologist Jo Anne Van Tilburg and geologist Steve Williams study an unusual, bearded statue lying face up with its head oriented downslope in an upper exterior quarry, Rano Raraku. *Photo by David C. Ochsner, 1984.*

Plate 5 ABOVE Diminuitive trachyte statue, re-erected after 1938 by Rapa Nui *vaqueros* wanting to protect it from grazing livestock, stands sedately on the slope of Pua Ka Tiki, Poike. *Photo by David C. Ochsner, 1989.*

Plate 4 LEFT Statue head of red scoriaceous material, its eye sockets filled with rainwater, lies in the foreground of Ahu Vai Uri and may be associated with nearby Ahu Tahai I, dated cal. AD 600–800. *Photo © 1991 by James L. Amos.*

Plate 7 ABOVE Anakena Beach, site of the fabled landing of Hotu Matu'a, is graced by a 4m tall statue reerected on Ahu Ature Huki (foreground) by the Norwegian Archaeological Expedition and Ahu Naunau, reconstructed by Sergio Rapu H. *Photo © 1994 by Russell Kord.*

Plate 6 LEFT Excavation by Patricia Vargas C. and the Universidad de Chile team in mythic Poike ditch found no evidence of massive human cremation suggested in legend. *Photo © 1991 by James L. Amos.*

Plate 8 RIGHT Entombed in at least three lava flows superimposed on the red earth, the ancient palms of Rapa Nui left their distinctive trunk prints as irrefutable proof of their existence. Averaging 45 cm in diameter, print sizes suggest that *Jubaea chilensis* may not have been the only palm present. *Photo by Jo Anne Van Tilburg, 1994, through the courtesy of G. Velasco, discoverer and documenter of the prints.*

Plate 9 ABOVE Submarine microhabitats off Rapa Nui
support only between III and 140 species of fish, not all of
which are sought or taken. *Photo courtesy of the Cousteau
Society, 1976.*

Plate 10 BELOW A superbly fashioned Rapa Nui basalt
fishhook frames the eye of a freshly speared fish. *Photo ©
1991 by James L. Amos with permission, Museo Antropológico R.P.
Sebastián Englert.*

platform has more than one building phase. The statue fragments incorporated into the walls may have come from an earlier phase but may also be from phase 1 or 2 of Platform 1. Neither of the platforms appear to have possessed lateral wings or a frontal ramp, nor were the front walls embellished with red scoria fascia. None of the statues wore *pukao*.

Platform 3 held four statues between 4.90 m and 5.40 m tall. Each statue wore a red scoria *pukao* and the *ahu* front wall held a red scoria fascia. The front ramp was paved with huge rounded basalt cobbles laid in horizontally linear patterns. An unusual feature of Akahanga's construction is that these cobbles run flush up to the lower front wall, an architectural detail seen in the Marquesas Islands but rarely on Rapa Nui. Platform 4, which held five statues between 5.45 m and 5.60 m tall, each wearing a *pukao*, was built to span and unite Platforms 1 and 3, although the connection between the two is out of alignment. Two smaller, secondary *ahu*, one with a statue, are related to Ahu Akahanga and are part of the elaborated ceremonial complex. Another *ahu*, where a statue 5.45 m tall was to be erected, lies nearby.

The evidence at Ahu Akahanga strongly suggests that the statues of Platforms 1 and 2 were lying more or less in their current positions while the statues of Platform 3 and then Platform 4 were standing erect. In our study of this site, we have conjecturally reconstructed the *moai* to illustrate proportionate size relationships. Some details of *ahu* corner construction and platform interaction are speculative without excavation, but the range of alternative strategies for the builders was limited. After all the statues on all four platforms were no longer standing and conversion of burial practices from cremation to *ahu* interment was complete, the final stage of ritual use of the site began. Some time after c.1600 and until well into postcontact time, Ahu Akahanga continued to be used for burials and other activities which incorporated the use of red scoria in tombs and the superimposition of petroglyph designs on fallen *pukao* and *ahu* fascia. Mutilation and destruction of sculpture is documented on many *ahu* sites. Removing statues and statue fragments from *ahu* sites, sometimes to bury them partially or to hide them, is relatively common. Specialised reuse of statues and statue fragments is also seen at habitation and other types of sites, and appears to be a function of ideological revival.

Thus we see at this single site, a continuum of use which spans several centuries and incorporates distinctive elements of architectural elaboration while retaining the same general site use plan. Details of *ahu* construction such as the corners, the relationship of beach cobble paving to the front wall, the joining of platforms and the use of red scoria fascia to unite visually Platforms 3 and 4 are site-specific to Akahanga. Further, the contemporaneous use of red scoria for both *ahu* fascia and statue *pukao* is evident. Each of the statues on at least three of the platforms stood on a base plate or plates. There is an apparent but quite gradual increase in statue height of some 32% over about 300 years. It is clear that there was a minor variation (up to about 50 cm) in height among contemporaneous sculpture, but the proportions of the statues never changed. This is in contrast to Ahu Akivi, for example, where seven statues were nearly exactly the same height. There is no evidence of dorsal designs on any of the Ahu Akahanga sculpture, but this may be a function of the pronounced erosion of these figures.

Architectonics of *Moai* and *Ahu*

The interaction between Rapa Nui image *ahu* and *moai* takes place between two planes, the earth and the sky. The plan of the *ahu* is horizontally rectangular, lying at right angles to the rectangular segment of lineage land. The vertically rectangular, flattened, cylindrical form of the *moai* stands erect on its flat basalt slab and reaches upward from the raised *ahu* platform to the realm of the sky.

The *moai* is a carved stone monolith in human male form. Only five to ten statues in Rano Raraku tuff, red scoria and basalt have either possible breasts or superimposed *komari* to indicate femaleness (plate 27). Because the *moai* was meant to be seen by relatively large numbers of people, monumentality is the defining characteristic of its presentation. Those placed upon *ahu* also functioned interactively with architecture. This public, architectural component of discrete social and ideological functions compelled the carvers to simplify the statue's lines to their emotional core. They then developed the form in terms of balanced masses and rhythmic linear repetitions. The originators of *moai* design were absolute masters of the components of traditional art as communication and use of line to convey emotion, and understood the social function of the form they had created.

Megalithic monuments, including the architecture/ sculpture complex of Rapa Nui, are socially active, symbolic structures which function in discrete historic contexts to give meaning and form to territorial space and natural/ supernatural relationships. Evolution of forms and changes in spatial patterns reveal, however tentatively, structural changes in the society. Research which documents in minute detail the development of the built environment, has the potential to delineate important aspects of these changes. Indeed, perhaps the greatest value of such documentation lies in its ability to tell us as much about people as it does about places.

Religion and ideology are, among other things, coping strategies.[37] They are employed as societies struggle to come to grips with the territoriality of humans and their resultant group competition, as well as with the reality of the resources presented to them by the natural world. That natural world is the immediate environment each society calls home. In this complex process, such organisational mechanisms as entitlements (land inheritance and hereditary status), socio-political promotions/restrictions on production and reproduction and the interactive relationships between men and women, leaders and led, are variously and continuously enacted, reinforced, reshaped and reinterpreted. As the evidence of Ahu Akahanga and many other sites illustrates, the developmental context of the *moai* concept reaches from Rapa Nui's Polynesian roots through its adaptations to Western contact. Throughout the context of the society's specific interactions with the island environment, we see some evidence of evolutionary social process reflected in the built environment.

The toppling of statues from *ahu* may have been, in some cases, the result of aggressive behaviour, but it also could have been a necessary, ideologically-dictated stage in the progression from one sculpture to another, larger one. That progression, as we have seen at Akahanga, could be quite gradual. The subsequent conversion of image *ahu* to semi-pyramidal forms and their use as sepulchres is a reflection of the changing social climate. This is also in keeping with the practice of interment in monumental structures which tends to emerge in periods of imbalance between many types of megalithic communities and their natural resources.[38] The superimposition of petroglyphic symbols and the destruction, decapitation, mutilation and reuse of statues well past the time when they stood upon image *ahu* is not necessarily evidence of rejection of the symbol through postulated social group competition. Rather, it may well be a reflection of the continuing regard in which these sites and objects were held by a small segment of the community and/or is a revival of previous ideological signs and symbols in a time of social dislocation.

The image *ahu* evolved as architecture along generalised lines which were dictated by the requirements of the statue cult. They were built of locally available materials by lineage and combined-lineage groups with varying skills, although a basic pattern was followed. The most complex and integrated structures were along the coast rather than in the interior of the island, and the most numerous of these were in the southeast coastal zone. The statues, in

sharp contrast, were only of Rano Raraku tuff and almost 'standardised' design, although variations (in particular in body/head shapes) are noted. They were finished to a level of professionalism which could only have been accomplished within a highly controlled context such as a restrictive craft 'guild'. The statues are present in the greatest numbers on the most complex sites and in the southeast coastal zone. The cumulative evidence suggests that statue design innovation or variation took place more often in the western, higher ranked sector of the island. This implies either control of the symbol through hereditary status privilege relative to the god represented, lineage control of the carving 'guild', a greater social acceptance of innovation or a combination of these and other factors.

When placed upon image *ahu*, the statues stood upon flat basalt stones, usually perfunctorily shaped to match the base shapes of the statues and which served as pedestals. These pedestals were not required to erect the statues successfully. In fact, their presence made the task of statue placement on the *ahu* platform somewhat more difficult and exacting. However, the purpose of the pedestals could have been functional in that it increased the height of the statues slightly or allowed for the heights of several statues on the same platform to be adjusted to fit a conceptualised whole. Notwithstanding this, the pedestals very likely also had a symbolic or ideological purpose.

In several of the ancient megalithic societies of island Southeast Asia, for example, the pairing of a vertical, 'male' stone with a horizontal, 'female' stone is well documented, and such pairings are also known in Oceania, particularly the Cook Islands and Micronesia.[39] As such, these stones make visible the ideological concept of active (erect), male principle relative to passive, female principle. The embedding of the upright stone or wooden pole in the mounded earth in many parts of Oceania is a direct fertility or procreative analogy often related to *kumara* planting, which also requires mounded earth to root the tubers. It is possible that setting a vertical *moai* upon a horizontal slab or embedding it in the earth accomplished the same symbolic action.

On many Polynesian islands the *marae* is conceptualised as a canoe and the chief the mast (*tira*). In turn, the sacred canoe of the chief was often compared to the body of the god Tane, with the mast signifying the erect male member. The canoe was thought to sail upon the vast waters of the sea as *marae*. The symbolism of creation and migration are intimately intertwined, and both are personified by the ritual act of procreation. Erecting a mast on a ship or a statue on a platform requires similar abilities, skills and tools, and calls to mind some of the same sacred imagery.

Throughout Polynesia, the depiction of the erect human male or male member implies power and hereditary, generational strength. Nautical symbolism on Rapa Nui is subtly expressed in the contours of some *ahu* walls and was continually and more graphically superimposed upon many statues and *ahu* sites in the form of marine type petroglyphs. It is not unreasonable to presume the interactive, metaphorical symbolic connection of *moai*, mast, sacred pole and chief.

The innovation of wings on some *ahu* has been reasonably suggested to be a practical solution to the problem of excess stone on the sites, possibly used in raising the statues to their positions on the *ahu*. It is also clear, however, that the stones used to pave the wings are quite small, fairly uniform in size and were carefully selected and placed to create an even surface. The wings may be, therefore, an architectural innovation totally unrelated to the problem of stone disposal. Visually, the wings extended the horizontally rectangular form of the *ahu*, widening the extent to which lineage lands were demarked.

At Vinapu William Hodges made sketches for his painting *A View of the Monuments of Easter Island*, illustrating '7 stone pillars, 4 of which were still standing, & 3 overturned'.[40] This was the first solid observation, corroborated by archaeological documentation from Ahu Akahanga and scores of other image *ahu* sites, to confirm that the oft-repeated comment that all statues were toppled from *ahu* at the same time is completely inaccurate. There is clear evidence that *ahu* renovation, in which walls were extended, elaborated or otherwise stabilised and improved upon, took place during late prehistory on sites which were allowed to retain fallen statuary more or less in place. Thus the island-wide, iconoclastic spasm of violence and warfare so often projected as the culmination of Rapa Nui prehistory can no longer depend upon the statue evidence to support its viability as a hypothesis.

K.P. Emory thought, and Métraux appears to have agreed, that the *moai* were an elaboration of upright stone slabs similar to those of the Tuamotus, Society Islands and Necker Island in Hawaii. These stone slabs were either back rests which held the place of chiefs on the sacred structures or memorials to deified ancestors. At Ahu Akivi a stone slab similar to these vaguely anthropomorphic uprights was recovered during excavation from the central platform fill. P.C. McCoy suggests that anthropomorphic or phallic-shaped stone slabs (*keho*) when placed upright and incorporated into the seaward walls of Rapa Nui *ahu* architecture, may in fact represent slab images similar to those known elsewhere in East Polynesia as *'eho*. Thus vertical slab masonry may not be merely an architectural tradition

but a sculptural tradition as well. Transition from abstract slab to realistic human form is reasonable to suggest but neither artistically automatic nor conceptually easily attained within Rapa Nui's precontact culture. This is especially true when we remember the conservative nature of Polynesian Societies and the nearly 1,000 years required before widespread adaptations in some aspects of material culture occurred in the Marquesas or Cook Islands. We are a long way from understanding what inspired, encouraged and allowed the emergence of the *moai* on Rapa Nui.

Significant keys to understanding *moai* meaning are formal and stylistic variation. Those *moai* which stood on *ahu* are overwhelmingly cut in the form of vertically rectangular cylinders (torso and head) with flat or nearly plane dorsal surfaces. Many of these statues become distinctly slab-like as they increase in size, including the majority of those standing on the interior and exterior slopes of Rano Raraku. There are a few red scoria *moai* which have *ahu moai* proportions and others which are more fully rounded in both head and torso shapes. Some (but not all) of the statue fragments in Rano Raraku tuff with more rounded contours appear to have come from some of the earlier architectural phases at Anakena and Tongariki, for example. There is one red scoria forked pillar or pole figure, of which there were undoubtedly others on Rapa Nui sites.

In short, while the varieties of *moai* form are somewhat limited, they appear to exist and co-exist on individual sites and probably on the island as a whole throughout the statue-carving sequence as it is currently outlined. A nonlinear, gradual transition from more fully rounded, life-like contours to the elongated and then greatly elongated half-cylinder may have been partially dictated by transport necessity, the use of the dorsal surface as a design 'tablet' or the functional presentation of the statue on its platform, although this is by no means certain. At this stage of research a hypothetical progression from upright slab to rounded, naturalistic form to *ahu moai* vertical half-cylinder to Rano Raraku elongated half-cylinder is reasonable but cannot be shown to be either definitive or inexorable on the island as a whole. Particularly with statues in trachyte and basalt, we may be dealing with late innovative or regressive trends within the conventionalised mode which are evidence of discontinuous stylistic variation and incomplete synthesis of design elements.

Ahu-related Ceremony

Organised religious ceremonies or rituals performed upon *ahu* grounds in front of erect *moai* were never observed or described by any of the early explorers. Neither is there any evidence to establish clearly that the statues themselves were ever actually worshipped as gods. Factors which might have made observation of *ahu* ceremony by Europeans unlikely include time, season of the year, the circumscribed or secret nature of some of the ceremonies relative to the newcomers' presence, and the very real possibility that such ceremonies were no longer a viable part of Rapa Nui ritual life. Captain Cook, for example, was a witness to public religious ceremonies in Tahiti and Hawaii, and in both places all such sites were assumed to be of symbolic and social importance at that time. In contrast, Lt. Pickersgill thought that the Rapa Nui did not 'pay that respect to them [the statues], that I should think they would do to a Deity'.[41]

While the Spanish saw no *ahu* ceremony during their 1770 visit to Rapa Nui, they did see and record an example of another sort of ritual behaviour. Following the Spanish erection of three wooden crosses and the singing of litanies led by priests in ceremonial garb, the Rapa Nui erected 'an idol about 11 feet high like a "Judas" stuffed with straw; it was all white, and had a fringe of black hair [made of rushes] hanging down its back. They put it up on stones and sat cross-legged around it, howling all night by the light of the flares'. The idol also had arms and legs, and the head had 'coarsely figured eyes, nostrils, and mouth'. The Spanish noted that 'on certain days they carry this idol to the place where they gather [the *ahu*], and judging by the demonstrations some of them made, we understood it to be the one dedicated to enjoyment [sex/fertility], and they name it *Copeca*'. Routledge says the figure was called a 'Ko peka'

(*kopeka* or *ati kopeka*), meaning either 'cross' or 'revenge or vengeance', and considered it to be used to mourn a death and perhaps represented a woman. In any case, what the Spanish seem to have witnessed is the *only* Rapa Nui ceremony ever recorded by Europeans in which an idol in human form and of monumental height was erected.[42]

Rapa Nui feasts (*koro*) and rituals associated with birth, seclusion and initiation of chiefly children were largely enacted at Orongo, Motu Nui and in large feast houses (*hare nui*) on lineage lands near *ahu* (fig. 63). Special grooming practices are noted for *neru*, young people who were kept in seclusion to acquire fair complexions, fed special diets to become corpulent and allowed to wear certain ornaments and insignia. Selected *neru* were consecrated at ceremonies to become *poki take* and *poki manu* (bird children). The *kaunga* feast was an opportunity for the young *neru* women to display themselves, and is associated with marriage, procreation and fertility. The short dancing paddle called *rapa* was carried by men in elaborate *kaunga* dances but is symbolically associated with women. Very similar treatment of special, usually high-ranking children is also known on Mangareva and Mangaia.[43]

The *paina* ceremony seems to have been an indirect part of funeral rites, usually held in memory of a dead parent. The feast was always held in the summer, at the first opportune moment after the death, when enough food had been

63 Sketch of a thatched structure which may be a *koro* house by the Mana Expedition to Easter Island, 1914–15. *Courtesy of the Museum of Mankind, British Museum.*

KORO.

aa. bb. Interior Partitions

accumulated to make an appropriate display. The exact timing of the feast was indicated by the position of the central stars of Orion. In the case of an especially important or honoured individual, the family and extended family accumulated and stored food for months or years in anticipation of the death rites. The *paina* feast and ceremony were both held on the *ahu*, and an *ivi atua* officiated. The focus of the ceremony was a very tall image in human form, constructed of plant material and covered with barkcloth. The image was erected on the court of the *ahu*, set up within a paved, sometimes slightly depressed circle. It was held in place by ropes, one of which passed over the *ahu*. In this way, *paina* pole images may be seen to relate to canoe masts, held in place by rope stays, and an association with the gods Rongo and Tongaroa is implied. The chickens to be distributed during the feast were placed at the feet of the image.

In addition to the figure which the Rapa Nui erected on Poike and which was seen by the Spanish, M. de Langle of the La Pérouse expedition actually saw a *paina* figure erect on an unnamed *ahu*.[44] The 3 m (ten foot) tall human figure was covered with white barkcloth (just as the Poike figure seems to have been). A smaller figure, about 60 cm (two feet) tall and apparently representing a child, was attached. Tepano and other Rapa Nui told Métraux that a *paina* figure they had seen was constructed by attaching circlets of reeds to a pole, with barkcloth then sewn onto this cylindrical framework. A circlet of frigatebird feathers was worn on the head. The eyes of the image were composed of white human bone and black shell, with black feather eyebrows. The form of the *paina* allowed a man (usually the son of the deceased) to climb into the figure and speak through the open mouth, eulogising his parent. The body of the *paina* was either white or stained yellow with turmeric and then painted. Tepano and the others remembered perpendicular lines on the neck to represent a male, while dots on the forehead and a black triangle (*retu*) on the cheeks indicated a female.

The images, after being removed from *ahu*, are said to have been carefully preserved, although none have ever been collected. Small, portable painted barkcloth figures are known however, and these have occasionally been suggested to be tattooers' models. They may also be commemorative or god figures. In the case of the *paina* images, it is not altogether clear how a figure associated with death was also associated with 'pleasure' (i.e. copulation/birth/fertility). The fact that one is in direct opposition to the other is obvious, reflecting the dual Polynesian vision of the world. The complexity of other meanings (including apotheosis) is not understood. It is possible that erecting a *paina* figure, which may have originally taken place in conjunction with erecting a *moai*, replaced or otherwise recalled the more costly erection of a stone statue.

6

Understanding Rapa Nui Society

Hotu Matu'a said, 'You are Kotuu, of Mata-nui, and your descendants shall multiply like the shells of the sea, and the reeds of the crater, and the pebbles of the beach . . .'

RAPA NUI LEGEND

Prehistoric Rapa Nui was a tribal society organised as a Polynesian chiefdom. Chiefdoms are usually understood as either simple (the more common) or complex. A simple chiefdom has a few thousand people, one level in the political hierarchy above the local community, and a system of graduated status ranking.[1] Complex chiefdoms, in contrast, organise thousands or tens of thousands of people into two political levels above the local community. Numbers of people incorporated into a chiefdom and territorial space are two of the major determinants of complexity. The best estimate of the Rapa Nui prehistoric (*c.* AD 1500, before European contact) population is 7,000 to 9,000, with island size only 162[2] km. On some islands social systems evolved after European contact into 'kingdoms'. Europeans encouraged and supported such evolution because it was usually easier to deal with one 'king' than several chiefs. An example of a complex chiefdom which evolved into a postcontact 'kingdom' is the Hawaiian islands.

Power and Status

Routledge's information from Juan Tepano illustrates that, regardless of population numbers, kin relationships were the basic method of social organisation on Rapa Nui, as in all tribal societies. She usefully defines kin groups and associates each with a specific part of the island territory, although her data and Métraux's do not fully agree.[2] Rapa Nui kinship connections were always known on both the father's side (patrilineage) and mother's side (matrilineage), but membership in the patrilineal descent group determined social status. All kin groups exchanged goods, wives and labour between them, and the patterns of exchange relationships were called *tumu*.

The Rapa Nui system of social organisation is called the conical clan, and is typical of Polynesia.[3] Ramages (local subgroups) are commonly formed through natural population increase and fission along collateral lines of common ancestry. In many Polynesian chiefdoms, and on Rapa Nui, the formation of lineages was also initiated through the division of island territory among kin by the ruling chief. This system is a reflection of domestic fission within the ruling family, and has been called 'heroic segmentation'.[4] It is a kind of 'centrifugal dispersion of the royal kindred'. Since all six of Hotu Matu'a's sons had the same ancestral reference, their status relationships (and those of their descendants) were defined by their birth order and maintained by the power which grew out of the land they were given by their father, the numbers of people on that land and their own heroic ambitions. In the normal course of history, lands originally distributed among Hotu Matu'a's six sons were redistributed to accommodate the formation of new ramage segments. Land redistribution could also be accomplished through forceful usurpation or political manipulation as a consequence of competition.

Households (*hua'ai*) lived informally and communally on hereditary lands usually shared by extended family (*paenga*). The shared land was called *henua poreko ranga* ('the lands where the ancestors were born'), with the senior male designated head of each household. As founder of his own lineage (*ure*), each senior male traced his own and his kin's path of descent from their common ancestor. He was physically and spiritually responsible for the wellbeing of all members of his family and extended family who lived on the land within his sphere, all of whom shared in and contributed towards familial resources and suffered through familial scarcities. His lineage bore his name and was ranked in place within each ramage (*mata*). Routledge referred to *mata* as clan or tribe and identified ten of them.

The term *mata* on Rapa Nui, Mangareva, Marquesas Islands and the Tuamotus means both the eye and the face. In Mangaia the term *matakeinanga* means a group of kinspeople but not necessarily a tribe. In Rakahanga individual *matakeinanga* were named and distinct, thus constituting a tribe. In the Marquesas Islands, the tribe was designated *mata'eina'a*. The Rapa Nui linguistic connection between the meanings of *mata* as eye/face and kin group is not fully understood. However, a somewhat similar relationship exists in Pukapuka in the name of Mata[a]liki, the major god of the i Tua lineage and the 'great god' of Pukapuka. There, *mata* and *ariki* (chief) combine to express the name of the god.

On Rapa Nui, each *mata* traced its origin, in ranked order, to the sons of Hotu Matu'a and through them to Hotu Matu'a himself, the Great Parent or founding ancestor of the entire island family (fig. 64). Beyond Hotu

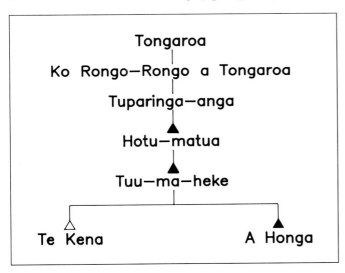

64 Genealogy of ruling A Honga lineage, Miru ramage, showing Hotu Matu'a's descent from the gods Tongaroa and Rongo, after Métraux (1940). *Drafting by Curtiss H. Johnson.*

Matu'a lay the shadowy realm of the gods, the mysterious and powerful pantheon of deified ancestors and mythologised culture heros. Two of these gods, Tongaroa (the creator) and Rongo (variously god of agriculture or war, depending upon the island in which he was found) were Hotu Matu'a's ancestors. Thus creation, fertility and fecundity were aspects of his powerful spiritual domain. On other Pacific islands, such as Fiji, the divinity of the chief was directly correlated with his role as founder of the island society.

As noted above, the largest political unit is referred to as an association or confederacy. Ko Tu'u Aro Ko Te Mata Nui (Ko Tu'u) was the western, higher-ranked unit with territories including Rano Kau. Hotu Iti Ko Te Mata Iti (Hotu Iti) was, in contrast, the lower-ranked unit in the eastern portion of the island. Rano Raraku was in the joint territory of the three principal Hotu Iti tribes. Such east/west divisions are known elsewhere in Polynesia, including Mangaia, Mangareva and Hawaii. Through several lines of evidence, it is very likely that the east/west division on Rapa Nui was very ancient, possibly inherent in the founding population. In all cases where the east/west division is documented, the east is always the lower-ranked sector.

Each Rapa Nui individual had a clearly established lineage position, defined by birth order and heredity within the household or nuclear family, the extended family, the ramage and finally, one of two confederacies within the entire island family. While the status-accorded birth order might be enhanced or diminished through alliances and relationships such as marriage or adoption, one's rank had an eternal and pervasive reality throughout one's life in society. Such a social system tends to stagnate over time unless it provides the means to facilitate some level of even limited social mobility. Leadership and distinction require acknowledgement, and the Polynesian concept of *mana*, or efficacy, is one of the institutional ideas which brilliantly addresses that need. *Mana* allows for the recognition, incorporation and utilisation of individual excellence or ability in social, political and religious contexts. It structures and makes possible a society in which heredity and achieved or ascribed status may interact. There are two types of *mana*, inherent and acquired.

Success in Polynesian societies was intimately linked to hereditary status, and the *mana* believed to exist within those people who were blessed with such status is called inherent. It is based upon genealogical priorities and the access to the gods and spirits which those priorities assure. Enhancing and balancing the concept of inherent *mana*, to a certain degree was the notion of acquired *mana*. Those fortunate individuals of varying social status who could demonstrate a certain level of skill in any activity, practical or esoteric, acquired *mana* commensurate with their abilities and the type of skills involved. Consequently, they achieved a certain enhanced status through the requisite social acknowledgement and appreciation of their achievements. Some were able to demonstrate *mana* in highly valued activities associated with spiritual life, and when this ability was combined with significant hereditary status the result was powerful indeed. There is a very strong indication that entrance into certain priestly or otherwise esoteric professions or activities on Rapa Nui was limited to the highest genealogical (and, therefore social) ranks of society. The competitive intensity which existed between inherited status and earned status, practical and esoteric skill, genealogy and power, complacency of tradition and challenge of talent is the tautly drawn, tensile strength of all Polynesian societies.

The traditions say that 'Tuu-ma-heke', the eldest son of Hotu Matu'a and the one upon whom highest hereditary status was conferred, returned to the homeland (*hiva*). Miru, either the next oldest son or grandson of Hotu Matu'a and next in line of succession, founded the highest-ranking *mata* on the island. The ranking elder of the Honga *ure* within the Miru *mata* was traditionally acknowledged to be the hereditary spiritual leader of the entire island family (fig. 65). As leader, he was designated paramount chief (*ariki mau*; Englert gives *ariki henua*), and contained inherently within his person an abundance of sacred, dangerous power (*mana*). In addition his behaviour, lifestyle, movements and even physical appearance were circumscribed by a series of rules and regulations which formed a complex and intricate *tapu* web which surrounded and separated him from ordinary mortals. He was descended from the most powerful of gods and, as such, contained within himself the most fearful potential for

65 'Queen' Eva (Ko Uka A'Hei A'Arero, 1840–1946) in *c.*1940s, wife of Rapa Nui 'King' Atamu Te Kena, who claimed direct descent from Hotu Matu'a. *Courtsey of Graciela Hucke Atan.*

harm as well as benefit. He interceded with the gods to produce material and spiritual wellbeing, and the most obvious evidence of his success was an abundance of food.

The *ariki mau* wore a barkcloth cloak, stained yellow with turmeric, several different types of feather headdresses, and an array of carved wooden symbols, among them the crescent shaped *rei miro* (figs 66, 67). His sacred loins were wrapped in a garment (*hami*) of red stained barkcloth, sometimes embellished with precious turtle shell. Similar symbols of status and rank were elaborated on other Polynesian islands to incredibly high levels, and that elaboration is characteristic of complex chiefdoms. On Rapa Nui, however, the early Europeans found it sometimes difficult to distinguish the higher-ranked individuals from the more ordinary by such accoutrements, although differences in the quality of barkcloth were noted. Sometimes body paint or tattooing alone were considered to be indicators of status. There is no evidence, however, that Europeans ever actually saw the *ariki mau* and class distinctions may have been more marked during the Ahu Moai phase of prehistory that they were at the time of contact.[5]

Traditions variously say that the *ariki mau* lived at Anakena or near Tahai, both in the western sector. Hotu Matu'a is said to have died at Orongo and been buried at Akahanga, thus associating the highest-status kin group again with the west but also with the east sector of the island. The *ariki mau* was the focus of increase, renewal and other rituals, seasonally receiving 'first fruits' and exercising his authority over nature to produce an abundance of food. He was able to perform sacred rites to control the weather, especially the bringing of rain, and to produce fertility. Wreaths and standards bearing long feather garlands called *maru* were carried before him in procession or presented to him in ceremony. The *ariki mau* was sacred to all and neutral in his social and political dealings. His obligation to society was the spiritual 'work' which he carried out in the name of all the people. The most powerful gods were both channelled through, and resided within, his being.

In this way, the *ariki mau* was similar to the *sau* on Rotuma (Republic of Fiji). There, the *sau* or king was an object of island-wide veneration. His role was to participate in the ritual cycle, the goal of which was to ensure prosperity.[6] The *sau* exercised no direct political power, although eligibility to the office was limited to those of chiefly rank. The duties of the *sau* are not fully known, but he was apparently obliged to eat gluttonously and to preside over and ensure the prosperity of the island as a whole. Evidence of prosperity was made manifest in human fertility and the productivity of the land, and the central symbol of

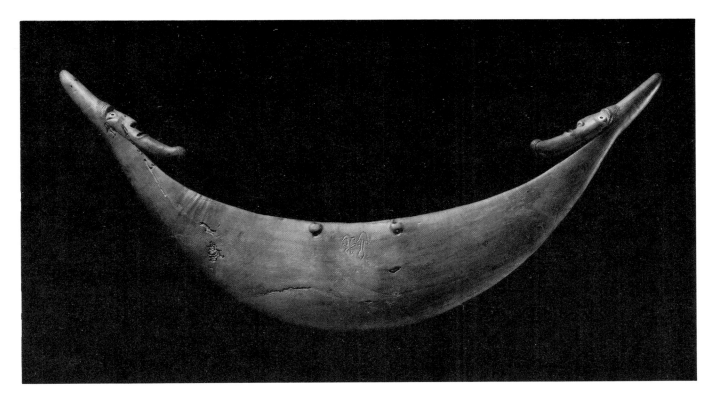

66 *Rei miro* (6847) presented by A.W. Franks, 1870, with two incised *rongorongo* type symbols. *Photo by Corson Hirschfeld with permission, Museum of Mankind, British Museum.*

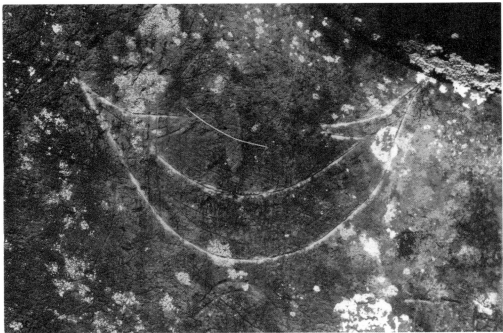

67 Incised petroglyph of a *rei miro*, Hanga Piko, Rapa Nui. *Photo by Jo Anne Van Tilburg, 1981.*

prosperity was food. The ultimate source of prosperity was the gods and the spirit world, but the chiefs in general and the *sau* in particular bore the weighty burden of primary responsibility in communicating with those gods. The task of intermediary was facilitated somewhat by the presumed familial relationship of gods and chiefs. The roles of both the *ariki mau* and the *sau* are in sharp contrast, for example, to the role of the *haka'iki* or hereditary chief in the Marquesas Islands. There, the genealogically senior *haka'iki* was only regarded as possessing limited sanctity, and played no active role in ritual. The powerful and feared inspirational chiefs (*tau'a*) were fully in charge of tribal ceremonial life.

In many Polynesian chiefdoms the paramount chief would periodically visit various of the island's district chiefs. He or she and an entourage of nobles, priests and others would descend upon their (occasionally reluctant) host for various feasts or special occasions, and the host was responsible for providing these guests with food and hospitality. Often the presence of the paramount chief at such events required the host to refurbish or otherwise elaborate ceremonial sites. In return for his or her hospitality the host was allowed to display visible evidence of the chief's presence or to conduct special ceremonies not otherwise possible or allowed. Thus the special relationship of the host/paramount chief was made visible to the entire community. In some islands or island groups paramount chiefs had no permanent abode but instead made a never-ending circuit of the island. On Rapa Nui the archaeological evidence of ceremonial site renovation and reuse, including the increased size of sculpture over time and placement of *pukao*, may be a reflection of this or a related type of ritual circuit. It is not unreasonable to assume that the *pukao* signal a special ritual and/or political relationship between lineage chiefs (as site owners) and paramount chief.

All members of the Miru were, theoretically, an aristocracy which bore the designation *ariki paka*, and the title *ariki* was reserved only for the Miru.[7] From Miru ranks were drawn the *tuura* (Métraux also gives *tahura*), those who worked to provide the *ariki mau* with his food and other goods, as well as the *haka paapa*, his personal retainers. The highest levels of the priesthood, called *ivi atua*, and some of the keepers of royal genealogy and history, called *tangata rongorongo*, were also drawn from the Miru *ariki paka*, although not exclusively. Talent and aptitude for learning the complex rituals and pursuing the requisite scholarship levels were assuredly recognised and rewarded. It is logically assumed that the *ivi atua* were responsible for performing the most esoteric rituals on the most complex *ahu* sites. The *rongorongo* experts were professional teachers. There is clear evidence throughout East Polynesia that the development of complex ritual architecture was, quite naturally, paralleled by a similar complexity in priestly functions.

The full duties of the *ivi atua* are not known, but their name (literally 'bone/god'; Métraux gives 'lineage of the gods') implies their association with burial ritual. Drawing the membership of a high-status priesthood from the highest-ranked kin group on the island is typical of many Polynesian islands, but the proportionate social relationship of heredity to achievement within the profession of *ivi atua* is not understood. Rapa Nui priests of lower grades were called *tangata taku* and were essentially healers

and casters of spells and charms, sorcerers who were greatly feared. Priests of all ranks were believed to be possessed by the god or gods called upon, and spoke in the gods' voices during supernatural rites.

The *ariki mau* was surrounded by *tangata honui* (important old men), to whom he distributed the fish caught by the *vaka tangata* (expert fishermen). The implication of the ethnographic and linguistic data is that chiefs or lineage heads who were not *ariki* (i.e. not Miru) were called *honui*. While the *ariki mau* held the highest social prestige and the most terrible spiritual power, each individual chief held political power appropriate to his hereditary status. That status, in turn, was reinforced and enhanced by economic success, demonstrated by the ability to amass surplus goods and command labour. This situation is similar to that of Mangaia, where a tribal chief of the highest rank (*ariki*) was always drawn from the Ngariki kin group.

Experts in any profession on Easter Island were called *maori*, and the widely known Polynesian term *tufunga*, or expert, was believed by Métraux to have been known formerly.[8] The word *tahonga* appears in one old chant associated with both an expert craftsman and a place. Carved wood egg-shaped or nut-shaped pendants are also called *tahonga*. They bear designs on them which are also present on the backs of the *ahu moai* and thus may be symbolic of the *tufunga* class of carvers, although they are also associated with initiation rites for children and Orongo. The names 'Tuu-hunga' and 'Tuhunga' appear in some lists of Rapa Nui paramount chiefs, and Métraux thought these individuals may have been experts rather than chiefs, but, of course, they may have been both. He also noted the inclusion of the god Tu or Tu'u in these names.

Expert stone carvers (*tangata maori anga moai ma'ea*) worked under the leadership of a master carver (*tangata honui maori*). They appear to have been organised into a 'guild' which crosscut lineage lines. 'They were a privileged class, highly esteemed, and their profession was transmitted from father to son'.[9] On other islands, professional crafts 'guilds' could rise to complex levels of organisation, with governing bodies, rules and insignia. The level of formal agreement in statue design attributes, the consistency of quality and the extensive time span in which such controls are evident, all strongly support the notion of a very well organised professional craft 'guild'.

Status levels or grades within professions were recognised, and *mana* commensurate with appropriate skills was acknowledged. Those men who chose the profession of warrior (*toa*), for example, were also called *paoa*, while those who achieved a higher level of fame and status through their success as warriors were called *matatoa*.

Hetereki was a famous *matatoa* whose name is retained in legend. The *kai tangata* or *paoa kai tangata* formed a special subset of warriors who were said to practise cannibalism. Warriors wore distinguishing feather headdresses or circlets of feathers.

The *matatoa*, as professional warrior, led the war forces in battle, not the chief. However, a chief who was also a great *matatoa* was a doubly feared and respected man, a possessor of inherent and acquired *mana* who could rise to the level of serious political challenger of the island-wide status quo. Clearly, temporal power occasionally passed into the hands of *matatoa*, but the extent and periodicity of that transfer is not known. There is a poor fit between the evidence of injury types found in the existing, late osteological record and the elaboration of the *matatoa* class as found in the ethnographies.

In assuming temporal power at a period somewhat late in precontact time, some *matatoa* are also thought to have assumed certain privileges of status generally reserved for the *ariki* class and possibly even to the *ariki mau*. Strong *matatoa* who were not chiefs but were members of a successful kin group or allied kin groups presented themselves as a formidable social threat to peace, forming secret societies and allying themselves with individual priests or sorcerers to practise extortion. Such a secret society was briefly described by one of the Catholic missionaries, and seems to have had Makemake as a patron and lower-level priests as practitioners of sorcery and visionary-type rituals. Similar societies are known in many parts of the Pacific, particularly in Micronesia, where members often dressed in bird costume. There is however, no specific indication that a *matatoa*, with or without genealogical validity, ever fully and completely usurped the spiritual role of the *ariki mau*. Métraux suggests that similar conditions existed on Mangaia, where only the temporal component of the *ariki*'s power passed to the hands of victorious warriors.

The general Rapanui term *hurumanu* means commoner. Polynesian societies would frequently produce refugees, landless or otherwise mobile segments of the population. These people were called *kio* on Rapa Nui (the term *kikino* was used in the Marquesas Islands).[10] While *kio* has frequently been interpreted to mean 'slave', it really means an individual who was forced, by strife or economic circumstances, into being temporarily landless or homeless. The numbers of people who were thus periodically adrift in society fluctuated a good deal, just as they do today in Western societies. Those who extended a hand to *kio* provided food and shelter, while the *kio* were obliged to labour for their hosts.

The Rapa Nui Chiefdom: On the Cusp of Change

Analyses of Polynesian societies have sought explanations for the fairly broad range of social system complexity documented in the precontact Pacific. Patrick Kirch has helpfully summarised the work of Marshall Sahlins and Irving Goldman, who sought explanations within cultural evolutionary frameworks emphasising ecological diversity and status rivalry, respectively.[11] Both scholars developed a typological approach to Polynesian societies, with Goldman typing Rapa Nui society as 'open' (along with Samoa, Mangaia, the Marquesas Islands, and Niue), and Sahlins suggesting that it fitted within his IIA category (as did Mangareva, Mangaia and 'Uvea). In both schemes, Rapa Nui and Mangaia have a great deal in common. Goldman says that the traditional Rapa Nui hierarchical system, as an 'open' society, was modified to allow military and political effectiveness and to exercise social control. As a result, the culture is said to be more strongly military and political than religious.

Both Goldman and Sahlins, to some degree, tend to form an understanding of the entirety of Rapa Nui social history based upon their reading of the limited, late ethnographic data, projecting a static picture of what was a more fluid and dynamic culture. There was also a lack of important demographic data in their analyses, and this problem remains with us today. Nevertheless, it seems to me that their insights are useful when modified by an approach which acknowledges the more recently understood archaeological record in the context of geography and ecology.

The most basic geographical factors to make an impact on Rapa Nui political development were the island's profound isolation and, of course, its size. From several vantage points, the whole island is tantalisingly visible and accessible, forming an area potentially controllable by a single political unit. Secondly, Rapa Nui lacks the deep valleys of some other high islands, making the visual and physical isolation of individual political units minimal to nonexistent. This facilitated communication and was probably an impetus in architectural development, but it also exacerbated social tensions. Finally, there is a clear disparity in the desirability of certain areas and the availability of specific resources, even on this small island. One result of this situation is, of course, competitive group behaviour, although this is not inevitable.

During the Rapa Nui Settlement and Development Phase I, broadly Polynesian social characteristics were in transition, interacting with the existing island environment to create the formative stages of Rapa Nui culture. That culture evolved throughout most of Ahu Moai Phase II.

Beginning at the end of Phase II and reaching into the Decadent/Restructure Phase III, it 'devolved' in response to intensive environmental stress.[12] Throughout this critical period, however, all lines of evidence confirm that ideology remained the crucial legitimiser of power and authority. Ideology was capable of evolutionary structural change as the perceived need for it by the ruling elite changed. Thus we see, beginning in the mid-1500s, the intensification of the birdman cult as a transformation of the more ancient statue cult. Writing in 1980, archaeologist Patrick McCoy said that 'it is not surprising that the Rapanui, faced with an ecological crisis that threatened their entire social order, if not their very lives, should take the initiative to fashion a new religion'. This initiative was *interrupted and redirected* by contact with Europeans. The culture responded, not in a collective way but in individual units, integrating this new experience and beginning to restructure itself yet again, adapting in small ways to the intrusion of the outside world. The cultural developmental pattern was interactive and responsive, defined by phases of transition, evolution, devolution, integration and re-structure.

Goldman's notion, in my opinion, of Rapa Nui 'open' society as 'more strongly military and political than religious' is overly simplistic and not fully accurate. The archaeological landscape is a profoundly graphic and lengthy record of the interaction between life and death, secular and sacred, social order and ideology, chiefs and priests. That record reveals an intellectual and social awareness of the nature and interaction of leadership, ideology and the ideological legitimisation of power. It is, I suggest, entirely too simplistic to postulate the *moai* as mere symbols of intense prestige rivalry created by the basic and obvious equation of competition, population and arable land.

Sahlins' structural similarities between Rapa Nui and Mangaian cultures are clearly drawn and, in fact, a nearly parallel situation of vacillating socio-political alignments legitimised by ritual in an atmosphere of tension and aggression existed in both places. One Rapa Nui ideological response to the social/ecological pressure for structural change in society was to create the birdman cult. In its early stages, participation was sharply limited, probably only to the highest-ranked chiefs (*ariki*) and priests (*ivi atua*). Further, there is good evidence that most members of both these groups were drawn primarily from the *ariki paka*, the Miru aristocracy. The competitive power struggle was initially between the secular and the sacred, chiefs and priests of the higher-ranked Western kin groups. Over time, of course, participation was extended to the Eastern kin groups and ultimately became more egalitarian. Particip-

ants continued to include chiefs and priests but also the highest-ranked *matatoa*. The resultant, acquired power was divided, as it had always been, between sacred vessel (the birdman, now in the traditional role of the *ariki mau*) and secular leader. The traditional hereditary (inherent), sacred power of the *ariki mau* diminished steadily. Ultimately, of course, the entire cult came to be dominated by the *matatoa* and the birdman was reduced, as was the *ariki mau*, to the role of empty symbol.

On Mangaia, secular power was competitively acquired by the Temporal Lord through prowess and achievement in warfare, while the maintenance of sacred, esoteric leadership was hereditary and invested in the two High Priests of the national god Rongo. The Ngariki tribe competed continuously with the more warlike Tongaiti, striving throughout most of Mangaian prehistory to maintain the position of Temporal Lord within their own tribe. Elsewhere in Polynesia Rongo is the god of agriculture, but in Mangaia he was the national god of warfare and the only god carved in stone. Two images of Rongo are said to have once stood on the Orongo *marae*, although these have never been documented and are now lost. The larger of the two images is said to have been decorated during ceremonies with a barkcloth cape or poncho and a headdress.[13]

The Mangaian High Priest officiated on the inland *marae*, where Rongo was represented by a triton shell trumpet, and had the duty of guarding the island from evil spirits approaching from the east. The second High Priest defended the island from spirits that came from the west. Wearing a special feather headdress, he officiated on the sacred *marae* called Orongo, which faced the setting sun on the shoreline. There, sacrificial human flesh was offered to the carved stone image of Rongo by the High Priest. The warrior who procured the victim was given a sacred belt and a gift of land.[14] The High Priests were neutral in the wars that took place, willing to perform the ritual to Rongo for the conqueror, no matter what his tribe. The High Priest's observance of the proper ritual placated Rongo and assured the success of the Temporal Ruler. The power of the High Priest was considerable, and he retained his sanctity as long as he restricted his activity to religious matters. His refusal to conduct the necessary legitimising rituals led to the 'venting of Rongo's anger upon the land', slaying among the masses and ultimately to famine.

After repeated battles and bloodshed had run their course on Mangaia, the drum of peace was sounded and the installation of the Temporal Lord was undertaken at Orongo. The ritual was preceded by six processions around the island. During one of these, all of the principal *marae* on the island were visited and a forked stick (*toko*) was erected on each.[15] The forked stick on Mangaia signified that the principal chief of the district in which the *marae* was located would function as a *toko*, a prop or support of the new Temporal Lord. The Temporal Lord asked the *toko* to 'prop up his rule, not with rotten sticks, but with ironwood', and begged them 'not to fell ... the tall palm which bore fruit [and] symbolised a long reign of peace'.

The ferocious warfare of Mangaia was avoided in the early stages of Rapa Nui prehistory and then circumvented and somewhat controlled by the institutionalised competition at Orongo. Later in time, the competition was less successful in defusing direct aggression. Warfare, although still poorly understood in terms of extent and type, became the rule. The stability which hereditary chiefships had provided Rapa Nui society was lost and the birdman rites were transformed into a vehicle more obviously to facilitate the socially acceptable (and ecologically required) division of acquired, secular power. The spiritual power of the hereditarily dominant tribe (Ngariki on Mangaia and Honga Miru *ariki mau* on Rapa Nui) attempted throughout to assert itself to legitimise the acquired secular power of the victorious warriors/competitors (dominated by the Tonga-iti on Mangaia and Hotu Iti on Rapa Nui).

Chiefly Power: Economy and Ideology

It has been suggested that there are three components of power in chiefdoms, and that these components are also alternative political strategies.[16] The components are economics, warfare and ideology. Each of these requires socio-political attention, and the proponents of strategies necessary to deal with them are traditionally chiefs, warriors and priests, respectively. Neither the strategies nor the groups which use them are mutually exclusive, however, and there is a clear overlapping, layered and interactive relationship between and among these distinctions. This means that a successful chief or paramount chief will demonstrate an ability to achieve economic surplus, concentrate force and maintain a justifying ideology. Successfully balancing these components is an intricate and complex

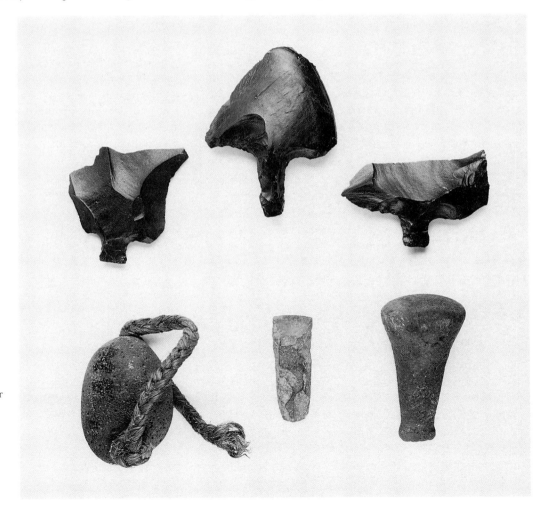

68 Rapa Nui stone artefacts related to subsistence and other activities include a sinker (1920.5–6.186, lower left), *toki* (1920.5–6.42), pounder (1920.5–6.183), and three obsidian *mata'a* (1920.5–6.63, 64 and 70). *Courtesy of the Museum of Mankind, British Museum.*

task. Obviously, one of the better strategies to pursue is to have the roles of highest-ranking chief, priest and warrior fulfilled by one individual or maintained within a single kin group.

On Rapa Nui, the archaeological evidence illustrates clearly that the control of subsistence production in agriculture and marine resources was intimately and strongly linked to the typical Polynesian scheme of hereditary land use rights (fig. 68). The need constantly to restate that ownership, generation after generation and in the context of a growing population and a changing natural environment, seems to have been one of the driving forces of *ahu* construction, although other social and religious motivations obviously existed. These ceremonial centres, most of which became increasingly elaborate over time, firmly relate ideology to economy, the supernatural to the natural. The *ahu* as lineage centres had, as one primary and original purpose, the establishment of group identity and solidarity. Their intent was to bind the lineage to the land, the people to the place, the place to the gods.

The Rapa Nui statue distribution data reveal that the extra-Rano Raraku *moai* are concentrated in largest numbers in the eastern, lower-ranked Hotu Iti territories (fig. 69). Semantic architecture, burials or other types of sites believed to be religious in nature (including *tupa* and rock art clusters) are distributed primarily or (in the case of *tupa*) exclusively in the coastal zone of both Hotu Iti and Ko Tu'u. The stylistic data suggest that innovation in statue design occurred sporadically and unevenly but primarily in the western, Ko Tu'u region. Therefore the *moai* as an object was widely available, proliferating over nearly the entire island but primarily in the coastal zone. It was acquired in largest numbers by the lower-ranked kin groups.

The competitive need to build larger and more elaborate *ahu*, and to erect taller and heavier *moai*, is clearly more frenzied and intense within Hotu Iti. One possible inter-

69 Distribution of monolithic statue sites relative to Routledge's (1919) kin group divisions. *Computer drafting by Gordon Hull.*

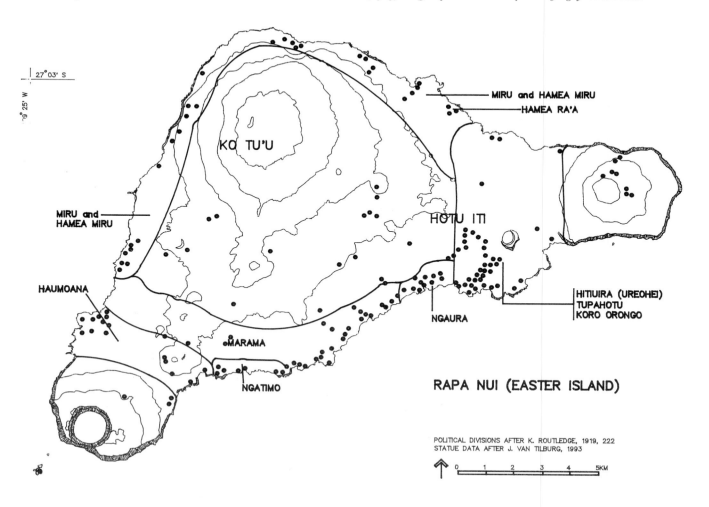

RAPA NUI (EASTER ISLAND)

POLITICAL DIVISIONS AFTER K. ROUTLEDGE, 1919, 222
STATUE DATA AFTER J. VAN TILBURG, 1993

0 1 2 3 4 5KM

pretation of this is that their hold on the land, and on the acquired status demonstrated by the megalithic complexes they constructed, was more tenuous than that of the western kin groups. The Ko Tu'u owed their status position in society to the more traditional, and thus more secure, hereditary acquisition of power. Their position was more assured, but retaining it definitely required the manipulation of an ideological symbol (the *moai*). That symbol was regarded as representative of the entire island family's religious beliefs but may have been more closely associated with the Western kin groups generally and/or the Miru particularly (i.e. Miru status yielded greater or more direct access to the god or gods accommodated by the statues).

If we follow this hypothesis, we can see that even though competitive strategies led to a generalised but probably gradual increase in *ahu moai* size over time, every statue reinforced the subordination of each individual lineage chief to the dominant paramount chief. Statue production itself was a strategy which re-established, each generation, the ancient social convention of subordination to hereditary rank.[17] Instead of regarding the situation as one in which each individual lineage is competing against every other lineage for enhanced social status, we see that the conflict is really between inherent and acquired power. This tension is variously articulated between lineages, perhaps combined-lineage units and even classes, initiating a measurable flexing of ideological muscle.

Sahlins suggested that the extent of chiefly food redistribution prerogatives was an aspect of social stratification and that stratification, in turn, was created by the production of food surplus. Further, he postulated that surplus production was positively correlated with the presence of craft specialists. He does not deal specifically with the issue of craft specialists and their status as a group relative to the power balance in society, but I believe this is an important question. On Rapa Nui a range of construction and stone carving skill is obvious on all *ahu* sites, implying that these structures were built with available local labour and guidance of varying levels of expertise. Stone carvers who worked to produce *moai* could theoretically come from any of the lineage groups. The carvers' 'guild' which produced the *moai* however, would have had certain inherent limitations on access. The highest levels would have been difficult to impossible to attain without either great personal talent or the blessing of inherited status. Who controlled the carvers' 'guild'? What was the status position of carvers relative to priests and chiefs? The carvers were obviously central to the creation of the *moai*, the main focus of religious belief and ritual. How central was the 'guild', in turn, to the political process?

Anthropologist Roy Rappaport is critical of Sahlins' proposition in general, although he does not discuss Rapa Nui specifically. He suggests that his own calculations of population densities on arable island and atoll lands discredit fully the notion that social stratification in Polynesia was correlated with or caused by high economic productivity.[18] He maintains that the economic and sustenance value of chiefly redistribution on high islands was slight. Rather, he believes that the true value of chiefly collection and redistribution lay in its potential and real ability to demonstrate to all members of society the dominant/subordinate nature of social relationships. In my opinion Rapa Nui settlement pattern data, the presence of craft specialists and probably craft 'guilds', the probable ability to produce immediate and cyclical food surpluses and the florescence of megalithic construction, taken as an interactive whole, encouraged increased social stratification to an as yet undefined level. Social complexity may not actually have risen on the entire island, inevitably and finally, to the highest levels as defined by either Goldman or Sahlins, but this is by no means either a fully considered nor clearly articulated research question as yet in Rapa Nui studies.

The ecosystems of high islands such as Rapa Nui were relatively safe from the natural catastrophes which often devastated the harsh environments of coral atolls. On the other hand, they were very vulnerable to soil erosion and depletion caused by land use policies which removed trees and other natural vegetation. Rappaport believes that the development of highly stratified societies such as Hawaii and Tonga was largely motivated by the need to protect the ecosystem from the degradation of land use policies. This would require, of course, that prehistoric societies were able to perceive environmental change as a trend rather than merely as a seasonal event, and then record those changes and transmit the information from one generation to the next. Non-literate societies are not usually able to gain such perspective. Still, if we follow Rappaport's reasoning, we can suggest that ecological degradation on Rapa Nui may be a partial reflection of the failure of the system to modify itself sufficiently towards greater stratification.

The cusp of change on which the Rapa Nui political system found itself was one in which the hegemony of one chiefly line gradually ceased to exist while at the same time, the changing demographics and decreasing resources of a finite, isolated island space required serious social re-organisation. Lineage heads increasingly found themselves responsible for growing numbers of people not directly related to themselves or their families. These people, unable or only occasionally able to avail themselves of traditional land use rights, peacefully sought to affiliate with chiefs who were visibly successful or powerful. At the same time, public works projects involving the *moai* became increasingly less supportable from a resource point of view and appreciably less effective in motivating group effort and maintaining group order.

Perhaps inevitably, the strategies employed by those without arable land or living space became more aggressive. There is very strong evidence within the statue data, however, that on at least two (and perhaps more) occasions somewhat late in time single chiefs were able to put numbers of people to work which far exceeded the normal extended family involvement defined for moving and erecting the average *moai* (see Chapter Ten). These chiefs were thus exacting tribute in the form of labour beyond that of familial obligations, attempting to move their segment of society tentatively towards greater stratification through political consolidation and leadership skill. Ultimately of course, these isolated efforts were not enough to deal with the multi-faceted, island-wide crises of ecology and European 'discovery'.

7

Hunger and Rapa Nui Prehistory

Food shortages do not necessarily lead to an obvious change in social structure.

PAUL E. MINNIS Anthropologist

Archaeologists commonly cite food shortages and associated social stress as a major causal factor in social change. Intensification of subsistence activities, settlement pattern shifts and increased warfare are widely believed to be common human responses to hunger. With the advent of new research techniques, the ways in which hypotheses are designed to test this notion have increased in sophistication, but cross-cultural studies are still very limited in scope. The interactive dynamics of environmental and sociocultural change are only beginning to be understood in Polynesian chiefdoms.

Concepts such as environmental carrying capacity and population pressure describe long-term trends. On Rapa Nui, the island itself and its superimposed archaeological record are mute evidence of the important interrelationship of people and the natural world. It is not enough, however, to understand this situation on an island-wide (global) level. If we are to learn anything at all about the Rapa Nui, we must search for the less obvious, more subtle evidence of specific organisational or coping responses in the face of these trends. Models for human response sequences to hunger have been developed, and some of these are instructive in our goal of understanding Rapa Nui behavioural change over time.

Food, Stress and Culture Change

Adaptation refers to adjustments that individuals, groups of individuals and entire cultures make to the ways in which their lives change in the natural, social and cultural environment.[1] Adaptations take place first on the individual level and then on increasingly more inclusive levels. They are made in response to real or perceived situations and forces, and have been characterised according to

their scope as transformations, modifications and adjustments.[2] A good example of adaptive transformation is the colonisation of new islands in Polynesia. Adaptive modification is less fundamental and minor or short-term adjustments are made most frequently in an attempt to maintain personal or group balance within a given culture.

Cultural selection interacts with environment to produce societal change. Selection can be either stabilising, directional or diversifying.[3] On Rapa Nui, the first stage of cultural selection took place at colonisation and was directional. It was partially made in response to the island environment as it was encountered and resulted in the elimination of some behaviours and the encouragement of others. One behaviour which was culturally selected and emphasised was stonecarving. The transference of ideological concepts and a high degree of adaptiveness to the richness of available stone resources and range of exploitation strategies resulted in the stabilising selection and development of *moai* cult ideology. Over time, new directional selection strategies were required to respond to crisis level ecological changes followed by the event of Western contact.

Resources, technology and social behaviour interact to produce and shape cultural adaptations. Long- and short-term changes in the environment and in evolutionary and revolutionary social processes exert the pressure which shapes the interaction. A model for such a system has been suggested by Karl Butzer, and it is applicable in many ways to the Rapa Nui situation (fig. 70). Island space, time and resources interact with the Polynesian form of neolithic technology and with social behaviour defined by controls and organisation, ideology, cultural attitudes and perceptions, and a hierarchical power structure. One goal of adaptation is to achieve a better fit between society and environment.

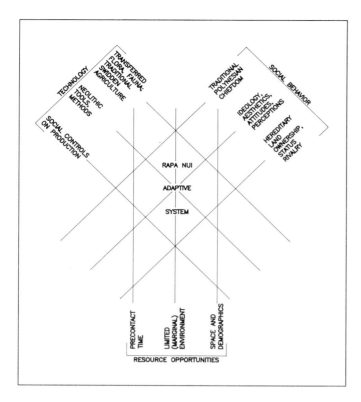

70 Hypothesised interaction of resources, technology and social behaviour to produce the distinctive Rapa Nui adaptive system. Adapted from Butzer (1982). *Drafting by Curtiss H. Johnson.*

The way in which the Rapa Nui people perceived food and the adequacy of the food supply, real or feared food shortages, and the repertoire of cultural responses at their disposal to deal with these factors directly affected their relationship with both power and ideology. Individual responses to hunger include sharing, fasting, reducing intake and changing preparation methods. We know appreciably nothing as yet about the presence or absence of these methods on Rapa Nui. Common community responses to food shortages in agriculturally based chiefdoms include diversification of the crop inventory, storage of food, storage/utilisation of famine foods, conversion of surplus into valuables which may be traded for more food and the cultivation, extension and development of social relationships which allow access to the resources of others.

The Rapa Nui ability to diversify their crop inventory was sharply limited. The plants brought with them at settlement were all they ever had, and it is likely that not all of the original inventory was successfully planted and nurtured into production. While the same plant inventory was available to all, the better agricultural land is on the south

coast, and more productive yields resulted when rainfall was adequate. Individual households could certainly diversify within the available range, and there is some scant evidence in the ethnography that specialised plantations of bananas and sugar cane production were developed. Households or combined households appear to have intensified plant production with the use of *manavai* late in time. The hypothesised use of Rano Kau for specialised agricultural use is not yet understood on a social level. On the whole, the preliminary evidence suggests that the plant economy was centred on an island-wide specialisation in sweet potato cultivation (fig. 71). In that overall context there was also some household level diversification and the exploitation of famine foods such as the palm nut.

Because Rapa Nui lacks a reef, the extension of land ownership reached out to sea, and six named and discrete fishing zones existed wherein specific types of marine resources were harvested. Various sorts of crabs, urchins, crayfish, slugs and shellfish were obtainable by scavenging in tidepools. The valued and highly desirable pelagic fish such as tuna were sought in a sea zone at least 1 km from shore and in waters more than 200 m deep (fig. 72). Expert fishermen sought these fish in the canoes commissioned and owned by the *ariki mau* who distributed the catch. The fishermen also fished at the request of others who paid them in food. Control of these fish as a resource appears to have always been more or less in the hands of the Miru. Recent excavations at Anakena, the seat of the Miru, by David Steadman and his Chilean colleagues reveal a very high percentage of dolphin/porpoise (Delphinidae sp.) bones (37%) at about 600–900 years ago, as well as a quantity of fish bones (23%). These scholars speculate that the decline in exploitation of marine mammals must have been rapid from about 500–550 years BP, suggesting it may have been related to the lack of wood required to build seaworthy canoes. Comparative percentages of faunal food resources at five excavated sites reveal a decidedly greater consumption of large, pelagic fish and porpoises in generalised Miru territory over that on the southeast coast.[4]

Storage of tubers on Rapa Nui is poorly understood but may have been accomplished by leaving them in the fields, and small caches of such famine foods as palm nuts have been found. Stored foods are vulnerable to raiding, stealing and reciprocal obligations (such as might be centred on statues), as well as to pests such as rats and insects. Consumption of low preference foods (such as seed tubers) during periods of food stress has the obvious result of decreasing future crop yields, thus compounding the hunger problem.

The two responses to food stress most difficult to detect

71 Graciela Hucke Atan preparing *kumara* and other tubers for a traditional *umu tahu* feast, Anakena. *Photo by David C. Ochsner, 1989.*

72 Rapa Nui fisherman with Yellowfin tuna catch at Hanga Piko. *Photo by Jo Anne Van Tilburg, 1991.*

archaeologically are conversion of goods to food through trade and barter and the cultivation of social relationships to allow greater access to food resources. There is some evidence that normal ritual mechanisms for food distribution within chiefdoms increase when stored foods are at their lowest level. Further, it has also been shown that in some chiefdoms, craft specialisation increased with the severity of food stress. One possible cause of this is that traditional peoples, including the Rapa Nui, tend to see the social environment as a causal part of the natural environment. Neglect of ritual duties causes imbalance in the natural world, and that imbalance can be righted by enacting, extending or increasing ritual behaviour.

Everything, of course, depends upon the type of rituals and whether they are time-dependent (calendrical) or event-dependent.[5] Calendrical rituals, by definition, have set times for their performance and do not increase during food stress. On Rapa Nui, the calendrical rituals of the birdman cult would have been automatically occurring and independent of socioeconomic variables such as food stress, even though they were centred on food acquisition. Event-dependent rituals such as the *paina* ceremony and perhaps some ceremonies involving the *moai* are sensitive to food stress, and may be postponed or rescheduled accordingly. Because the major, inherent goal of many event-dependent rituals is the maintenance or building of social bonds, they may also (and, in fact, often do) increase during periods of food stress.

During a period of increasingly severe famine as a result of hurricanes and a drought on the tiny Polynesian outlier of Tikopia, a range of modifications in ceremonial funeral behaviour, status indices, task specialisations and social obligations was enacted.[6] For example, more work parties were called upon to repair or enlarge communal property at the same time that ritual obligations were curtailed but still acknowledged. Strictly social occasions which did not require huge amounts of food presentation were increased in frequency, and information exchange and social integration was facilitated. Foods considered *tapu* were not eaten, but antisocial behaviour such as thieving increased, including from the chief. The order of responses to food shortages and then to famine increased both horizontally (spatially) and vertically (hierarchically) in society, beginning at the household level and then extending through the increasingly larger kin group units to the community at large. In other words, responses became progressively *more inclusive* with increasing stress severity.

In the light of this evidence, we might postulate that real or perceived food stress on Rapa Nui was, throughout history, an important aspect of the energy which fueled increased social integration. Further, we can suggest that increased craft specialisation and consequent *moai* production was a response to the conceptual link in the Rapa Nui ideology between ritual performance and natural order. The statue cult, especially if the rituals enacted upon *ahu* were both calendrical and event-dependent, served to engage food surpluses, facilitate exchange relationships, clarify and define social task specialisations, transfer information and increase the level of sociopolitical integration from the household up to the east/west territorial divisions.

Time, the Calendar, Sacred Geography and Ritual

The central symbol of prosperity throughout Polynesia is food. The abundance of food indicates that the political order is well established and functioning, while scarcity implies the opposite. The ultimate source of food is the spirit world. All chiefs, but particularly the paramount chief, have the basic and vital responsibility of acting as intermediaries with the gods, actively influencing them and ensuring their benign involvement in the fortunes of the island as a whole. The major sources of food on Rapa Nui were marine and bird resources and agricultural crops. Success in exploitation and production required that the chiefs and priests understood, controlled and were able to predict (to some degree) time, the weather and seasonal changes.

The placement of the *moai* upon lineage *ahu*, and the orientation of the sculptures towards the community and their plantations, offers nearly incontestable contextual support for the assertion that the sculptures probably functioned in rites concerned with agriculture. Beyond that however, the *ahu moai* also functioned interactively within many other real and symbolic parameters of island life. Most obviously, the *moai* had a relationship to the sacred geography of the island in time and space and as part of the natural and spiritual worlds. Because of the material used, it had a primal relationship with Rano Raraku. This relationship was symbolically emphasised over time as the numbers of statues retained in the quarries and erected on the interior and exterior slopes increased. Another basic relationship of the *moai* was to the east/west division of island space and to the lower-ranked/higher-ranked lineages that occupied those respective territories.

According to E.S.C. Handy Polynesian dualistic philosophy associates west with the realm of darkness and death, the night, the left or weak side of humankind, the inferior aspect of nature and the negative, female principle. Associating these qualities with high status leadership and hereditary privilege is in some ways odd (and Handy may be in some error here). However, these are precisely the connotations of the Rapanui name Miru. Miru is known in Hawaii, New Zealand, the Society Islands and on Mangaia in the Cook Islands. On Mangaia Miru was called 'ruddy Miru' and his skin was believed to be red. In New Zealand Miru was a goddess. Miru is definitely associated with death and the release of the soul or spirit. He/she is ruler of shades and ghosts, king of the underworld and the lower regions. The mortuary function of the *moai* is illustrated by the context of the statues relative to burials or cremation on *ahu* sites.

In Hawaii, the rising of the Pleiades was the signal for the beginning of the Makahiki, a major harvest festival which centred upon Lono (Rongo). For Rapa Nui, as for the Maori, the Mangarevans and the rest of the people of the Southern Hemisphere, the rising of the Pleiades is

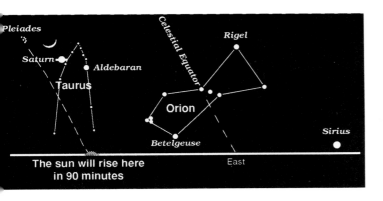

73 The eastern Rapa Nui sky 90 minutes before sunrise at the time of June solstice, AD 1500. Rising at 2:43 am, azimuth 64°33', the Pleiades are 18° above the horizon at the end of astronomical twilight. The Pleiades, crescent moon, Saturn, Aldebaran, Orion's Belt and Sirius are visually aligned. *Courtesy Will Kyselka.*

almost simultaneous with the Austral June solstice. The Rapa Nui calendar begins with the month of Anakena (the name of the landing site of Hotu Matu'a). Anakena was said by Thomson to mean August, but Métraux corrected that to July.[7] Taking into consideration the conflicting evidence of the timing of Orongo ceremonies and based upon consultation with noted Pacific astronomer Will Kyselka, I think it is probable that the Rapa Nui ritual calendar, as that of the Maori, Mangarevans, Samoans, Tongans and other Polynesians began in July following the rising of the Pleiades.

On Rapa Nui and many other islands, the Pleiades were called Matariki. The Rapa Nui ethnographies say that 'old men' watched the stars on Poike, from a cave on the west coast or from near an *ahu* where six boulders represented the Pleiades (in other words, on several different types of sites in more than one locale).[8] The Orongo rituals are thought to have begun in the AD 1400–1500s, and the use of Orongo as a ritual site intensified some fifty years later. If we take AD 1500 as a baseline, we find that the sun's declination was 23°26', while the declination of the Pleiades was 22°37'. This means that the Pleiades led the sun into the sky by about two hours, and that the two risings were over the same geographical feature a mere 0°49' apart.[9] The ethnographies do not mention Orongo as a site from which the skies were watched. Let us presume however, on the basis of the site's special qualities and uses, that the old men may have watched the skies from Orongo (fig. 73). In the year AD 1500, they would have seen the Pleiades at 18° above the horizon at the end of astronomical twilight on *hua*, the twelfth night of the moon in the Rapa Nui month of Te

Maro (The Loincloth). The Rapanui word *hua* means 'the same, to continue' and 'to bloom, to sprout, to flower', with a germ sense of both plants and human progeny growing and thriving. If the night was clear, the Pleiades would have risen steadily and visibly for some time before the morning twilight washed the constellation out.

The rising Pleiades led a twinkling procession of bright stars into the sky: Aldebaran first, then the stars of Orion (called Tautoru by the Rapa Nui). Sirius (Reitanga in Rapanui), at a declination of 16°42', is the brightest star in the sky on this and every other morning, and travels a path that takes it over the centre of Polynesian culture, Tahiti. The Pleiades set at 2:00 pm in the afternoon of that day and in the direction of the solstitial sunset, but the event was not visible. If the sunset was viewed from Poike it would have taken place in the direction of Anakena, the name of the first month of their calendar, the landing place of Hotu Matu'a, the birth place of the island culture and the traditional home of the *ariki mau*.

A few small, mostly unelaborated and other larger *ahu* appear to have been aligned with Poike and the position of the sun at solstice (fig. 74).[10] While it is inconceivable that the initiated keepers of esoteric knowledge on Rapa Nui would not have been aware of the movements of the sun relative, at least, to the solstice, we are not sure of the extent to which Poike's peak was an element of sacred geography. Juan Tepano's association of the peak's name (Pua Ka Tiki) with a demon and solar or lunar eclipse was, according to Métraux, unsubstantiated and uncertain. Neither is there any evidence to conclude that all Rapa Nui *ahu* as a group were constructed to serve as solar observatories, or that any of the discrete archaeological features at Orongo (including Hoa Hakananai'a) were individually associated with the sun. The seasons on Rapa Nui are understood as wet and dry. There was not a significant need to use the sun to schedule highly specific agricultural planting and harvest times, since most staple Rapa Nui crops were grown almost continuously all the year round and probably largely stored in the fields. In the absence of an urgent practical need to monitor the sun, was there a ritual need?

Astronomers who have studied the world's megalithic cultures, wherever they exist, have often suggested or detected alignments of significant structures with the solstice positions of the sun. Megalithic construction throughout Southeast Asia was widely but erroneously believed, for many years, to be the product of a single 'sun cult'. The very real importance of the sun to the ancient built environment is most clearly understood in well-documented, urban clustered and highly developed cultures

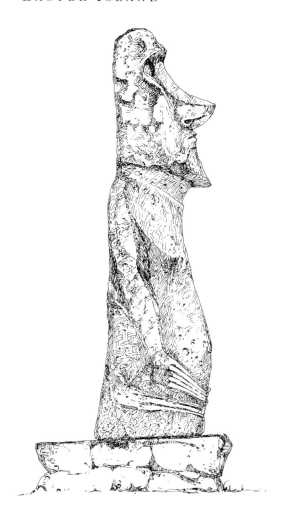

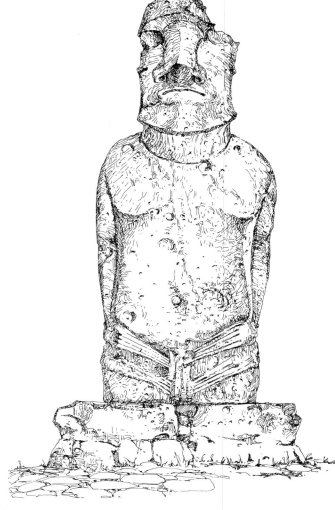

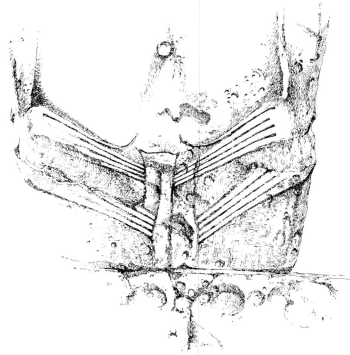

74 Re-erected *moai* at Ahu Huri a Urenga (5–297) is 3.34m tall. The *ahu* is suggested to be 'solstice oriented' (Mulloy 1975a). *Drawing by Cristián Arévalo Pakarati.* BELOW RIGHT Detail of recarved hands (5–297). *Drawing by Cristián Arévalo Pakarati.*

(such as the Andean) that have cosmologies in which time was believed to be cyclical, regenerative, and dependent upon human activity for its recreation. In those cultures, the ruler was believed to be, in effect, the sun god whose accession brought about the conjoining of time, nature and history, not in metaphor but in sacred reality. In the absence of those documented solar-centred cosmologies, the significance of the sun's position relative to architecture or megalithic sculpture is either poorly understood or dubious.

Polynesians, in sharp contrast, held a very different view of the world, of time and of creation. They believed that the time of origins was in the past, a completed event which might be metaphorically referenced or otherwise commemorated. It was not their belief that those essential origins would take place repeatedly in the future or that the very existence of the secular world depended upon the proper seasonal, human reconstruction of the sacred world in ritual. The Polynesian emphasis was on procreation as an inceptive act which generated both the sacred and natural worlds from a primal void. Thereafter the death/rebirth of nature and some gods was a cyclical event in which humans participated through ritual, but did not control as a creative or recreative act. Solar associations with chiefs are noted in Mangareva, Hawaii and in Mangaia, where honorific titles included sun imagery. In the words of Marshall Sahlins, however, such associations were 'more a question of the sun as the king than the king as the sun'.

It is highly probable that the serendipitous association of the Austral June solstice, the azimuth of the rising Pleiades and the geography of Poike relative to Orongo interacted significantly with the Polynesian understanding of time to define/modify the progression of the Rapa Nui ritual calendar and the development of Orongo as a ritual centre. In keeping with practices in other parts of Polynesia however, it is not likely that solar movements *alone* were of major consequence in Rapa Nui ritual, although the shifting sunlight path bisects the island along the important east/west axis. The stars and the moon, on the other hand, including Sirius and especially the Pleiades and Orion, are clearly and unequivocally recorded as significant signs of time passing. It is likely that monitoring the growing seasons and timing bird and fish migrations on Rapa Nui required an interactive set of skills common among Polynesian mariners and weather predictors.

Throughout Polynesia, the moon was recognised as a feminine being and Hina was the moon goddess, as she was on Rapa Nui. The moon's rising, setting and changes of shape were a part of life, love, myth and consciousness. Various crescent and other lunar shapes (especially when executed in marine shell) are widely employed in Polynesian aesthetics. They are prominent in Rapa Nui tattoo designs, *kohau rongorongo* signs, on the neck of the *moai*, in petroglyphs and in the form of the wooden *rei miro*. Time was organised on Rapa Nui, as elsewhere in Polynesia, into nights of the moon. Generational time was measured by distance from the founding ancestor. The moon was the feminine, cosmic counterpart of the masculine sun, and balance between these two forces produced harmony in nature.

Carving, transporting and erecting the *moai* required substantial economic resources, and each successfully completed stage of the work would have been the occasion for redistribution of food resources and the activation of stored foods. Polynesian societies inherently seek a balanced share of resources, and one solution to imbalance is exchange. The *moai* was a major facilitator, motivator and visible token of that exchange. The timing of virtually all activities involving the *moai* would probably have been dependent, to some extent, upon the predictions of weather change, and the winds were significant indicators of those changes. Unfortunately, we have no real evidence of these or other sorts of guidelines which may have been used by priests or chiefs relative to megalithic activities. The ideological system structured and validated what was essentially an interactive dynamic between real or perceived food stress, the communal attempt to seek economic equilibrium and the desire of hereditary leadership to control and maintain the resource base and thus the sociopolitical *status quo*. All of this was accomplished on the island's tiny geographical stage, within the marked rhythm of sunlit days and moon-drenched nights and under the starry canopy of Southern Hemisphere skies.

Death, Warfare and Cannibalism: A Reassessment

In the Polynesian way of thinking death, no matter how it came, was caused by evil spells or magic, demons or gods who were angry. These negative factors were compounded by the danger to humans of the soul or spirit released from the body to wander among the living. The legacy of death was fear and fear was alleviated by ritual. If the person taken by death was a powerful chief, it was obvious that no one was safe and the priests had failed. The departed soul, the evil spirits and the angry gods could be placated and won over by impressive displays of mourning. In many parts of Polynesia burial rites were accompanied by incredible displays of sacrifice, violence to self and others, destruction of property, special modes of dress, changed or altered vocabulary, sham battles, wailing and much more. Often such displays were followed by singing, dancing and eulogies. On Rapa Nui during historic times the grief and sorrow of mourning (*timo*) was expressed by family members who wore special feather headdresses, rattled flat bone clappers (*etmoika*) and shouted loudly.

It was nearly universally believed that a rapport between the deceased's spirit and his/her physical remains existed forever. Burials of many types are recorded, including canoe burials. The preservation of skeletal remains, particularly when the deceased was of high status or distinction, was very important. Caves were often used to hide remains and prevent desecration. It was generally customary for temples or other sacred sites to be renovated or otherwise enlarged or improved as a means of commemorating the deceased. Erecting poles or posts, in honour of the departed or to represent the soul of the departed is documented in New Zealand, where cylindrical wooden chests carved with stylised divine or heroic human figures stood upright (sometimes in communal burial caves) and contained the bones of honoured ancestors. The *moai* is a central figure in Rapa Nui mortuary practices.

Human remains retrieved from Rapa Nui burials have the potential for telling us a great deal about the dietary and social practices of the Rapa Nui late prehistoric and proto-historic population. Scientists George Gill, Douglas Owsley and their colleagues have collected complete metric data and conducted other analyses of a well-documented sample of 464 skeletons from archaeological contexts and museum collections.[11] All of this material is from post-AD 1680, and some of it extends well into the historic period. Most was retrieved from cave and *ahu* interments, many of which were secondary burials of the Decadent/Restructure Phase III. Evidence from several megalithic cultures suggests that interment in monuments (such as *ahu*) tends to emerge when there is an imbalance between people and their critical resources.[12] Other types of burials, however, are known.

Prior to the use of caves and other extra-*ahu* areas the Rapa Nui both exposed the dead upon *ahu* and practised cremation, although some specific details about cremation and post-cremation practices are not known. Cremation sites consist of usually rectangular, slab-lined pits called *avanga* or cleared, low mounds over which small beach pebbles, obsidian flakes, coral and red scoria were scattered. The most well-defined cremation pits are usually found at the rear of *ahu*. The exact time frame for cremation is not known for all parts of the island, but it was early, extensive and assuredly occurred during the 1200s and through the final phases of *ahu* use at the large coastal centres. Cremation is not widely practised in Oceania. It is documented for Indo-Malaysia, Near Oceania (where it is associated with small-scale megalithic remains on Bougainville) and Chatham Islands but is not known elsewhere in East Polynesia.

Routledge recorded the methods by which the dead were exposed upon *ahu* (fig. 75). The body was wrapped and tied in mats of barkcloth or rushes. It was exposed for an unknown period of time near the house of the deceased, a common Polynesian practice, then later carried on staves to the *ahu*. On the *ahu*, the carrying frame with the bundled corpse was 'offered up' by being elevated on four Y-shaped posts, between which two transverse bars rested at each end. Occasionally, only two Y-shaped posts were used. These were held in place by inserting them into drilled

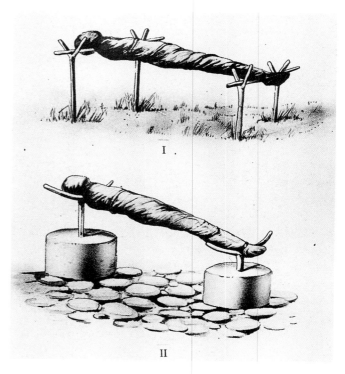

75 Two methods of elevating a wrapped corpse on forked sticks illustrated for K. Routledge by Rapa Nui informants, 1914–15. *Courtesy of the Museum of Mankind, British Museum.*

holes in two stones. The stones were frequently red scoria cylinders, usually recarved *pukao*. The use of nearly intact *pukao* in burials is known at Vai Mata, Tautira and Tongariki.[13] Red scoria stone scattered in crematoria and burials and *pukao* used in burials tie the material, the colour and the object to the deceased specifically and to death/burial generally. The *pukao* may have been an indicator of status level in death as well as in life. Some crania of high-ranked individuals were incised or painted red with sacred designs, including the *komari* (figs 76, 77).

The available Rapa Nui skeletal sample is definitely Polynesian, very probably East Polynesian with a close relationship to the Marquesas Islands. The famous Polynesian 'rocker jaw' characteristic is present but not dominant in the crania corpus as a whole (figs 78, 79). The physical appearance of the founding Rapa Nui cannot, at present, be fully reconstructed. The men, even the older ones, were described by Europeans as generally tall, muscular and well-proportioned with regular features, even, white teeth, black hair usually cropped short and beards (fig. 80).[14] They were thought to be generally strong, lithe and capable swimmers. Many had their ears pierced and lobes extended. Cook recognised the physical resemblance between the Rapa Nui and other Polynesians he had met in the Pacific Islands.

The women were always described in what we would today regard as sexist terms, said to be everything from 'not bad looking' to 'quite attractive', with one of the most extravagant descriptions coming from E. Belcher in 1825 (fig. 81). He said a Rapa Nui woman was a 'perfect Venus in form and with as delicate hands and tapered fingers as Europeans, face and nose a la Gricque'.[15] The Rapa Nui women seen by Europeans were frequently said to be enticing or alluring, offering their sexual favours or being bartered to Europeans by Rapa Nui men assumed to be their relatives. These women are all described as young and attractive, wearing their hair long and usually having their bodies painted red. In 1795, Captain Charles Bishop described the Rapa Nui in the clichéd phrases of the times as 'children of nature' and a 'happy race'.[16]

Admixture of Rapa Nui with Europeans is demonstrated in three late Rapa Nui male skeletons with Caucasian characteristics.[17] The presence of syphilis, the scourge of the Pacific, is noted in about 6–7% of the late sample of both males and females. Syphilis, of course, is a sexually transmitted disease, and it is frequently assumed to be carried to 'primitive' populations by Western exploring parties and ships' crews. Recent investigations in New World studies however, suggest that in some cases the reverse may have been true, and the question is not fully resolved in the Pacific. On all three of his voyages Captain Cook vainly attempted to control venereal diseases by

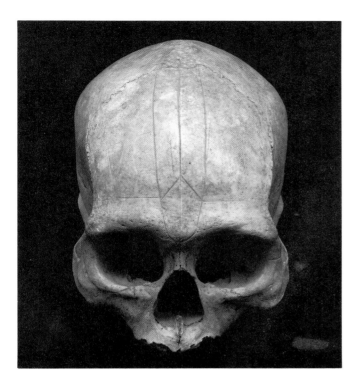

76 Rapa Nui cranium (USNM 31064a) with incised *komari* (vulva) design consisting of an elongated oval surrounding a central Y-shape. *Photo by Corson Hirschfeld with permission, Department of Anthropology, NMNH, Smithsonian Institution.*

77 *Moai* head of red scoriaceous material at Tahai (8–134–01) with carved *komari* superimposed. *Drawings by Cristián Arévalo Pakarati.*

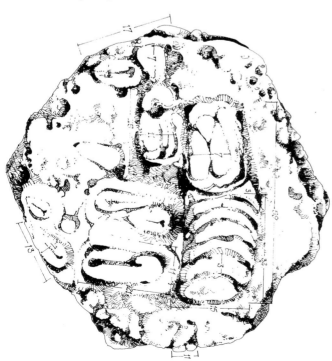

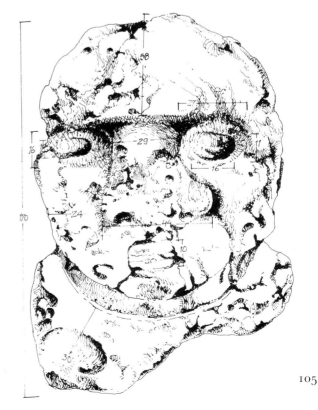

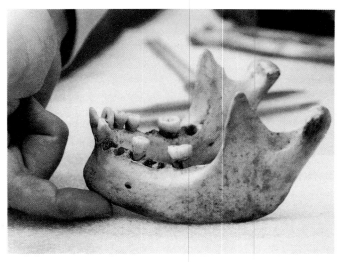

78 Dr. D. Owlsley of the Smithsonian Institution measures a cranium collected on Rapa Nui. *Photo by Corson Hirschfeld with permission, Department of Anthropology, NMNH, Smithsonian Institution.*

79 Detail of 'rocker jaw', a defining characteristic of the Polynesian population. *Photo by Corson Hirschfeld with permission, Department of Anthropology, NMNH, Smithsonian Institution.*

80 Rapa Nui man drawn on Cook's second voyage, 1774. *Courtesy of the British Museum Department of Prints and Drawings.*

81 Rapa Nui woman drawn on Cook's second voyage, 1774. Note tattooed forehead. *Courtesy of the British Museum Department of Prints and Drawings.*

limiting contact between his crews and Pacific Island women. There is some evidence that syphilis was transmitted to nearly half of Cook's crew on their first visit to Tahiti by women infected earlier by Wallis's and Bougainville's crews, who are said to have introduced the disease there. Syphilis is also thought to have been spread from Kauai to Maui by women who had contact with Cook's men only on Kauai. On Rapa Nui, it is not yet known if the disease was present in the population prior to European contact or introduced by Europeans.

While male/female intercourse is the most frequently occurring means of transmitting syphilis, same sex transmission is also possible. This is especially interesting in the light of a comment made by E. Belcher in the mid-1800s.[18] He describes thirty or more women, sitting 'like seals' on a rock on the shore of Hanga Roa. They were 'singing and accompanying the voice with [their] arms like sirens alluring one into danger'. On another rock nearby was a similar number of young boys 'from 13 to 17 but these did not attract so much attention'. A possible interpretation of this information is that some Rapa Nui were prepared to offer or barter sex without regard to the sexual preference of their visitors. Sex in Pacific islander interactions with Europeans was used for both socioeconomic and religious purposes, and the class of the women involved varied with these purposes.

An interesting finding of the Gill-Owsley osteological research is that adult Rapa Nui present in the sample studied demonstrate an extraordinarily high percentage of dental caries, reflecting their limited diet in late protohistoric and historic times. The frequency of caries is 27.1%, more than double the normal frequency among prehistoric farming and horticultural populations. The sugar content of such foods as sugar cane, sweet potatoes and taro is suggested to be the cause of this situation. For the rest, the Rapa Nui appear to have been a fairly healthy population, with little infection evident.[19] Some arthritis is present, as well as ectocranial porosity which appears to have been chronic. While no severe malnutrition is evident, such mild osteoporosis is the probable result of iron and calcium deficiency. This means, in general, that the Rapa Nui had an adequate calorie intake from a diet lacking in some nutrients.

Raiding and warfare may assuredly increase during times of food stress, but this is not always nor automatically the case. Occasionally, the reverse is true. In some Polynesian chiefdoms, the response to food stress is to call a truce in order to focus more fully upon food production. The Rapa Nui osteological sample also reveals a pattern of multiple, non-fatal injuries and wounds possibly sustained

through hit and run aggressive behaviour. While there is clear evidence of killing, there is also ample evidence of healing. Depression fractures from blunt force trauma are frequent, but there is little evidence of fight to the finish events. Douglas Owsley's opinion is that individual killings may have been events which made a social impact, causing much talk and entering the oral literature where they then became inflated to the proportions of battles, creating the substantial number of oral traditions which deal with warfare. No mass burial grounds or cremation sites are known archaeologically which would suggest a single, huge battle event. The legendary Poike ditch, as we have seen, did not serve such a purpose.

The period of Rapa Nui prehistory from at least AD 1680 and extending into the historic era was one in which jealousies and rivalries over land, food, status and women, grudge fights, revenge taking and other negative social interactions appear to have resulted in the need for individuals and families to run and hide, to defend their property and possessions, to threaten to attack their neighbours and to take individual lives. The historic behaviour of Torometi toward the Catholic missionaries and Angata and her followers toward the Europeans at Mataveri seem to be reasonable examples of how Rapa Nui people might act out their aggression. Probable indicators of negative social trends include changed settlement patterns, neglect, disuse or changes in use of semantic architecture, the reuse of stone from semantic architecture in vernacular structures, changed burial customs and changes in material culture. There is, to date, virtually no evidence of warfare in the sense of large-scale confrontations with specially assembled armies such as were known in Hawaii or elsewhere in Polynesia.

Characteristically, Polynesian warfare was conducted to maintain chiefly power and prestige and at the same time, to extend political influence. Revenge was a frequent motive, and certain types of ceremonial rivalries might have existed for many generations. The typical and most preferred form of combat was hand-to-hand with clubs, and the Rapa Nui *paoa* is similar in form to the New Zealand *patu* (fig. 82). In some islands formal, combative contests between two or more warriors were held in front of observers gathered for the occasion, and sham battles were fought on Rapa Nui. Stone throwing very often greeted Europeans, and slings were sometimes used to hurl missiles with deadly accuracy. Spears were more often used in Melanesia, where skirmishes were conducted as a result of clan or village feuds or for headhunting.

The Dutch and the Spanish clearly state that the Rapa Nui whom they saw were completely unarmed. Although

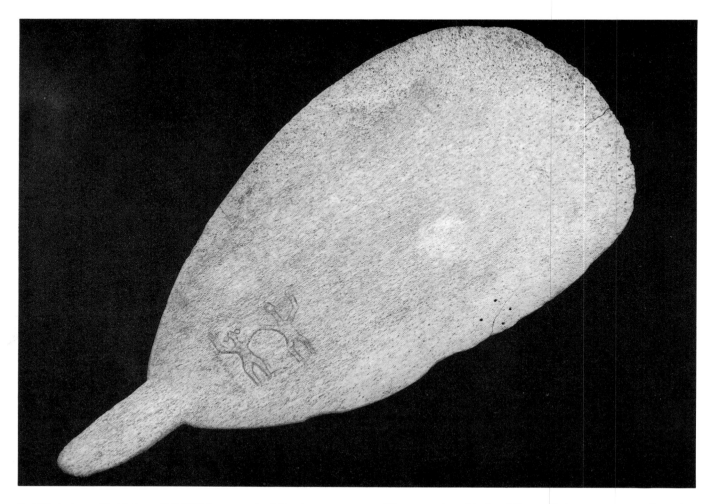

82 Whale bone 'fetish board' (USNM 129,742) of the *paoa* type with two incised *rongorongo* type figures. Called *timo ika*, it was said to be used by sorcerers. *Photo by Corson Hirschfeld with permission, Department of Anthropology, NMNH, Smithsonian Institution.*

they never saw any weapons, the Spanish certainly saw conspicuous wounds on many Rapa Nui. When the murderous altercation between the Rapa Nui and the Dutch took place, the Rapa Nui only threatened to throw stones, and the chief who took control was taking charge of a crowd, not leading an army. In the Vaihu area of the southeast coast Cook's officer Edgcomb shot a Rapa Nui man in the back after he had snatched a bag and fled. Before any of the other Rapa Nui could respond, one man threw off his cloak and ran round the Englishmen, gesturing and talking, thus preventing an altercation. Aside from these examples, there is no evidence of a war leader ever taking charge of a group of men believed to be warriors and either ordering them to fall back or to attack as a group.

There are two kinds of Rapa Nui spears, one a throwing spear and the other a shorter, thrusting spear. Both are made of a shaft of paper mulberry wood to which a flaked obsidian spearpoint (*mata'a*) was attached (hafted) by first wrapping the tang of the spearpoint with white barkcloth and then tying it to the shaft with cord (fig. 83). Six types of *mata'a* have been distinguished by shape, and five of these have Rapanui names, suggesting their specialised use. The most common is called *mata'a rei pure rova* or *mata'a arokiri*. The overall form of this spearpoint is the same in outline as prehistoric Lapita obsidian blades.[20] Métraux was aware of this similarity but the documentation of Lapita, of course, was not then available to him. Thus he was forced to discount the similarities in Rapa Nui and Melanesian artefact form and material.

Flaked tool manufacture is a skill which approaches an art in many cultures, but the manufacture of *mata'a* does not appear to have been controlled to produce an object of great beauty or utility which would befit a highly regarded warrior or artisan class. Instead, most appear to vary according to the probable time invested in their manufac-

83 Obsidian *mata'a* of the *mata'a rei pure rova* type (EP 17) hafted to a shortened wooden shaft. *Courtesy of the Museum of Mankind, British Museum.*

ture, their purpose and the skill level of the individual tool maker. A single *mata'a* of basalt is known, as is an obsidian implement which may be a ceremonial knife. Métraux speculated that this implement might have been used for cutting up large fish or human flesh.[21]

There is absolutely no doubt that *mata'a* proliferated widely on Rapa Nui in late archaeological and surface contexts. Neither is there any doubt that these contexts were within a time of probable economic difficulty and certain change in the natural and social environment. The current classification of *mata'a* was made by H.D. Skinner and is based upon 194 specimens in the Bernice P. Bishop museum. An extension of this preliminary research, studies of obsidian sources, artefact contexts, forms and other related matters are long overdue and badly needed. Without these studies, it is difficult to know which *mata'a* were certainly weapons, the distribution of those which were weapons, and to extrapolate from that some insight into their use in warfare or in such activities as sham battles.

Until this is done, it is facile to continue to cite the huge number of *mata'a* alone as evidence for a high level of undefined warfare on Rapa Nui.

Cannibalism (anthropophagy) is a charge frequently levelled at Pacific islanders and partially substantiated to varying degrees in Fiji, New Zealand and elsewhere. Cannibalism is mentioned in Rapa Nui ethnographies and at least one European account exists, but those tales may be exaggerated as in the case of warfare. The archaeological evidence for cannibalism is present on a few sites. Analysis of this evidence is only preliminary in most cases, making it premature to comment on the scope and intensity of the practice as a cultural phenomenon. As in New Zealand, human bone was often used by the Rapa Nui for several utilitarian purposes, such as the manufacture of fishhooks and small tools. How that bone was obtained in all cases, however, is not known. A preference for hiding human skeletons in caves or under a heavy cover of stone on *ahu* in late prehistory and into historic time may reflect the need to protect skeletons from desecration.

Cannibalism has been called the 'divine hunger'.[22] In the Pacific, human flesh is commonly equated with the flesh of both fish and pigs, and the word for fish (*ika*) is frequently applied to sacrificial victims, whether eaten or not. There are two basic types of cannibalism, exocannibalism (the cannibalism of enemies, slaves or victims captured in warfare) and endocannibalism (the cannibalism of relatives). Primary motivations for cannibalism include chronic and prolonged hunger stemming from famine and ritual requirements. Employing cannibalism as a response to hunger is not an automatic human choice, but requires the support, facilitation and reinforcement of a cultural framework practically and ideologically congenial to the practice.

It has been demonstrated that cannibalism is more likely to be present in politically homogeneous than heterogeneous societies, and less likely to be present in areas where agriculturalism has proceeded to optimum heights. Endocannibalism (which includes mortuary cannibalism) occurs in tribal societies where the consumption of human flesh objectifies the continuity and perpetuity of the clan, and where the ancestral legacy in the form of procreative power is linked to the preservation of ancestral bones and skulls in shrines, cult houses and ossuaries, and in the related rituals performed on these sites. Bones preserved and used in this way do not enter the larger public political domain but are, instead, meant to validate relations only internal to the ancestral domain. Such an endocannibalistic use might be postulated on Rapa Nui, for example, for preserved Miru skulls linked ethnographically with the perpetuation of hereditary status, fertility and fecundity. According to the work of Douglas Owsley the incised and painted symbols most often employed are anthropomorphs, fish or birds.

The preservation of a deceased individual's body parts is not always linked unequivocably to cannibalism. Before Captain Cook fell under the dagger of a Hawaiian warrior on the shore of Kealakekua Bay he had been greeted as a divine guest by the chiefs and priests of the islands. Regarded as an incarnation of Lono (Rongo), god of fertility and harvest, Cook and his party had inadvertently traced the seasonal Makahiki festival's ritual circuit. Ultimately he was slain amid a crowd of thousands assembled at the ritual centre of Lono's cult. Cook's remains, delivered to the English one week after his death, consisted of bones stripped clean of flesh but excluding those of the back and jaw. These were said to have been burned with the torso. Whether any of his flesh was consumed by Hawaiians is not known. Cook's hands, with the flesh intact, had been carefully salted for preservation.

Motivations for exocannibalism are complex and varied, embedded in the ideological constructs of individual societies, but certain patterns are discernible. On the simplest level, exocannibalism was practised as part of revenge taking, status enhancement or the seeking of spiritual protection. The Polynesian notion that ingesting one's victim or portions of one's victim (such as the eyes in Marquesas Islands and Hawaii) also allowed for the absorption of the victim's spiritual power (*mana*) was a factor in ritual cannibalism. This was not, however, a widespread practice but was, instead, confined to certain chiefs and priests in complex ritual settings.

Apparent remains of cannibalistic activities are known on Rapa Nui from both ceremonial and non-ceremonial contexts, but was the activity exocannibalism or endocannibalism? This is a crucial question with important ramifications for understanding Rapa Nui culture. Was famine cannibalism used as a means to satisfy basic human nutritional (protein) needs in a time of sharply limited food resources? As with warfare in general, the extent, intensity and social role of cannibalistic behaviour remains a matter of speculation. Any hypothesis that the Rapa Nui consumed human flesh on any widespread, extensive level remains to be demonstrated archaeologically.[23]

A final important revelation of the osteological data lies in the discernible patterns of what anthropologists call endogamous and exogamous breeding. Métraux suggested that Rapa Nui kin groups practised tribal endogamy, marrying only within their own kin. In contrast, Routledge says that 'in remembered times there were no group restrictions on marriage, which took place indiscriminately between members of the same or different clans'.[24] Incest, a socially acceptable and frequently ritually required practice at the highest levels of some Polynesian societies, probably existed. Genetic flow from the territory of Anakena, controlled by the Miru, towards the lower-ranked southeast coast is suggested by the extant data, illustrating probable extra-immediate kin contact. I take this as further evidence of increased and extended sociopolitical alliances somewhat late in time.

The Rapa Nui Aesthetic

Plaiting the real and the imagined defines all art.

JOHN FOWLES Author and Lover of Islands

The idea of exploring historic relationship through continuity in the arts is relevant to the complex but, as yet, somewhat formative field of Polynesian art and aesthetics. Cultural continuity can be established by comparative study when there is historical continuity between archaeological artefacts and ethnographic objects.[1] Building upon the notion of inheritance from a common source (Lapita), we can use art objects from other Polynesian islands in our study of Rapa Nui art. In all cases, these objects must be related to their original social and aesthetic contexts.[2]

Traditional Polynesian art is a significant component of traditional society, and profoundly reflects the order, organisation and values of that society. Objects, body decoration and various of the performing arts were made, used, presented and displayed within a social structure which had an inherent inequality created and reinforced by genealogical rank or achieved status. Hence, an 'aesthetic of inequality' has been shown to have existed.[3] This aesthetic can be seen in unequal access to clothing, ornamentation, living sites and quarters. Further, inequality is evident in the distribution of valuables during ceremonial exchanges, access to sacred places, performances and ceremonies and the awarding of special status to artists. In this way, the actual availability of esoteric information, encoded in highly traditional art forms executed only by the initiated and entitled, was sharply controlled.

Rongorongo and Its Oceanic Heritage

The Lapita ceramic and non-ceramic aesthetic tradition has discernible characteristics, at least five of which are evident in Rapa Nui art. First among these is symmetry (as a property of regular patterns and as a factor in perception). Indeed, symmetry is a basic and underlying feature of Rapa Nui style. The other qualities are repetition, redundancy, the use of the human form and the depiction of physical transformation. Bird and human representations appear as single forms but are also often integrated.

Archaeologists have recovered an anthropomorphic sculpture from a Lapita site in the Mussau Islands. (fig. 84). Small and highly stylised, this image has arms indicated by incised lines at the front of the body only, legs (each with a line indicating possible feet) and a double horizontal line across the front which may represent a loin cloth or ceremonial belt. The arms terminate at the midpoint above the (non-indicated) genitals, creating a line which repeats that of the chin. The head/face is elongated and ovoid,

84 Small, stylised human image of heavy bone retrieved from archaeological context, Lapita culture, Mussau Islands, Bismarck Archipelago. *Drawing by M. Davidson. Courtesy of P.V. Kirch.*

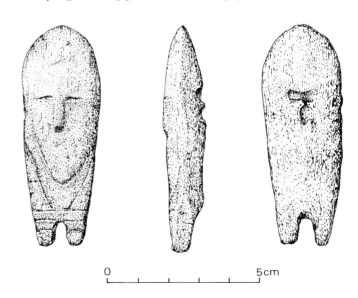

0   5cm

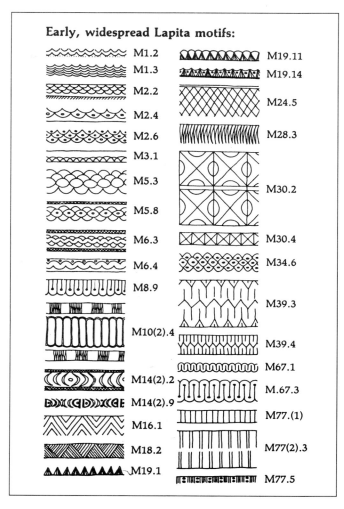

Early, widespread Lapita motifs:

〜〜〜〜〜	M1.2	〈〈〈〈〈〈〈〈	M19.11
〜〜〜〜〜	M1.3	〈〈〈〈〈〈〈〈	M19.14
✕✕✕✕✕✕	M2.2	╳╳╳╳	M24.5
❖❖❖❖❖	M2.4		
❖❖❖❖❖	M2.6	〰〰〰〰	M28.3
❖❖❖❖❖	M3.1		
❖❖❖❖❖	M5.3		M30.2
❖❖❖❖❖	M5.8		
❖❖❖❖❖	M6.3	⋈⋈⋈⋈	M30.4
❖❖❖❖❖	M6.4	❖❖❖❖❖	M34.6
⊔⊔⊔⊔⊔	M8.9		M39.3
	M10(2).4	∪∪∪∪∪	M39.4
		⌒⌒⌒⌒⌒	M67.1
◐◐◐◐	M14(2).2	⊔⊔⊔⊔⊔	M.67.3
	M14(2).9	‖‖‖‖‖	M77.(1)
⋀⋀⋀	M16.1	‖‖‖‖‖	M77(2).3
◣◥◣◥	M18.2		
▲▲▲▲▲▲	M19.1		M77.5

85 Early, widespread Lapita pottery decorative motifs. *Courtesy of R.C. Green.*

and the eyes are slits.[4] At another site on Reef Island, a fragment of a human figure in baked clay has a design which probably represented a tattoo etched into the buttocks on both sides, and a bird's head of modelled pottery from Santa Cruz Island dates to 1400 BC.[5]

Lapita ceramic designs are small in scale, applied to pottery within bounded and well-defined zones and forming patterns which are repetitive, continuous or discontinuous and bilaterally symmetrical (mirror image) (fig. 85).[6] Most designs are stamped or incised into the pot surface with special tools in a process not unlike those used to produce designs on barkcloth or the human skin. The repetition of patterns adheres to formal rules. Sometimes, for example, the designs are repeated in one direction only. Motifs are sometimes superimposed upon other motifs. Similarly, repetitious, symmetrical, geometric designs enclosed within

horizontally, vertically or diagonally bounded zones are found on a variety of Polynesian artefacts of great artistic distinction, including ceremonial adzes associated with the god Tane from Mangaia, ceremonial paddles and food scoops from Ra'ivavae and war clubs from Fiji. While the use and surface decoration of pottery decreased with the movement eastward into Polynesia, the application of design motifs to other types of both utilitarian and ceremonial objects did not.

Design tablets called *kupeti are suggested to relate to Lapita pottery decoration. These began to be used in Western Polynesia at some unknown point in late prehistory.[7] Usually composed of multiple bands of motifs, some of which were either superimposed or mirror image, the tablets were utilised to produce basic barkcloth designs by passing them in repetitious, linear movements over the surface of the barkcloth. There is variation in the linear patterns depending upon the island region.

Western Polynesian design tablets were manufactured from pandanus leaf, or fibrous coconut-leaf sheaths and midribs. In Samoa and elsewhere the leaf tablets were replaced by carved boards after European contact. The *kupeti did not reach Eastern Polynesia, but the rigid alignment of repetitious designs on the *kohau rongorongo* may be a Rapa Nui adaptation, innovation or invention which demonstrates a retention of the linear, bounded design pattern as an aesthetic idea (fig. 86). The Rapa Nui ethnography suggests that designs cut or impressed into the smooth, shiny surfaces of banana leaves with any of a variety of sharp obsidian, shark's tooth, bone or even metal tools may have sometimes served as teaching surfaces in the instruction of *rongorongo* symbology.[8]

While the *kohau rongorongo* as objects were certainly never meant to function in the production of barkcloth designs, their use as mnemonic devices in ritual would be a remarkably functional and creative cultural reintroduction or reinvention of a design concept out of which, at another place and time, the *kupeti idea emerged. On the basis of present information, most scholars concede the probability that the *kohau rongorongo* are postcontact innovations growing out of established ritual practices and prompted by the act of 'signing' the treaty of annexation with the Spanish in 1770.[9]

An unknown number of the tablets existed during missionary times, and all of the collected examples are from that era. During that very same period, there was a substantial indigenous movement of resistance to Christian authority led by Torometi. In times of rebellion or resistance in preliterate societies it is common to revive ancient but perhaps neglected esoteric symbols. It is less usual to

Plate 11 Orongo's basalt rocks on the summit of Rano Kau are profusely sculpted with haunting images associated with the *tangata manu* cult. *Photo by David C. Ochsner, 1989.*

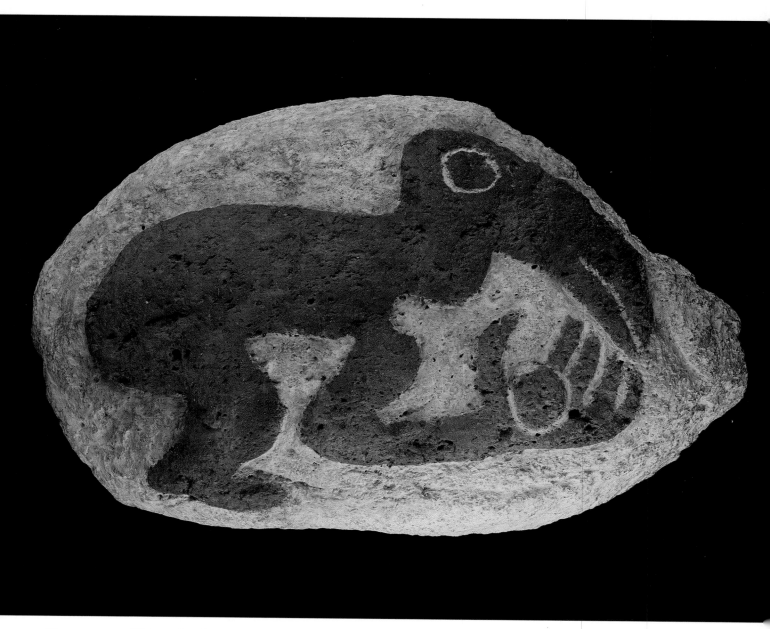

Plate 12 ABOVE White painted stone with birdman figure carved in low bas-relief (BM 1920.5–6.1) was collected at Orongo by the Mana Expedition to Easter Island, 1914–15. Length of carving 36.5 cm. *Photo courtesy of the Museum of Mankind, British Museum.*

Plate 13 RIGHT Juvenile frigatebird (*Fregata minor*). Physical characteristics and contexts of these birds when depicted in petroglyphs differ, possibly relating the figures to variant purposes, ceremony types or ages of their makers. *Photo by Mandy Etpison, Republic of Belau, Micronesia.*

Plate 14 ABOVE A Lan Chile flight departs Rapa Nui, winging its way over the impressive ancient stone *ahu* wall at Vinapu. *Photo © 1991 by James L. Amos.*

Plate 15 RIGHT Ahu Tahai (foreground) and Ahu Vai Uri, restored to their final construction phases, appear to be relatively simple rectangular platforms with *poro* paving from the front, while at the rear a complexity of interrelated retaining walls and ramps stabilize and dramatize the seaward construction. Types and extents of *ahu* walls are dictated by a range of varying factors on each site. *Photo © 1994 by Russell Kord.*

Plate 16 ABOVE The late Amelia Tepano Ika was a beloved link with the past, a much sought-after teacher of the art of *kaikai*, string figures made and presented with accompanying chants. *Photo © 1991 by James L. Amos.*

Plate 17 RIGHT Cristián Arévalo Pakarati, Amelia Tepano Ika's grandson, recreates body paint designs for the annual Rapa Nui arts festival, 1992. *Photo by Jo Anne Van Tilburg, 1992.*

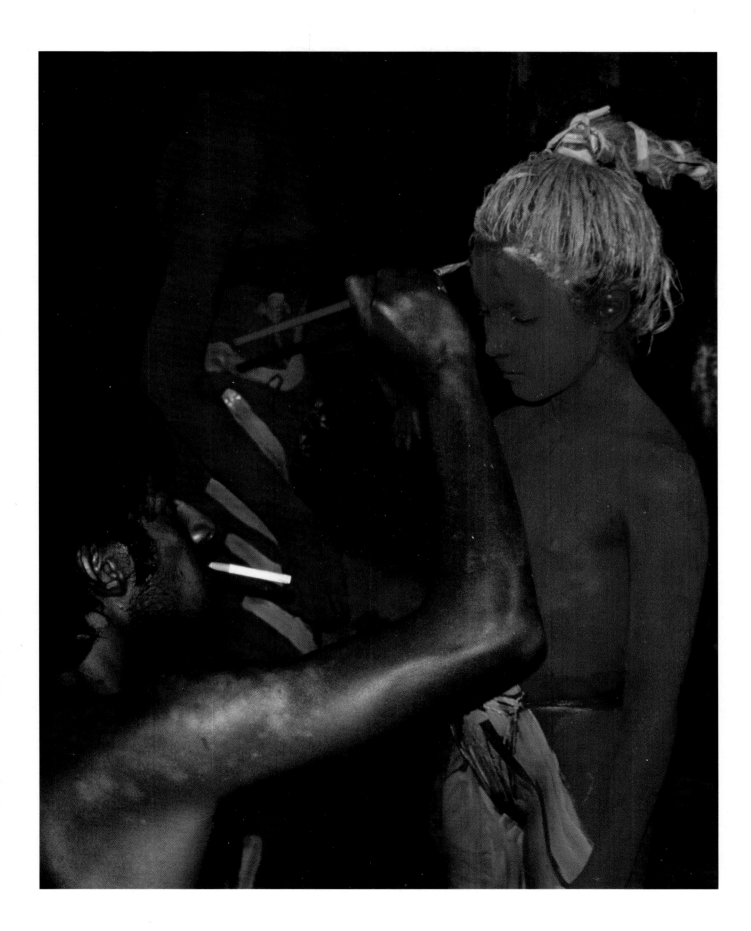

Plate 18 The meaning of a dramatic, red-painted anthropomorphic face, sculpted from the stone wall of a cave containing burials and other painted petroglyphs, is unknown but probably related to birdman cult ritual. *Photo by David C. Ochsner, 1989.*

Plate 19 Headdress (53541) of wood, fibre and painted barkcloth is distinctly reminiscent of Makemake type petroglyph faces but also alludes through design details to the *tangata manu* woodcarvings. Acquired by Boston Museum in 1899. *Photo courtesy of the Peabody Museum of Archaeology and Ethnology, Harvard University, Cambridge, Mass.*

86 Detail of carved symbols on a *kohau rongorongo* (USNM 129,773). *Photo by Corson Hirschfeld with permission, Department of Anthropology, NMNH, Smithsonian Institution.*

create totally new symbols; very often an existing symbol, symbol system or method of symbol presentation from outside a given culture is appropriated (as Angata did when she wore a red cross round her neck during the Rapa Nui 'rising').

In modern times (the 1930s) a seventeen-year-old woman named Gaidiliu emerged as a charismatic leader to take charge of a rebellion of the Naga people against the British. The Naga comprise a tribal society in the mountains of Assam, on the Burma/India border. Prehistorically, these people raised stone megaliths and enormous, Y-shaped wooden posts to deified chiefs. Their society was formed and has been influenced to unknown degrees by both Austroasiatic and Austronesian-speaking peoples, with the Austronesian influence more recent. The Naga rebellion was political, but the means by which it was

legitimised were ideological. Gaidiliu announced that a new day had dawned, new religious practices were required, and sacrificial animals and food as tribute were demanded. Gaidiliu claimed supernatural powers, assuring her followers that the bullets of the British would not harm them. In very nearly all respects, Gaidiliu and Angata were central and similar figures in nearly parallel events which differed, obviously, in scale, context and time. Their rise and influence, however brief, was a function of the underlying similarities in the sociopolitical structure of each society as well as the similar tensions and needs of the times.

In the Pitt Rivers Museum, Oxford, there is a set of notebooks which Gaidiliu filled with regular and repetitive symbols resembling writing but in no known language.[10] Pages of the writing were said to enhance her power and were 'read' by messengers to her followers. The acts of writing and reading were believed to be magic. In conditions of deprivation and destruction over which people feel they have little or no control, preliterate societies will sometimes adopt symbols of literacy and incorporate them into ritual or political acts. The conflicted and traumatised Rapa Nui society in the 1800s was also an intellectually demanding and stimulating time. Innovating, reviving or otherwise creating *rongorongo* out of such an environment is quite possible.

Routledge, Métraux and Englert were all led independently and reluctantly to the conclusion that the meanings of *rongorongo* symbols, and the way in which they functioned as mnemonic devices for chanters during ceremony, were taken to their graves by the *tangata rongorongo* (fig. 87). They also recognised the problems associated with having such a small sample of objects with which to work. Apparently, only between twenty-five and thirty original *kohau rongorongo* fragments exist, and Barthel believes that approximately 120 basic design units are combined in various ways to produce between 1,500 and 2,000 compound symbols. Notwithstanding the apparent problems, Barthel and his colleagues have worked tirelessly to reconstruct symbol meaning using linguistic models and extra-island comparisons, starting from the assumption that the symbols are ideograms which also, at times, held and conveyed meaning as sounds.[11] Other researchers also have cautiously moved toward the notion that *rongorongo* symbols are a mixed ideographic and phonetic system.[12]

A significant problem in understanding even the most apparently realistic (as opposed to metaphorical) symbols is that we know very little about how the Rapa Nui regarded the natural world. Elsewhere in Polynesia shells, birds, plants, fish and even insects had a place in life's creative scheme. The virtues, dangers, vitality and allure of such

KOHAU RONGO-RONGO (Tablets)

RÉSUMÉ OF EVIDENCE

Kohau	Kapiere	Jotefa	Kitimuti	Tomenico	Tehaha	Langitopa	Romanahé
Hakiri	(b)x	x		x	x	x	x
Atua Matua	(a)X	x			x		
Timo	x	x					
Ika	x	x			x(2)		
Hauwa	x		x		x		
Toa	x	x			x		
Tangata	x						x
O-te-pua	} x		x				
Manu				?			
Také	x	x		x	x	x	
Katagnivek	x						
Rauhiva					x		
Puré	(mast)	(roof)	x		(roof)		
O-te-ranga	x		x	x		x	
Tau	x		x	x			x

87 Katherine Routledge collected data from seven old Rapa Nui men regarding 15 named *kohau rongorongo. Courtesy of the Museum of Mankind, British Museum.*

entities were often invoked in ritual. Most had a name or a symbolic image, usually frequently changed, and many were variously depicted in several forms of art, including petroglyphs and tattoos. This was undoubtedly so on Rapa Nui, where even the lowly centipede was associated with the powerful *matatoa* class of warriors and depicted in tattoo. The once dynamic, changing quality of *rongorongo* symbols, now static and locked forever in wood, is a substantial barrier to scholarship. In my judgement, a possibly fruitful research direction might be to study *rongorongo* within the existing corpus of knowledge about zoned, linear, repetitious, small scale surface decoration on Lapita ceramics. Tests of repetition, redundancy, symbol and pattern symmetry might be applied. While exact parallels in design motifs obviously will not exist, elucidating the specific and comparative rules of ordering and using surface space may prove helpful in understanding the rules defining *rongorongo*.

In Polynesia, it has been shown that the carver of sacred images, the tools used by the carver, the material from which the object was being carved, the object itself and the histories and genealogies of each were inextricably bound together in the process of artistry. The web which was woven to enclose the profoundly creative act of carving, tying it to the ancestral gods, was sacred chant. This 'integral association of visual and verbal modes of expression' is widespread in Polynesia and 'a fundamental characteristic of Polynesian art and aesthetics'.[13] Two widely documented methods of associating chants with objects or symbolic movements to produce performance art include dance and string figures (*kaikai* on Rapa Nui) (plate 16).

Competitive recitations by learned and initiated *tangata rongorongo* took place at Orongo during the bird cult rites, at Anakena once a year at an unknown date, and variously throughout the year at the new moon or last quarter of the moon. At Anakena, the *tangata rongorongo* apparently arranged themselves in parallel rows facing the *ariki mau*, who sat on a seat said to be either of stone or made of *rongorongo* tablets, depending on the source (all of this information came from Routledge's informants). At the end of the recitations, the *ariki mau* was said to stand on a platform borne by eight men to address the *rongorongo* men on the performance of their duties.[14] Today competitive recitations during the yearly Rapa Nui arts festival called Tapati Rapa Nui centre on *kaikai* only, and the participants are almost always women.

Métraux pointed out the similarities between the *tangata rongorongo* as an institution and the Maori schools of learning (*whare wananga*), the *tuhuna o'ono* of the Marquesas and the *taura rongorongo* of Mangareva. In the Marquesas, these individuals were ceremonial priests as well as master chanters and tribal bards, while in Mangareva they were more like a class of 'intellectuals', attending feasts organised by the chiefs to recite genealogies and transmit cultural information to their students. Each of these experts carried ceremonial sticks, staffs or clubs during recitations. If we consider the specialised information which informants have said was included in various types of *kohau rongorongo*, it seems apparent that the Rapa Nui *tangata rongorongo* could be either or both specialist priest and 'intellectual'.

Lavachery and others have suggested that some *rongorongo*-type designs occur in petroglyphs. The increase in scale of both design and surface, the change in media, the indicated variation in skill and possibly in social level of the maker and the decrease in control of technique and tool is evident in these incised petroglyphs as compared to incised wood carving or even bas-relief petroglyphs. This does not necessarily mean that petroglyphs and *rongorongo* symbols are coeval, although the late archaeological and ethnographic contexts of both suggest to me that this is quite probable. Nor does it mean that the *rongorongo* carvings inspired the petroglyphs, or the reverse. What such similarities assuredly demonstrate, however, is the pervasive value of repetition and the ubiquity of certain design forms in Rapa Nui aesthetic expression, articulated within a consistent but evolving belief system.

Hybrid and Morphosis Images

An important quality of Rapa Nui art is what I call transformation or morphosis attributes. Morphosis is a Greek word which means the action or process of changing or forming. In many Rapa Nui woodcarvings, some stonecarvings and some petroglyphs we see that faces or bodies change from human to bird or other forms depending on such variables as the angle from which the carving is being viewed. This sculptural quality has been called visual punning, but such a term inaccurately implies that the artisan's intent is humorous when, in fact, something far more important is indicated.[15] Morphosis carvings depict a being changing to another being, and cleverly involve the viewer in the process of that change. These objects depict physical transformations which are the probable result of such supernatural actions as spirit possession. The best known of the morphosis figures is the birdman or *tangata manu*, the earliest of which was collected in 1828, and a probable morphosis figure is etched on one of the skulls examined by Doug Owsley. The lizard/man *moko* is an especially graphic and dynamic example of the morphosis principle. *Moko* are usually described as being worn, but some have also been catalogued as clubs. All known *moko* are postmissionary. The perceptual dynamism of Lapita pottery designs are ancestral (and far more sophisticated) forerunners of the concept of morphosis in Rapa Nui art.

In Lapita pottery we see the importance of how symmetry and repetition are used by talented craftspeople to influence how the eye recognises shape and perceives form. Perception is a process which includes the physiology of vision but is also dependent on selection conditioned by the social environment. In other words, we are taught what to see. This teaching obviously varies with culture, but it also varies within cultures and especially between status levels of probable hierarchical cultures such as Lapita and, of course, Polynesia and Rapa Nui. Once we train our eyes to the challenge of perception created by the symmetry of these designs, we recognise minimal fundamental units of structure previously ignored. These fundamental units include the human eyes/face, the avian beak/face, the conjoining of human/bird forms and the seated, full human figure.[16]

Human faces (sometimes called 'masks') on pottery are known from some of the earliest Lapita sites (*c.*3400–3000 BP), and a discernible change in these designs over some 1,000 years has been suggested (fig. 88). Further, relationships between the Lapita face design and 'transformations' of this design in various, later art styles of Melanesia and the Dong Son metal work of Roti have been noted.[17] Faces have been classified by M. Spriggs as either single or double. Double faces seem to be, in general, earlier (*c.*2750 BP) than single faces, and a progression toward greater abstraction over time is indicated, although the data are scant. The more complex, curvilinear, double face forms of Western Lapita are included within a class called Type 1. Four types of designs (star, circle, cross and herringbone) form elements which have been reasonably interpreted as depictions of earplugs. The faces, as in all Lapita pottery surface decoration, appear in repeated, contiguous and linear arrangements within bounded and well-defined zones.

Three reconstructed Type 1 designs from Western Lapita sites are among many examples of perceptual complexity.[18] One design (Type 1C from site RF-2) is an arrangement of full and partial concentric circles placed on either side of a central triangle shape (fig. 89). The circles are joined by spanning concentric lines above the triangle. This design may be perceived as a triangular human face with elaborate earplug ornaments, the whole then framed within a curvilinear design. Depictions of the human face as triangular occur in many Oceanic and several Polynesian contexts. The design may also be perceived as a partial face or 'mask' consisting of a pair of eyes formed of concentric circles and a triangular-shaped nose, hence its double face designation. Beyond this, however, I perceive that the entire form also possesses distinctly avian qualities, suggesting the eyes and sharply pointed beak of a bird (fig. 90).

88 Lapita pottery sherds with face design and small circles defining spatial zones were excavated by R.C. Green at site RF-2, Reef Island, southeast Solomons, 1971–2. *Courtesy of R.C. Green.*

90 *Tangata manu* woodcarving (N 736–204), early nineteenth century, is a fine example of a human/bird morphosis figure. *Museum of Anthropology and Ethnography named after Peter the Great, St. Petersburg. Photo courtesy J.T. Seaver-Kurze.*

The presence of the eyes/nose 'mask' in various artistic traditions in Oceania does not necessarily mean that a masking tradition existed in any or all of these areas, and there is no evidence that it did on Rapa Nui.[19] The interaction of the cultural/ideological value placed on the human head and eyes with the artistic value of the zoning technique in pottery manufacture may be at least partially responsible for creating an iconic value for the human face 'mask' and its subsequent presence in other media. Interestingly, the human face petroglyphs in the Marquesas Islands emphasise the eyes/mouth more frequently than the eyes/nose, and are a distinctively insular innovation which relates most obviously to Marquesan bone and wood carvings in a variety of simple to elaborate forms. Further, curvilinear rather than linear design elements seem to predominate in Marquesan rock art.[20]

89 Reconstructed Type 1C design, Lapita pottery sherds from RF-2. Type 1 designs are thought to date before 2750 BP. *Courtesy M. Spriggs.*

Rapa Nui Style: Icons and Ideas

Rapa Nui art encompasses the full spectrum of Polynesian art forms including tattoo and body painting, barkcloth, featherwork, shell work, woodcarving, stonecarving and basketry. Performance art (singing, dancing, reciting) has evolved greatly over the years and through outside Polynesian and European influence. Stonecarving includes three dimensional monolithic and portable stone sculpture and rock art. Rock art is two-dimensional, carved into natural rock, semantic or vernacular architecture or sculpture. Rock carvings are called petroglyphs and rock paintings are called pictographs. Painted petroglyphs occur in several different locations on the island.

Examples of Rapa Nui art are in three main locales. The island itself remains the central 'museum' for Rapa Nui art, with the largest part of the corpus of monolithic sculpture (887 examples to date) and rock art (3,993 examples) remaining on display *in situ*. The off-island ethnographic collections I have reviewed in many of the world's museums are eclectic, and include samples of several object types, although few non-stone and non-wood artefacts have survived in good condition. There are many privately-collected objects in small collections such as that of the Royal Geographic Society. Portable stonecarvings of

undocumented, historic or modern contexts are in many museums, and others have been collected by the survey in habitation or agricultural contexts. It is possible that stylistic antecedents of monolithic sculpture may be present among these pieces, some of which may have been design or practice maquettes.

A creative adaptation of Rapa Nui artistry to shortages in traditional materials and the introduction of modern tools and materials (such as trade cloth in the nineteenth century, beads and iron nails even earlier) is widely evident in the extant collections. The distinction between 'evolved traditional art', 'folk art' and 'airport art' on Rapa Nui is yet to be made in all categories of artistic expression.[21] Many of the objects collected and purchased are of dubious value for scholarly study, and an informed, critical analysis of this material remains to be undertaken. Recently, valuable scholarly efforts have been made to identify

91 Tattoos, here lavishly present on the Rapa Nui man Rano, later called Tepano, may have inspired incised marks superimposed on *moai* and painted designs on barkcloth images. Note stylistic continuity with fig. 81, although 'arms' and a vertical element have been added to some dots on the forehead to create an anthropomorphic form. Dots may be outliners or zone definers as are circles in some Lapita pottery. *Photo after Stolpe (1899). Courtesy of the Bernice P. Bishop Museum.*

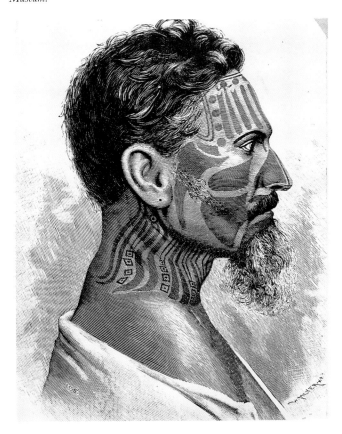

the earliest objects in various type categories of wood-carving.[22]

A discernible aspect of the Rapa Nui three-dimensional carving aesthetic is the preference for vertically rectangular, cylindrical forms. The richly decorated surface was not a goal of Rapa Nui craftsmanship in the same way it was, for instance, of Maori woodcarvers or Marquesan tattooers. Instead, restraint in the treatment of the surface is obvious, and fine, even and smooth finishes in both wood and stone carvings are a hallmark of Rapa Nui work. In general, geometric designs and linear use of space is evident, although curvilinear designs (circles, spirals, partial or concentric circles) are frequently applied to rectangular forms. There is good evidence that tattoo was a lavishly complicated and highly evolved art form, with the richest designs reserved for the face and neck (fig. 91).

In keeping with the widespread Oceanic belief in the spiritual value of the human head and face, Rapa Nui craftspeople emphasised the heads of monolithic stone statues by disproportionately enlarging and elongating them relative to the bodies. The heads of some fallen *moai* were occasionally engraved with partial human faces of the Makemake type, pairs of human eyes, *komari* or small, *moai*-like figures in a redundant emphasis or reemphasis of the head's value. Similarly, the heads of woodcarvings were also carved with a variety of symbols, some of which are found in the petroglyph corpus. This accomplished the same sort of emphasis, but the relative influence of petroglyph designs on woodcarvings in general is not known. The crescent-shaped *rei miro* pendant was enhanced with a superimposed, carved crescent.[23] The spiritual importance of head, eyes, hands and spine is illustrated in the sculptural and detail emphasis given to them in Rapa Nui arts, and the redundancy of that message is made clear when forms having the same or similar meanings are then superimposed.

The prehistoric Rapa Nui design vocabulary continued to be manipulated during historic times, augmented by introduced influences of the pre- and post-missionary era to create realistic, abstracted and metaphorical designs and objects. A decided tendency toward control of line and form and standardisation in both wood and stone carving was sought, with varying degrees of success. Precontact symbols, when fully and highly standardised, were raised to iconic levels of meaning. The monolithic *moai* were among the more fully standardised of all Rapa Nui art objects. The bas-relief birdman of Orongo rock art was relatively standardised in attributes but varied in form, suggesting either that the carvers of that image were allowed, perhaps even expected, to express variation within the accepted style range or that they were individuals of varying skill and/or understanding. In spite of evident design controls each object and class of objects (including the *moai*) contains formal and stylistic differences which may be, in part, attributed to inevitable variation.

While the conceptualisation and aesthetic development of the *moai* and various other Rapa Nui objects were assuredly highly creative endeavours, the repetitious, redundant production of exact or nearly exact replicas of these objects was in the hands of artisans, not artists in the Western sense of individualised communication/reception through art. Craftsmanship and the ability to conform to a standard model was the desired norm. Individual skill levels and/or creativity were tolerated or allowed to the extent of producing the form variation described in the statue study for example, but true innovations emerged only under encouraging social circumstances. Rapa Nui art objects were meant to function as part of the socialisation process, and were highly traditional in form and use. The *moai* were not individually created. They were executed within a defined socioreligious context.

Colour and Material

The traditional Polynesian colours of red, black and white were used, with a decided preference for shades of red. Red as a colour is called *mea* or *meamea*, and appears to have been highly valued by the Rapa Nui, who sought earths and made plant dyes which they could use to paint objects, rock art designs, some *moai* and their own bodies and hair (plates 17, 18). In particular, reuse of a few statues by applying red or white paint (as at Ahu Akivi, Vinapu and possibly Tongariki) was probably a reflection of the significance of body paint during ritual. There is virtually no evidence, however, that statues were painted in elaborate patterns similar to that suggested by Lavachery. In addition to paint, a few statues also have etched lines, pit-shaped depressions, or petroglyph designs on the throats, bases, torsos and faces. Some of these designs, especially the circular pits and lines, relate to tattoos (fig. 92).

Red and red-brown mineralised tuffs are found on Poike and elsewhere on the island as well as on Motu Nui, and pigment, called *ki'ea*, is made when this material is mixed with the water and sugar from sugar cane. Another pigment, called *marikuru*, is white (*teatea*) and was made with unoxidised tuff. Yellow or orange was obtained by grating the root of turmeric (*Curcuma longa*, called *pua* on Rapa Nui) and mixing it with sugar cane juice. Black (*kerekere*) completed the complement of the four essential colours in Rapa Nui (and Polynesian) art and ritual.

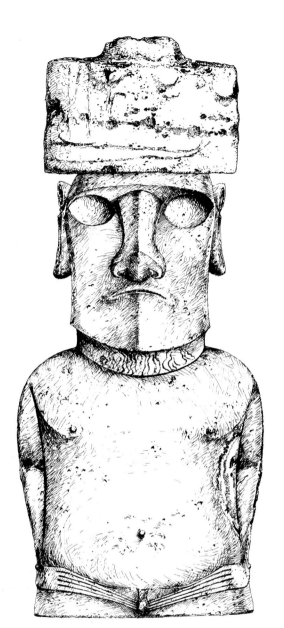
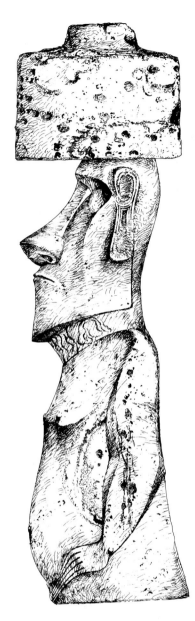

92 Conjectural reconstruction of broken and damaged *moai*, Vinapu (2–210–04), drawn earlier by Palmer (fig. 35). Note incised lines on neck, painted crescent on left side and cupules on the *pukao* and left arm, added after the statue fell. *Drawing by Cristián Arévalo Pakarati.*

The Rano Raraku tuff when freshly quarried is a very light orange-red, occasionally appearing quite yellow. This colour weathered and changed over time to a grey-black, and the colour change may have been a factor in the need to create new sculpture. The red scoria utilised in some sculpture and *ahu* fascia is distinctly and sharply different from Rano Raraku tuff in hue and also in texture. At Anakena, the beach cobbles used to pave the ramp of Ahu Naunau had an oxidised white finish, and may have been specially selected and used for this quality. The white of the paving, the red of the *ahu* fascia and *pukao* and the reddish-yellow of the *moai*, still visible today, would have created an inherently colourful architectural/sculptural complex.[24] The *toromiro* wood preferred for woodcarvings was also red-

dish. While the lavishly red-feathered birds of other islands were not present on Rapa Nui, chicken feathers of several colours but mostly red/black and white/grey were widely utilised. Barkcloth appears to have been an especially valued and scarce material during historic times and probably earlier.

The Human Body as Art Object

The realistically presented human body, discretely executed human body parts (such as hands, feet, eyes and female genitals) or abstract expressions of the human torso, head and face are overwhelmingly emphasised in Rapa Nui art. This observation is consistent no matter what the medium, and includes three-dimensional wood and stone sculpture, many ceremonial or status artefacts and two-dimensional rock art (plate 19). The largest category of extant objects is the three-dimensional, realistic human figure executed in stone, wood, barkcloth and vegetable material. Others are wood ceremonial paddles and staffs which represent human figures, composite human/non-human (hybrid) and morphosis figures in both stone and wood, and pendants (some of which represent parts of the human body such as the hands or feet).

Realistic human figures include the *moai*, the large *paina* figures made of vegetable material and erected on *ahu* sites,

painted barkcloth portable figures, portable stonecarvings and woodcarvings (plates 22, 23). Woodcarvings include the well-known and widely collected emaciated male called *kavakava* (plate 20), the realistic male human called *moai tangata*, and the female or male/female composite called *moai pa'apa'a* (figs 93, 94). The earliest *kavakava* was collected in either 1804 by Lizjanskij or 1811 by Von Kotzebue. The *moai tangata* and *moai pa'apa'a* figures were collected from about 1870 or 1871 to the early 1900s. A possible prototype for the moai pa'apa'a may have been collected on Cook's second voyage.[25] The time frame for the extant and

93 Two morphosis woodcarvings with inherent anthropomorphic characteristics include the lizard or *moko* (96–1194) and the *tangata manu* (1928.5–17.1), here shown with the wooden human hand (EP 32) collected on Cook's second voyage. *Photo courtesy of the Museum of Mankind, British Museum.*

94 Three anthropomorphic woodcarvings include (from left) the highly abstracted *rapa* (6846), examples of which were seen used in improvised 'dancing' by crewmembers of HMS *Topaze*, the *moai tangata* (EP 24) and the *pa'a pa'a* (EP 23). Each of these carvings bears details also present on *moai*, including the marked clavicle, inlaid eyes, joint markers and dorsal designs. *Photo courtesy of the Museum of Mankind, British Museum.*

documented human male and female woodcarvings thus begins only in 1804 or 1811.

The *'ao*, the *rapa* and the *ua* are ceremonial objects which evoke the human face and trunk (fig. 95). On the surfaces of the *'ao* and the *rapa* we find the human face indicated by a bas-relief line meant to represent the eyebrows/nose. This precise detail is found on the backs of the *moai*, outlining the spine and shoulders. Thus, the interchangeable symbolism is fully anthropomorphic, indicative of both a face and a backbone. Thomson collected an *'ao* which was painted red and white to represent realistically a face and headdress (plate 21). Interestingly, ears are represented on these paddles by round earplugs, just as in Lapita pottery.

Ceremonial paddles were observed in 1868 being used by men in dancing. One of these dances was staged for the crew of HMS *Topaze*, held in the presence of Catholic missionaries. It was said to be somewhat improvised and very unstructured, involving jumping in the air and twirling or waving the paddles. Any observed use of the *rapa* collected on Cook's voyage was not described, and certainly

95 Rapa Nui chief's stave (E 1216) called *ua* has facial characteristics also present on some *moai* fragments recarved as faces. *Royal Albert Memorial Museum, Exeter. Photo courtesy A.L. Kaeppler.*

no dances were witnessed. It seems clear that the paddles could be held upright (that is, with the head/face at the top) or reversed, and the consequent ability to present the object from various angles and positions was certainly an important part of the meaning of the symbol in movement.

The *rapa* are similar in form to the *'ao*, but appreciably smaller. None are painted in the same graphic way as the *'ao* collected by Thomson, although one quite small, very lightweight *rapa* in the collection of the National Museum of Natural History, Smithsonian Institution is painted completely red. The *rapa* have, at the midsection terminus of the bottom paddle, a small projection which appears to be either representative of a phallus or an elongated clitoris. Thomson attached the name 'Mata Kao-Kao' to the painted red and white *'ao* he collected. He also recorded the term 'Mata Kao' for a similarly anthropomorphic object described as a 'skull oar', said to be very old and highly prized by the islanders. The object is formed of a long stick or pole to which is lashed a carved form vaguely similar to that employed in some parts of Polynesia for canoe bailers, but which is more graphically evocative of the human face. The Rapa Nui word *kao* definitely refers to female genitals, suggesting that the sexual reference of at least these two objects is female (fig. 96).[26]

It seems likely that some Rapa Nui art objects of several types were produced in enlarged dimensions and proportions after contact and during an unknown span of time. Such a preference for increased size over time, of course, is indicated in the dimensions of the monolithic statues, but has also been suggested to be a quality of postcontact Pacific art objects.[27] The *rapa* attributed to Captain Cook's 1774 voyage, for example, is only 43.5 cm long, while one brought back less than 100 years later on HMS *Topaze* is nearly double that length (81.5 cm). Several different types of pendants in various museum collections are also in startlingly increased proportions over the majority of others in the same category.

The famous human hand given or traded to Mahine by the Rapa Nui and then given to Forster, now in the collection of the British Museum, is perforated. Whether the perforation was meant to allow the hand to be hung in house rafters for safekeeping or to be worn is not known. The carving represents the left hand and the fingernails are clearly seen. The left side of the body is associated in Polynesian thinking with the common and unsacred, destructive influences, death, darkness, the female principle, west and night. These qualities are often part of both black magic and healing practices, and in rites of witchcraft, sickness or marriage the left hand, believed to be *noa* or void of *tapu*, is always used. It is not unreasonable to suggest

96 Sketch of tattooed or painted 'ao on a Rapa Nui woman who came out to meet HMS *Portland* on its first call to the island, 1852. *J. Linton Palmer. Courtesy Royal Geographical Society.*

that this carved hand was part of the accoutrements of a Rapa Nui priest or priestess as healer or sorcerer.

A very small but well-carved human foot in the collection of the Bernice P. Bishop Museum was also apparently worn as a pendant, although it is very likely a good deal later than the carving of the hand.[28] Another fragment of a woodcarving preserved and recycled as a pendant consists only of a human leg and vulva. This carving emphasis on discrete body parts reminds me of the metal and wood objects called *milago* which are common in Catholic, Spanish-speaking New World countries. They are all associated with healing and grew out of missionary era influence on traditional practices.

Petroglyphs of human hands and feet only are known but rare, and one anthropomorphic petroglyph has legs fully indicated. The hands and feet of barkcloth figures are very stumplike, sometimes with nails indicated. Two monolithic statues, a portable stone statue and a large, bas-relief petroglyph all have hands indicated only by raised, rounded forms lacking any details. All of the rest of the *moai* have highly detailed and beautifully carved hands and fingers. Only two statues in Rano Raraku quarry, one of which is Tukuturi, possess legs and feet. One basalt and one trachyte statue from two other sites have partial legs indicated.

Many of the crescent-shaped *rei miro* carvings, worn as pectorals by men and women of rank, are accented with human heads on each point of the upturned crescent, creating a somewhat whimsical (to the Western eye) 'man in the moon' quality. The upturned crescent is said to be a standardised East Polynesian convention meant to represent the human figure with upraised arms which, in turn, is thought to represent the gods who were believed to hold the sky safely in place above the Earth.[29] The addition of human heads to the crescent becomes, therefore, a redundant device, graphically restating anthropomorphic symbolism. The form of the *rei miro* is similar to but distinct from painted and carved crescent shapes superimposed upon *moai* and which appear to represent watercraft. The crescent shape is associated with the moon in most Polynesian art, and is interpreted as the moon by scholars working with *rongorongo*. The moon was universally regarded in Polynesia as feminine and the goddess Hina was associated with it. Time was reckoned by the nights of the moon. The *rei miro* is thus a complex statement of status and rank, religious belief and a time-linked reference.

The eye (*mata*) as a feature was nearly always detachable from the sculptural form and occasionally depicted as a detached object in rock art. In fact, it is the eyes, perhaps more than any other feature of the human form, which consistently receive special attention and treatment in all classes of Rapa Nui art. The eyes/nose or eyebrows/nose are often highly abstracted, and the conventionalisation of the human face was reduced to a single curved line motif on the dance paddles and dorsal surfaces of the *moai*. The treatment of the eyes on the *moai* is positively correlated with site type and is a chronological marker of stylistic development. The eyes/nose alone are often used to represent the creator god Makemake in rock art. In the cases of both the *moai* and the birdman petroglyphs, the eyes and the hands are emphasised by the sculptors. It is the attributes of the hands and feet alone which are selected to define the human presence in the bird/man symbols.

Male sexual characteristics are rarely realistically illustrated or graphically depicted in stonecarving. The genitals of the *moai* are modestly covered by a representation of the Rapa Nui loincloth called the *hami*. The presence of graphic male sexuality in the *kavakava* and other woodcarvings, as well as in one barkcloth figure, may well be a late stylistic innovation, encouraged through trade with Western seamen or whalers in the 1800s. The addition of loincloths to cover the genitals of some of these figures has been suggested to be a missionary influence, indicating the probable responsiveness of the Rapa Nui carvers to the demands of outsiders.[30] Importantly, there is clear evidence of sexual ambiguity or sexual integration in woodcarvings, where *moai* facial features and beards are sometimes present on figures which also have human vulvas indicated. The idea which gave genesis to this convention is echoed in the superimposition of female *komari* as petroglyphs on *moai* and in the features of Tukuturi, the kneeling statue of Rano Raraku.

In sharp contrast, female genitals are often graphically illustrated in rock art, stone carvings and some woodcarvings. In fact, the *komari* or vulva form is the most frequently occurring, discretely executed symbol in the documented rock art corpus (excluding cupules or small pits). Sheer numbers of examples alone attest to its importance. The *rapa* and *'ao*, as we have seen, may also be associated with female sexuality. The *komari* symbol, whether it appears in the outline of the foundations of *hare paenga*, incised onto portable stone artefacts, superimposed upon woodcarvings or *moai* or etched into the living rock, is one of the most meaningful symbols of Rapa Nui spiritual life.

Metaphor and Meaning

Rapa Nui art, like all Polynesian art, is metaphorical. Objects which were esoteric symbols were meant to function in a variety of ways, but the focus was nearly always on genealogy, history, mythology and the relationships between past, present and future which the ancestors, the chiefs and the gods represented. These symbols were manipulated in performative contexts which had metaphorical or allegorical significance. Visual metaphors are not easy to recognise or comprehend in their full complexity when the viewer is separate from the culture in which these symbols exist.[31] In many cases, such metaphors are not even fully understood outside of certain initiated or privileged levels or segments of the culture producing them. In fact, Polynesian languages (including Rapanui) had built-in linguistic devices which shaded, obscured or hid meaning. According to R. Langdon and D. Tryon this process is called metathesis by linguists, and the Rapanui word *ponoko* describes it.

The presence of a high degree of conventionalisation in any art object tells us that object very probably has a metaphorical function. In order to reach the level of conventionalisation, the object 'must contain elements which are aesthetically congenial to the large majority of the people supporting art production over continuing generations. The nature of what is aesthetically congenial is determined by the basic personality structure of the people'. This means that the conventionalisation by Rapa Nui artisans of symbols such as the *moai*, the *komari*, the birdman and human eyes/face associated with Makemake was acceptable to the larger community. Do the natures of these symbols as objects tell us anything about the personality or attitudes of the Rapa Nui people?

There is a good deal of literature on this topic. For example, scholars have suggested that the tendency to depict human arms close to the body, as we find in all examples of Rapa Nui art forms, reveals mild introversion. Depicting long human hands and noses, also a Rapa Nui art trait, is said to illustrate ambition and 'phallic aggressiveness'. Generally compressed design in the human figure is said to suggest introversion, obsessive and/or compulsive traits. By the same token, symmetry is thought to express rigidity and constraint. Most of these projections are drawn from the psychological literature, and few if any of those who apply these guidelines to 'tribal art' or 'primitive art' demonstrate any grasp at all of the complexity, variety or socioreligious function of art styles in tribal societies. In the same way, the rather facile attribution of art style to the 'collective unconscious' or 'shared memory' derives from Jungian theory.

It is clear, however, that visual forms in art have meanings which can be analysed and verbalised. Further, some of these meanings are cross-culturally valid.[32] It is important to remember that in order to relate these meanings to other aspects of society, culture and personality, the contexts in which the art styles occur must be fully documented, examined and understood. In the case of Rapa Nui, as we have seen, this is only possible to a limited extent. Objects divorced from their performative context on Rapa Nui, or from the well-documented performative contexts in larger Polynesia, are only incompletely known. Rapa Nui art style as represented by the *moai*, woodcarving and rock art has been studied by several scholars on the level of 'low-order meaning', which is based upon distinctions between forms that are then ordered into types and other sorts of categories. We can attempt to understand 'higher-order meaning' by refining appropriate categories and media, seeking similarities and then employing metaphor to understand these similarities. 'Highest-order meaning' is only expressed when the objects are in their performative context, being used in ritual. It is clear that 'highest-order meaning' is not directly available on Rapa Nui.[33]

In all artistic media on Rapa Nui, the materials chosen to make art objects were not randomly selected. They were utilised for the qualities of colour and texture that they brought to the work, but they also had inherent attributes of value and status. Exclusivity of material (as in the use of Rano Raraku tuff for the vast majority of monolithic sculpture), relationships of association (as in the use of Rano Kau basalt for petroglyphs and perhaps some statues associated with the birdman cult), and restricted availability (as in barkcloth or certain types of wood

images) were factors which lent significance to objects. Stonecarvings, woodcarvings, barkcloth objects and even body painting and tattooing were meant to function within a living context of motion and sound. They were intended to be perceived as part of an artistic and performative whole, and their value was in proportion to the ability of the maker, status of the user, history of the object, ceremonial use and perception and response of the community.

Rapa Nui art style is recognisably Polynesian in form and emphasis, with shadowy hints of very ancient iconographic connections which are apparent in the corpus of documented Lapita designs and Western and Eastern Polynesian objects. That style is also, however, unique to Rapa Nui, without direct comparative reference elsewhere in Polynesia. It has evolved within the context of Rapa Nui as an isolated place, produced, in large part, by trained artisans whose goal it was to control and faithfully replicate form and substance, establishing and maintaining continuity with the shared past through ceremonial objects. In this way, Rapa Nui art is as Polynesian as is the distinctive Maori woodcarving or the specialised Hawaiian featherwork. Rapa Nui artisans were keepers of traditions encoded within the objects and images they created, historians of shape, colour, texture and material. As artisans, they were the key to the preservation of belief, the transference of culture and the maintenance of the social structure.

9

Spirit in the Stone

The king has been born! Bare of all coverings is he who is lofty as a rainbow

LEONARDO PAKARATI Prayer for the newborn

The *moai* is an icon which exemplifies the funda-mental Polynesian concern with genealogy, gener-ation, status and respect. It grew out of the Rapa Nui past but was articulated in the public present of prehis-tory, a cultural motivator and modifier of group behaviour. Current archaeological projections are that approximately 1,000 statues were produced over some 800 to 1,300 years on the island as a whole, or about one for every seven to nine people at peak population estimates. The *moai* was standardised to a level which has been characterised as 'mass produced'. Is a 'mass produced' sculpture considered to be art? From a conceptual point of view, it may be. From a production point of view, it probably is not. From an historical point of view, the *moai* certainly employed the materials of art as well as the Rapa Nui society's visual language of communication. It was an organic part of the culture which produced it. The *moai* gave visual expression to a cultural set of ideas and ideals and then, for a time, perpetuated them. The form of the *moai* did not demon-strate or embody the changing reality of personal perspec-tive, as one expects of 'art'. Rather, it was a reassuringly familiar, straightforward and clean-lined image which was a predictable, stable and unvarying feature of the natural/supernatural landscape for many generations (plate 24). Visually, it was as a word repeated in a chant, a step re-peated in a dance. It was myth made visible in support of the traditional social status quo.[1]

Gods, Chiefs, Master Carvers and Icons

The Rapa Nui gave Captain Cook a few personal names for some monolithic statues (fig. 97). The German Captain Geiseler and then Katherine Routledge also recorded some names, mostly descriptive or derisive and probably of no great antiquity. The names of the two monolithic statues in the British Museum were probably coined on the spot by Rapa Nui people in response to questions from HMS *Topaze* crewmembers.[2] George Forster noted that the statues were 'erected in honour of their Kings', and thought the *moai* similar to Polynesian *tiki* (which, in fact,

97 Sketch of a *moai* standing on an *ahu* but facing incorrectly over the rear retaining wall, possibly at Vinapu. Cook's second voyage, 1774. *Courtesy Staatsbibliothek Preussischer Kulturbesitz.*

they are). He disagreed with the Dutch, who thought that the statues were 'idols'. Forster astutely understood that Polynesian carved figures were not, in the true sense, idols to be worshipped or which could confer benefits directly through such worship.[3] In the same way, Paymaster Thomson of USS *Mohican* was technically incorrect in his suggestion that the statues were 'effigies of distinguished individuals'.[4]

The Spanish recorded the word *moay* as applied to monolithic statues. Captain Cook said that the Rapa Nui would sometimes prefix 'the word Moi, and sometimes annex Areekee' to the names of statues.[5] The Rapanui word *moai* is equivalent to the Hawaiian *mo'i*, which is applied to individuals at the apex of the hereditary, sacred social pyramid.[6] Further, the main image on Hawaiian sacrificial altars was designated *mo'i*, as was the highest-ranking chief or king, and the variant *mohai* meant temple offerings. Moi was a legendary and powerful high-ranking priest who officiated at the most complex religious sites.

If we accept Cook's statement that the title *ariki* was sometimes attached to the names of individual *moai*, and if Métraux is correct in believing that the *ariki* title was never held by tribes other than the highest-ranked (western) Miru, it is logical to assume that the *moai* as an object or symbol was associated with the Miru.[7] This is especially indicated when we recall that Cook never left the western shore of the island and only saw statues in the vicinity of what is now Hanga Roa.[8] The word *moai* is thus functionally similar to the word *ariki*. Both designate an individual chief or head of a descent group and the class of which that chief is a member. If we presume that the *moai* is a symbol of the dominant Miru, why was it distributed throughout the island and why did it stand in greatest numbers upon *ahu* built by subordinate, non-Miru lineages?

The most obvious answer to that question is that the statue was acceptable to the entire island family as the symbol of a universally shared idea. Beyond that however, the answer lies in the relationship of the Miru ramage to the others on the island, in the relative status accorded kin groups through hereditary rank and in the definition of master carvers as a class. The statues were meant to demonstrate graphically lineage rank as a defining fact of life, just as the *ahu* defined lineage land ownership and therefore social status. Status and rank, *ahu* and *moai*, earth and sky are the interrelated and supportive components of a single Rapa Nui socioreligious idea. The combined function of the *ahu* and *moai* as a single semantic architecture concept is to define space and time on both horizontal and vertical planes. The non-static nature of the *ahu*/*moai* complex in terms of size and elaboration is a reflection of an evolving

social environment. The causes of that evolution are many and complex, but they are recognisably Polynesian. One of them was assuredly a competitive need to state and restate human relationships to land, gods and chiefs within a changing social context which materially rewarded the achievement of growth and success in these relationships.

Moai are not portrait sculpture. They do not represent the actual visages of specific chiefs or gods as individuals, even though some of the statues may have borne personal or descriptive names. Rapa Nui religious beliefs were not theomorphic. That is, they did not conceive of humankind as formed in the precise physical image of a deity, as do Christians, for example. Neither were their gods only in anthropomorphic form. Rather, their theophanic construct was one in which gods could manifest or reveal themselves in many ways and many forms, temporarily abiding in natural or manmade objects of many types. The sacred nature of those objects was dependent on their ability to accommodate spirits and gods, and the history of that accommodation was cumulative for each object.

The statues were commemorative images commissioned by the sons of lineage heads or by the lineage heads themselves, but the original creation of the symbol and its subsequent 'standardised' reproduction was in the hands of the appropriate, initiated experts. Those experts were master craftsmen who had risen through the necessary levels or grades of their respective professions, enabled by their training, dedication and talents to create *moai*, commune with their patron god and conduct or participate in the associated rituals. Experts may have been drawn from the lineage of the commissioning chief but could also have come from other lineages since, as we have seen, the carvers' 'guild' crosscut lineage lines.

The production of *moai* was assuredly consecrated labour, and the omens, offerings and ceremonial requirements of that labour can be assumed to have been extensive. Chants, incantations, sacrifices and prayers would all have been involved and even the lowliest apprentice or labourer was consecrated to the task at hand. Throughout every stage of work signs of success or failure would have been sought and heeded. Weather experts were consulted and rain was especially regarded as an omen. Purification with water, turmeric or fire and smoke protected the work from evil spirits and, on some islands, experts were required to live and sleep (but not necessarily eat) in the sacred place where the work was being conducted. Special *tapu* were placed on women and sexual conduct. If all went well and the work was not abandoned due to ritual or technical error or other evil signs, the final consecration and dedication of the *moai* on its *ahu* site was achieved.

These ceremonies, as elsewhere in East Polynesia, would have been in the hands of high-level temple priests, but craft experts and all who had participated in the sacred work were directly or indirectly involved.

Increased statue numbers, height and weight over time and correlative variations in the elaboration of *ahu* architecture are competitive, visible strategies employed by lineage heads and designed to appropriate, demonstrate and reinforce subordinate lineage-based claims to dominant ancestral, hereditary power. The success of those claims was dependent on three socioeconomic factors. Firstly, agricultural resource production, the economic base which allowed lineage heads to commission statues and to compensate all those involved for their efforts, needed either a crop surplus or exchange commitments (or a combination of both) sufficient to each carving/building task. The relationship between statue production and food production was intimate and profound. Secondly, the skills of master carvers and transport specialists had to evolve over time to accommodate and motivate the demand for larger and heavier statues. Thirdly, the charisma, leadership and *mana* of individual lineage heads had to inspire sufficient confidence in the success of each construction endeavour. The cumulative evidence suggests that those southeast coastal zone lineages most removed from the central, hereditary power source were, ironically, comparatively more productive and thus relatively successful in their drive to appropriate ancestry.

The creative reference for the *moai* was, I believe, the paramount chief (*ariki mau*), a human icon who held within his sacred body the traditions, histories and very spirits of the shared heritage of the entire island family. The *moai* and the *ariki mau* are analagous forms into which the gods entered and temporarily dwelt, producing an incredibly powerful, sacred, advantageous and dangerous transaction between humans and gods. The tranquillity, passivity and lack of dynamic tension in the sculpture suggests that the *moai* is a somewhat neutral vessel, a receptacle for several different spiritual entities drawn from varying grades or levels of power and which may be used by generations of chiefs from different lineages. The *moai* could have accommodated a range of gods and spirits called into the stone in response to the words and gestures of chiefs and priests who held different levels of power and who officiated on *ahu* of varying degrees of elaboration.

Who were those gods? We don't know for certain, and can only hypothesise on the basis of limited evidence placed within the larger Polynesian context. The genius of Rapa Nui artistry is such that the *moai* was an adaptable and thus somewhat enigmatic symbol. Anthropomorphic form, monolithic scale and interaction with architecture placed on lineage lands are important clues to meaning. Polynesian gods inhabited a universe in rank order, just as Polynesian people did. The great transcendent Creator or Supreme Being of the universe (called Tangaroa or Io) was followed by the superior gods and these, in turn, by clan gods/goddesses and a range of other entities.

We know, for example, that the Rapa Nui knew and preserved the names of several of the greatest Polynesian gods, most importantly Tangaroa and Rongo. Tangaroa was a deity of primal importance throughout Polynesia, variously the creator and master builder of the universe, lord of the seas. His brother was Tane, First Man and primal procreator, lord of the forests and trees and patron of carvers. Tangaroa is given as one of the divine ancestors of Hotu Matu'a and may have been incarnate in various sea creatures such as seals or porpoises.

Rongo is a fascinatingly complex god whose name in all of its dialectical variations in Polynesia has meanings associated with sound and especially with speaking and listening. Societies of singing, dancing and chanting are associated with Rongo, as are objects which make noise or music, such as the shell trumpet in Mangaia. There is good evidence that Rongo's original importance was as the god of rain, usually called Hiro. Rongo is given in Hotu Matu'a's genealogy after Tongaroa, and Hiro is associated with a natural stone called Pu O Hiro, originally located in the vicinity of Ahu Mahatua and which produces the sound of a shell trumpet when blown. In some islands, Hiro is the patron of thieves and may have been such on Rapa Nui.

It is not unlikely that one of the gods of the *moai* was the Rapa Nui incarnation of Rongo, the powerful and transformational god of agriculture, whose voice was heard in thunder. In New Zealand, Rongo was the god of the sweet potato. In Mangaia, Rongo was the source of all food but also became the god of war. Lono (Rongo), the focal point of elaborate agricultural rites in Hawaii, was apparently believed to have been reincarnated in Captain Cook. The murder of Cook and the preservation of his severed hands were ritually dictated acts related to the birth/rebirth of Lono and that god's ability to provide food. Ono (Rongo) in the Marquesas was the patron of ritual chanters. Rongo's sign was often the rainbow, and as patron of peace and agriculture he was on the left side of cosmic duality. Tu, god of warfare, warriors and sacrifice was associated with the powerful and often threatening right side (*mata'u*) of man. The interactive sphere in which Rongo and Tu jointly functioned, that of peace and war, plenty and scarcity, hunger and satiation, life and death is a balanced and complementary measure of the close sociopolitical relationship between these two gods and between food and power.

The *moai* which stood upon and dominated lineage lands was, I believe, intimately related to agricultural production and food redistribution. The function of the *ariki mau* was to assure the bountiful production of all crops, fish and chickens for the entire Rapa Nui Island family, and that of the *tangata manu* was to attract birds and the fish they followed to the island's rocky shore. The *moai* when filled with the power of Rongo assured fertility, growth and bounty. An aspect of Rongo's power in some island societies was healing. As the central figure in ancient and widespread variants of fertility concerns, Rongo and his various incarnations received 'first fruits' offerings in ceremonies such as the Makahiki festival in Hawaii. When the nature of the spirit which filled the *moai* was required by society to change from peace to war, from the defining essence of Rongo to that of Tu, the ceremonies on the *ahu* and the associated emblematic symbols would also naturally have changed as well.

The god of the *moai* also could have been the lineage god of the Miru. As we have seen, Miru is a god or goddess associated with sickness, witchcraft, death and the 'realm of the shades' in New Zealand, Cook Islands, Tahiti and possibly Hawaii.[9] On Mangaia this god is the patron of thieves. The ability of gods and goddesses of powerful lineages to be elevated to national or island-wide status was only occasionally enacted in Polynesia, but it did happen. More often, powerful lineages attached themselves genealogically to the traditional creator gods, as did Hotu Matu'a. In historic times local tribal patron gods, which were deified spirits of somewhat recent origin, superseded the ancient creator gods in Marquesas Islands, Cook Islands and New Zealand. In Mangaia, as we have seen, Mata[a]liki, the major god of the dominant lineage, became the great god of the entire island in exactly the same way that the chief of that lineage was the supreme chief of the entire society. The attribute similarities between Makemake and Mata[a]liki are highly suggestive of a cognative relationship.

It is probable that the original identification of various Polynesian superior gods was occupational, and that the gods of some occupations also became the patrons of entire clans or tribes. If such a situation existed on Rapa Nui, then the patron god of the Miru ramage was probably associated with carving as an occupation and thus might have been Tane himself, traditional patron of woodcarvers, or a variant. Rapa Nui traditions say that Tu'u Ko Iho was a legendary, expert canoe builder and culture hero. He

is associated with Hotu Matu'a, expert craftsmen, carving and the god Tu. Métraux believed that Makemake was the Rapa Nui version of Tane (as in New Zealand) and had absorbed, as well, the personality of Tiki (as in Mangareva and the Tuamotus).[10] In both the statue and the birdman cults, carving was the defining central feature of ceremonial function.

The Sky Propper

The erect *moai* is a product of a transcendental aesthetic which allows it to function in a multiplicity of ways, serving both secular and sacred purposes. In the sacred realm, it facilitates the transfiguration of gods and the apotheosis of humans. Its fundamental purpose is to make visible the invisible processes whereby the gods are called through ceremony and ritual from the supernatural world into the sacred *marae* space. In the secular realm, it is the chiefly 'post' or 'prop' around which all in the earthly world is ordered and on which all depends. It stands erect between the earth and the sky, separating or 'propping' one above the other while, at the same time, uniting and providing access for god and man to the natural and cosmic worlds. The *moai* thus mediates between sky and earth, people and chiefs, and chiefs and gods.

The higher-ranked of the two largest political units on Rapa Nui was the Ko Tu'u Aro Ko Te Mata Nui. This is literally translated as The Mast/Pillar/Post [standing] Before the Greater Tribes. Toko te rangi, or Sky Propper, is named by Métraux in his corrected Miru genealogy as the thirteenth king of Easter Island and as one of the lineages or subgroups of the Miru (fig. 98).[11] Although we have no record of the Sky Propper legend on Rapa Nui, other Polynesian legends of the Sky Propper are widely known,

98 Genealogy of the Toko-te-rangi lineage of the Miru *mata*. *After Métraux 1940. Drafting by Curtiss H. Johnson.*

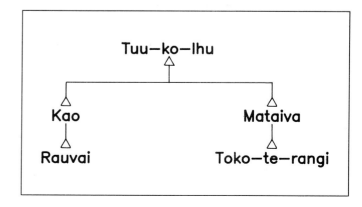

and they are formative elements in the basic cosmogenic theory of Polynesian belief. Sky (*rangi*) and Earth (*papa*) lay in primal embrace, and in the cramped, dark space between them procreated and gave birth to gods such as Tane, Rongo and Tu. Just as children fought sleep in the stifling darkness of a *hare paenga*, the gods grew restless between their parents and longed for light and air. The herculean achievement of forcing Sky to separate from Earth was variously performed by Tane in New Zealand and the Society Islands, by Tonofiti in the Marquesas and by Ru (Tu) in Cook Islands. After the sky was raised high above the earth, props or poles were erected between them and light entered, dispelling the darkness and bringing renewed life. One detail which is iconographically of interest is whether the god responsible for separating Earth and Sky did so by raising Sky with his upraised arms and hands, as in Tahiti and elsewhere, or with his feet as in New Zealand.

The actual props, pillars or posts which separated the sky and earth are called *toko* in New Zealand, *to'o* in the Marquesas Islands and *pou* in Tahiti. In Rapanui *tuu* and *pou* are known, with *pou* meaning column, pillar or post of either stone or wood. Sometimes the word is applied to a natural rock formation with postlike qualities which serves as an orientation point. The star Sirius is called Te Pou in Rapanui and functions in the same way. One monolithic basalt statue is called Pou Hakanononga, a somewhat obscure and probably late name thought to mean that the statue served to mark an offshore tuna fishing site. The Rapanui word *tokotoko* means pole or staff. Sacred ceremonial staves, such as the *ua* on Rapa Nui, were called *toko* in Polynesia. Based upon the fact that *toko* in New Zealand also means 'rays of light', it has been suggested that the original props which separated and held apart Sky and Earth were conceived of as shafts of dawn sunlight.[12] In most Polynesian languages the human and animate classifier is *toko-*, suggesting a congruence of semantic and symbolic meaning between anthropomorphic form and pole or post.[13] Tane as First Man and the embodiment of sunlight thus becomes, in the form of a carved human male figure, the probable inspiration for the *moai* as sacred prop between Sky and Earth.

The *moai* as Sky Propper would have elevated Sky and held it separate from Earth, balancing it only upon his sacred head. This action allowed light to enter the world and made the land fertile. Increasing the height of the statues, as the Rapa Nui clearly did over time, would symbolically increase the space between Sky and Earth, ensuring increased fertility and the greater production of food. The proliferating image, consciously or unconsciously, must have visually (and reassuringly) filled the dangerously empty horizon between sea and land, just as the trees they were so inexorably felling once had. Those trees, source of food and construction materials, were the abode of spirits sometimes thought to be incarnate in birds. Trees, masts, sacred posts and Tane are symbolically one and the same in many Polynesian societies. Thoughtlessly eliminating trees from the island, in ways which were not solely dictated by uncontrollable competitive or vengeful destruction, would mean that the trees were of small or no value in the Rapa Nui philosophical construct (a highly unlikely possibility).

Following Métraux's reasoning Makemake as the transformed Tane also embodied the personality of Tiki. There was thus a redoubled emphasis on maleness, on fertility and procreative genesis. The Rapa Nui belief system as currently understood emphasised the generative, procreative attributes of Tiki within the physical (male) context of Tane. The ethnographies clearly state that Makemake was the Creator God, the Supreme Being. Is Makemake then cognate with either Io or Tangaroa? Because of the confusion and disorientation of Rapa Nui culture during the period in which the ethnographies were collected, borrowing or other influence from Europeans and Polynesians alike and the pervasive impact of missionary thinking on religious data this question is still open.

The central spiritual focus of the statue cult was to catch or entrap the dangerous and powerful spirits of deceased individuals. In this process they sought to control them and to facilitate their transformation. Another focus, and one which is evident in the birdman cult as well, was to attract the gods and spirits back to the earthly realm. This was accomplished by producing a proper vessel within which these entities might interact favourably with humans and with nature. Vessels for spiritual interaction were of many types and their uses and the levels of power they could accommodate were correspondingly varied. Wood carvings, portable stone carvings, trees, stones and other natural objects, priests, healers and sorcerers were all such vessels. Most prominent in the hierarchy of sacred vessels were the *ariki mau* and the *moai*, the incarnate *tangata manu* and the carved petroglyphic images of the birdman. On an island denuded or nearly denuded of trees, providing a suitable abode for the gods and spirits became a vital, aesthetically creative and intensely competitive, seductive Rapa Nui quest.

The Iconography of Power: The Chiefly Body

The way in which the human body is depicted in three-dimensional sculpture varies significantly in the many and varied cultures of the world. The idealisation of the human/god figure in the Greco-Roman aesthetic tradition contrasts sharply with the static human form in many pre-Columbian New World cultures. The sculpted human body in sub-Saharan Africa, where the majority of images are not intended to represent real people (even though they are named and understood to be 'portraits' of real people), is very different from the compact, relatively standardised passivity depicted in Egyptian sculpture. The emphases of posture, scale, form and iconography expressed by artisans in all of these cultures grow out of social conventions and the dictates of ideological beliefs peculiar to each traditional society.

In an effort to find an artistic source for the Rapa Nui *moai*, some scholars (including especially Thor Heyerdahl) have compared them to the monumental sculpture of Tiwanaku in Bolivia. Superficially, this seems reasonable. These superb human figures, carved in basalt and often finished to a high, polished sheen, are authoritative, severely geometric abstractions, usually carved as cylinders with flat backs. Shallow, incised or low bas-relief surface carving often ornaments them, and the huge round eyes and rounded navel are prominent features. They are often adorned with depictions of ceremonial belts or sashes, and

their standing, full frontal position, arms held tightly at their sides, facilitates their incorporation into architecture. They stand in the architectonic context of Tiwanaku's mythic, urban environment on the Island of the Sun in Lake Titicaca.

From about 300 BC until about AD 1100, this highly ordered and densely populated Andean centre produced a sculptural style which had, in part, evolved out of the earlier aesthetic traditions of coastal and Amazonian cultures. An important synthesis of these styles took place within Chavin, which preceded Tiwanaku, flourishing from 900 to 200 BC. The monumental sculptures of Tiwanaku are part of a series of vast public works produced by a highly stratified (three classes) society of farmers, herders and fishermen. Their remarkable sculpture was but one aesthetic link in a complex and intense symbolic system growing out of and supporting a remarkable history of political achievement.

99 *Moai* re-erected on Ahu Naunau, Anakena, with unique spiral designs on the buttocks. *Drawing by Cristián Arévalo Pakarati.*

There is no question that the generalised diffusion of Andean art styles was made possible by long-distance trade between the Pacific coast and the highlands, and the presence of the sweet potato in Polynesia is apparent and real evidence of prehistoric contact between the continent and the Pacific islands. However, even though the extent of trade and travel along the South American coast and into the near shore Pacific is not yet fully delineated, and though the sculptural tradition of Tiwanaku is impressive and somewhat reminiscent of some Marquesan monolithic wood sculpture, there is a near zero likelihood that the Rapa Nui sculptural form was imported intact or influenced directly from Tiwanaku. Portable artefacts from South American cultures (including, especially, textiles and pottery) are not known, to date, from Polynesian archaeological contexts, and once proposed linguistic links have been examined and largely rejected. In short, a vaguely similar monumental sculptural style from a completely different and distant cultural context cannot support, without corroborative evidence, the notion of South American presence on prehistoric Rapa Nui.

How did Rapa Nui artisans depict the human body in monolithic sculpture? The shapes of Rapa Nui *moai* vary, and these shapes define statue type categories. The majority have heads and torsos which are each vertically rectangular cylinders, flattened on the back, and the proportionate relationship of the head to the torso is one third, although occasionally it approaches one half. This emphasis is in keeping with the Polynesian belief in the sanctity of the chiefly head, as is the Rapa Nui penchant for preserving and occasionally superimposing sacred designs on the skulls of Miru chiefs. Statues with rectangular head shapes are also known to have torsos in trapezial or, more often, inverted trapezial forms. Examples of these statues are usually large and heavy, and some on Ahu Tongariki are typical. Vertically rectangular torsos occasionally have square heads or rectangular faces and heads which are rounded at the back. The rectangular flattened cylinder is, very clearly, the numerically preferred *ahu moai* shape.

The unvarying pose of all *ahu moai* is an erect, frontal posture, torso truncated at the waist with arms held tightly at the sides and hands meeting on the lower abdomen, fingers directed at a central design motif called the *hami* (fig. 99). This posture is common in Cook, Austral and Society Islands art, and in the Tuamotus is considered a burial posture. Tukuturi has his hands resting on his thighs. As representative of the human body form the *ahu moai* is recognisably realistic, although certain features of proportion and posture are exaggerated or unnaturally emphasised. These stylistic features are components of the Rapa Nui aesthetic and visible markers of ideological emphasis.

The Face, Head and Neck

The facial features of the *moai* are extraordinarily well sculpted, balanced in harmonious spatial relationships and framed on the sides by curved facial planes, the emphasised line of the jaw and the elongated, elaborated ears. On a few statues, a beard is indicated. The ears universally begin 10 cm down from the top of the head, and the distinctive notch which distinguishes the body of the ear from the elongated lobe is always placed exactly across from the

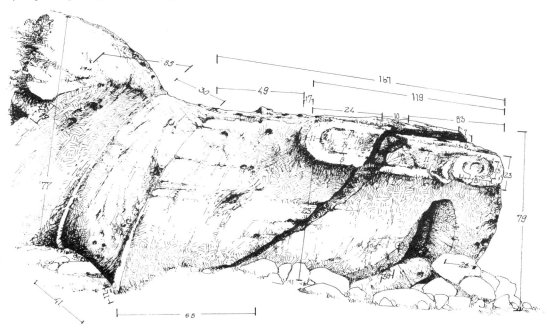

100 Fallen and broken *moai* on Ahu Vaihu with detail of ear design and dimensions. *Drawing by Cristián Arévalo Pakarati.*

corner of the eye (fig. 100). There is a slight flaring out of the earlobes from the face at the bottom, and their configuration is usually vertically rectangular, although some are more round or oval. Statues at Tongariki and elsewhere have circular indentations in the middle of the bottom of the lobe, some of which may have had discs of obsidian or other materials inserted. A few statue heads of Rano Raraku tuff, trachyte and red scoriaceous material are known which have realistic, rounded ear shapes. The trachyte head is from Poike and the others are from such sites as Anakena and Tongariki, where they appear to have been related to construction phases which are earlier than those which supported *moai* with elongated ear lobes.

The head is connected to the body by a neck which is delineated at the front but never the back. The neck is defined by a ridge which curves in a semi-circle from each shoulder at the front, creating a crescent or *rei miro* shape. On Hoa Hakananai'a and a few other basalt and Rano Raraku tuff statues the clavicle is indicated at the front. The statue heads are all set forward slightly on the shoulders. Tukuturi, the famous kneeling statue of Rano Raraku, and Moai Hava have their faces turned slightly upwards. Métraux quotes a Rapa Nui legend in which carvers from Hotu Iti (eastern sector) journeyed to the western sector to seek the advice of a master carver. They were perplexed about how to resolve the difficult problem of carving the statue neck. He advised them to seek the answer by viewing their own bodies. They did so, and discovered that the model for the statue neck was the penis (*ure*). This legend supports to some extent the phallic nature of the statues, but it also associates design experts or master carvers with the higher-ranked western sector of the island.

The dominant facial features are the eyes and nose, just as they are in petroglyphs, dance paddles and portable carvings. The nose in profile is most often straight or concave, broad at the nares with expertly carved nostrils elaborated as bas-relief fishhook shapes. The profiles of the distinctive *kavakava* carvings, in contrast, feature strongly dominant, convex noses. Both *moai* and *kavakava* traits are markedly exaggerated versions of actual Rapa Nui facial features currently visible in the population and detectable in the osteological sample. There is an implied phallic symbolism of the nose which is only evident on statues in certain positions in Rano Raraku quarries, and is not perceivable either from the front or in profile when the statues are erect upon *ahu*.[14] The forehead is narrow, convex and well-defined. The mouth is narrow with compressed but clearly separated, slightly upraised lips. On one basalt statue the mouth is more rounded, with lips slightly parted. Another has a slightly upturned lip line. There is a

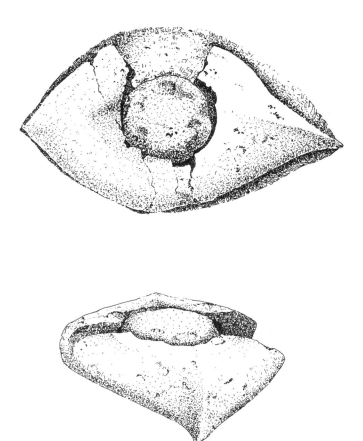

101 Coral and red scoria *moai* eye components were retrieved during the restoration of Ahu Naunau directed by Sergio Rapu H. *Drawing by Cristián Arévalo Pakarati with permission, Museo Antropológico R.P. Sebastián Englert.*

102 Detail of flaked obsidian disk possibly used as either eye or ear inserts in wood or stone monolithic carving. *Drawing by Cristián Arévalo Pakarati with permission, Museo Antropológico R.P. Sebastián Englert.*

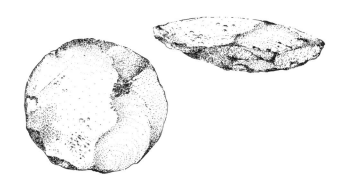

disproportionately small distance between the mouth and the nose on all *ahu moai*. This characteristic, combined with a very slight widening of the curved line which defines the jaw, causes the jawline to be emphasised.

The eye sockets of the *ahu moai* are always carved in an oval shape. Their outer edges are always flush with the side plane of the face and flat. The back of the socket is not plane and the bottom of the socket has a slight ridge, allowing for a coral and red scoria insert to lie comfortably within at a very slight upward angle (figs 101, 102, plate 25).[15] The flat outside 'corner' of the eye socket accommodates very well the elongated, teardrop shape of the eye insert, giving an emphasised size to the eyes. Round eye sockets are most often present on red scoria statues, and these may have been fitted with flaked black obsidian discs. Eye sockets in the precise form of the *ahu moai* are also on red scoria statues, however, and it is probable that Hoa Hakananai'a and one other statue of basalt may also have had eye inserts. Tukuturi has bas-relief eyes with indented pupils in the exact form of most petroglyphs. A natural rock feature incorporating a water source called Vai A Heva on Poike was enhanced to produce a megalithic head/face sculpture. It also has bas-relief eyeballs with indented pupils, as does a free-standing boulder carving (Monument 1) at Orongo associated with the creator god Makemake (figs 103, 104).[16]

The treatment of the facial features is a significant indicator of chronological placement of sculpture. In contrast to the sharply delineated, elongated and flattened facial planes of the *ahu moai*, those stone carvings which have bas-relief eyeballs with indented pupils set in more rounded, naturalistic faces with pronounced cheeks, whether free-standing sculpture or petroglyphs, relate in style to the wood staves called *ua* and to *kavakava*. These attribute innovations are a result of limited aesthetic experimentation, discontinuous variation and/or incomplete synthesis which took place in monolithic carving but was articulated to a much greater degree in other media, such as rock art and woodcarving. In short, Tukuturi and a few other statues, *pukao* recarved as faces and the rock sculpture at Vai A Heva are probably contemporaneous with the rise of the birdman cult and the Makemake faces of Orongo (AD 1400–1500 or later).

Although *moai* on *ahu* had eye sockets carved to accept eye inserts and hold them safely, if temporarily, in place, no European artist or observer ever saw them. Only two sites, Anakena and Vinapu, have yielded fragments of *moai* eyes, although it is possible that they lie undiscovered on other unexcavated sites. It is highly likely that these eye inserts were only placed in the statues during specific

103 Monument 1, Complex A, Orongo is carved in the style of some petroglyphs as well as woodcarvings. The presence or absence of indented pupils in petroglyph eyes may have a meaning similar to the presence or absence of eye inserts in *moai*. When excavated in 1955 this carving did not have indented pupils (E.N. Ferdon, Jr., pers. comm. 1994). *Drawing by Cristián Arévalo Pakarati.*

104 Small trachyte head called Puoko Tea Tea, carved in the style of Monument 1 (see Fig. 103), has a brow ridge typical of many woodcarvings and lacks indented pupils. *Drawing by Cristián Arévalo Pakarati with permission, Museo Antropológico R.P. Sebastián Englert.*

ceremonies, and that those ceremonies were only held on certain important sites. Even though statues on *ahu* had carved eye sockets, some may have vainly awaited eye inserts if the appropriate ceremonies were never held. Statues in Rano Raraku and along the transport roads may have lacked carved sockets not because they were incomplete but because the statues were not on lineage lands or not meant to function in ceremonies on lineage lands which required eye inserts. The placement of the eyes in the *moai* may have been for the purpose of making visible to the amassed multitudes the spiritual 'awakening' of the gods, as in *marae* ritual in the Tuamotus.[17]

The gaze of the Polynesian chief was fearful. It projected dangerous *mana* from his sacred head and especially his eyes, the 'symbolic site of subjection'.[18] The heat of the sun and the light of the stars combined to form the brilliant gaze of chiefly power (plate 26). Such a gaze was more than mere commoners could bear, a luminous shaft which caused them to fall prostrate in the company of the most exalted chief. The eyes of sacrificial victims and breakers of *tapu* were put out in many island societies, and in the Marquesas Islands, the Tuamotus and Hawaiian Islands priests would often ingest the eyes of high-status victims, thus ingesting their *mana*. The eyes of the statues looked out upon the lands and homes of the people, but could the people look upon the statues when the eyes were in place? Certainly, the relationship between godly power, the statues and the land was made most profoundly manifest when the statues' eyes were open. In the Tuamotus, a chief laid his claim to the land by saying 'I turn my back in one direction, I turn my back in the opposite direction, all that I see belongs to me'.[19]

The Torso, Hands and Backs

The front of the torso is marked by bas-relief nipples and navel (*pito*), each of which averages 10 cm in perfect diameter. The nipples are the termination of curved (or occasionally more chevron-shaped) lines which extend from the front of each arm just below the shoulder. These are not female breasts, although one red scoria figure at Vinapu, one statue in the quarry and one bas-relief basalt carving have breasts which are raised and rounded, appearing more feminine (plate 27). There is a statistical indication that the right nipple is placed slightly higher than the left, although this is only evident to the naked eye when the erect statues are viewed from certain perspectives. Rapa Nui ethnographies emphasise typically Polynesian practices associated with cutting the navel cords of newborns and then burying them on lineage land. The navel cord is a graphic representation of the ancestral connection which

ties the past to the present, the gods with humans, humans to the land. The emphasis on the balanced relationship of nipples to navel is a recognition of their natural relationship in birth and sustenance and, by extension, acknowledges the chief's role in sustaining life by virtue of his control of nature.

The hands of the statues are extraordinarily well carved in bas-relief, enlarged and out of proportion. They lie flat upon the lower stomach. A raised, round joint marker of exactly the same size as the nipples and navel is placed on each wrist, and the bend in the arm at the elbow is indicated, giving the arms a realistic appearance. The thumbs are raised in graceful curves, pointing to and visually emphasising the navel. The disproportionately long fingers are separated by single or double incised lines and the nails are not indicated. This is in contrast to the carved wooden hand collected by Cook's party. While the carving emphasis on the hands of the *moai* and the woodcarving indicate the general iconographic significance of this part of the human body in Rapa Nui thinking, the esoteric meaning of the woodcarving may not necessarily be the same as that represented in the *moai*.

The *moai* fingertips do not meet directly, but lie next to

105 Detail of incised hands and *hami* on a statue in Rano Raraku. *Photograph by Lorenzo Dominguez, 1960. Courtesy of Sra. Clara Dominguez.*

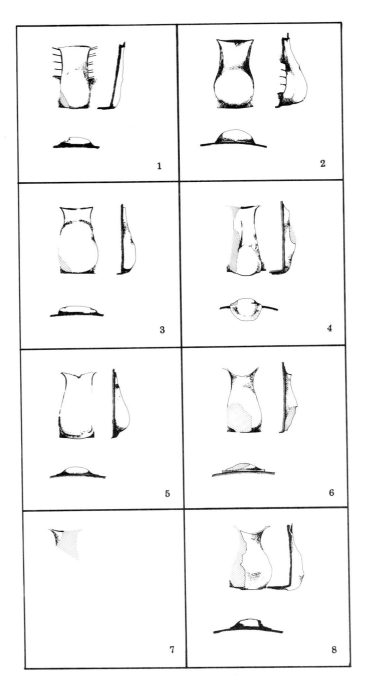

106 Variation of *hami* sizes and shapes found on statues documented at Ahu Tongariki. *Drawing by Cristián Arévalo Pakarati.*

107 A coconut leaf *malo* from Pukapuka in the Cook Islands, said to be everyday garb. A similar garment may have inspired the *hami* on *moai. Courtesy Bernice P. Bishop Museum.*

the centrally placed *hami*, a Rapanui version of the Polynesian *maro* (*taura* in Rapanui) (fig. 105). This garment, made of fabric or vegetable fibre, was occasionally elaborated with feathers or turtle shell during historic times. Red-stained belts called *taura renga* were worn by women, and the basalt statue Hoa Hakananai'a was said to be adorned

with one during rituals. The *hami/taura* was worn to conceal the genitals. Occasionally, *moai* genitals are indicated even though the garment is present. There are twelve variations of *hami* shape, and the way they are depicted on the *moai* most resembles a Cook Islands garment of coconut leaf (figs 106, 107). The hands are unrealistic in that they are overlarge and the lower edge of the wrist is decidedly curved. This latter convention gives the hands, especially on the larger statues, the distinctive sweep of birds' wings. The birdman petroglyphs have human hands and, conversely, the *moai* have winglike hands. The hands/*hami* design motif is an allusion to the lifegiving *mana* of the chief, concentrated in his hands and loins (recall the preservation of Cook/Lono's hands).

A few *moai* (between fifty and seventy-five) were elaborated with bas-relief designs on their otherwise flat backs (fig. 108). These designs, called 'ring and girdle' by Routledge, may represent either a garment, a tattoo or the raised welts produced in branding, a variation of tattoo. In my opinion, the purpose of the designs is either to signal

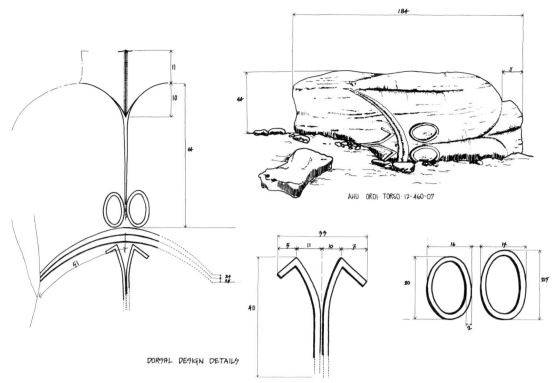

AHU OROI · TORSO · 12-460-07

DORSAL DESIGN DETAILS

108 Detail of dorsal design found on one broken statue at Ahu Oroi (12–460). *Drawing by Raúl Paoa Ika.*

109 BELOW Eight variations of dorsal designs on monolithic *moai*. *Drafting by Johannes Van Tilburg.*

membership of the lineage chief in a specialist class or to mark the site as one on which a particular type of ceremony was held or at which a particular grade of priest officiated.

On one site only, that of Ahu Naunau at Anakena, the *moai* also have beautifully executed bas-relief fishhook designs on their buttocks. These fishhook designs are the same as those used to indicate the nostrils, and fishhook petroglyphs are frequently present in the western sector of the island. Stone fishhooks (*mangai ma'ea* or *mangai kahi*) may have been ceremonial, although Métraux thought them to have been somewhat widely available and functional, used with large fish in general and tuna in particular. Unlike *mata'a*, stone fishhooks are laboriously and beautifully fashioned. Elsewhere in Polynesia fishhook imagery is associated with sorcery, black magic and soul catching. It is possible that such meanings also exist for the symbol as carved in stone on Rapa Nui.

There are eight documented variations of *moai* dorsal designs, and they probably have multiple individual, conjoined and interacting meanings (fig. 109). The statue's back is first divided into two design realms by one, two or three bas-relief curved lines which arch across the small of the back and end at the wrists. These lines, if we consider

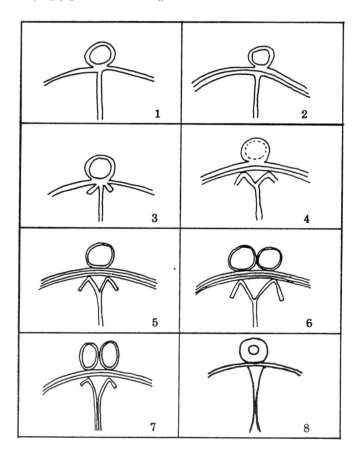

110 *Moai* (survey no. 89) on the exterior slopes of Rano Raraku with bas-relief Y-shape carved on the chin. *Photo by Lorenzo Dominguez, 1960. Courtesy Sra. Clara Dominguez.*

them related to the *hami*, could represent the sacred loincloth of chiefly authority. They might also be, as some Rapa Nui informants have thought, a representation of the rainbow as both a natural and a symbolic phenomenon.[20] The lines are surmounted at the midpoint by one or two bas-relief circles. Below the curved lines we find either a Y-shaped or more elaborated and possibly later M-shaped form. Both the Y-shaped and M-shaped motifs appear in Lapita pottery designs. The Y-shaped design is a component of the *komari* motif and is, perhaps more importantly for this discussion, carved in bas-relief on the chins of some *moai* (fig. 110).

These dorsal designs are all part of the original conceptualisation of each individual *moai* on which they are found. They can be seen on statues in the quarry, along the transport roads and on *ahu*. The designs are always superimposed upon the incised line of the spine/shoulders. That line, while it marks the sacred spine of chiefly genealogy, also represents the anthropomorphic face reduced to highly schematic outline, just as it does on the wood dancing paddles (*'ao*), pendants (*tahonga*), some rock art designs and other objects.

A reasonable interpretation of the concentric circles is that they represent an 'eye' or 'eyes', similar to those depicted on birdman petroglyphs. In Marquesas Islands stone and wood sculpture anthropomorphic eyes are enlarged and either oval or perfectly round, carved in bas-relief and nearly precisely similar to the way in which the circles on the backs of the *moai* are carved. The M-shaped design then becomes the 'body and wings' of a frigatebird. The placement of the frigatebird motif allows it to transcend and symbolically unite both upper and lower design realms. There is no question that similar schematic designs represent frigatebirds in other parts of Oceania, such as in Solomon Islands rock art and Australs Islands wood-carvings. In Samoan tattoo the Y-shaped motif' (*ngongo*), which can be either in an upright or lateral position, is said to represent a tern.[21]

What is the significance of the Y-motif? What in Polynesian material culture may have inspired it? 'Fork shaped' implements, sticks and posts were widely utilised in Oceania for a variety of construction, fishing and other tasks.[22] Y-shaped posts framed houses and were the supports for funeral biers on many islands, including Rapa

111 Forked stick images called *eketea* from Mangareva are associated with death and fertility (Waite 1993). The upper image (NN) is in the Mission Museum, Brain-le-Comte, Belgium and the lower (AU2167) in The Vatican, Rome. *After Buck 1938, 451, figs. 59–60.*

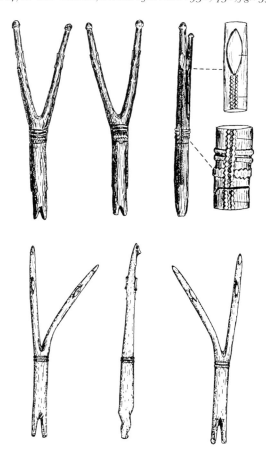

Nui. They rode as ornamental crests on the mastheads and pilasters of Fijian canoes. As we have seen, the Y-shaped form was the emblem both of a god and of a high-ranking carpenters' guild on Samoa. It is quite possible that the Rapa Nui Y-shape design may have a similar significance.

For the best-documented esoteric meaning of the Y-shape we must look to Mangareva, where 'forked stick' wands and 'stick man' effigies called *eketea* were used in mortuary, fertility and initiation rituals conducted by priests (*taura*) at which *rogorogo* and wood craftsmen participated (fig. 111).[23] These interesting objects were highly abstract depictions of the human form which had legs or legs and feet indicated and carved decorative bands around the midpoint. One example has oval 'eyes' carved on each of the two parallel parts forming the upright forks. In Mangaia, the forms of the 'forked sticks' erected on *marae* during the initiation of the Temporal Lord are not known. It is very clear however, that erecting these 'forked sticks' represented the visible commitment of the individual district chiefs to act as *toko* (prop or support) to the Temporal Lord as he undertook his duties.

The forms of the Mangarevan *eketea* and the Mangaian ethnography suggest that the connotation of 'forked stick' figures in each place combined to be both political and religious. The relationship was of dominant to subordinate political power but may also have been, in a broader sense, the intimate genealogical association between chiefs and the god or gods who raised and held Sky above Earth. If we further broaden the 'forked stick' symbolism to incorporate its use by the Samoan carpenters' guilds, we may speculate that the Rapa Nui Y-shaped design carved on some *moai* served visually to restate the meaning of the *moai* as Sky Propper, the chief as sociopolitical 'prop' and the intimate relationship of an artisans' guild with both. Forked or plain sticks, sometimes with streamers attached, were used or carried by Rapa Nui priests (fig. 112 detail).

If the concentric circles on the backs of the statues are considered only in relation to the multiple strands of the rainbow/*maro*, the resulting motif may represent something similar to what is called in Pukapuka a 'soul catcher', part of the spiritual paraphernalia of priests (fig. 113). Enmeshing, enfolding or otherwise entangling an individual's soul was part of black magic. In Tahiti and New Zealand, string figures (called *kaikai* on Rapa Nui) were employed in the black arts. Priests involved with sickness/healing or with mortuary ritual were feared as threats to community wellbeing but also, on the more positive side, could perform the useful function of catching and holding an escaped soul and returning it to the body. The cords which wrap the *moai* body thus trap and hold the fearsome spirit in the stone.

112 ABOVE Idealised engraving of a drawing by Duché de Vancy illustrates several small vignettes of activity, including the artist's self-portrait, Rapa Nui women with trade goods and the first depiction of actually measuring a statue. *Photo of a lithograph in private collection, J. Van Tilburg.*

RIGHT Detail of a Rapa Nui man holding a pronged stick. Assuming it was not casually collected as some sort of a measuring stick, this may be a 'forked stick' of authority.

Hoa Hakananai'a, the basalt statue from Orongo, presents unique and significant evidence of Rapa Nui social change encoded within its form and design (fig. 114). It documents the retention of 'classic' sculptural form beyond the Ahu Moai Phase II of Rapa Nui prehistory while, at the same time, illustrating the choice of fine, black basalt over Rano Raraku tuff as a sculptural material. In the process, it dramatises a shift in ideological focus from lineage sites to Orongo.

The petroglyphic tableau on its back depicts the *manupiri* position of two *tangata manu*, suggesting a cooperative alliance of two factions or the succession of power within one faction over time. The heraldic positioning of the Sooty Tern symbol, mouth opened in sound, may represent the ritualistic predictions of *ivi atua* or oratorial pronouncements of *tangata rongorongo* during the course of birdman ceremonies. The carved *'ao* and perhaps a *rapa* represent the power of the ascendent clan. The link between the

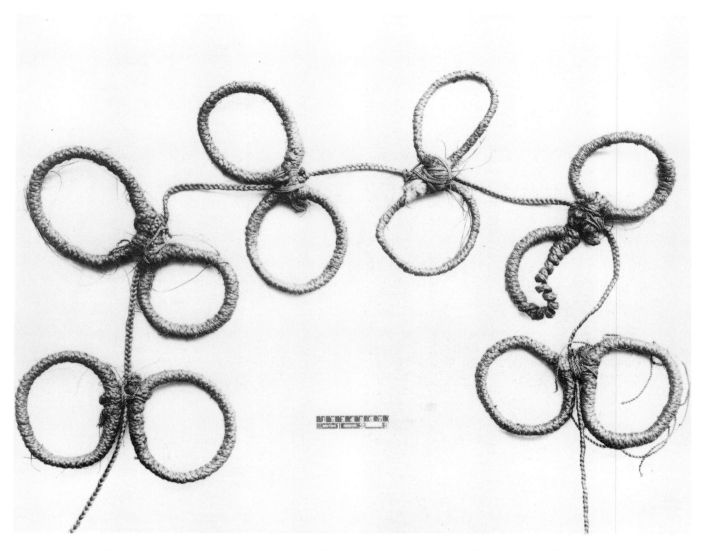

113 Soul catcher from Pukapula, Cook Islands, collected by Rev. Ellis. A similar idea or object may have inspired the 'ring and girdle' design on the *moai*. *Courtesy of the Bernice P. Bishop Museum.*

komari design and Orongo is as clear as is the link between the birdman design and Orongo, and as it is used here may indicate a comment on the presence of two female deities thought to participate in birdman rites. The broadly interpretive meaning of the *komari* is, without doubt, fertility and fecundity but may also include *tapu* removal or imposition, initiation and healing. There is the possibility that these carvings constitute an informational code in the tradition of *rongorongo*.

The Pukao

Pukao are red scoria cylinders quarried at Puna Pau and transported to *ahu* where they were carved to their final forms and placed upon the heads of between fifty and seventy-five *moai*. There is a positive correlation between the presence of dorsal designs and *pukao* on statues and red scoria fascia on *ahu*. Further, the petroglyphs superimposed upon both *pukao* and fascia are all similar. I interpret this to mean that dorsal designs, *pukao* and red scoria fascia are components of a single motivation meant to distinguish the *moai* and *ahu* on which they appear from the rest of the religious sites. They would, therefore, distinguish the lineages which owned those sites from all others, placing them in a special relationship to the *ariki mau*. The rituals conducted on *ahu* where these features are present would have differed from the rituals conducted on *ahu* where they are lacking. The meaning or importance of *pukao* extended into protohistoric or possibly historic times.

In the Marquesas Islands a great stone was sometimes placed upon the head of a carved image to signify mourning. In many parts of Oceania round and/or cylindrical shapes are often indicated on the heads of images, and the

Labels on the drawing (right):
komari / y symbols
rapa or 'ao
manutara
'ao
tangata manu
komari
'ao or rapa
tangata manu
dorsal design variation 5

114 LEFT Dorsal view of basalt statue called Hoa Hakananai'a, collected by HMS *Topaze*, 1868. *Courtesy of the Museum of Mankind, British Museum.*

RIGHT Detail of petroglyphs superimposed on the dorsal side of Hoa Hakananai'a. *Drawing by Ben Burt, Museum of Mankind, British Museum.*

exact meaning of these shapes varies greatly. What do the *pukao* represent? Various scholars have suggested that they represent hats or feathered crowns.[24] The Rapanui word *hau* can mean hat or cap. A magnificent headdress of red chicken feathers in the Pitt Rivers Museum, Oxford was collected on Cook's voyage and might reasonably be considered the material culture object which the stone cylinders are meant to depict. The *pukao* also may represent hair dressed in a topknot (*mono*), possibly braided and wrapped around the head and then coloured red with earths or pigment. In Western Polynesia a warrior is told to 'tie up your hair and gird on your *malo*' before taking part in battle.[25]

All of the *pukao* were placed upon the heads of the statues in such a way as to project out over the eyes, and are best suited for the *ahu* statues rather than those standing on the slopes of Rano Raraku. Some *pukao* which are intact possess protruding knobs on their top surfaces and possibly represent lengths of cloth wrapped turban-style around the head and knotted snugly in the middle at the top. Such a turban would protect the head from natural and supernatural harm and, at the same time, shade the eyes and face. The *pukao* forms at Anakena are unusual.

Since the Rapanui word *pukao* cannot be shown to mean exclusively either hat, crown, headband or topknot, I am drawn to the hypothesis that the *pukao* were conceptualised as representions of barkcloth turbans. On Rapa Nui turbans may have been replaced by dressed, red-painted hair. The reason for such replacement may have been the scarcity and value of the fabric. In 1827 Rapa Nui of apparently high status were observed wearing a 'Species of head dress like a Turban'.[26] Barkcloth turbans are documented from Fiji (where they are associated with navigators) and several parts of Polynesia. In Mangareva they were wrapped around the heads of high-ranking men during feasts of initiation and warfare. A Mangarevan chant describes a 'turban of wondrous style' worn by women when they met 'Tiki-the-father' 'through whom women lose their virginity and by whom all was created'. In Tahiti red and yellow turbans and on Mangaia red turbans were worn by men during funeral rites.

Thus we see that elsewhere in Polynesia turbans are known to indicate status as well as to have been worn during rituals of initiation or mourning, as preparation for warfare or in rites centred on fertility. It is possible, for example, that the *pukao* signalled the transformation of the *moai* from a vessel congenial to the benign spirits of peace and plenty to one more suitable for aggression, warfare or sacrifice. Alternatively, the Rapanui word *kao* means cloth or clothing (as does *hami*) but also means female genitals. Barkcloth was the premier product of female labour, a highly prized and ceremonially important material, frequently presented as a gift on important occasions of life or death. If the *pukao* was associated with female fertility or other symbolism in some way, placement of it on top of the male *moai* by inserting the head of the statue into a carved hole (*pu*) in the *pukao* then becomes a metaphor for procreation. If the *pukao* were associated with warfare they might be visual emblems of political alliances or conflicts. Whatever their exact meaning, the *pukao* served both to extend the height of the statue and make a strong statement about the ability of individual lineages to marshall resources and procure labour.

The Perfect Chief

The reddish colour of Rano Raraku stone and the use of red scoria for some monolithic sculpture suggests a link with other islands in Polynesia such as the Australs and Marquesas Islands, where red stone was similarly used. Red scoria sculptures, while few in number, show an enormous time span on the island and a similarly large spectrum of design change. The desire to carve sculptures in red or with a reddish hue, using material which was superior to red scoria, was probably a major factor in the choice of Rano Raraku stone. All of this, and the documented use of red paint in body painting, rock art and artefacts supports the value of the colour red on Rapa Nui. Red, the sacred colour of Oceania and in Polynesia, the colour of 'chiefly possessions and whatever is most precious' was a key aspect of statue iconography.[27]

In my opinion, a reasonable interpretation of the use of red stone in anthropomorphic sculpture is that it refers graphically and directly to red-coloured or ruddy skin. Miru as ruler of death and the lower regions was said in Mangaia to be called 'Ruddy Miru'. A legendary figure sometimes called Tahaki was known over most of Polynesia including Tonga, New Zealand, Mangareva and the Tuamotus.[28] Tahaki's red skin was a source of both great sexual attraction and enormous admiration and envy. He wore a red wreath on his hair and carried a staff of red feathers. In the Tuamotus, Tahaki is associated with cannibalism. Tahaki was the 'perfect chief', clever, powerful and virile. He sailed a great canoe called Rainbow through the seas and the skies, and had the power to control the elements. He could heal the sick and resuscitate the dead in battle. His status allowed him to achieve great weight because he had generous access to food, and his long nails were the trademark of chiefly idleness. His eyes were the sparkling stars.

The consistently integrated archaeological use of red scoria for *moai* not placed upon *ahu*, for *ahu* fascia and for *pukao* suggests that a link exists between these practices, and that the practices may be associated with death, sacrifice, virile chiefly power and perhaps with the concept of Tahaki or the Rapa Nui equivalent of Tahaki. While Rano Raraku stone is also reddish in colour, it was reserved for the highest-status sculptures (those actually erected upon *ahu*). Colour was an aspect of the symbolism of the *moai*, but not the defining attribute.

Sex as Metaphor

We have noted in Rapa Nui art forms a definite reluctance to depict male genitals in direct and graphic form, unless we are dealing with historic objects. In contrast, we see that depictions of female genitals (*komari*) in art approached standardisation of form and an iconic level of meaning. The *komari* form is found superimposed upon symbols regarded as male, including the *moai* and the rock art form of the *tangata manu*, or birdman. We have recorded a single site in which a *moai* was expertly recarved to depict a bas-relief *komari*, thus successfully converting male form to a female symbol in monolithic scale and at a very high level of probable meaning and function (fig. 115). This graphic and realistic *komari*, found at Ahu O'Pepe in the eastern sector of the island, was very likely the focus of late ritual which involved a master carver, ten or more earth ovens

115 Bas-relief *komari* expertly carved from a fragment of *moai* torso at Ahu O'Pepe (20–1), Rapa Nui. *Photo by Jo Anne Van Tilburg.*

(*umu pae*) and at least 100 people. The ethnographies suggest that the event was a *koro*, and that possibly the *poki manu* or child/bird was the focus of the rituals.

The Polynesian concept of sexuality was not separate from procreation. Procreation was a physical process but also a metaphysical construct. The natural world was generated through procreative energy and articulated as both graphic and metaphorical references to copulation. Fertilisation was a cosmic lightning bolt, a ray of sunshine, 'the joy of issuing forth from silence into sound'.[29] Man's cosmic parents were Rangi (the Sky) and Papa (the Earth), and all of nature was a dualistic world composed of male qualities and associations in opposition to female qualities and associations. The harmonious balance of these opposites was the obligation of the gods personified in the sacred chief, who embodied all of these forces within his own powerful being. That being, in turn, had opposing right (sacred, strong) and left (weak) sides, positive and negative energy, active and passive natures. The male principle was associated with light, the colour red, positive and active energy, occult knowledge, the strong right side, the east and day (*ao*). The female force was associated with dark, the colour white, negative and passive energy, common or non-sacred knowledge, the weak left side, the west and dark (*po*). Interactions between male and female power were highly charged and dangerous intimacies between opposite spirits and competing social forces.

Tane is the universal male principle. As First Man he was the power which 'warms the body of the Earth Mother, and is the cause and conserver of all life'.[30] He was procreative *mana*, the embodiment of male power activated in the context of the real or symbolic sex act. Such symbolic acts, in the form of poles erected on religious sites or implanted in the earth, were an important element in Polynesian ritual, and there is good evidence to suggest that they were a part of Rapa Nui ceremonial life. Images or objects of a sacred nature which are also symbolically phallic were usually referred to in Polynesia as *tiki*. In Rapanui, *tiki* means a master of any skill or art, as does *maori*, although the antiquity of the term is not known. Englert says that a master sculptor was called *tiki moai*, and recorded a reference to Makemake as Tiki Makemake.

There is a metaphorical connection between the statues, everything straight, tall and erect in nature, the human male and the erect male organ. There is a metonymic connection between the statues as symbols, the statue-making process (including tools and transport), male craft or other activities in general and the personified creator god. Each time a *moai* was erected upon the mounded, sacred feminine earth 'heaped up' and enclosed within *ahu* walls on ancestral lands, the primal metaphor of procreative/creative genesis of man and nature was expressed and made visible before the assembled community. The beauty of the perfect chiefly body was united with the Earth designed to stand at the centre of society. That beauty was expressed in a form which was masculine but very subtle. The ability of this masculine form also to embody feminine qualities or entities was a ritual component of the *moai* as the society's ultimate and most subtle morphosis figure.

In some parts of Polynesia, images which were definitely androgynous were created. Some Rapa Nui woodcarvings have this quality, suggested by the presence of beards and vulvas on the same figure (fig. 116). Tukuturi has a beard and an inverted triangle in place of the more usual, male *hami*, but the *ahu moai* are not androgynous. The *actual* sexuality of most Rapa Nui chiefs throughout prehistory was probably male, and the *symbolic* representation of the *moai* was perceived by the community as male. Notwithstanding that, the spirits enticed into the statues, and the qualities those spirits expressed, could be either male or female, masculine or feminine, depending on the ritual need of the community. This is in keeping with the broader Polynesian notion of masculine/feminine aspects of an integrated human nature.

The presence of female sexual characteristics in art and objects of material culture should not necessarily be taken as evidence of political power on the part of women, either individually or as a group. Neither can it be read as proof of the status of individual women as heads of lineages, although the acknowledgement of matrilineal heredity which was present in the society would make status achievement on the part of women somewhat accessible. Certainly, we have the evidence of Angata and her circle of women agitators as an example of female ability to usurp and exert power in leadership roles usually held by men. Rather, emphasis on female sexual characteristics suggests that the Rapa Nui society clearly valued and celebrated the feminine aspect of procreation, healing, *tapu* removal and fertility. The power goal however, was control over productive and reproductive forces by a hierarchical, male-dominated society.

Space and Place

We have no direct ethnographic information on how the spatial requirements of ritual sites were determined, divided or otherwise organised on Rapa Nui. Archaeology demonstrates that the rectangular form of the *ahu* was the norm, and that this form could be extended by the addition of wings. Height was sought through mounding the earth or using the natural configuration of cliffsides or bedrock. A rectangular space perpendicular to the *ahu* served as the ceremonial 'plaza'. Habitation and cooking activities were kept at a distance from the *ahu* and highest-status houses

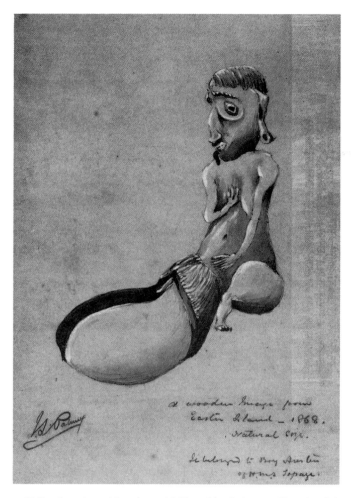

116 Woodcarving with enlarged *labia*, said to belong to 'Boy Austin' of HMS *Topaze*. Watercolour by J. Linton Palmer, 1868. *Courtesy of Royal Geographical Society.*

Mother. As late as 1934–35, Maria Ika, the wife of Juan Tepano, composed and sang a song in honour of the statue Pou hakanononga as it was taken from Rapa Nui to Belgium. In it, she alluded to the sexual magnetism of the statue, urging the foreigners to 'put it on an ahu where the Belgian girls will see it'.[31]

Just as the Polynesian chiefs could contain within themselves the power of various gods, those gods and the associated power were of many types. A male chief could embody and express both masculine and feminine power. In Fiji, the king actually appeared as both male and female. The task of masculine power was to create nourishment and then provide it to kin in the form of food. One task of feminine power was to attract and transform virile, divine generative force. Another was to draw off the negative forces of sickness or evil spirits and to remove *tapu*. The beauty of the *moai* was as the beauty of the chiefly body. Both were

Plate 20 A carved wood *kavakava* (53743) possibly collected in 1835 was acquired in 1931. Its eyes are partially filled with red material and its skull is embellished with intricate carvings (cf. Seaver 1988, 234). *Photo © 1991 by James L. Amos with permission, M. H. de Young Memorial Museum.*

Plate 21 Painted *'ao* (USNM 129, 749) called 'Mata Kao-Kao' was collected by Paymaster W.J. Thomson, 1886. Each side is painted in a distinctive pattern related to, inspired by or inspiration for rock paintings on sites associated with birdman cult ritual. *Photo by Corson Hirschfeld with permission, Department of Anthropology, NMNH, Smithsonian Institution.*

Plate 22 Seated figure (53543) of wood, fibre and barkcloth is painted in dramatic orange-red, white and black designs similar to known tattoo patterns. Acquired by Boston Museum in 1899, the figure is 41 cm in height. *Photo courtesy of the Peabody Museum of Archaeology and Ethnology, Harvard University, Cambridge, Mass.*

Plate 23 Melodramatic, with a posture far more tortured, tense and expressive than its counterpart figure (Pl. 22), this painted barkcloth image (53542) nonetheless has a similar facial expression and the same attached eyes, teeth and nails. Painted lines on the throat and the stippled facial dots of this and the barkcloth headdress (Pl. 19) occur on some *moai* as incised lines and cupules. Acquired by Boston Museum in 1899, the figure is 30.5 cm in height. *Photo courtesy of the Peabody Museum of Archaeology and Ethnology, Harvard University, Cambridge, Mass.*

Plate 24 With astonishing artistry, prehistoric Rapa Nui sculptors executed forms of harmony and simplicity to create an image of soaring power and solid presence. *Photo by David C. Ochsner, 1989.*

Plate 25 RIGHT Coral and red scoria *moai* eye in the foreground of Ahu Naunau, Anakena, from which it was retrieved during restoration of the site directed by Sergio Rapu H. *Photo by Jo Anne Van Tilburg with permission, Museo Antropológico R. P. Sebastián Englert, 1994.*

Plate 26 Empty eyesockets of a bearded statue standing now near Ahu Tongariki and in the shadow of Rano Raraku are magically filled with sunbeams. *Photo by David C. Ochsner, 1989.*

Plate 27 Statue lying in the upper, exterior quarries of Rano Raraku is one of the few on the island with feminine attributes. *Photo by David C. Ochsner, 1989.*

Plate 28 Rapa Nui's computer generated terrain is crossed by an icon representing an ancient statue in-transport over optimum Path 1. *Computer graphics and program by Zvi Shiller and Satish Sundar. Photo by Jo Anne Van Tilburg.*

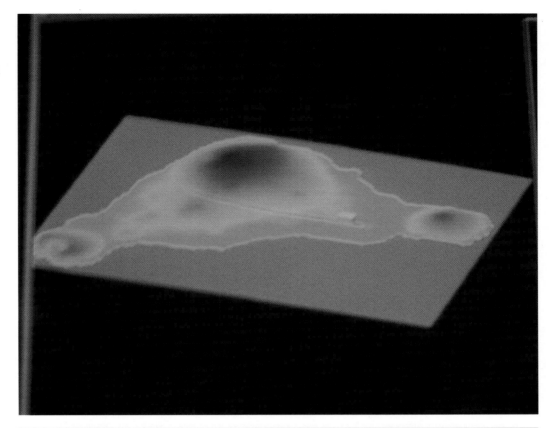

Plate 29 Modern computer technology allows us to generate a model of how the average statue may have been erected on appropriately sited prehistoric *ahu*. On some large coastal sites, the statue's position may have been prone and its approach to the *ahu* would have been made from the front. *Computer image by Michael Ohara with Jo Anne Van Tilburg.*

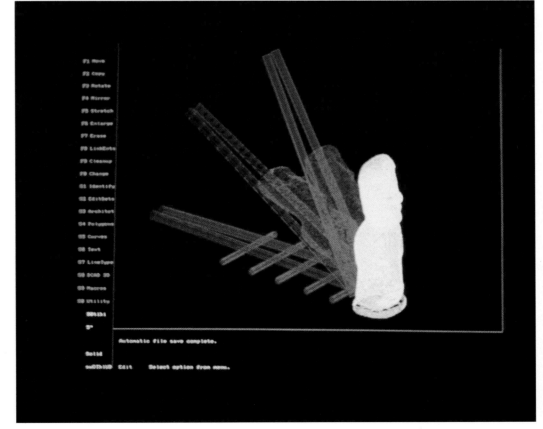

Plate 30 The magnificent *moai* of Ahu Tongariki are being reerected in an internationally funded project directed by Chilean archaeologist Claudio Cristino F. *Photo with permission, Jo Anne Van Tilburg, 1994.*

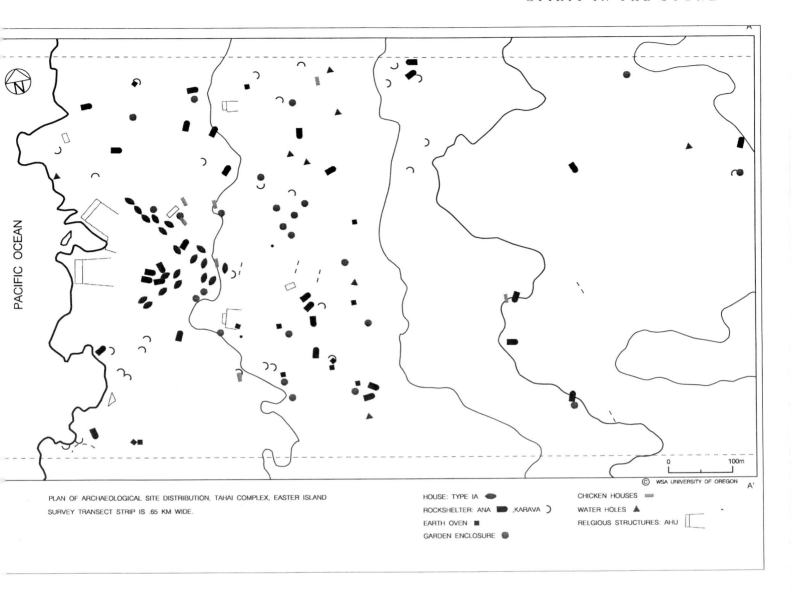

PACIFIC OCEAN

PLAN OF ARCHAEOLOGICAL SITE DISTRIBUTION, TAHAI COMPLEX, EASTER ISLAND
SURVEY TRANSECT STRIP IS .65 KM WIDE.

HOUSE: TYPE IA ●

ROCKSHELTER: ANA ■ ,KARAVA)

EARTH OVEN ■

GARDEN ENCLOSURE ●

CHICKEN HOUSES ▨

WATER HOLES ▲

RELGIOUS STRUCTURES: AHU ⌐

© WSA UNIVERSITY OF OREGON

117 Plan of archaeological site distribution and spatial relationships, Tahai complex, Rapa Nui. Transect strip is 0.65 km wide. *Courtesy of W.S. Ayres.*

(*hare paenga*) were closest to it (fig. 117). The relationship of the *ahu* to the female, earthly principle embodied in the lineage land is clear. The *ahu* defined the parameters and relationships of the lineage ritual and living space, bordered and faced it. The *moai* dominated it.

If we follow the organisation of space documented in other Polynesian societies, we know that ritual spaces, canoes and houses were all divided along a right/left, front/back scheme. The right side of all such structures is considered to be the most important. Areas were designated 'feminine' and 'masculine', just as were objects, tasks and foods. Thus, space was divided between men and women, men's tasks and women's tasks. The coastal or shore area of an island was more desirable, hence more important, than the inland areas, and status often decreased relative to distance from the shore. On some islands, including Rapa Nui, the centre of the island was the realm of the spirits. Various places on an island, certain rocks, trees or tidepools were named and set aside as forming or lying within distinct spatial entities. Such entities on Rapa Nui included the major geological sources and most highly evolved ritual sites, including Rano Raraku and Rano Kau, and probably Puna Pau and Poike as well.

Throughout Polynesia, space is ordered in such a way that the dual spiritual order and the hierarchical class system is always expressed and reinforced. The cardinal directions were always noted, and the west/east division in many islands is obvious and ancient. Antagonistic or opposing relationships of cosmic directions are deeply rooted in Polynesian navigational and astronomical lore. In surprising contrast to the symbolic association of west with female and east with male, where such divisions are noted the west is the seat of hereditary power. In Hawaii the oldest and most senior lineages are located in the western islands of Oahu and Kauai, but the historic dynamism of the system was in the east, with Maui and Hawai'ian chiefs who were able to 'differentiate themselves from local competitors, or even from their own dynastic predecessors, by appropriating ancestry from the ancient western sources of legitimacy'.[32] The dynamic of east/west division on Rapa Nui may have been similar to that of Hawaii.

The *moai*, a symbol created and controlled by expert carvers and directly associated with the entire island family, was acquired in greatest numbers by the lower-ranked lineages of the east and nearly exclusively displayed in the coastal zone and in Rano Raraku. Acquisition of the *moai* as *ahu* site symbol may be interpreted as an attempt to 'appropriate ancestry' in order to enter into the social mainstream of resource redistribution, alleviate food stress and achieve status. When this attempt began to reach the level wherein serious sociopolitical imbalance was created, a shift in ideological practice was initiated by the ruling elite, and rituals were relocated from lineage space to the already sacred and established pan-island spaces of Rano Raraku and Rano Kau. There, the same forces and the same manipulators of those forces enacted ancient but transformed rites. The major difference was that the ritual spaces were now less directly tied to ancient lineage lands and rivalries, and the resource focus had shifted and/or broadened. The proliferation of carved *tangata manu* petroglyphs at Orongo and the similar concentration of large, late statues embedded in the exterior slopes of Rano Raraku serve equally to emphasise and reinforce the importance of each place.

Orongo has long been recognised as the sacred site it is, and the implied importance of Rano Kau is clear. Rano Raraku, on the other hand, has been consistently regarded by Western eyes as a more secular place, a 'production centre', 'statue factory' or, oddly, a 'maternity ward'. Such a distinction does violence to the Polynesian view of natural and supernatural, and denies the concept of 'sacred work' and all associated with it. Work in the quarries to produce sacred images would have been integrated with ceremonies and other observances to consecrate tools, carvers, other workers and each stage of the work. Areas or sectors of the quarry would have been occasionally *tapu* for a variety of reasons. We are, in fact, a very long way from fully understanding the way in which space and resources in the quarry were apportioned.

For example, nearly the entire outside parameter of Rano Raraku crater is ringed, between 50–75 m contour levels, by evenly spaced *hare paenga* of overall similar sizes. Nearly all of the structures still retain evidence of attached pavements and most have *umu pae* associated. Such an order of space and relationship of structures is definitely not coincidental. If these structures were meant to house master carvers, chiefs or priests, those individuals clearly had an agreed-upon pattern of design and location. Since many of the *hare paenga* appear to be somewhat late in time, probably even after the peak period of statue manufacture, they may represent the presence of the same class of ritual experts who inhabited the similarly-shaped stone houses of Orongo. This suggests the ritual interrelationship of both sites. At the very least, it is clear supportive evidence for the presence and influence of high-ranked individuals and the sacred nature of Rano Raraku.

Some 40.3% of the statues in Rano Raraku are found on the interior and exterior slopes, the majority of these standing erect or nearly erect. Those on the interior generally face west or northwest, while those on the exterior almost all face south or southwest. Because they are embedded, and because the extent of detritus which has accumulated around them is so great, we have very few measurements of the total height of any of the standing statues. It is, however, beyond doubt that the numbers and sizes of most of these statues could not have been accommodated on the existing *ahu*, none of which are prepared to receive them. While there are many unanswered questions with regard to Rano Raraku, in my opinion some or all of the standing statues, especially those with perfunctory pavements, artefacts or burials associated, were never meant to be moved further. The erection or embedding of statues on the slopes of Rano Raraku is an especially graphic example of the pole/mound, male/female procreative metaphor of Polynesian beliefs. I believe that Rano Raraku and Rano Kau, the standing *moai* and the birdman petroglyphs probably functioned in analogous ways during late prehistory, as Routledge originally suspected.

Tukuturi and one other statue in Rano Raraku depart from the island-wide norm in posture. Both are carved in a kneeling position with hands placed upon the tops of their thighs. This posture is unusual but has clear stylistic antecedents in the larger corpus. Several statues show evidence of the development of both legs and the kneeling posture, although the position of the hands on the abdomen does not vary. The most important of these are in the western sector of the island, carved in basalt and red scoria.

Attempts to date Tukuturi have not, to date, been satisfactory, but the best data suggest that the statue may have been carved near the time of the arrival of the first Europeans.[33] Tukuturi is, in fact, the single statue on the entire island which best fits the ethnographic descriptions of a birdman, bald pate and all. As such, it is the only fully realised, three-dimensional sculptural example of the conceptual transition from *ahu moai* and the god or gods thus represented to the incarnate *tangata manu*. The statue remains on the slope of the quarry from which, I suspect, it was never intended to be moved. Its presence there and its physical appearance, sharply distinct from the *moai* with which it is surrounded, suggests to me that it is an attempt to make a clear visual statement about both the time and the place. That statement concerns the birdman cult, the use of the quarry in the birdman cult, and is about the relationship, in unity and opposition, of east to west, Rano Raraku to Rano Kau, Tukuturi to Hoa Hakananai'a and heredity to acquired leadership status.

The horizontal and vertical organisation of place in Polynesia has been called a 'mythical charter'.[34] In this charter, gods and people ordered their worlds to reflect the order of the universe. The ritual maintenance of this charter was the vital and essential task of all members of society. The order of space and the use of it in ceremonial centres, inside houses, in settlement patterns and elsewhere reflected a similar order in the hierarchical patterns of society, and each was a link which strengthened the whole. The magical and religious nature of the great, water-filled craters which dominate the Rapa Nui landscape stemmed from their natural configurations and from ancient beliefs in the nature of the cosmological world and the passage of man and gods from one level of that world to another. Just as George Cooke, on the *Mohican* expedition, recognised a symbolic relationship of the craters to the human navel, the Rapa Nui assuredly saw these places as mythic centres of creative and procreative power.

The Rapa Nui shared their island with all other members of their families and extended families, with those who were closely related and others who were more distantly known. The island, it should be remembered, was also the abode of benevolent and malevolent spirits. Those numerous and dangerously mobile spirits moved about and through the natural and supernatural world and had access to every corner of the landscape and seascape. The spiritual adventure that individual Rapa Nui chiefs embarked upon when they began to carve and erect increasingly larger statues must have been one which was viewed by many not only with awe but with alarm as well. Enticing incredibly powerful spirits into increasingly larger stone images and then concentrating those images in the specific geographic locale of Rano Raraku may have operated as a control strategy meant to minimise negative spiritual events as well as to consolidate and strengthen the power of the *moai*. Without carved eye inserts, the ritualistic meaning and function of the *moai* in Rano Raraku would not have been the same as it was when the statues stood, eyes open and intact, on the *ahu* platforms.

Many Oceanic societies, it has been said, 'employ the aesthetic at the boundaries of the moral'.[35] The beauty of persons and objects, such as the hereditary chief and the carved stone *moai*, stands central to the place where the constituted social group intersects with 'mythical charter' and 'moral order' of the conjoined real and philosophical worlds. The dynamic tension between heredity and achieved position, inherent and acquired *mana*, is dramatised in the *moai* as increasingly more dominant sentinels erected to maintain the boundaries of sacred spaces and reinforce the claims of charismatic and effective lineage leaders. The monumental human form of the *moai* reveals the Rapa Nui aspiration toward permanence in place and time, a taste for harmonious and ordered symmetry of aesthetic expression and an intellectual and spiritual quest to seek answers for the life and death questions posed by the world they and their religious beliefs had created.

Beyond Belief: Moving the Moai

The power apparatus will achieve more if the human machine can be revved up.

ANDREW BARD SCHMOOKLER Philosopher

In all organisms, locomotion is increased by a bad environment.

KONRAD LORENZ Behaviour Theorist

A perplexing question for most seekers of the Easter Island 'mystery' is, 'How were the statues moved?' The research program which we have undertaken to understand the technological methods utilised on Rapa Nui to transport and raise the megalithic *moai* has moved through essentially six procedural levels, all growing out of the statue inventory. Our first task was to define, statistically and stylistically, what the statues looked like, how they were similar and how they were different. To do this, we first inventoried the statues in the field, filed the descriptive data and then classified the statues in morphological types. Secondly, we documented regional centres of production and looked for island-wide patterns of distribution. Thirdly, we defined the statistically average statue, the one which was most widely produced, most often erected on *ahu* and most extensively distributed. Fourthly, we then isolated a single example of that average statue and documented it photogrammatically. Fifthly, we used dynamic motion planning and robotics programmes to determine three of the most viable transport routes from Rano Raraku quarry to the site on which our average statue stood. Finally but most importantly, we constructed a model of the Rapa Nui sociopolitical unit which would have been capable of commissioning, producing, transporting and erecting the statue. The goal of this research is not to focus on the transport failures, those statues lying between quarry and various *ahu*, all unprepared to receive them, but to seek the norm, hoping to achieve a broad-based understanding of Rapa Nui society at its most widely achieved functioning level.

Megalithic Methods

Ancient methods of heavy transport are not really as 'mysterious' as they would seem, at first glance, to be. The late Robert F. Heizer, California archaeologist and scholar, was prompted by his own work among Olmec ruins to investigate the physical and historical evidence dealing with moving heavy weights in prehistoric societies.[1] In the southeastern lowland of Mexico in the first millennium BC, members of the Olmec culture successfully moved scores of sculpture, stelae and 'altars' carved of basalt and weighing up to 36 tons. Through personal observation of Mexican workmen at La Venta, Heizer determined that stone columns weighing between 1.5 and 2 tons could be carried, suspended from poles in rope slings, by thirty-five men. Similar feats were accomplished in modern times and are well documented from Colombia, Madagascar, Tonga, the Marquesas Islands and elsewhere (fig. 118). Confident of these observations, we took them as our starting point. Therefore, any statue weighing up to 2 tons, on any Rapa Nui site anywhere on the island, could have been carried there from Rano Raraku or any of the other regional quarry sites.

There are ninety-two statues which have, to date, been coded as in-transport by the survey. Of these, forty-seven are located outside of Rano Raraku quarry zone (fig. 119). We have metric data on forty-four of them, the largest of which is 9.3 m total length (figs 120, 121). The mean length of in-transport statues is 5.79 m. The tallest statue successfully raised upon *ahu* is called Paro. It stands 9.8 m in total

118 Method used by the Naga people to move a stone slab weighing less than two tons. *Photo by Ursula Graham Bower, 1941. Courtesy Pitt Rivers Museum, Oxford.*

119 BELOW Prone *moai* recorded as in-transport lies on a remnant of the prehistoric road from Rano Raraku to the south coast. *Photo by David C. Ochsner, 1983.*

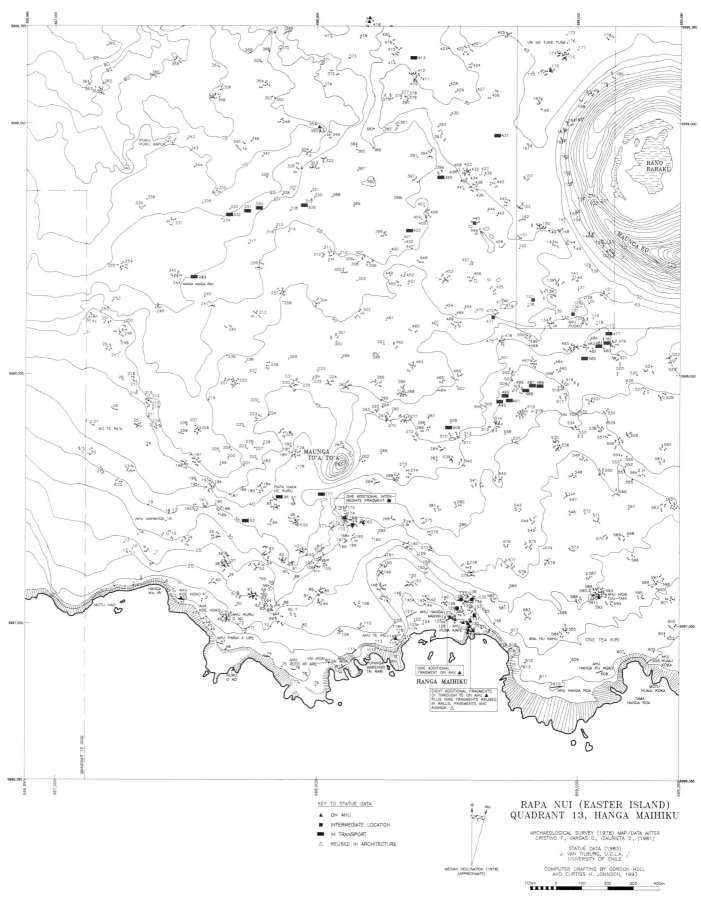

RAPA NUI (EASTER ISLAND)
QUADRANT 13, HANGA MAIHIKU

ARCHAEOLOGICAL SURVEY (1978) MAP/DATA AFTER
CRISTINO F., VARGAS C., IZAURIETA S., (1981)

STATUE DATA (1983)
J. VAN TILBURG, U.C.L.A. /
UNIVERSITY OF CHILE

COMPUTER DRAFTING BY GORDON HULL
AND CURTISS H. JOHNSON, 1993

KEY TO STATUE DATA

▲   ON AHU

■   INTERMEDIATE LOCATION

▬   IN TRANSPORT

△   REUSED IN ARCHITECTURE

MEDIAN DECLINATION (1978)
(APPROXIMATE)

100m   0   100   200   300   400m

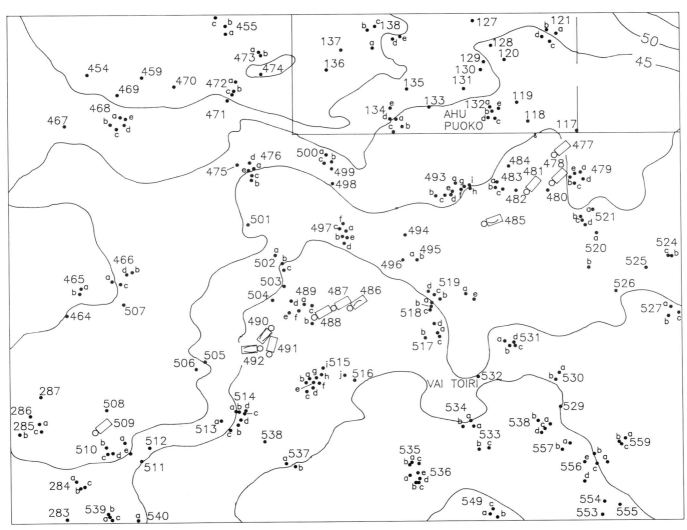

120 OPPOSITE Distribution and location type identifications of 62 monolithic statues and statue fragments in Quadrant 13. *Base survey map computer drafted and edited with additional data after Cristino F. et al. 1981, by Gordon Hull and Curtiss H. Johnson with Jo Anne Van Tilburg and Patricia Vargas C., 1993.*

121 ABOVE Detail of Quadrant 13 illustrating varying positions and orientations of eleven statues. *Base survey map computer drafted and edited with additional data after Cristino F. et al. 1981, by Gordon Hull and Curtiss H. Johnson with Jo Anne Van Tilburg, 1993.*

length and is located on Ahu Te Pito Kura within the Miru territory of the northeast coast. Another statue only 1 cm taller was successfully transported to Ahu Hanga Te Tenga on Ngaura lands on the southeast coast, but fell and broke, possibly during the task of erecting it. An enormous *pukao* is associated with Paro, while there are none now present at Ahu Hanga Te Tenga. In terms of *ahu* statue height, these two sites represent the remarkable equality attained by two lineages on opposing west and east confederacy lands at a point relatively late in prehistoric time. Paro was said to have been toppled during warfare between rival east/west factions, and Routledge thought the event took place some-

time in the generation preceeding that of her oldest informants (mid to late 1800s).

My research model required the statistically determined average *moai*, drawn from a subset of 134 statues. These statues all have the best and most complete metric documentation, including crucial dimensions needed to determine volume and weight, and all were either in-transport or had been successfully moved to *ahu* on every part of the coast. Our 'reference *moai*' is found at Ahu Akivi, a restored coastal zone *ahu* lying about 140 m above sea level on the southwestern slope of Maunga Terevaka (fig. 122). It has a total height of 4.05 m. It is 1.60 m wide at its base, 1.48 m

122 Ahu Akivi platform and statues after restoration by W. Mulloy and his team, from the northwest, with ramp excavation incomplete. *Courtesy G. Figueroa G-H.*

wide at its head and has a depth through the body at mid-point of 92 cm. It has a total volume of 5.96 cubic metres, a centre of gravity at 1.36 m and a total weight of 12.5 metric tons. The statue was carved of Rano Raraku tuff and was moved, along with six others nearly precisely the same, to Ahu Akivi where it was raised upon the second phase *ahu* platform sometime after AD 1400 and probably between the early and mid-1600s.

Wherever in the prehistoric world stones of similar dimensions and weights were moved, whether it was Egypt, Stonehenge, Assyria, Teotihuacan or anywhere else, methods which are almost identical are suggested to have been used successfully. These methods have been tested in a surprisingly large number of experimental archaeology projects which focus on methods, time, labour expenditure and food/energy requirements. There is, in fact, a wealth of literature on this very well-discussed topic.[2] In all cases, the preferred method of transport (with only minor variations) was to place the stone in a horizontal position, attach it to a wood sledge and then haul it over rollers and/or sleepers by workers pulling on ropes made of vegetable material. Similarities in methods used between otherwise unrelated cultures are the result of independent invention manipulating such variables as the simplicity of materials and availability of workers. The magnitude of production achievement was related to the complexity of social structure, and the cultures which produced the most extensive public works projects were large, complex chiefdoms or highly evolved states. Rulers of such societies had access to nearly unlimited natural resources, extensive amounts of forced tribute and conscripted labour.

In Polynesia, as we have seen, stone construction was most extensive in East Polynesia, and the chiefdoms which accomplished the most complex projects were structurally somewhat varied. In Tonga, West Polynesia, the formal dualism of the chiefdom produced a division of power between sacred and secular chiefs and a very well-preserved and documented building tradition of great note. In the thirteenth century AD, the Tu'i Tonga, twelfth hereditary ruler of Tonga, built the impressive ceremonial centre of Lapaha, subsequently elaborated with high-status residences, earthwork fortifications, megalithic burial mounds and an enormous dock to accommodate inter-island voyaging canoes. The expansion and complexity of the built environment at Lapaha appears to parallel a growing complexity in the structure of the Tongan dualistic chiefdom.

The eleventh Tu'i Tonga constructed the enigmatic memorial called the Ha'amonga Trilithon.[3] Two basalt uprights, each weighing twenty to thirty tons, are set at least 60 cm into the ground. These are spanned by a horizontal stone 'beam' of similar proportions, firmly anchored into the mortised tops of the upright pillars. A 'detailed and logical' description of how the great stones were cut and moved is preserved in Tongan tradition, as is a legend explaining why the structure was built. The Tongan builders worked in basalt and coral 'sandstone' (beach rock), hauling both on wooden sledges with the use of sennit ropes, wooden rollers, blocking wedges and ingenious methods of leverage. The uprights were set in place with the aid of an earthen wall built perpendicular to the excavated pits which were ultimately to hold the pillars.

In the Marquesas Islands huge stones and cut stone slabs which measured up to 3.6 m (12 feet) long were used in the construction of terraces and platforms, at which the Marquesans excelled. Stones too large to be easily carried were rolled with the use of levers and inclined platforms. The cut slabs (usually of a coarse-grained red tuff) were transported by suspending them between stout poles resting on the shoulders of men walking in single-file over narrow trails. Ralph Linton observed six men carrying a slab over a metre (four feet) long with relative ease, and frames required to transport huge quantities of food to ceremonial sites are said to have been carried by sixty men. Skids or rollers were apparently not used on the challenging terrain, but may have been used in the quarries. A problem detected by Linton in Marquesan transport methods was that of constructing a frame strong enough to bear the weight of the slab and large enough to allow all of the bearers to grab hold. Examples of how such frames may have been constructed are well-documented among the Naga and Ao Naga.

On Rapa Nui, members of the 1955 Norwegian Archaeological Expedition attempted to work out the problem of statue transport and a 'bipod' method was postulated by Mulloy for Paro.[4] His proposal, which he offered at the time as speculative, is an overly complex solution with potentially major problems in execution, but nevertheless has been widely cited. It requires that the statue, to which a Y-shaped and inexplicably curved 'fork-sledge' is attached on the ventral side from neck to base, be transported prone, with the whole then suspended by ropes from the weakest point of a very tall (c. 9 m) bipod. The convex surface of the statue's belly and sledge combined was said to act as a fulcrum as the statue was rocked forward. This notion was based upon observations of two or three of the larger statues lying along the transport road which have protruding bellies. Leaving aside the formidable problem of strong, properly shaped wood resources, the statues, in general, lack sufficient depth through the midsection to make the fulcrum idea feasible. Further, the two logs or tree trunks required to construct the bipod need to be nearly double the length of those used in the horizontal method I propose below.

An alternative solution was actually implemented on a statue at Anakena. A supine statue, fortuitously of the requisite average size (4 m) and weighing 'about 10 tons', was attached to a Y-shaped sledge made from a forked tree trunk 'with cross pieces over the runners'. The sledge design, unfortunately, was not fully documented but was said to be the idea of Pedro Atan. He reportedly said such sledges 'were used to move the large blocks of stone on the *ahu* into position'.[5] Such Y-shaped sledges are very useful and practical and have been used by the Assam to move large stones in modern times. In fact, a particularly fine series of photos documenting their design was published in the 1940s.[6] It is doubtful that Atan's Y-shaped sledge is the product of traditional knowledge. Nevertheless, it is a practical and reasonable solution to the problem of statue transport. An important requirement, of course, is the availability of a forked tree branch of the requisite size.

A third proposal, that the statues were moved upright by 'tilting' them on their bases, using ropes attached to their necks, is associated with a literal interpretation by Leonardo Pakarati of Rapa Nui legends saying that the statues 'walked' to the *ahu*.[7] Heizer's research illustrates that, wherever megalithic monuments occur, beliefs that the stones 'can will themselves to move or remain fixed' are widespread.[8] This results from the magical and religious function of these monuments, but also is especially true when the extant culture is disassociated from the remains, for whatever reason. In Micronesia, I was repeatedly told by Belauans that stone megaliths, about which many spiritual concerns still remain, moved alone. The Rapa Nui 'walking *moai*' legend is very likely a similar phenomenon.

The upright, tilting method was actually tried on two smaller than average statues. One of these, moved a few feet by a crew of workmen under the direction of Heyerdahl and his colleagues, visibly damaged the base in the process and raised a cry of protest in the community and among scholars. A similar and nearly simultaneous project employed a full-scale but poorly designed and inaccurately proportioned concrete statue model which was placed upright on a small wooden platform and the whole placed upon short rollers. This method was superior to the tilting method, but still incredibly dangerous. The logistics of any upright method suggested to date are daunting to impossible on the rolling Rapa Nui terrain.

The patterns of breakage on the larger than average statues lying along the southeast coast transport road and relatively close to the quarry suggested to Routledge that they had stood upright in place to form a ceremonial roadway. One of these statues, excavated at the base by A. Skjølsvold and his colleagues, had a pavement associated with it, thus partially substantiating her claim and not, therefore, requiring an upright transport method as an explanation for breakage.[9] My own examination of the in-transport statues, many of which are broken at the necks (the weakest point), is that Routledge may well have been right in her assertion.

Fully 42.6% of statues documented outside Rano Raraku quarry zone including those in-transport are lying prone, 31.9% are supine and 8.1% are lateral (table 4). The majority of prone and lateral statues are lying with their heads oriented away from the quarry and in a generally southwest direction (table 5). If erect, they would have faced toward Rano Kau. Supine statues are oriented more to the northeast. If we assume that, regardless of position, the statues were transported heads first (as extended corpses are in many cultures) the majority (52.3%) were

TABLE 4 Easter island monolithic statue count and percentages by position in which they are found.

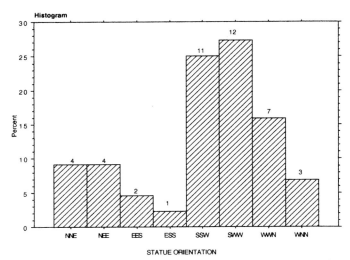

TABLE 5 Percentage distribution of 44 in-transport statues by compass orientation of the heads. *Histogram by Gordon Hull.*

destined for the southwest portion of the island.

In addition to the documented stone construction techniques of Polynesia, the ethnographies contain important data on methods of canoe construction and the organisation of people required to accomplish this important work. We can imagine that the process of building a large voyaging canoe or deep-sea fishing canoe for an important *ariki* was probably similar in many ways to that of commissioning, carving and transporting a statue. When Europeans entered the Pacific, the great double voyaging and war canoes were few in number, seen mostly in Samoa, Tonga and Fiji. Estimates of size vary, but a canoe 36 m long, more than three times the length of the largest statue successfully transported, was known in Hawaii. Hulls of some canoes are estimated to have weighed significantly more than average *moai*.[10] Construction of such vessels was in the hands of master craftsmen with hereditary status and specialised knowledge, and the task took from two to seven years. The work progressed in accordance with the availability of food, and Fijian craftsmen said '*a tata tu i kete* (the chopping is in the belly)'.[11] Sometimes the canoes were built inland, where the best timber was available, and had

Position		Frequency	Percent	Cumulative frequency	Cumulative percent
0	Unassigned	6	1.6	6	1.6
1	Prone	163	42.6	169	44.1
2	Supine	122	31.9	291	76.0
3	Vertical	61	15.9	352	91.9
4	Lateral	31	8.1	383	100.0

Easter Island monolithic statue count and percentages by position, exclusive of Rano Raraku sector.

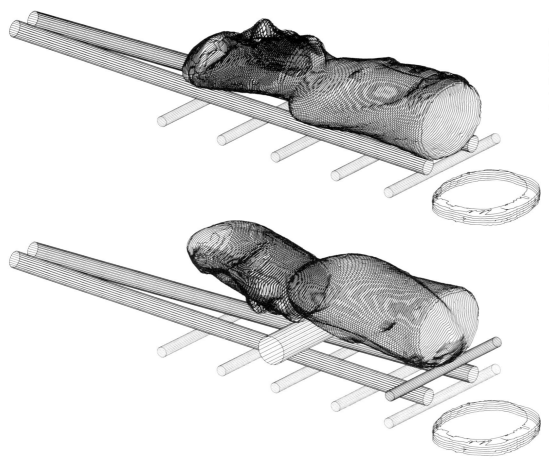

123 Conjectural methods for moving a supine (upper) or prone statue of statistically average size using only rollers, two wooden beams or two beams with two cross pieces of different sizes. *Computer drafting by Michael Ohara with Jo Anne Van Tilburg.*

later to be hauled overland to the beach. In Fiji, the great canoes were launched over the bodies of men, sacrificed to serve as rollers as the vessel slid into the water.

How They Did It: A Model

Statue 01 at Ahu Akivi, a particularly good example of the statistically designated average statue, was chosen for the research model. All of our metric, photogrammetric and other data documenting this statue enabled a professional sculptor to create a 1/10 scale model of the statue. From the scale model, a professional set designer carved a full-scale (4 m tall) statue out of plastic foam. The purpose of this research was to document fully and exactly how and in what order a professional, working from a model as Polynesian canoe builders often did, would tackle the problem of creating a sculpture out of a rectangular block. This process was documented on videotape, and lent great insight into carving methods. The 1/10 scale model was then used to experiment with a variety of transport methods, and a laser scan of it produced a three-dimensional computer image. At the same time, a topographic map of Rapa Nui was digitised, producing a three-dimensional compu-

ter map. With the aid of a specially designed computer programme, we sought the optimal path over which Statue 01 was moved to Ahu Akivi.[12] The value of this method is that it is precise and accurate but does not require using or putting at risk, in any way, an actual statue. Related to this process, we were able to arrive at the number of people required to do the work, the time involved, the amount of energy each person was required to expend and the number of calories needed to produce that energy. The result is a model of how the average statue was transported and what it cost to do it.

My approach to the problem of transport was to assume that the Rapa Nui craftsmen had at their disposal generations of Polynesian expertise in marine exploration and canoe construction. This knowledge would have been retained within the framework of occupational 'guilds', but would also have evolved over time to accommodate the nature of the task and changing resources. It would have been used to develop methods for handling the statues in ways similar to constructing, transporting and launching the great canoes. Thus we can presume that widely known principles of the fulcrum, lever, forked lever, balance beam, pivot and moving pivot would have been easily adapted to problems of statue transport.[13] Ancient skills in the production of stone tools, strong cordage and lashing methods would have been employed, as well as known techniques of raising and securing masts using side, back and fore stays. Basic materials such as wood from the *Sophora toromiro* and *Thespesia populnea* and palmwood from the *Jubaea chilensis* offered a range of specialised attributes, with their use depending on such variables as the age of the tree, the dimensions of trunks and branches and elasticity. Cordage of acceptable dimensions and tensile strengths could have been produced from *Triumfetta semitrolaba*. Using and frequently recycling available wood and fibre materials, it is most likely that a basic repertoire of transport methods was adapted to each individual statue weighing more than 2 tons.

We sought an economical, reasonable and basically straightforward method for moving the *moai* which would be in keeping with Polynesian capabilities and known methods (fig. 123). We allowed the actual attributes of the statue to partially dictate our hypothesis. I thus believe that the average statue was moved in a supine position on its flat back. Could the prone or lateral positions of some of the in-transport statues be the result of transport methods? One of our original hypotheses was that if the transport process was interrupted or abandoned before the statue reached the *ahu*, it may have been rolled over before removing the valuable rollers beneath. Experiments now show however, that the statue could have been levered up high enough to remove the rollers without actually turning it completely over.

In a supine transport method rollers 10 cm in diameter are sufficient. The easiest way to transport a prone statue is to increase the diameter of the rollers to at least 25–30 cm. Another way is to insert two crossbeams of the same diameter between the statue and the two non-parallel transport beams supporting it, raising the face and nose sufficiently far from the ground to avoid damage. The design of the statues suggests this placement of crossbeams, but doing so reduces the number of contact points between the statue and its transport beams, placing mild to severe stress on the vulnerable neck area especially. Thus it is possible that at least some of the breakage noted on some in-transport statues does not have to be attributed to an upright position but may have been caused by the accumulated stresses to the neck while attempting to move them in a prone and horizontal position. Prone transport places the statue at higher risk of breakage, is more expensive in terms of resources and unnecessarily complicated. None of the variations on prone transport we have devised thus far are fully satisfactory. The evidence does not allow us to

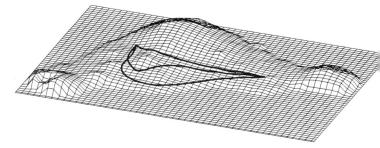

124 Three-dimensional map of Rapa Nui terrain with alternative statue transport paths from Rano Raraku to Ahu Akivi. Path 1 (the shortest) is at the top. *Map and pathway calculations by Zvi Shiller and Satish Sundar.*

postulate a single scenario for positioning and breakage of all the in-transport statues.

The statue was transported only during the dry season and only over a dry, hardpacked track. Wet tracks are impassable with this sort of load and wet tuff weighs an average of 10% more and breaks more easily than dry. From five to forty rollers of 10–20 cm in diameter would have been required to ease the statue along the track, and occasionally sleepers of similar size may have been substituted. *Jubaea chilensis* trunks are known to reach 1.8 m in diameter, a size considerably in excess of that required by this model. However, the recent discovery by G. Velasco of many fossil palm trunk prints averaging 35–45 cm in diameter clearly proves that wood appropriate to our transport model was present at some time on the island. In the absence of rollers, the statue would need to be dragged as a dead weight, an unlikely event due to the high degree of stone damage involved. If it did happen, friction would have to be kept at a coefficient of .2, and water would be the most logical aid to reduce friction, although palm fronds or sap could also have served.

The next step was tracking the optimum transport path, and I invited Zvi Shiller and his students at UCLA's Laboratory for Robotics and Animation to participate in the next stage of research. Using their own research expertise in optimum path studies, and with no knowledge of Rapa Nui's surface archaeological remains, they then discovered and traced on their digitised map three possible paths for hauling Statue 01 from the exterior slopes of Rano Raraku to Ahu Akivi (fig. 124). Path 1 was the optimal in that it was the shortest and most direct route (10.1 km) (plate 28). Although it required the largest maximum number of people (seventy), the required energy expenditure was lower than the other two routes because it took the least amount of time (4.7 days). The path ran westward and directly inland, through terrain which was probably hot but only sparsely or seasonally inhabited. Fortuitously, it approximates a portion of a conjectured track branching from what Katherine Routledge called the 'western image road'.

The other two routes are viable but less attractive for some very specific reasons. Path 2 was longer (13.4 km), took more time (6.2 days), and sixty-eight people were required. Energy expenditure, however, was higher than Path 1. Path 3 was the longest (15.2 km) but the terrain was much flatter, the air cooler and more pleasant, and the number of people required (sixty-three) was slightly smaller than either of the other paths. Total energy expenditure, however, was the greatest of all three possible routes. Another important factor which may have mitigated against the choice of Path 3 is that, although it ran conveniently along part of the traditional south coast transport route, it also passed through one of the most densely populated parts of the island, probably necessitating an impressive amount of political expertise on the part of the Ahu Akivi chief. At various points along the way of all three paths, both gravity and friction hindered the statue as it moved up and down slopes, but this could have been handled with holding ties. The projected number of people involved in all three routes varied only slightly and depended on terrain difficulty, with the average for Path 1 being forty-eight (fig. 125).

On all three paths traced, the maximum force required to pull the statue was 2.5 tons when the statue was in a horizontal position. In an upright position a statue with a

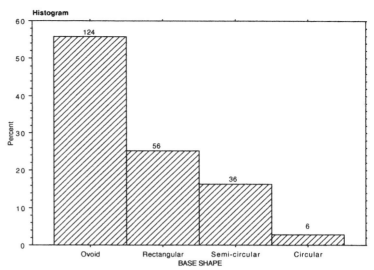

TABLE 6 Percentage distribution of statue base shape for 222 statues throughout the island. *Histogram by Gordon Hull.*

rectangular, plane base required 2.3 tons of force to tilt, an order of magnitude which offers no appreciable gain in efficiency. Significantly, the total friction force is the same for both upright, tilting method and horizontal method because the total weight is the same. Some 61.8% of *moai* base angles recorded are plane but only 24.7% are rectangular (table 6). This presents a serious problem for the success of the upright, tilting method. In an upright position, the statue's total weight is unsafely distributed between only two pivot points, and these points are most securely present on a rectangular base. The weight distribution is then alternated right and left as the statue is tilted, in contrast to the horizontal, supine method of even distribution of weight over the statue's entire length. Most importantly, an upright statue, either tilted or pulled on a wooden platform over rollers, will fall more than 50% of the time on a 10° to 20° slope. In short, moving a statue upright over the Rapa Nui terrain defies the laws of efficient motion and terrain reality. It appears to gain nothing in terms of energy and risks everything in terms of safety.

There are, theoretically, several ways the statues may have been moved. Some of these are more reasonable than others but all require tests of reason, simplicity and archaeological and resource context for their validity. Just because a method may be conceptualised in the contemporary mind does not mean it is a justified projection on the Rapa Nui past. If someone can demonstrate that a hypothetical statue could be placed on a wooden sledge and then lashed upright standing on its head, does that mean it was actually done? Archaeologists seek to understand

125 Plot of the number of persons and amount of time (days) required to transport one average statue from Rano Raraku to Ahu Akivi over path 1. Variation of manpower requirement relative to terrain difficulty. *Created by Zvi Shiller and Satish Sundar.*

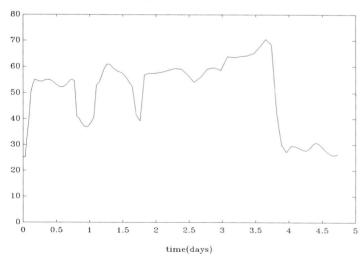

time(days)

human behavioural variability as it sketches patterns which allow inferences about social processes in the context of time. The statue documentation data have consistently revealed patterned responses to the research questions posed thus far. Thus we focus on the pattern rather than the exception.

Precontact Rapa Nui society was tradition bound. It was also innovative and experimental enough to allow or facilitate its initial adaptation to a new island environment at settlement and then to the changes over time in individual and societal ability to exploit that environment. Their heritage as Polynesians shaped to some extent most if not all of their cultural/ecological interactions. The Rapa Nui used statue transport methods transferred from other construction industries but also a range of other applicable possibilities when necessity dictated. The hypothesis presented here is replicable, testable and embedded in the archaeological reality and cultural possibility of Rapa Nui as currently understood.

What It Cost: Economic Impact

Culturally dictated gender specialisation in labour tasks was probably associated with *moai* production. Although women (and even children) would have been involved in many ways, our transport method presumes that the actual hauling of the statue was done by men. Just as we calculated the average *moai*, we calculated the average Rapa Nui man best qualified to perform the work of transporting and erecting the average *moai*. This Rapa Nui 'reference man' was between the age of eighteen and thirty, in generally good health. He was 172.7 cm tall and he weighed approximately 70 kg. His standard nutritional requirement would have been 2,880 calories per day, of which he would have expended roughly 50% in energy.[14] On this diet, he would have been able to maintain body weight, but how much labour-related energy could he have produced?

Human strength which would be applicable to the task of moving the *moai* is understood as either static or dynamic. Static strength is the maximum force which can be exerted continuously but for a brief period of time. It is, for example, measured by pushing against a heavy object. Weight and height are positively correlated to this type of strength, which means that the heavier a man is, the better his performance at static strength tasks will be. An example of a person with great weight/static strength capability would be a *sumo* wrestler. Dynamic strength, in contrast, relates to the strength of the trunk and the arms, and is a force which is repeated or exerted continuously in tasks

such as pulling or pushing. In these tasks the largest and heaviest men perform less well, and a key issue is balance. We presume that more men were involved in pulling than in pushing tasks during the work of transporting the *moai*.

Our Rapa Nui 'reference man' was physically very well-qualified for the task of transporting and erecting the average *moai*, and could pull the weight of the statue more easily than he could push it. In general, when working in a crew of men on the transport task, he could be, quite literally, expected to pull his own weight. Our conservative estimate is that he was capable of producing one-third horsepower.[15] Factors which affect work performance are age, sex, environment, adaptation and motivation. Motivation has been shown to be one of the most highly significant variables impelling an individual to action, and has been described as the key to the success of many work projects. Assuming good physical health, nutrition is the other vital concern.

The number of individuals directly involved in the transport task was not static but varied over the course of time relative to terrain difficulty. A safe estimate is that between fifty-five and seventy men, each capable of pulling their own body weight, would have been able to move Statue 01 from Rano Raraku to Ahu Akivi. One good, concerted pull on the hauling ropes could have moved the statue a single 5 m increment (the length of the statue/frame). This pulling activity was followed by pauses to accommodate manipulating the statue, moving the rollers, tightening any lashings or otherwise adjusting the process. The work of moving the statue from Rano Raraku to Ahu Akivi could have been accomplished, depending on which of the three possible paths was chosen, in from five to seven days, calculated on the basis of a five hour workday (the norm for these sorts of projects). This time need not all be consecutive, of course, and variables which might affect this figure are ritual observations, logistics of food supply and weather.

Who were the men who moved the Ahu Akivi statue, and where did they come from? What resources were required to support them and how were those resources obtained? We know that the typical Rapa Nui family can be assumed to have had nine members. Using data from precontact Western Polynesia, we also know that individual extended families could be expected to have forty-five to fifty people.[16] Virtually every member of these groups contributed some form of productive labour to the economic life of the whole. It has been estimated that 65% of males and females between the ages of ten and sixty-five constitute the average available extended family 'work force'.[17] Conservatively, eight males of appropriate age and vigour per extended family would have been available to take part in *moai* transport. Thus, if we presume that males only were actual participants and the rest of the family functioned as a support group, we see that 8.7 extended families (between 391 and 435 people) would have had to join forces to work and provide food for the seventy workmen as they hauled the statue over Path 1.

An optimum daily diet of about 2,880 calories for our Rapa Nui 'reference man' would have been one from which only 25–35% of the calories was provided by fat.[18] In order to replace the energy and body tissue he was expending in the work task, he would have needed 65–75 g of protein and 15 g of iron, in addition to calcium, phosphorous, carbohydrates and various vitamins. The osteological data, as we have seen, suggest mild calcium deficiency existed in the population. Ideally, while performing the work required to move the average *moai*, each man should have consumed either 200 grams of chicken or an equal amount of non-oily fish (preferably tuna or something similar) to provide himself with 500–600 calories of protein. In the event of a total lack of protein, the work task still could have been accomplished. Converting carbohydrates to energy is, in the short run, more efficient in the human body than converting protein first to carbohydrates and then to energy. In the long run, a lack of protein will result in discernible health deficiencies, including muscle atrophy, which clearly would be disadvantageous for statue transport tasks. Two staple Rapa Nui crops, 1,000 g of sweet potatoes and nearly half that of bananas, would have provided our Rapa Nui 'reference man' with the minimum 2,000–2,200 calories.

Studies show that work performance is affected by a lack of nitrogen in the diet and that, in fact, nitrogen loss is the determining variable in protein intake demands which, in turn, influence maximum work performance. Rapa Nui legends always speak of payment for work in terms of fish, lobsters and eels. Where could the required 500–600 calories of protein per worker come from? Although recent research suggests the possiblity of some palm trees growing on the south coast as late as AD 1600s and wood is surmised here to have been available for statue transport, the bulk of the Rapa Nui, at the time of the Ahu Akivi project, probably did not have enough adequate vessels available to them to secure large fish. Smaller fish and eels, available close to the shore or in tide pools were attainable, and lobsters can be secured by diving deeply in areas such as Akahanga and Tongariki. Excavation data from reported sites (Runga Va'e, Papa Te Kena area and Anakena) reveal that chicken, rat and human bone are greatly in evidence during this period, with rats especially important. Either

the requisite protein came from these sources or, more likely, it was not always available. Native birds and marine mammals, important sources of fat and protein several centuries earlier, had been virtually eliminated from the diet.[19] Unfortunately, no faunal data were reported from the Ahu Akivi excavations.

Another key factor in avoiding fatigue during work is water intake, which must balance loss in order to avoid dehydration. Water deficit results in a marked increase in pulse rate, body temperature and physical discomfort, causing a similarly marked decrease of tolerable work time and performance. Because it was preferable to transport the *moai* over dry rather than wet roads, we presume sunny weather, making the environment and prolonged work times a possible cause of increased risk of dehydration. Bananas, sweet potatoes and sugar cane have a very high water content, but drinking water would have been absolutely essential. Water exists, of course, at Rano Raraku where the work project began, and at Terevaka, near the destination, and gourds were available to carry it.

We calculate that seventy Rapa Nui men moving the *moai* to Ahu Akivi over Path 1 would have collectively required a total of 201,600 calories per day in order to do the job. The average sweet potato yield, using traditional Pacific methods, is three to six tons or 3,000,000 to 6,000,000 calories per acre. Where banana is cultivated in plantations using traditional methods, as it was on Rapa Nui, the yield varies from four to eight tons or 2,800,000 to 5,600,000 calories per acre. Although Métraux believed that, in historic times, the typical Rapa Nui family was capable of supporting itself on the yield of two acres, the average Pacific island agricultural land use in precontact time was .5 acre per person or about twenty-two to twenty-five acres per typical extended family. At a calculated yield per acre for each of the agricultural staples, the single Rapa Nui chief who commissioned the Ahu Akivi Path 1 transport task would have been required to have political and economic access, above and beyond his normal requirements, to the productive yield of an additional 1.5 to 3.0 acres of cultivated sweet potatoes and between 1.6 and 3.2 acres of bananas. If we consider the normal fallow/productive ratio, the number of accessible acres per crop must be roughly doubled to between three and six.[20]

Beyond this, however, he would also have required a stored surplus at least equal to what he was expending in order to pay for whatever limited animal protein he was able to secure. Food of all types, but especially that *perceived* as feast food, was needed to participate in various other social and ritual obligations inevitably associated with the project. Polynesians distinguish between life-sustaining subsistence, famine foods and foods perceived to be special, worthy of feasts and presentations where generous displays of food, rather than merely adequate amounts, are the ceremonial norm. In the Rapa Nui community today the chief yardstick of social success is still an overladen table, and tuna and lobsters are the most impressive and valued food served. The Ahu Akivi chief thus required food first to engage the requisite master carver or carvers, feed the workmen, meet the daily nutritional needs of family and involved extended family (the support network for the transport task), trade for desirable foods not immediately available to him and 'feed the gods' as well. All in all, it is a conservative estimate that access to the agricultural resources provided by 50 acres, or approximately double the extended family norm, was required to complete the Ahu Akivi transport task.

Ahu Akivi is located in the Ko Tu'u or western confederacy and was associated with an extensive community which lay between the *ahu* and Ahu Tepeu on the shoreline some 2.6 km distant.[21] North and east of Ahu Akivi lies an expanse of good agricultural land. To the immediate west, a broken and cracked lava flow provides numerous pockets of good soil and natural underground tubes in which fresh rainwater is regularly trapped. Collapsed lava tubes by the score have been modified as *manavai*. The most extensive occupational area was located on the northeast of this flow, and clusters of *hare paenga* attest to the use of this area by the highest ranked individuals. Food preparation, presentation and consumption associated with *moai* transport tasks took place in the vicinity of the *ahu* not along the transport roads.

Ahu Akivi is within the territory of the Miru, hence the chief who commissioned the average statue was entitled to bear the title *ariki*. Further, as a Miru he would have had access to marine resources, however scant they may have been, augmenting his apparently ample agricultural resources. Over the course of time from AD 1442 to the early 1600s, the first stage construction at Ahu Akivi was renovated to a second stage platform capable of holding the seven statues ultimately erected upon it. In those *c.*200 years it is possible that eight chiefs (at twenty-five years per generation) could have existed. The memory of each of seven Ahu Akivi chiefs may have been commemorated by the act of a single chief, as their direct descendant, who conceptualised and ordered the production of seven identical *moai* as part of a single engineering effort.

The total time span for the Ahu Akivi statue effort was dictated by resource availability, the weather, a peaceful social environment, political acumen, ritual success and many other factors. It clearly could have been accomplished in the single lifetime of one dedicated chief and his highly motivated extended family, even during a phase of prehistory in which adequate protein was probably not always available to the workers involved in the task. This would have had *actual* effects on physical wellbeing, but would also have been *perceived* as a negative reflection on the chiefly ability to provide, thus reverberating on sociopolitical power and status and challenging basic ideological assumptions. In this way, the direct impact of resource scarcity is indirectly felt in the intellectual and actual community, and change results.

126 Re-erection of one prone Ahu Akivi statue from the front of the *ahu* during site restoration, 1960. *Courtesy Gonzalo Figueroa G-H.*

It is significant to note that the completion of Ahu Akivi took place just prior to the time when the legendary battle of the Long Ears and Short Ears at Poike ditch is said to have taken place. Such a battle, conceived of in myth as a major, island-wide confrontation, would have assuredly rendered the Ahu Akivi accomplishment impossible. Safe passage over lineage lands for the statues in-transport from Rano Raraku to Ahu Akivi, peaceful co-existence facilitating exchange of food and other goods, sociopolitical stability and an environment encouraging megalithic tasks dependent on the acceptance of supportive ideological priciples and ideas logically could not have existed while, at the same time, one half of the island population was incinerating the other at Poike. Certainly, life on one part of the island varied from that on another because of variable population and resource factors, but not on the scale implied by the Ahu Akivi/Poike battle juxtaposition in pre-history. What was accomplished at Ahu Akivi is a visible archaeological fact. The Poike battle is either a myth or a partial distortion of history.

The final and by far the most difficult aspect of the Ahu Akivi megalithic task is positioning and then erecting the statue upon the *ahu* (fig. 126). Each statue approached Ahu Akivi base first, in a supine position and from the rear, not the front, of the *ahu*. A gently sloping earth ramp may have been required to bring the statue level with the top of the platform, and the base was then positioned upon the pedestal.[22] The statue was probably now securely lashed to the two transport beams, although friction continued to act in favour of keeping the statue and the beams in contact. A partial wood frame may have been constructed to protect the statue from contact damage. Using rocks, earth, rope stays, wedges and levers, the statue was raised to an angle where it was then guided slowly into place, using its own centre of gravity and the length of the transport beams as positive factors (plate 29). A major problem, in addition to protecting the statue, was to control the pace of the statue's movement, and highly expert guidance was required. Any scars on the sculpture's surface were abraded out with coral. The time required for positioning and raising the statue on the *ahu* was variable, but took double the transport time, perhaps as much as twenty to thirty days. No *pukao* were worn by the statues at Ahu Akivi.

In the cases of Paro and the Hanga Te Tenga statue, we can increase the transport task investment by a factor of 6.5 but balance it, to a certain extent, by the fact that the distances travelled from quarry to both *ahu* were less than half of that to Ahu Akivi. The question of raising the cylindrical *pukao* has not yet been addressed in this study, but we currently postulate that they were raised, one end at a time, on a scaffold of increasing height. A team of about ten men using levers and the guidance of experts would have been required.[23]

The Price They Paid

On Easter Island, it seems clear that 'individualised' work parties formed of combined, co-resident family groups or cooperating extended family units, directed by expert craftspeople and functioning in the short-term, achieved wide success in attaining the 12.05 m ton island norm. Further, approximately 10% of the time these discrete units were able to exceed the norm to, in two cases only, a maximum of 81 tons. If we consider the sheer numerical magnitude of the island-wide accomplishment, as well as the morphometric and iconographic qualities of the statues, we are faced with the realisation that all of this 'individualised' effort had a single motivating esoteric idea. Further, the attributes which defined the *moai* as premier symbol of that idea were highly controlled, implying strong ideological directive.

If we assume that transport and use of multi-ton stones, in both architecture and sculpture, are the palpable evidence of the exercise of authority in socially stratified populations, we see that the individual Rapa Nui chiefdom functioned best when it didn't require people to move stones which weighed appreciably more than 12.05 m tons. We also see that chiefly authority could occasionally succeed in requiring people to move stones which weighed 59 to 81 m tons. In those few cases, the food resources were made available through the political leadership of the commissioning chief, and the numbers of people involved at all levels in such tasks would have increased proportionately. How were these people pressed into service? There are two possibilities. One is coercion and the other is implied gain. I favour implied gain (security and sustenance) based on the non-hereditary affiliation of large numbers of people with specific, successful chiefs. That means that in some cases people were living on lands not hereditarily their own, under the protection of chiefs to whom they then paid tribute in the form of labour. Such a situation where land control was in the hands of chiefs rather than descent groups, is a first step toward class distinctions more fully articulated in places such as Tonga and Hawaii.

The cumulative data describing the Polynesian cultural fabric imply subtle threads of underlying factors and persistent sequential temporal trends. That sequence increasingly appears to be one of strong, internal order and slow, conservative change evolving through intensified competition towards more rapid change and increasing fragmentation.[24] On Rapa Nui, that pattern is directly implied. We recognise that the local ecosystem, long regarded from the perspective of constraints present, also offered unique possibilities. Rano Raraku was an important natural resource for which a unique and socially defining purpose was created. The use and management of that resource was achieved through articulated social patterns, aspects of which are of great antiquity. The extraordinary chiefly leadership variously exerted to accomplish the ideological purposes for which Rano Raraku was exploited evolved and changed within the context of the island as a place of finite space and time.

But in the course of time, the motivating idea itself, the social order which gave birth to the idea, and the evolution of the society urged by the exercise of chiefly authority in the name of the idea, initiated a downward spiral of natural resource availability which is clearly and unequivocably visible in the cumulative record, although the exact time frame and the pulsating flow of change/recovery cycles are not yet defined. There is no question that the extent of damage done to the island's natural resources was profound. From the point of view of human exploitation and degradation of the ecosystem and extinction of bird species, and partially because they lived in a marginal environment on a geographically isolated island, the Rapa Nui are at the extreme of the Polynesian spectrum. The price they paid for the way they chose to articulate their spiritual and political ideas was an island world which came to be, in many ways, but a shadow of its former natural self.

The proportionate impact of human and natural events and forces on the Rapa Nui environment is only partially understood. Humans transformed Pacific Island environments by introducing new biota, depleting or exterminating bird species and clearing land by burning and cutting trees. Selective overuse changed plant communities. Inland soil erosion and coastal deposition depleted or filled water resources. Nature, however, also took its toll through drought, cyclones and long-term regional climatic change. Understanding the interactive nature of environmental change on Rapa Nui is a crucial factor in interpreting the archaeological record. For example, burning vegetation clearly had a negative impact on the land but also encouraged nutrient recycling. Deforestation on Rapa Nui is correctly presumed to have been largely the result of human activity, but disease and/or pests may also have been factors.

Perhaps most important, however, in terms of understanding that individual Rapa Nui chief at Ahu Akivi and the society of which he was a part, is how the Rapa Nui reacted to natural events, some of which they had brought upon themselves and from which there was no escape. For many years and based on only limited evidence, it has been written that the Rapa Nui response to natural disaster was concomitant social disaster. In other words death, destruction, cannibalism, warfare and social dislocation. My reading of the statue evidence, the contextual archaeological record and ecological data, the temporal evidence of Ahu Akivi and elsewhere and the ethnographies, suggests to me that this conclusion is not, on present evidence, wholly valid. This is not to deny the presence of any or all of the incarnations which human aggression might take in a desperate world. Rather it is a plea for a more rigorous examination of the evidence on all fronts and an abandonment of oversimplified interpretations and generalisations about an entire culture which are no longer defensible.

Out of 'decadence' or cultural 'devolution' came unmistakable attempts at restructure, times of reinvention and innovation on established ideological and political themes. While those themes, by their very archaic nature, remained limited, what flexibility they did possess was activated and exploited in an effort to find a way out of the crisis. The (from our perspective of time and place) short-sighted aim of those efforts however, did not change, but remained the retention of power by hereditarily dominant political units.

Epilogue

A distinction has been made between the cognised or perceived environment and the real or operational environment to describe ways in which prehistoric island populations interacted with their circumscribed ecosystems.[1] The cognised environment of the founding Rapa Nui is not known and probably cannot be fully reconstructed, although aspects of it may be hypothesised within the Ancestral Polynesian construct and known East Polynesian context. The operational environment of Rapa Nui is increasingly better understood, and includes limited dry land floral and faunal resources, fluctuating population densities, natural events and competitive/cooperative human behaviour patterns. Island communities in general are intensely anthropocentric attempts to occupy and fully exploit simplified and limited ecosystems with short food chains.

On each island at settlement, ecological conditions were a given.[2] The traditional land use systems each group of voyagers/settlers transferred, innovated and employed were just as profoundly a part of their cultural baggage as were their religious beliefs. Scholars have noted certain baselines of diversity, variability and conformity throughout the Pacific in all aspects of art, material culture, subsistence systems and cultural norms. This does not imply that a fully homogeneous social system was laid down like an archaeological grid over the entire island-patterned sea, but instead suggests the evolution of a modulated set of variations on established themes. The settlement of the Pacific islands was accomplished largely at the expense of discrete ecosystems. On tiny Tikopia alone, it has been estimated that prehistoric settlers moved one million m[3] of soil.[3]

It has been suggested that there is a positive correlation in some parts of the Pacific between the intensity of land use and the intensity of craft production. In the Western Pacific in particular, the movement of craft products through exchange and trade is intimately connected with the redistribution of land, food and thus with status. This interactive relationship between ecology, production and the social needs met by exchange appears also to be present on Rapa Nui. Statue production was an innovated cultural response that grew out of established social patterns, ancient food production systems which were introduced at settlement and the limited opportunities offered by island resources. Some of the major adaptive accomplishments of Rapa Nui prehistory unfolded during about 1,000 years between the establishment of the land use system and the beginning of an ecological crisis sufficiently serious to require major cultural readjustment. This sort of pattern, if not typical, is greatly similar to that discernible on other islands. The years which followed on Rapa Nui, however, were also ones of creative social growth in an altered environment and, although progress has been made, we do not yet understand at all the full complexities of Rapa Nui relationships with either each other or their environment.

Neither can we yet draw a clear and sharp functional distinction between ideology and power or spirituality and religion. The complexities of Rapa Nui society are enormous, especially when considered within a paradigm of environmental change, religious coping and the success or failure of adaptive social response. Ronald A. Heifetz, Lecturer in Public Policy at the John F. Kennedy School of Government, has said that people fail to adapt for at least three reasons: first, they may not see, understand or fully grasp the significance of the threat before them, and therefore cannot see its ramifications; second, the challenge may simply be too great for the culture's adaptive capacity, something that cannot be known until all options have been tried and failed and third, the anxiety, pain or conflict involved may be too stressful.[4] From our perspective now as cultural outsiders, with the benefit of history and time on our sides, we can see where the Rapa Nui went wrong. But we can also see within the archaeological record evidence that changes were made to meet challenges when they were recognised and understood.

Scary Parables and Metaphors for Disaster

The ethnocentric projection of Western metaphor upon Rapa Nui history is fashionable today, and Rapa Nui has been cited often in a series of 'scary parables' and metaphors for disaster.[5] It has been called 'the island that self-destructed' and a metaphor for the behaviour of the human species on planet Earth. This assertion grows logically out of the Darwinian notion of islands as 'laboratories' for scientific study. It reflects the obvious and real ecological concern that all thinking people today share, but is also a profound denial of the 'fatal impact' of European intrusion into the Rapa Nui world. The seven-statue project at Ahu Akivi may have been completed just one to two hundred years or less before Roggeveen set foot on the island. Clearly, at least one *ariki* among many was still able to exercise leadership and marshal wood, staple foods and human resources sufficient to accomplish megalithic tasks within a distressed and depleted natural environment.

The metaphor for disaster, as I see it, is a projection of Western values which emphasises the self-destruction of the Rapa Nui culture over the actual, near-annihilation of it by contact with the West. Although the hard data of pollen diagrams, fossilised palm nuts, landsnail remnants and bird bones are mute testimony to environmental devastation, they are not enough to construct a paradigm of decline which ignores or denies the social restructuring and readjustment strategies of the Rapa Nui, some of which we have discussed in this book. Such a model of 'indigenous decadence', contrary to the still sporadically fashionable but equally wrongheaded 'noble savage' concept, is a sort of apocalyptic fatalism. It incorporates the dark Victorian certainty that man is unworthy of God, an idea implicit in the postcontact religious conversion of Pacific peoples.[6]

The interpretation of Rapa Nui cultural 'collapse' is traditionally symbolised by the fallen statues. We now know, however, that the destruction of the statues cannot all be attributed to a mighty wave of iconoclastic rebellion and resultant anarchy. Statue production is usually described as an 'industry', Rano Raraku a 'factory' and those who functioned in that 'industry' are seen only as operational links in production. The ideological realm of the artefact itself is made to be subordinate to the technological realm, a projection of Western values which fails utterly to consider the Polynesian world view and the functional differentiation of ideological objects. The intimate involvement of art with politics, which is assuredly present on Rapa Nui, cannot be understood if it is reduced to cliché.

To do so denies history the opportunity to see and understand the island's culture in terms of the unique yet familiar ways it behaved and evolved. It reinforces an extant and primary metaphor of 'primitive society' as a mirror in which we see ourselves, a dehumanising and ultimately elitist notion first put forward in the nineteenth century and today restated with a new arrogance. That is not to deny that some aspects of these scary parables are valid, nor to suggest that metaphors are without value as a learning strategy. I merely react to the demeaning of data which is implicit and suggest that, in their simplistic projection, such metaphors are ultimately yet another form of cultural collecting.

While collecting exotic objects was a preoccupation of antiquarians during the nineteenth century, the contemporary world seems to focus upon the collecting of entire cultural identities. It is no accident that 'ecotourism' and 'ecoindustries' have arisen in an era which also has seen dismal projections of environmental disaster in a context of urban conflict and moral uncertainty. Puritan notions of human worth are intimately and seductively interwoven in Western intellectual history with the idea of personal profit. Rapa Nui and other islands are especially hospitable sites for acting out such beliefs.

What is the real metaphor of islands? *The Tempest* is Shakespeare's great seafoam voyage of the mind, a free-floating metaphorical sail to a 'bare island' lying as a planet in oceanic space.[7] The stormy sea of life has stranded the playwright's metaphorical sailors and with them the powers, hopes and limitations of all humans. This universal myth demands that the reader use his or her own intellect to fill the sails of imagination and enter into the realm of self-discovery instead of merely 'collecting' and intellectualising 'primitive' peoples, places and histories. *The Tempest* teaches us the tragedy of an isolated and 'bare' inner human life, no matter where that life is led.

Who Owns the Rapa Nui Past?

Since the mid-1950s archaeology and tourism have been critical to the economy of Rapa Nui.[8] Out of the fine work of Katherine Routledge, Alfred Métraux and all those who were part of Thor Heyerdahl's Norwegian Archaeological

Expedition grew the dedicated efforts of many scholars, and the work being conducted on Rapa Nui today owes much to these pioneering investigators. Archaeology has enhanced Rapa Nui cultural pride, serving to support the Rapa Nui people intellectually as a new generation leads a renaissance of interest in their Polynesian past. Thanks to the popularity of the *Kon-Tiki* saga Rapa Nui became a tourist destination and a kind of 'archaeo-tourism' evolved.

Beginning in the 1980s, the cumulative impact of twenty years of scholarship and heightened cultural awareness allowed the Rapa Nui people to become less dependent on the *Kon-Tiki* myth as a means of attracting tourists. Recently and at a vulnerable juncture in their history, another outside influence of potentially great import was introduced. A multi-million dollar film being produced by American actor Kevin Costner will be called *Rapa Nui*, and promises to be a history of romance and adventure in the style of Romeo and Juliet. Directed by Americans, employing Australians and funded by English investors this can only be described as an 'eco-film'. It is an affectation of Hollywood that by descending on a tiny island with tons of equipment, hundreds of people and millions of dollars they will produce an 'honest' and 'real' film. Instead they are creating a fantasy which takes great liberties with history in the name of entertainment. The script repeats yet again the fictional battle between the Long Ears and Short Ears, and features 'walking *moai*' and icebergs inexplicably on the horizon. This film is a powerful tool for the distortion of the Rapa Nui past. Its impact on the aesthetics of the island is as yet unknown, but the potential for cultural destruction is profound.

Cosmopolitan, ambitious and well-aware of Western ways, most Rapa Nui people understood the value of the *Kon-Tiki* myth to their economy. In the same way, they have allowed this film to be made. The problem, of course, is that the world and the younger Rapa Nui will now see this beleaguered island's history through the distorted lens of Hollywood myth-making. Scholars who usually talk to each other for a long time before they talk to the public about their ideas, are faced with the challenge of raising their voices and lending the balance of reason to the power of cinematic fantasy.

The *moai* continue to be links with the past, as they always have, even though a strict continuity of purpose or intent is no longer present. They offer us the opportunity to view human activity both in terms of events surrounding construction of individual sites and in the broader processes of cultural change inspired by and reflected in those events. They are a constant reminder of the importance of site protection if scholars and the Rapa Nui together are to continue to learn. Recently a number of commercial and bureaucratic proposals have been made to the Rapa Nui people and Chilean government to restore various *ahu* and *moai*. The scientific validity of some of these projects is doubtful, and the danger that the island will be littered with ill-conceived and/or failed projects is great. Determining the direction of Rapa Nui archaeology from now until the end of this century is a challenging task, and a major concern is statue preservation. The complete cooperation of Rapa Nui leadership, national and international agencies and the entire concerned scientific community is required to set a course which will benefit both science and culture.

Rapa Nui rises upon the horizon of world history as both a puzzle and a revelation. The *moai* are artefacts which have transcended their primitive time frame and limited island realm to enter into the consciousness of contemporary life. In that process, they have become imbued with Western cultural beliefs and values, just as they were once filled with the prayers, power and spiritual *mana* of the ancient priests and chiefs who caused them to be created. They have been metaphorically moved about, like giant, clumsy chess pieces, upon the chequered board of cult archaeology and pseudoscience.

Today, as I write, some of the finest and most beautiful *moai* are rising again to stand upon the restored site of Ahu Tongariki (plate 30).[9] Though cast down, they refuse to remain still and silent. As objects of scholarship they are imperfectly understood, and a great deal more work remains to be done. As tokens of human energy in the name of ancient beliefs and as iconographic and emblematic symbols of ancient power relationships, the *moai* are dynamic objects of continuity with the Rapa Nui past. As echoes reverberating from the thunder and dust of falling stone, the voiceless *moai* remain palpable evidence of Rapa Nui cultural achievement, not failure.

Endnotes

A Note on Orthography

1 Krupa 1982, 43–119.
2 Hotus y Otros 1988; Paté *et al.* 1986; Englert 1978; Green 1988; Krupa 1982; Langdon and Tryon 1983.
3 Kirch 1990b, 51, n.5; Sahlins 1985, 1, n.1; Van Tilburg 1992a, xi; Graves 1993, 5, n.1.

Prologue

1 I penned a brief notice on the death of José Fati P. from cancer in 1989 (*Rapa Nui Journal*, Fall 1989, vol. 3, no. 3, p. 12).
2 Terrell 1989, 123.
3 Frazer 1963.

Chapter 1

1 Mrs. Scoresby Routledge, *The Mystery of Easter Island*, 1919, 6. *Mana* is a widely known Polynesian word which means 'supernatural power or efficacy, transferred from the deities to the chief by virtue of his descent' (Kirch 1984, 288). The Routledge (n.d.) papers are in the RGS archives. Additional important published works are Routledge 1917, 1920, 1921.
2 'The only place where I feel you could do something epoch-making is Easter Island – but I quite realize the difficulties ...' (Letter from T.A. Joyce, British Museum, to the Routledges, 1910; RGS Archives: K. Scoresby Routledge Correspondence, 1910–13).
3 From a review of the Routledges' book *With a Prehistoric People: The Akikuyu of British East Africa*, August 1910. Notes compiled for Mrs. C. Kelly, Royal Geographical Society, London. Copied and sent to Mr. John Lipscomb by former archivist Mrs. C. Kelly, 22 April 1991.
4 Letter to Dr. Merrily Stover, Department of Ethnography, British Museum from Pauline Adams, Librarian and Archivist, Somerville College, Oxford, 28 June 1990.
5 RGS Archives: K. Scoresby Routledge Correspondence, 1910–13.
6 Wheeler 1954; Ceram 1975; Daniel 1981; R.R. Marett advised Routledge on excavation methods and suggested she concentrate on the caves. B.G. Corney emphasised collecting *kohau rongorongo* (five letters from R.R. Marett to K. Scoresby Routledge, 31 May to 8 Dec. 1912, RGS Archives: K. Scoresby Routledge Correspondence; see 21 June 1912).
7 H.R. Mill, *The Record of the Royal Geographical Society, 1830–1930*, 1930, 226–31. The first meeting of the RGS in Lowther Lodge was 14 April 1913. Routledge's (n.d. [1925]) will provided for publication of her papers and subsequent placement with either the British Museum or Royal Anthropological Society.
8 In the 'halcyon spring of 1914', the mechanical novelties of the twentieth century were 'a matter of course'. 'Small and efficient expeditions' of exploring and mapping, such as the Mana Expedition, were encouraged by the RGS and facilitated by the wireless, the establishment of Greenwich meridian time and the ability to define longitude.
9 The RGS admitted women to membership on 15 January 1913 (Mill 1930, 182–6).
10 Some of this frustration found its way into her published work. About a gale (called *pampero*) off the coast of Brazil, she wrote that 'it has been made painfully clear to me that my presence on deck when things are bad is an added anxiety; this is humiliating, and will not, I trust, apply to the next generation of females' (Routledge 1919, 50). She also ruefully noted an English newspaper article in which the expedition was described as being composed of 'single-minded men of science' (ibid., 152). A note in the monthly journal of The Archaeological Institute of America, *Art and Archaeology* (August 1916, 125), by R.V.D. Magoffin describes the work of an 'English explorer, W. Scoresby Routledge' with no mention of Katherine's participation. Among the weekly editions of papers Katherine arranged to have waiting at their ports of call were two published by two different Women's Suffrage societies.
11 Letter to K. Scoresby Routledge from Miss Mabel Peacock (RGS Archives: K. Scoresby Routledge Correspondence, 1910–13). I have received dozens of similar letters following the airing of the BBC's *Easter Island: The Secrets and the Story*. Adapted in the US as 'The Mystery of Easter Island' by *NOVA*, WGBH, Boston.
12 Journal in the hand of K. Scoresby Routledge, 26 April to 31 August 1915 (RGS Archives: K. Scoresby Routledge Papers 4/1/2). By modern standards, the Routledges' excavation techniques are deplorable. Judged by the conflicting practices of the day, they are within the norm (Wheeler 1954, 11, 15, 17).
13 Wheeler 1954, 7.
14 'The night *Mana* crossed the Equator is unforgettable; the yacht, borne along by the newly caught trade wind, raced through the water with the very poetry of motion. The full moon made a silver pathway over the sea and lit up not only the foam from the vessel's bows, but also her white sails, which were faintly reflected in the dark sea; the masts and rigging stood out black against the deep blue sky, while over all was the Southern Cross. What has been said of sunset from shipboard is still more true of moonlight and starlight nights. Then ocean and sky become a whole of marvellous beauty, and of majesty beyond human ken; always suggesting questions, always refusing the answer' (Routledge 1919, 120; see also 118).
15 Palmer 1869, 1870a,b deals with the location of Hoa Hakananai'a and Moai Hava; for a complete discussion see Van Tilburg 1992a.
16 News of WWI had reached the island, prompting Lt. Ritchie's departure to return to duty.
17 Routledge 1919, 176.
18 In speaking of both the statues and the ruined *ahu*, Routledge (1919, xi) noted that it was 'not till after some six months' study could they even be seen with intelligent eyes'. This observation is supported by my own experience in the field.
19 McCoy 1976a, 14. McCoy described both *ahu* and *moai* as 'religious monuments', a designation since clarified, with 'statue' becoming a discrete category; see Dominguez 1968 for some statue details; Campbell 1974 for some *ahu*; see Mulloy 1961, 1968, 1970a, 1973, 1975b; Mulloy and Fiqueroa G.-H. 1978.
20 Information on the geology of Rapa Nui is drawn from Bandy 1937; Chubb 1933; Fisher 1958; González-Ferrán and Baker 1974; González-Ferrán 1987; Baker 1967; Bird 1988.
21 The survey first reported 391 statues in the Rano Raraku quarry zone (Cristino F. and Vargas C., 1980, 213; Cristino *et al.* 1981). In 1984 the count was increased to 394 (C. Cristino F., pers. comm.) and then again to 396 (Vargas C., 1988, 134); see Cristino *et al.* 1988. In 1993 I took the measurements of a statue head/face exposed accidentally by the American film crew then working on the island. Thus, 397 statues are known.
22 I worked from a list of statue site numbers which was then incomplete, published survey maps and McCoy n.d. [1968]. My recording forms were first used in 1982. They were revised twice (1983 and 1989).
23 Vargas 1988, 136–8; González *et al.* 1988.
24 Van Tilburg n.d. [1991], 1992a, 1993a.
25 Williams n.d. [1984]; Charola 1990 for comments on stone preservation.
26 Van Tilburg and Lee 1987.
27 Lee 1986, 1992.
28 Vargas C. *et al.* 1990, 14; Van Tilburg 1992a, 13; McCoy (pers. comm.) notes a trachyte statue in Quad. 4.
29 Three Rapa Nui informants with whom we worked shared the opinion that the statue may have been erected by the first Rapa Nui *vaqueros* who worked for the Williamson, Balfour Company on Poike in an effort to protect it. One was certain that it was erected after 1938 and was originally located on Ahu Moroki (Alberto Hotus C., pers. comm. 1991; Van Tilburg 1992a).
30 cf. Heyerdahl and Ferdon 1961; Heyerdahl 1975.

Chapter 2

1 Denning 1980; see Hooper 1985, 11 for note on European contact effects in Hawaii; see Peacock 1987 for Belau, Micronesia.
2 Hooper 1985, 10.

3 The accounts of Roggeveen's 'discovery' of Rapa Nui are found in the following principal sources: 'Brievin en pepieren van Batavia Concerneerende de West-indische Schepen den Arend en Thienhoven in Dato 30 November 1722' (V.O.C. No. 11.126), in the collection of the Koninklyke Biblioteek, The Hague. The material pertaining to Easter Island begins on 6 April 1722. These handwritten pages were copied from the original text in Java by several different clerks of the East India Company and sent to Holland. The original log and/or journal in Roggeveen's own hand has *never been found*, and therefore all Roggeveen quotes, wherever they appear, come from a secondary source. A printed version of the Koninklyke Biblioteek text was published in Middleburg in 1838, and is entitled *Dagverhall de Ontdekkings-Reis van Mr. Jacob Roggeveen*. This text was translated into English by Corney (1908) and Sharp (1970). C.F. Bouman's journal (really a log) was edited and published in Dutch by F.E. Mulert (1911). Another Dutch language volume entitled *Jacob Roggeveen En Zijn Reis Naar het Zuidland* was published by L.W. De Bree (1942) and includes illustrations from *Tweejaarige Reyze rondom de Wereld . . .*, a volume published anonymously in Dordrecht in 1728. It was somewhat widely available and may have been read by both George Forster and Captain Cook prior to their visit to the island. There is virtually no evidence that this volume was written by Roggeveen, and it may be the first truly pseudoscientific account published in a long line of such books inflicted upon Rapa Nui. Cook also may have read accounts by Dalrymple and Behrens, neither of whom he held in high esteem as dependable historians or observers, and Forster knew Roggeveen's material through Dalrymple but also had read a 1739 account in French called '*Histoire de l'Expédition de Trois Vaisseaux*' (Beaglehole 1969, 338, n. 2; Forster 1777, I, 557).

4 Sahlins 1985, 41; Mosko 1992 examines 'heroic history'.

5 Corney 1908; Gaceta de Lima 1771; Fillippi 1873; Routledge 1919 233–5; Mellén-Blanco 1986; Gana 1870.

6 Sahlins 1985, 60.

7 Mahine (Hitihiti) was also called 'Oediddee, Oedidee, O'Hedidee', and was a native of Bora Bora (Joppien and Smith 1985, 178, fig. 2.70). He was about 17–18 years old, and was taken on board the *Resolution* at Raiatea on 17 September 1773. He spent seven months aboard, travelling to Rapa Nui, New Zealand and Tahiti. Mahine and Cook's party traded Tahitian barkcloth with the Rapa Nui, who admired it greatly. Forster (1777, I, 581) reports that the beautifully carved wooden hand in the collection of the British Museum was given to Mahine who gave it to Forster, Sr. (Kaeppler 1978a, figs. 315, 316). Cook reported that a Rapa Nui man who boarded ship when it was anchored off Hanga Roa fathomed (measured) the length of the English ship, 'and as he counted the fathoms we observed that he called the Numbers by the same names as they do at Otahiti (Beaglehole 1969, 339). From this, it appears that communication between Mahine and the Rapa Nui was possible, justifying Cook's foresight in bringing him. Forster (1777, I, 601) quotes Mahine's opinion to the effect that 'the [Rapa Nui] people were good, but the island very bad'.

8 'As they passed along, they observed on a hill a number of people collected together, some of whom had spears in their hands; but, on being called to by their countrymen, they dispersed; except a few, amongst whom was one seemingly of some note. He was a stout well-made man, with a fine open countenance, his face was painted, his body punctured, and he wore a better Hahou, or cloak, than the rest. He saluted them as he came up, by stretching out his arms, with both hands clinched (*sic*), lifting them over his head, opening them wide, and then letting them fall gradually down to his sides. To this man, whom they understood to be the chief of the island, their other friend gave his white flag; and he gave it to another, who carried it before them the remainder of the day' (Cook 1777, 281; Beaglehole 1969, 341). Forster (1777, I, 588) says the Rapa Nui man was 'Ko Toheetai of Waihu', and that he didn't want the Englishmen to go on. He wore a 'cap' or 'diadem' of long, shining black feathers.

9 McCall (n.d., 1976, 1980) has convincingly demonstrated the intense and manipulative interest of the Rapa Nui in securing trade goods; see also Van Tilburg 1992a for overview.

10 Zuhmbohm 1868, 219, 1879, 279–80; Routledge 1919, 206; Métraux 1940, 44–5; McCall 1976, 67.

11 Métraux 1940, 44–5; Porteous 1981, 14.

12 Cameron 1987, 208; see also Porteous 1981, 6.

13 Métraux (1940, 45) characterises the work of the missionaries as successful; McCall (1976, n.d., 24) asserts that the Rapa Nui conversion to Catholicism may have been, in the beginning, nothing more than a cultural overlay. This is at least partially supported by Clark (1899, 144), who says that when he arrived aboard the *Sappho* in 1882 no trace was visible of the missionaries'

work and no religious ceremonies or observances were seen. Trotter (1974, 104, footnote) reports that Bellwood believes Mangaians 'may have professed conversion to the missionaries but still held to old customs in secret'.

14 Seaver (1988) suggests that placing fibre loincloths on Rapa Nui woodcarvings of the nude male figure may represent missionary influence. She also suggests that breaking off the penises of such carvings are post-missionary acts visited upon some figures which may be pre-missionary (Seaver pers. comm., 1990).

15 The original report of La Pérouse's expedition was published in Paris in 1797, in 3 vols. It contains reports by others including M. Bernizet, M. Rollin M.D. and M. de Langle. This was translated into English by Hamilton in 1799. The original French work was condensed into one volume by F. Valentin in 1838. The 14th edition of Valentin includes a supplement of notes describing the Rapa Nui from the journal of M. Rollin, ship's surgeon on the *Boussole*. The whole was translated and edited from the French by J.S. Gassner (1969).

16 Skjølsvold (1961c, 274) describes European trade items in Anakena cave (E-10), and Smith (1961b, 260) reports finding a 'small blue glass bead'. Roggeveen (in Sharp 1970, 91) tells of the two strands of blue beads given to the Rapa Nui man who paddled out in a tiny outrigger to meet and board one of the Dutch ships.

17 In the letters of Eugène Eyraud to the head of the Congrégation des Sacrés-Cœurs de Jésus et de Marie, Eyraud speaks of Torometi, his tormentor, who apparently lived in 'Apina Nui', ancestral lands of the Huki of Hau Moana Miru (Englert 1964; McCall n.d., 27). Uhi [yam] A Torometi is a place name in Quadrant 3, Hanga Roa.

18 I presume this connection between Torometi and HMS *Topaze* on the basis of Torometi's reported character and a watercolour/sketch done of him by J. Linton Palmer while Torometi was at church aboard the *Topaze* as it lay at anchor off the coast of Hanga Roa, 1868 (Van Tilburg 1992a, fig. 47).

19 The specific date of sale is '1.11.1869'. Torometi is also listed with two other individuals ('Kory, Cutano') as selling land in 'Hangapiko, Apina, Vai Kapua, Vinepu' (*sic*) to Dutrou-Bornier on '9.7. 1873' for '100 francs each' (Porteous 1981, 60, tbl. 1,3). See McCall n.d., 28.

20 Cooke 1899, 692. Someone named 'Kaitae', said by Thomson (1891) and Cooke (1899) to be about eighty years old and a descendant of the last king of Easter Island, is a mystery. Métraux (1940, 92) tried to identify him further in the 1930s, showing his photo to Rapa Nui of advanced years, but oddly, neither the man nor his name were known. Routledge had tried earlier to locate him with the same result. It is possible that 'Kaitae' was actually an incorrect spelling of Kaituoe, a name which appears in the Miru genealogies where it is associated with Christian Schmidt (Hotus *et al.* 1988, 234). Another man named Huki was 'remarkably well-informed regarding everything pertaining to the island' (Cooke 1899, 701); Englert 1974, 51.

21 Van Tilburg n.d. [1984]. A large *kavakava* figure collected by Admiral Byrd's (1935) Second Antarctic Expedition during its brief stopover on Rapa Nui was sent to me by Ms. Noreen Meager of New York in 1983 for my comment. A photo of the piece which I gave to J. T. Seaver Kurze was identified on the island as having been carved by Juan Tepano.

22 *Declaracion del Natural de Isla de Pascua y Cacique, Juan Tepano*, 7 August 1914 (Hotus *et al.* 1988, 319). Veriamo's second marriage was to 'Esteban Rano' (ibid., 127); see also McCall 1980, 93–4; Seaver (1988, 88) wrongly gives 'Juan Tepano Hito', reflecting an error in a typescript entitled *Genealogia Isla de Pascua 1886–1981*, Documentos de Trabajo No. 2 C.D. Universidad de Chile, Centro de Estudios, Isla de Pascua, E. Edwards n.d. (J.T. Seaver Kurze, pers. comm., 1992). A legend called 'The Floating Tree', about an old man named Rano living in the vicinity of Tongariki, was recorded by Métraux 1940, 376.

23 Tepano served in 'Regimiento No. 2 "Maipo" in Chile (Hotus *et al.* 1988, 302–3; see also Englert 1974, 52; Porteous 1981).

24 Porteous (1981, 72–3) gives Bishop Edwards' 1916 statement that the lepers, 'men and women, young and old . . . appear to be walking corpses, brutally mutilated'. Juan Tepano's sister was confined at that time to the colony with another ten to twelve individuals (*Declaracion de Matias Hotu*, Hotus *et al.* 1988, 305), and 'las viejas Eva y Catalina' appear to have been the most frequent bearers of alms to the colony (*Declaracion del Natural de la Isla de Pascua, Daniel Maria Teave Haukena*, ibid., 311). This Eva may be the Rapa Nui 'queen' baptised in 1882 and married to Atamu Te Kena (Englert 1947). Métraux (1940, 22) says that in 1934 there were twenty-two lepers on the island. He also incorrectly says the disease is endemic. Leprosy was introduced to Rapa Nui from Tahiti in 1888 and is not endemic (Englert 1964, 67, 78). Thus Pontius's (1969) 'neuropsychiatric view' of Rapa Nui *moai* style is not supportable.

25 Routledge 1919, 145.

26 ibid., 149.

27 *Declaracion de Matias Hotu*, Hotus *et al.* 1988, 308.

28 Kirch 1984, 7; Howard 1985, 41; Bellwood (1978, 117–22) discusses the value of Aitutaki (Cook Islands) oral traditions for archaeology, suggesting that validity depends upon each being, independently and in their own right, strong and reliable; Terrell 1986, 1–8 briefly discusses the legend of Hotu Matu'a; see Sahlins 1985 on the 'anthropology of history'.

29 These traditions are reported in Thomson 1891, 528–9; Routledge 1919, 280–2; Métraux 1940, 69–74; Englert 1970, 130–5, 1974, 96–7 for genealogy of Ororoina, given as 'Ororoine'. Métraux's analysis of this story includes the somewhat unreliable data of Vives Solar; see Murrill 1968, 66–8 for an analysis of this story relative to studies of human physical remains.

30 Routledge 1919, 280 calls the groups 'Hanau Epé' (Long Ears) and 'Hanau Momoku' (Short Ears).

31 See, for example, Heyerdahl 1952.

32 Englert 1978, 180, 201. Englert also follows Thomson in the use of 'raza' or race with no justification.

33 Smith 1961c; Vargas *et al.* 1990, 4–5.

34 Kirch 1984, 267; see Spriggs and Anderson (1993) regarding natural fires/forest clearance, carbon and human occupation of islands. These authors reassess radiocarbon dates, giving cal. AD240–660 for Poike (K-502). They argue against this date's utility for determining human presence on the island in that it lacks a clear cultural context.

35 Routledge 1919, 282.

36 Métraux 1940, 74.

37 Beaglehole and Beaglehole 1938, 379; Van Tilburg 1992a.

38 'Englert 1970, 129–35; Behrens in Corney 1908, 133; Roggeveen in ibid., 9. The man is described by Bouman (in Sharp 1970, 91, n.1) as 'a man well into his fifties, of the browns, with a goatee after the Turkish fashion, of very strong physique'. Upon landing the day after the Rapa Nui man departed the Dutch ship, the Dutch fired upon the Rapa Nui in fear, killing or wounding at least a dozen. Behrens (in Corney 1908, 134) says that 'among the slain lay the man who had been with us before, at which we were much grieved'. See n. 16, above.

39 See n. 16 above.

40 Borofsky 1987, 152; Wagner (1981, 11) says that 'as the anthropologist uses the notion of culture to control his [or her] field experiences, those experiences will, in turn, come to control his [or her] notion of culture. He [or she] invents "a culture" for people, and *they* invent "culture" for him [or her]'. Further, 'the study or representation of another culture is no more a mere "description" of the subject matter than a painting "describes" the thing it depicts'. The profound and unconscious, often symbolic, interaction between anthropologist and subject/informant makes an impact on the subjective in the 'invention of culture'. Apropos of this, Juan Tepano's son told E.N. Ferdon Jr. that his father and Métraux often disagreed. 'Métraux would ask Juan about some aspect of Easter Island culture and when [Juan] would try to explain it to Métraux he would often contradict him. Juan finally got fed up with it and kicked him out of the house' (E.N. Ferdon, Jr., pers. comm. 1993). The Rapa Nui people, always eager to please, often tend to tell outsiders just what they want to hear.

CHAPTER 3

1 'The canoe of Hotu-matua had landed also. When he landed, the child Tuu-ma-heke was born to Hotu-matua in the land [called] the Navel-of-the-land'. Métraux 1940, 65.

2 Kirch 1984, 67.

3 The Eastern Lapita subgroup is distinguished from the Western Lapita subgroup primarily on the basis of pottery design motifs. Eastern Lapita, isolated from the Western subgroup by the large water gap between Fiji and the New Hebrides, developed a distinctive repertoire of dentate-stamped and other designs on a wide range of vessel forms. Over time, designs were simplified, ending with the final pottery phase of Polynesian Plain Ware bowls. See Donovan 1973; Green 1979a,b, 1989a,b, 1993; Hunt 1988; Sharp 1988; Kirch 1984, 44–53 for overview.

4 Kirch 1987, 163; 1990c; see also Kirch and Hunt 1988; Green 1982, 1989a, b; 1991; Spriggs 1984; Gosden *et al.* 1989; Green and Anson 1991; Spriggs and Chippendale 1989; Terrell 1989.

5 Bellwood 1985, 102–29.

6 Green 1982; Spriggs 1984; Kirch and Hunt 1988; Gosden *et al.* 1989, 577.

7 Spriggs 1984.

8 Kirch 1984, 56; Green 1982, 16.

9 See Kirch 1984, 41–69 for a thorough discussion of the probable cultural attributes of Ancestral Polynesia, from which this brief description is drawn.

10 Finney 1979; Finney *et al.* 1989; Kyselka 1987; Irwin 1989, 1990; Irwin *et al.* 1990. For South American settlement theory, see Heyerdahl 1952; for evaluations or critiques of this theory see Skinner 1958; Suggs 1960; Golson 1965; Lanning 1970, 175; Emory 1972; Kaeppler 1976a; McCoy 1979; Van Tilburg 1987b; for overview, Bellwood 1987; for voyaging models, Rolett 1993. Population experts suggest that 50–100 people per vessel were required to produce viable settlements. Finney (pers. comm. 1993) believes 25–50 people were sufficient. See also Finney 1993, n.d. [in press].

11 For a concise overview, see McKie 1991; Jones 1991; Bellwood 1985, 82–5; for a more technical report on Polynesian genetics see Hill and Serjeantson 1989. DNA testing in Fiji may determine at what point interbreeding between Polynesians and Melanesians may have taken place.

12 Jones 1991, 52.

13 Kirch 1986, 9. The discussion presented here depends partially on Kirch's synopsis. See also Kirch 1991b for brief review of Marquesan prehistory; Rolett 1993; Spriggs and Anderson (1993) examined available radiocarbon dates for East Polynesia and suggest a revised (later) chronology for the entire area, including the Marquesas Islands.

14 Green 1993; Rolett 1993.

15 See Spriggs and Anderson 1993.

16 Green 1993; Sinoto (1966) established a preliminary cultural sequence in the Marquesas Islands. It is this sequence which Kirch (1986) has reassessed on the basis of his reinterpretation of the archaeological evidence. See also Bellwood 1970; Spriggs and Anderson (1993) argue for later East Polynesian settlement.

17 Green 1993, 222.

18 Kirch 1984; Green 1988; Spriggs and Anderson (1993) assert that linguistic and archaeological data are not independent of one another and suggest a colonisation date for Rapa Nui 'towards the end of the 1st millennium AD'. Cristino (pers. comm. 1994) maintains that sites dating earlier than AD 800 on Rapa Nui are not known anywhere on the island and probably do not exist. Tahai dates may be interpreted at the more recent end of the suggested range. As elsewhere in East Polynesia, the earliest Rapa Nui dates may be lost due to natural forces or sampling error. The gap between linguistic and archaeological evidence is significant and requires more attention.

19 Métraux 1940, 55–6; Thomson 1891, 526–9.

20 According to Métraux (1940, 56–8, 61–2) every version of Hotu Matu'a's legend speaks of two canoes. Routledge's version says that two canoes (hulls?) called respectively *Oteka* and *Oua* were bound together, but 'as they came near the land the cord which united them was cut' (Métraux 1940, 62). In an Aitutaki folktale, two brothers sailed with their party aboard a single double-hulled canoe. When they arrived at Aitutaki, the hulls were separated and each brother landed on a different part of the island (Duff, Appendix 1 in Trotter 1974, 144). Finney (pers. comm. 1993) says that most Polynesian languages refer to double canoes in the plural.

21 Métraux 1940, 315 notes the presence of 'Atua-metua' or God-the-parent in a Rapa Nui creation chant, but urges that this name not be confused with Atu Motua (Father-lord or First-lord) of Mangareva. However, the First Parent or Great Parent reference of Hotu Matu'a, 'Atua-metua' and Atu Motua is obvious. A date of AD600–800 is currently suggested at Anakena (C. Cristino, pers. comm. 1992).

22 Métraux 1940, 56–8.

23 Trotter 1974, 83.

24 Bellwood 1979, 6; Rapa Nui was formed by the concentrated action of submarine volcanoes lying some 3,000 m below the surface of the Pacific. Easter Island, Sala y Gomez, San Feliz and San Ambrosio are widely spaced islands in a related chain associated with a defined 'Easter hot line'. The 'absolute ages of the volcanic structures ranges from 3 million years old to recent', and the islands are associated with the same 'hot spots' of volcanic activity which affect the Nazca Plate (González-Ferrán 1987, 39; Fisher 1958). The nature and extent of prehistoric seismic activity is thought to relate to some *ahu* wall variation and possibly to positions of fallen statues on *ahu*, though this has not yet been demonstrated (González-Ferrán, pers. comm. 1994).

25 McCoy 1979, 135; Cristino *et al.* 1981, 1. The figure cited in the text follows archaeological literature. Other sources consulted give other figures. For example, Castilla y Oliva (1987, 19) have 163.7 km² while González-Ferrán (1987, 42), in the same volume, gives 173 km². Terrell (1986, 14) says that the average Pacific Island is only 60 km²

26 Fuentes 1913; Métraux 1940; Skottsberg 1956; Kuschel 1953; Heiser 1974;

Flenley 1979; Etienne *et al.* 1982; Dransfield *et al.* 1984; Flenley and King 1984; Flenley *et al.* 1991. Fossil prints of palm trunks average 45 cm in diameter, suggesting the presence of more than one type of palm or that, if a single species existed, it may not have been *Jubaea chilensis* (G. Velasco, pers. comm. 1994).

27 Roggeveen in Corney 1908, 15.

28 J.P. Harrington and Fernando in Hudson *et al.* 1978, 27–31; McLendon and Lowy 1978, 308, fig. 4; Wallace 1978, 453, fig. 7.

29 Yen 1974.

30 Hather and Kirch 1991; Kirch *et al.* 1992; see Spriggs and Anderson 1993, 211 for comment on Mangaia and Cook Islands dates.

31 Campos and Peña 1973; Mataveri, at the base of Rano Kau, is associated with the Ao, the ascendent lineages in residence during the birdman rites. Its name is said to be 'place of the centipede', and a Rapa Nui man sketched by Captain Charles Bishop in 1795 bears some sort of six-legged, tailed creature (lizard, centipede or other insect?) as either a tattoo or painted design (Van Tilburg 1992a, 71). The lizard (*moko*) is an important historic Rapa Nui wood-carving form; see also Bierbach and Cain 1988. The Polynesian symbolism of the lizard is variable but often associated with death and the underworld as, for example, in Mangaia.

32 The Polynesians also widely introduced a species of land snail (Kirch *et al.* n.d. [in press]).

33 Ayres 1985; Odhner 1922; Di Salvo *et al.* 1988; Newman and Foster 1983; Osorio and Cantuarias 1989; Randall and Cea 1984; Rehder 1980; Santelices and Abbott 1988.

34 Santelices and Abbott 1988; Di Salvo *et al.* 1988.

35 D. Steadman, pers. comm. 1992; Schlatter 1987.

36 Ayres n.d.; see Kirch 1984 for brief overview; Green 1993 reviews methods for outlining sequential change over time; see Spriggs and Anderson 1993, who have drawn Easter Island radiocarbon dates into more question as a result of their analysis (see n. 18, this chapter). In general, more dates from non-*ahu* sites are needed.

37 This synopsis of birdlife is based on the work of D. Steadman and his Chilean colleagues, and is drawn from numerous conversations with Steadman.

38 A recent popular work erroneously reports a find of dog bones at Anakena (Bahn and Flenley 1992, 91).

39 The date for Tahai I used here (GaK-2866) is based on the assessment of W.S. Ayres. See also Ayres n.d., 1973; Mulloy and Figueroa 1978; Van Tilburg 1986a, 1992a, notes 18 and 36, this chapter. I am willing to accept this date and its implications as not inconsistent with other evidence. The frustrating problem for my own research is that the inability directly to date statues requires reliance on *ahu*-associated dates, which may not accurately reflect either the time of construction or the placement of statues. Each site must be fully studied as a discrete entity and then integrated into a reasonable projection for the corpus as a whole. In my own opinion, statue style information is a highly reliable indicator of general time frame. There is one re-erected statue of Puna Pau scoria and a total of three scoria heads in the Tahai area.

40 Population estimates were made by nearly all historic observers; for reliable archaeological estimates of population see McCoy 1976a, 1979; Stevenson 1984; Stevenson and Cristino F. 1986.

41 The east/west political division is based wholly on Routledge's (1919) data but accepted by Métraux (1940) and upheld in modified form by Hotus *et al.* 1988.

CHAPTER 4

1 The term 'cult' as used throughout is defined as a 'system of beliefs and ritual connected with the worship of a deity, a spirit or a group of deities or spirits' and is not taken to mean 'a religion regarded as unorthodox or spurious' (*Webster's Third New International Dictionary*, 1981).

2 Métraux 1940, 311–14; Makemake's birth in the sea may relate this god to Tangaroa.

3 Métraux 1940, 314, 320–3 for creation chant.

4 Buck (1934, 119) says that in Mangaia the priest was the *pi'a* or receptacle of the god; Handy 1943; Williamson 1924, 1933; Balfour 1917; Esen-Baur 1983; Barrow 1967, 191; Lee 1986, 1992.

5 Beaglehole and Beaglehole 1938, 308–9, 19, n. 3; Borofsky (1987) gives Mataaliki and discusses the antiquity of the legends associated with this god.

6 The data describing petroglyph counts and range of distribution cited here are drawn from Lee (1992); see also Geiseler 1883, Lavachery 1935, 1939; Klein 1988.

7 Routledge 1919, 261; she seems to have obtained this information from Wilkes (1845, 330) and did not actually witness this number of birds on Rapa Nui herself; see also McCoy 1978b, 193–214; Van Tilburg 1992a, 57. The time frame for Orongo rituals is hopelessly confused. Routledge (1919, 262) says that 'the coming of the tara inaugurates the deep-sea fishing season' and that, until that time, 'all fish living in twenty or thirty fathoms were considered poisonous'. Métraux (1940, 173) says that during July, August and September 'fishing was prohibited by a tapu and fish caught at that time were considered poisonous'. Tuna were considered to be forbidden all year round except in summer. He also says that small amulets of stone shaped like fish were charms for fishermen (ibid.).

8 Churchill 1912, 206; Routledge 1919, 262.

9 Harrison and Seki 1987, 310; Pennycuick 1987, 58; Croxall 1987; Churchward 1959, 519 says that a flock of seabirds resting on the surface of the sea have one or two others flying above on the lookout for fish. These birds are called 'manu-o-kaho' in the Tongan language. Polynesians recognised seasons marked by the rising of the Pleiades, and in Tikopia it is said that when the Pleiades rise 'the Ocean begins to bite'. Often, winds are coordinated with the appearance of the Pleiades in Polynesian lore (Hye-Kerdal 1955, 205).

10 Harrison and Seki 1987, 322.

11 Lee 1986, 273; 115, fig. 31; 191, fig. 71; 192, fig. 72; 272, fig. 101; ibid. 1992; see also Armstrong 1965.

12 Steadman 1989, 200 reports that habitat alteration through clearing of trees and the introduction of non-native plants, predation by humans and introduced mammals and diseases carried by non-native birds are the processes of extinction everywhere in Eastern Polynesia; Steadman and Kirch 1990; Steadman n.d. [in press]; McCoy 1978b; see also Johnson *et al.* 1970.

13 McCoy 1978b.

CHAPTER 5

1 The words cognatic and cognate are frequently used in anthropological and linguistic literature, and are increasingly used in art history. Objects or ideas which are closely related logically through certain specifiable factors are said to be cognate. They have the same or similar nature, qualities or elements through borrowing or ancestral origin.

2 Smith 1961b; Ayres 1973, 1988; Cristino F. and Vargas C. 1980; Cristino F. *et al.* 1981; McCoy 1973, 1976a, 1979; Vargas 1993. Description of settlement pattern from McCoy 1976a, 129–39. Comments on the change, consolidation and distribution of southeast coastal patterns from Stevenson 1986; site type totals and distribution in the survey to date from Vargas (pers. comm. 1992); Vargas 1993 gives subtotals within a specific study area.

3 McCoy 1976a, 23–6; Bernizet (in Hamilton 1799, 347) describes houses, gardens and settlements and says that the houses and 'morais' were connected by networks of paths which were 'solid and totally free from stones' and about 'a foot and a half' wide.

4 University of Chile survey data.

5 Many *taheta* are far too small for water storage, and may have been used for body painting or other ritual, especially those in proximity to *ahu* or on statues. The similarity of some stone bowls to Lapita pottery form was recognised by McCoy, Green (pers. comm.) and others and has been noted by Kirch (1984). Fully 71% of known water holes or wells and 81.8% of catchment basins are in the coastal zone of the defined University of Chile study area (Vargas 1993).

6 McCoy (1973, 1978a) recorded thirty-three ovens near Orongo; at Ahu O'Pepe at least ten are present and may have been used in *koro*-type rituals (Van Tilburg and Vargas C. n.d. [1988]).

7 Métraux 1940; McCoy 1973; Kirch 1984, 108; Green 1993.

8 Englert 1970, 49–50. Nuku Kehu is said to have built a house 160' long called Tupo Tu'u. Excavation of the house site said to be Hotu Matu'a's failed to establish its exact foundation extent, and it may have been both unfinished and never occupied; Skjølsvold 1961c.

9 Mellén-Blanco 1986, 183, 141, fig. 5.

10 Métraux 1940, 199, fig. 17. The illustration presents 'two small pillars' at the entrance to a *hare paenga*, at least one of which definitely appears to be a dorsal view of a *moai*. Métraux (ibid.) points out the carved doorposts of some Orongo houses in comparison. Such carvings marked important communal houses or high status buildings in much of Polynesia.

11 This is the contemporary Rapanui word we were given; Métraux 1940, 199 gives *paepae*.

12 Metraux 1940, 197.

13 Gassner 1969, 17; Métraux (1940, 196) quotes the description given by La Pérouse's engineer. A 'small piece of round stone pillar which supported side of door or small cave or stone shelter' is in the Rapa Nui artefacts collection of the Bernice P. Bishop Museum (n.d. Catalogue of Polynesian Collection of J.L. Young. Original typescript, Bernice P. Bishop Museum). It is a portion of a perfectly round, smooth, dark grey basalt post.

14 Métraux (1940, 197) says that the 'number of knots used in lashing should be odd, for fear of bad luck'.

15 ibid., 199 quoting George Forster; Routledge 1919, 216. Rollin (in Hamilton 1799) says 'mats', 'trifling utensils' and 'small wooden images' were inside the 'huts'. He also notes the presence of rats.

16 Routledge 1919, 201, 195, fig. 15c. The terms 'pillow' and 'phallic stone; female' are applied to a naturally rounded cobble into which *komari* have been incised (Métraux 1940, 258, fig. 42e,f calls it a 'good luck object'). This object (B4454), in the collection of the Bernice P. Bishop Museum is from the J.L. Young collection. Young's catalogue entry describes this stone as 'Maea Momoa: Phallic stones carved with conventional figures of the vulva feminai used in the ceremony of the Hakatoro Repe ...''. See also Young (1904), where he discusses 'phallic stones' as 'Maea momoa' or 'Maea hika', and says that the old Rapa Nui men in Tahiti maintained that the stones were part of 'Hakatoro repe' or rites centred on the elongation of the clitoris. His description of similar rites in other islands suggests that Rapa Nui artefacts usually described as 'sinkers' may also have been part of such rites; see Hanson 1982 on female genitalia and *tapu* removal.

17 Kirch 1985, 79, fig. 52. There appears to be some question about whether this house 'looked the way it does in [Kirch's] illustration' (P.C. McCoy, pers. comm. 1993).

18 Métraux 1940, 201–2, 417; Ferdon 1981; Emory 1975, 172–3, fig. 146 and cover; Van Tilburg 1992a.

19 Kaeppler *et al.* 1993; Henry 1928, 426.

20 Egenter 1992.

21 Bellwood 1985, 151; Graves and Sweeney 1993.

22 Smith 1961a; Ayres n.d., 1973, 1988; McCoy 1976a; Stevenson 1984, 1986; Stevenson and Cristino F. 1986; Beardsley 1990. The first inventory of *ahu* was conducted by Thomson (1891) followed by Routledge (1919), who made the first classification of *ahu*; Englert (1974) broadened the descriptive survey. For comparative analysis in Society Islands see Garanger 1967; Green *et al.* 1967; Orliac 1984; Henry 1928; Descants 1990; for the Tuamotus see Emory 1934, 1947, 1975; Stimson 1933, with whom Emory frequently disagreed; for Hawaii see Emory 1928; Malo 1951; Buck 1964; Ellis 1969; Kamakau 1976; Kirch 1985, 1990a,b; Cox and Davenport 1988; Cleghorn 1988; Valeri 1985; Stokes 1991; for the Marquesas see Linton 1925; Handy 1927; Heyerdahl and Ferdon 1965; Skjølsvold 1965; Sinoto 1970, 1979; Kirch 1991b; for Cook Islands see Duff 1968.

23 Hooper (1981, 6–7) discusses the 'field of meanings' of *afu* and its cognates in Polynesia.

24 ibid.; Firth (1981, 53) is critical of this linguistic evidence for the conceptualization of Tikopian belief, although he concedes that a primal female, the archetype of women, was a 'lineage and clan goddess, oriented to food production and maintenance of health and welfare primarily for the group concerned but also .. for the prosperity of the community as a whole'; Rapa Nui legend says the female spirit Hina-popoia (Hina-the-heaped-up) was created by Makemake as Tiki from a heap of sand (*ahu-one*). Their offspring, Hina-kauhara or Hina, is a sexually ambiguous spirit which has the useful ability to transform herself from female to male. Hina is a widely known goddess connected with Tane or Tangaroa and the moon.

25 Duff (Appendix 1 in Trotter 1974, 143); Sahlins (1985, 6) says that 'creation, migration and parturition are so many versions of the same story'.

26 Hicks 1988, 141, fig. 147; Van Tilburg 1992a, 19.

27 Bellwood 1985, 151.

28 Sahlins 1985, 62–3.

29 Heyerdahl and Ferdon 1965; Bellwood 1970; Green 1993 for overview; McCoy (pers. comm. 1993) questions the commonly-held view that the distinctive slab masonry of Rapa Nui image *ahu* was a retaining wall in the earliest *ahu*. He believes that vertical (upright) slabs became, through the addition of chinking, platform facings designed to support increasing statue size.

30 Buck 1927; Trotter 1974; Bellwood 1978, 199.

31 Cook (1777, 294) described the wall of a coastal *ahu* (probably near Hanga Roa) as 'at the brink of the bank facing the sea, so that this face may be 10 or 12′ or more high, and the others may not be above 3 or 4. They are built, or rather faced, with hewn stones of a very large size ...'. He also notes that 'the

side walls are not perpendicular, but inclining a little inwards ...'. See n. 34, this chapter.

32 Routledge 1919, 230–1; boat symbolism is also seen in 'Miro-o-orne', 'earth ships' where Rapa Nui gathered during historic times to 'act the part of a European crew, one taking the lead and giving orders to the others' (ibid., 239). The participants, sometimes up to one hundred in number, wore garments of European sailors as 'stage props'. The focus of these activities was the 'gods', 'men who came from far away in ships'. Routledge says that the 'cult went back at least three generations' (to *c.*1844) and the early voyagers 'were therefore taken for deities in the same way Cook was at Hawaii'. The religious nature of these ceremonies is not really known.

33 Quarrying, shaping and fitting of stone blocks in Inca masonry is described by Protzen 1985, 161–82, 1986, 94–103 and V.R. Lee 1986, 49–85; Skinner 1955, 292–4.

34 In the hypothetical reconstruction of Ahu Tahiri at Vinapu, Mulloy (1961) suggests that six of the seven statues on the site were all standing at the same time, the end of the so-called Middle Period. He suggests that, at Vinapu 2 during the same time frame, nine statues of an extended size range were all erect at the same time. At Ahu Vai Uri, he placed four statues and a fragment of a very small torso erect on the restored *ahu*, again postulating a contemporaneous relationship. The evidence of Ahu Akahanga suggests that statues of slightly different heights might have stood erect at the same time on a single site, but the range of height variation at Vai Uri is so great as to give one doubts. Further, the shapes of the statues differ markedly, something which is also not usual. I think therefore, that the statue placement at Vai Uri may not be accurate and am doubtful that Mulloy's conjectural restoration is fully correct at Vinapu. At Ahu Akivi, restored to its second construction phase, contemporaneous placement of all seven statues on *ahu* is assuredly accurate.

In addition to Cook voyage documentation that statues on one *ahu* were standing while others on the same platform had fallen, de Langle (in Hamilton 1799, 331) says that 'in the course of the morning we visited seven different platforms, on which were statues, erect or reversed [fallen], and differing from each other only in their size, and the greater or less decay they had undergone from the duration of their exposure'. Size differences noted probably refer to the standing vs the fallen statues, but may also mean those standing relative to one another.

35 Stevenson 1986, 74–5; dates are from obsidian hydration analysis. Earlier dates are expected; see also Stevenson and Cristino F. 1986; Stevenson *et al.* 1988.

36 Reuse of statues and statue fragments takes many forms, including incorporation in architecture. Mutilation and damage of megalithic monuments is a common cultural practice wherever they occur (cf. Grove 1981).

37 Schaefer and Gorsuch 1993 find three dispositional styles of religious coping: self-directing (active individual/passive god), deferring (passive individual/active god) and collaborative. These vary with situational variables of loss, threat and challenge. All three are individual styles, but may also be social styles. When perception of stress is highest there is a greater reliance on collaborative style coping (in which both god/gods and individuals/societies take active roles). I offer the suggestion that the prehistoric Rapa Nui religious coping style was probably variously all three, with the *moai* evidence of society-wide collaborative religious coping enacted on a lineage or multi-lineage political level.

38 Hodder 1984, 52.

39 Van Tilburg 1991; in Tikopia, 'a flat stone which receives religious veneration ... on the *marae* was regarded as the embodiment of a female deity', a variation of Hina (Hye-Kerdal 1955, 200); see n. 8, Chapter Seven, this volume.

40 Joppien and Smith 1985.

41 Beaglehole 1969, 34. Behrens (in Corney 1908, 136) says the Rapa Nui 'relied in case of need on their gods or idols which stand erected all along the sea shore in great numbers, before which they fall down and invoke them'. A reference to possible ritual behaviour was made by Roggeveen (in Corney 1908, 150) as he observed from offshore. He says he saw some Rapa Nui 'squatting on their heels with heads bowed down, they bring the palms of their hands together and alternately raise and lower them'. Forster (1777, I, 553) suggested that 'the fires which the Dutch interpret as sacrifices, were only made use of by the natives to dress their meals; and though the Spanish suspected them to be a kind of superstition, they were, perhaps, equally mistaken, because the scarcity of fuel obliged the inhabitants to be careful of it, and to prevent their provisions being uncovered after they had once been put under ground with heated stones'. Cook (1777, 280, 292) reports that 'we frequently saw ten, or a dozen, or more such fires in one place, and most commonly in the mornings and evenings'. The Spanish recorded the impression that the Rapa Nui did not want them to walk near the statues or *ahu*, and 'could not bear to see us smoke cigars ... I asked one of them the reason, and he made signs that the smoke went upwards' (Don Juan Herve [in Corney 1908, 126]). Various *tapu* associated with ceremonial sites, especially when mortuary rites were practised, are widely reported throughout Polynesia. The prohibition on smoke may relate to a *tapu* on cooking, and there may be a link between the smoke from the Spanish cigars and the smoke from a functioning crematorium. Finally, the use of smoke and fire to discourage or drive off evil spirits is common in Polynesia (Handy 1927, 51–2).

42 Corney (1908); Mellén-Blanco 1986; Routledge (1919) utilised accounts from the *Gaceta de Lima* (1771) and Fillippi's (1873) monograph in her summary of the data, translated for her from the Spanish by Corney (Van Tilburg 1992a).

43 Luomala (1986, 16) says that, in Mangareva, 'parents and guardians groomed their favorite children for the beauty show of girls and boys, always a part of any festival. The children were cooped up in dark caves to protect their complexions from the sun, and stuffed with fattening food'.

44 Métraux 1940, 343–50.

CHAPTER 6

1 Earle 1991, 3; Green (1993, 226–7) suggests three criteria in the analysis of chiefdoms: scale of integration, centrality of decision-making and degree of stratification. Earle (ibid.) cites Renfrew to say that chiefdoms are either group-oriented or individualising, with group definition dependent upon corporate labour constructions. Individualising chiefdoms distinguish elites by status defining objects, housing and burials. The problem with the group oriented vs individualising dichotomy is that it is not always clear cut. Status distinctions are made in nearly all cultures (including Rapa Nui, although elaboration of objects, structures, etc. varied, was resource dependent and not, in late times, always marked), but not all cultures evolve corporate labour projects which develop into megalithic complexes on the scale of Rapa Nui.

2 Routledge 1919; Métraux 1940, 119–28.

3 Kirch 1984, 31.

4 Sahlins 1985, 44.

5 Behrens (in Corney 1908, 136) saw men he took to be priests who had their heads 'wholly shaved and hairless', an attribute of the *tangata manu*. In Mangaia Turi the Bald was the child of Tangaroa and Hina (Hye-Kerdal 1955, 217); see also n. 33, Chapter Nine, this volume.

6 Howard 1985, 41, 67.

7 Métraux 1940, 90, 135–6.

8 ibid., 90–1, 136–7; *tohunga* is the East Polynesian form.

9 ibid.

10 Kirch 1991b, 127.

11 Goldman 1970; Sahlins 1958; Kirch 1984, 34–7; Green 1993; Graves and Sweeney 1993; Mosko 1992.

12 Kirch 1991b, 14; Kirch suggests that the scale of integration in Marquesas Islands parallels that of Mangareva, Mangaia, 'Uvea and Rapa Nui, especially in the role of the warriors relative to chiefs in battle and the 'eclipse' of chiefly power by priests. Environmental degradation and destruction of the means of production is thought to result from an involuted cycle of prestige rivalry.

13 Marae Orongo (MAN.29) in the Keia district, Mangaia (Cook Islands) is said to be 'perhaps the most celebrated [*marae*] in the Cook Islands' (Bellwood 1978, 159). An 'altar' on this *marae* was said to be used for human sacrifice. See also Buck (1934, 112–24) and Duff (in Trotter 1974, 122), who says that Orongo (on the west side of the island) was built by 'dark haired people', succeeding 'red haired people' who built 'Marae Iva Nui on the east side of the Island'. A folktale from Rarotonga recorded by Roger Duff (in Trotter 1974, Appendix 1, 141–2) says that a sacred garment called '*Tia-tua* (*Tiputa*)' and worn by the god Tonga'iti had protective powers.

14 Buck 1934, 112–24; see also Van Tilburg 1992a.

15 Buck 1934.

16 Earle 1991, 9.

17 Rappaport 1979a, 18; see also Barth 1987, 59.

18 Rappaport 1979a, 20–3.

CHAPTER 7

1 Minnis 1985, 17

2 Butzer 1982, 288–94.

3 Kirch 1980a, 122–3, 1980b.

4 Ayres 1985, 1988; D. Steadman, pers. comm. 1993.

5 Rappaport 1971.

6 Firth 1959, 88.

7 Métraux 1940, 51–2.

8 ibid.; Routledge 1919, 235; in Tikopia a flat rock called Matariki and associated with the appearance of the Pleiades serves as an obstacle in ritual spear or dart throwing games on the sacred *marae*. Fertility and sacrificial rites are associated in much of Polynesia with the death/rebirth of some gods and with nature, and the Pleiades often are the sign to begin ritual or calendric cycles.

9 W. Kyselka, pers. comm. 1993.

10 Mulloy 1973, 1975a; González 1984; Ferdon 1988; Lee and Liller 1987, 1988; Liller 1990; see also Luomala 1971.

11 Gill *et al.* n.d. [1983]; see also Murrill 1965, 1968.

12 Hodder (1984, 52) citing others.

13 Van Tilburg 1986b describes a circular, stone-paved mound with associated *pukao* recarved as a basin. We found this at Vai Mata in 1984, and José Fati maintained it was a *hare oka*. We reported it to Claudio Cristino, who later excavated it and found an extended burial (late 1600s). Associating a *pukao* and a *moai* head with a burial is also known at Ahu Tongariki (A.G. Drusini, pers. comm. 1993). Routledge (n.d.) says that a statue head was used to mark a child's grave at 'Vai Hee' (Vaihu). Three sketches in her files are enfolded in a single wrapper marked 'to be redrawn' and show a statue head standing erect on a paved surface. The head depicted has a pecked circle on the left side of the face and stands today on the exterior slope of Rano Raraku. It is obviously not the statue which stood at Vaihu.

14 Cook 1777; Forster 1777; Roggeveen (in Corney 1908); Behrens (in Corney 1908). Descriptions of men's hair are interesting in the light of suggestions made that *pukao* represented hair styles. '... the hair chestnut coloured and limp, some have it black, and others tending to red or a cinnamon tint' (Don Francisco Antonio de Aguera y Infanzon in Corney 1908, 96); 'the hair of their heads, and the beards of some of them, were short, although others wore it long, and hanging down the back, or plaited and coiled on the top of the head in a tress' (Roggeveen in Corney 1908, 15); 'smooth hair and short beards' (Don Juan Herve in Corney 1908, 136); Behrens (in Corney 1908, 136) appears to have seen men 'having the head wholly shaven and hairless' whom he took to be priests, but they may have been birdmen; see Van Tilburg 1992a, n. 38.

15 Belcher n.d. [1825–7].

16 Roe 1967, 40–1.

17 D. Owsley, pers. comm. 1992; a few characteristics described as genetically Amerindian were detected by Gill and his colleagues in the late Rapa Nui skeletal sample as early as the 1980s, raising some unanswered questions. The practice of cremation destroyed early skeletal evidence, and that collected rarely has a clear archaeological context.

18 Belcher n.d. [1825–7]; Van Tilburg 1992a, 94, n.7.

19 D. Owsley, pers. comm. 1992; Owsley *et al.* 1985a, b.

20 Métraux 1940, 165–8, figs. 3,4,5; Newton 1988, 14–23; Métraux (1940, 413–4, 168) also suggested that the *mata'a* appeared as a *rongorongo* symbol. Routledge (1919, 223–4, fig. 92) gives descriptive names of *mata'a* shapes. She also notes caches of spearpoints and says 'the art of making' *mata'a* was then 'practically extinct', with only one of her informants still able to work obsidian; the employment of at least some of the collected *mata'a* in sham battles (on or associated with *ahu*) rather than in actual warfare is at least possible. In many parts of Polynesia spear throwing games and sports evolved from dart throwing. These activities were frequently held on *marae*, and their purposes varied.

21 Métraux 1940, 282, fig. 50; see also Van Tilburg 1992a, 166, fig. 28. This object (B2195) was acquired in 1920 as part of the Rev. William H. Cox collection. Rev. Cox apparently lived some 18 years in Melanesia, and his collection is dominated by Melanesian objects, casting some doubt on the origin of this piece. Métraux accepted its Rapa Nui provenance. Appropriate testing of the obsidian is the only method of confirming that this axe is, indeed, from Rapa Nui. Beardsley *et al.* 1991 confirm four sources for Rapa Nui obsidian (one of which is Motu Iti) and demonstrate that sourcing of this material is possible. C. Cristino F. (pers. comm. 1983) has speculated that the blade described here is from Moto Iti obsidian. In another situation, a spectacular and unique basalt adze long thought to have been from Rapa Nui may possibly be Tahitian (A.L. Kaeppler, pers. comm. 1992; see also Van Tilburg 1992a). See also Stevenson *et al.* 1988; McCoy 1976b.

22 Sanday 1986; comments on the nature and types of cannibalism made here are drawn from her research.

23 Kirch 1984, 277.

24 Routledge (1919, 221) notes the fluidity of movement over lineage and confederacy boundaries, although 'each person knows his [or her] own clan'.

CHAPTER 8

1 Green 1979a, 15, 1979b.

2 Kaeppler n.d. [1975], 1989.

3 ibid. 1989, 212.

4 Kirch 1987, 175, fig. 10.

5 Green 1979a, fig. I-2.

6 Golson 1971; Mead *et al.* 1973; Sharp 1988; Spriggs 1990; Green 1982, 16 points out that more than pottery defines Lapita sites, and says that the elements of the Lapita cultural complex derive from local, intrusive and innovative sources, assembled in Near Oceania between 3,500 and 3,200 years ago.

7 Green 1979a, 26–7.

8 Thomson 1891, 516; Routledge 1919, 214; Métraux 1940, 390; Barthel 1958.

9 Corney 1908; Gaceta de Lima 1771; Fillippi 1873; Routledge 1919, 233–5; Mellén-Blanco 1986; for the derivation of *rongorongo* from the Spanish experience see Routledge 1919, 202; Emory 1972; for a similar situation in Micronesia see McKnight 1961; Firth (1965, 267, fig. 8) illustrates marks of ownership on communal sago ovens in Tikopia which are unusual but of note in this context and related to kin groups.

10 Jacobs 1990, 160–2.

11 Barthel 1958, 1978.

12 Guy 1988, 321–4.

13 Kaeppler 1989, 217.

14 Métraux 1940, 390–1 quoting Routledge 1919, 245–6; competitive games, sports and contests were complex rites enacted on sacred sites everywhere in Polynesia. They were highly symbolic activities often associated with seasonal renewal or with mourning.

15 Lee 1986, 1992; Seaver 1988.

16 Spriggs 1990.

17 Newton 1988.

18 Spriggs 1990; single face designs include Figs. 18, 20, 26, 28; Fig. 18 is an example of a face and a 'mask'; Fig. 2 illustrates a seated, full human figure; Fig. 4 is a composite of full figure and 'mask'; Figs. 9 and 15 illustrate avian characteristics.

19 Teilhet 1979.

20 Millerstrom 1992.

21 These terms are from Kaeppler 1979b, 185, 1989.

22 Seaver 1988; Forment 1981, 1991.

23 Kaeppler (1980, 9–10) suggests a congruence of meaning between the human form and upturned crescents. It is her opinion that this symbol, called *hoaka* in Hawaii, was a stylised East Polynesian convention for 'the gods who were responsible for the important task of holding up the sky'.

24 Noted by Sergio Rapu H. at Ahu Naunau; the East Polynesian idea that First Man (Tane) was fashioned from red earth by the gods may account for the use of red body paint and the preference for red wood and stone in sculpture; Métraux 1940, 314.

25 Kaeppler 1979a, 89; Joppien and Smith 1985, 264; Seaver 1988; Attenborough 1990.

26 Thomson 1891, 537–8 gives the term 'Mata Kao-kao' for the red and white painted double-bladed *'ao* and 'Mata Kao' for an object which he describes as a 'skull oar' (USNM 129746). He gives the meaning of 'Matakao' to be 'Clitoris' (ibid., 548). Englert (1978, 193) says that *matakao* means 'remo' [oar, paddle], 'utero' [uterus, womb] and 'matriz' [main or principal and mother, as in mother tongue]. Further, he says that *kao* means 'costado; canto o borde; los labios menores de la vulva, las llamadas "ninfas"' (ibid., 165). In English, the meaning of *kao* is, therefore, 'side, flank, on the edge or border of; song, chant; female genitals'; *kaokao*, as in Motu Kaokao, describes a sharply perpendicular form (ibid., 165–6). In Rapanui *komari* means vulva, as *komar'i* does in Marquesan. In Mangareva however, *komari* refers to the spawn of certain fish (Langdon and Tryon 1983). The linguistic data suggest that, while the *rapa* were used by men during historic times, their symbolism was feminine/maternal and marine; see Bierbach and Cain 1988 on the meaning of *'ao*.

27 Kaeppler 1979b.

28 Artefact B4553 in the Bernice P. Bishop Museum collection of Rapa Nui artefacts. Called a 'fetish', it is from R.T. Aitken, Dominick Expedition, and entered the museum's collections in 1921. See also *1500 Jahre Kultur der Osterinsel*, 1989, 66, 251. The carving was photographed and lent to the exhibition organised by the Senckenbergischen Naturforschenden Gesellschaft in Frankfurt, which subsequently travelled to Brussels. The photo clearly shows that the foot had an attached cord which was missing when the artefact was returned to the Bishop Museum (Tony Han, pers. comm. 1992) and is not now present.

29 Kaeppler 1980.

30 Seaver 1988; 1993 for discussion of continuity in contemporary Rapa Nui woodcarving.

31 Hatcher 1974.

32 ibid., 9, 17.

33 This useful distinction between levels of meaning is drawn from Rappaport 1979a, 126–8.

CHAPTER 9

1 I have developed my interpretation of *moai* meaning over several years, expressing some of these ideas in Van Tilburg 1986a,b, 1987a,b, 1988, 1990, 1992a,b and Van Tilburg and Lee 1987. This discussion draws upon that material, but some of my ideas have evolved and, I hope, have been refined by new thinking and new information. The reader must realise that my interpretation, while I believe it is an informed one, is just that: my interpretation. New research will obviously shed new light on these ideas, requiring rethinking. Such is science. Such is life.

2 Van Tilburg 1992a.

3 Forster 1777, I, 600; Beaglehole 1969; in Tikopia upright stones on *marae* are said to be an 'embodiment' or 'confirmation' of the chief gods (Hye-Kerdal 1955, 200). Others were meant to commemorate victorious throws in ceremonial dart or spear throwing.

4 Thomson 1891. In Pickersgill's report to Cook (Beaglehole 1969, 340) it is said that the statues 'were erected to the memory of their chiefs; for they had all different Names and they allways call'd them Areekes which I understood to be King or Chief; and they did not seem to pay that respect to them, that I should think they would do to a Diety'.

5 González (in Corney 1908) confuses the word 'Moi' as describing an *ahu*. The term *moai* in all current Rapanui usage is clearly applied to the *ahu* statues, but also sometimes takes on the generic meaning of carving when applied to woodcarvings. Portable stone anthropomorphic carvings are called *moai ma'ea*. Barthel (1978) gives *mo aringa ora* or 'living face' for the *moai*, although the antiquity of the term is not known. He concedes that the etymology of the Rapanui word *moai* 'causes considerable difficulty' and suggests that it was 'based upon their function [to represent ancestors] and comes from '*mo ai*, which means for the progeny, for the descendants'.

6 Kaeppler 1980, 8. See also Kamakau 1976, 130–1, 146; Valeri 1985, 60, 271; Malo 1951, 178; Buck 1964, 522)

7 Métraux (1940, 90, 128) says that 'there is no evidence in literature or in modern traditions that the *ariki* title was held by tribes other than the Miru' and that the Miru 'reserved to themselves the title of *ariki* because the king was always a Miru'. In Pickersgill's report to Cook (Beaglehole 1969, 341; see n. 8, Chapter Two, this volume) we read that a chief of Vaihu on Marama lands of the Ko Tu'u (western confederacy) bore the Miru related title of *ariki*.

8 Cook 1777.

9 Handy 1927, 119; in New Zealand and Cook Islands Miru is 'goddess of Reinga or Hades'; on Mangaia Tane was the son of Miru.

10 Métraux 1940, 314.

11 ibid., 88–94; see especially the revisions and corrections of genealogical relationships on page 91. The direct historical value of genealogies on Rapa Nui is limited, and names of kings are frequently mixed with names of gods, titles, etc. While the record is certainly clouded, Métraux's corrections relative to Toko te Rangi are acceptable.

12 Handy 1927, 18.

13 Krupa 1982.

14 Van Tilburg 1986a.

15 Red scoria and coral eye components were retrieved from the vicinity of Ahu Naunau at Anakena during restoration work supervised by Sergio Rapu H., although no stratigraphic or other documentation has been published to date. These are now in the Museo Antropológico R.P. Sebastián Englert, Hanga Roa. Similar coral eye components were mistaken for bowl fragments by Mulloy (1961) during his work at Vinapu (Van Tilburg 1986b). The first published reference to the possibility that the statues had inlaid eyes was by Francis A. Allen in 1884 (Van Tilburg 1986b, 27, n. 9). The paucity of coral on Rapa Nui causes me to doubt that 269 (the number of *moai* on *ahu* to date) sets of coral eyes ever existed. Perhaps other materials were also used.

16 It is difficult now, because of erosion, to make out the exact form of Tukuturi's eyes. They are best seen in a (to my knowledge) previously unpublished photo taken just prior to the statue's excavation (Skjølsvold and Figueroa G-H 1989, unnumbered photo facing page 7). They are described in Skjølsvold (1961a). There is no question of their formal relationship to Makemake petroglyph eyes or to the eyes of the free-standing sculpture of Orongo (Monument 1). Ferdon (pers. comm. 1994) is certain that the Orongo sculpture lacked indented pupils when it was excavated in 1955.

17 Emory 1947, 66–8. The 'awakening of the gods' prayer, which follows the cyclical refurbishing (weeding) of the *marae*, was addressed either to Tane or a plurality of gods. It speaks of the canoe of Tane, Hiro and three stars, one of which was Te Toki, the craftsman's adze. Another Tuamotuan prayer for the consecration of the chief calls up the ancestral gods with the words: 'Let your eyes open in the world of light, Let your eyes open in the world of light!'. The literal opening of the *moai* eyes clearly took place on Rapa Nui. There is a linguistic connection between the eye (*mata*), the kin group (*mata*), the spear-point (*mata'a*) and the highest ranked warriors (*matatoa*) who stood on the right side (*mata'u*) of the chief (Van Tilburg 1986b).

18 Sahlins 1985, 18.

19 Emory 1947, 7.

20 When Routledge (1919, 187) showed the 'ring and girdle' design to some Rapa Nui, they told her it was completely new to them. The 'rainbow' interpretation was made by Leonardo Pakarati to members of the Norwegian Archaeological Expedition (Heyerdahl and Ferdon 1961).

21 The Samoan tattoo motif, which is considered to be of some antiquity, is called a tern (*ngogno*) or 'bent knee'. When used by women the design is termed *malu* and is an organizing motif for other, usually very simple patterns (cf. Buck 1930, 656–7, fig. 337g, 337p; Greiner 1927, pl. XXVI Ba); Jefferson 1956 illustrates Chatham Island dendroglyphs, 'stick figure' anthropomorphs which bear clear similarities to Rapa Nui Y-shaped and M-shaped motives. The Rapa Nui designs are related, in my opinion, to zig-zag and double zig-zag designs which are highly stylised human figures. These appear in minute geometrical and repetitious patterns on ceremonial paddles from Ra'ivavae (Haddon and Hornell 1975, 155, figs. 98a,b). Painted double zig-zags appear on the sails of the oldest documented Maori canoe (ibid., 209, fig. 140a).

22 The 'forked stick' has a role in canoe construction, fishing, bird netting, barkcloth manufacture, etc. in Polynesia. As a symbolic form, Y- shaped designs occur frequently in Polynesian art. The basic component is the chevron. Greiner (1927) notes the Y shape in Tongan barkcloth and tattoo, and in Marquesan depictions of the human form. See Kaeppler (1989, 215–6) for a review and critique of this work. A tattoo in the Cook Islands is called *manutahi* and is placed on a man's back at the spine. It consists of two parallel, vertical lines and branching, slanted lines on each side, forming a series of Y-shapes (Buck 1927, fig. 309). Y-shaped designs occur in Fijian barkcloth patterns, where they probably represented stylised human figures with upraised arms when vertical and stylised animal figures when horizontal (Kooijman 1972, figs. 413–7). In broader Oceania, comparable elements are found in southeast Solomon's tattoo designs (Ivens 1927, 84a). In Micronesia, an echo of the design is seen in canoe figureheads of the *manugutsig* type in Yap and the *faten* type in Truk (Haddon and Hornell 1975, fig. 238). Most interesting but further afield is the analysis of forked or Y-shaped posts in the megalithic culture of Assam (Hutton 1922, figs. 1,2). Areas in Oceania where fruitful iconographic comparisons might be made are those with an underlying Lapita presence, a point which Kaeppler (1976b, 198) has made with regard to dance.

23 Buck 1938, figs. 50, 60; Waite 1993; 'stick man' motives are widespread in Polynesia, frequently seen in Hawaiian and Marquesan rock art, and are also present in Tahiti. The simplicity of form of these 'stick figures' does not imply that they are primitive, formative or childish. Often the 'stick figure' is reduced to the 'short hand' of the zig-zag or double zig-zag, as in the Australs, New Zealand and Cook Islands.

24 Rivers 1920, 301; Churchill 1912, 201; Englert 1978, 233; Routledge n.d., 6.

25 Beaglehole and Beaglehole 1938, 403.

26 Cuming n.d. [1827–8]; Forster 1777, I, 584 presented some Rapa Nui working in *kumara* fields with 'a present of a small piece of Taheitee cloth, which they immediately wrapped about the head'. Contemporary Rapa Nui are adept at fashioning wreaths of plant leaves or vines to wear on their heads when in the sun.

27 Luomala 1986, 139; in Mangareva, where there was apparently no red pigment, *kura* was broadened from meaning red to refer to anything precious or special reserved for chiefs.

28 Luomala 1986.

29 Sahlins 1985 quotes lines more fully seen in Handy 1927, 22.

30 ibid.

31 Métraux 1940, 358; Forment 1983; Barthel 1958 describes female characteristics in stone sculpture.

32 Sahlins 1985; 'dualistic systems where the social community is divided into two exogamic halves reflect in mythical form the polarity of the world which, whether in cosmic or classifying antithesis, assigns each thing to its proper side' (Hye-Kerdal 1955, 205). In Tikopia a male/female, north/south division is sharply drawn. Although on Rapa Nui (as in Hawaii, Cook Islands and elsewhere) the emphasis is on the east/west division, the north coast possessed the hospitable and beautiful site of Anakena, home to the highest-ranked Miru. Anakena and Orongo at Rano Kau are in direct spatial opposition to one another.

33 Tukuturi was shown to Skjølsvold (1961a) by Rapa Nui as a statue which was different or unusual; it was subsequently excavated and reerected. A recent attempt to date the figure has not proved satisfactory (Skjølsvold and Figueroa 1989). My analysis of the cumulative stylistic data and the best of the available chronological data suggests that the statue may have been sculpted in the 1500s and very possibly 'some time around the arrival of the first Europeans' (Skjølsvold and Figueroa 1989, 27; Van Tilburg 1992a). The name Tukuturi (sometimes written Tuturi) was coined on the spot and refers directly to the kneeling posture. Perhaps worth noting is that Turi, a legendary Cook Islands ancestor, was brother to the mythical 'Tawhaki' (a variant of Tahaki), a Maori ancestor. In Mangaia Turi the Bald was the child of Tangaroa and Hina (see n. 5, Chapter Six, this volume).

34 Kaeppler *et al.* 1993.

35 Sahlins 1985, 17.

CHAPTER 10

1 Heizer 1966, 821–9.

2 For Egypt, see Dunham 1956, Tellefsen 1970, Flinders Petrie 1930, Isler 1976, 1987; for Stonehenge, ramparts, ditches and earthworks see Wheeler 1954, Atkinson 1956, Ashbee and Cornwall 1961; for overview see Heizer 1966, Erasmus 1965; for Tonga see McKern 1929; Ferdon 1987; for transport in general see Thorp and Williams 1991.

3 McKern 1929, 65.

4 Heyerdahl 1958, 149–50; 1989; Skjølsvold 1961a; Heyerdahl and Ferdon 1961; Mulloy 1970b; for critique of Mulloy (1970b) see Cotterell and Kamminga 1990; Bernizet (in Hamilton 1799, 352) says that 'with regard to the difficulty of transporting and erecting these large masses, without the assistance of machines, when we reflect, that, by the help of the arms, ropes, two levers, and three wooden levers, it is easy to transport and lift the most enormous blocks, this difficulty will totally disappear'.

5 Skjølsvold 1961a, 370–1; Ferdon 1987, 318 n. 39 says that the manpower estimate of 150–80 given by Skjølsvold and Heyerdahl in their published works does not coincide with his. He remembers between 75–100 men and women participating, an estimate much closer to our own figures in the computer transport experiments (E.N. Ferdon, Jr. pers. comm. 1993). Mulloy 1970b, 9 quotes Skjølsvold's numer of 150–80 islanders and does not contest it, saying that he observed the demonstration.

6 von Röder 1944–9, pl. 1, figs. 2–4.

7 Heyerdahl *et al.* 1989; Pavel 1990, 141–4. Both Routledge 1919 and Métraux 1940, 304 inquired among the Rapa Nui for transport descriptions but none were forthcoming. Métraux (ibid.) concluded that they were 'unable to explain the methods used by their ancestors for transporting the stone images.' Roussel was told that a chief with *mana* empowered the statues to walk, and Palmer heard (possibly from the missionaries) that the chief so named was Tu'u Ko Ihu. Zuhmbohm was told that the being responsible was Makemake. Métraux (ibid.) attributes one version of the 'walking *moai*' legend to Isidore Butayein in 1901, and *ivi atua* are said to be the ones responsible for repeating the charms required to move the statues. There is little doubt that all of the versions of this tale refer to ritual acts and spiritual power in the form of chiefly and priestly *mana*. Virtually none of the extant references can be shown to be of demonstrable antiquity and none deserve to be literally interpreted as technological explanations.

An upright transport method was advanced by Love (Rock Springs [Wyo.] Daily Rocket-Mirror, Wed., Dec. 16, 1987) which required tilting a poorly designed concrete statue replica on its base. Love claimed in the 1987 BBC documentary (see Chapter One, n. 11) that all statues were moved upright by tilting them on their bases and that this movement caused visible and serious damage to those bases. He also said that all of the statues in transport possessed such damage. Our descriptive data clearly refute this last assertion, a fact of which I informed him. He then wisely modified his transport method to incorporate a platform ('pods') of short logs, the whole then moving over rollers (Love 1990, 139–40). On the log platform twenty-five men were able to move the statue model forty-five metres in two minutes over flat terrain. The method is thus viable but slower than our proposed one metre per second for a horizontal statue. A sloped surface, misplaced rollers or any number of other miscalculations could, by Love's (ibid. 139) own admission 'cause disaster'.

8 Heizer 1966, 828.

9 Statue 13–477 was excavated at the base and head/face (Heyerdahl *et al.* 1989, 36–63). At a depth of '25–40 cm' an arrangement of stones was encountered which the excavators interpreted as a 'foundation' or 'plaform'. Thirty-eight stone *toki* were associated, as were four large stones standing on edge. A similar excavation of statue 13–504 did not reveal a 'platform' or 'foundation'. An uncalibrated ^{14}C date of 180–110 BP was obtained on a carbon sample 'found underneath one of the pavement stones behind statue 478' (ibid., 63 unnumbered footnote to the conclusion).

10 Hadden and Hornell 1975

11 ibid., 328.

12 Shiller and Gwo 1991.

13 Adam 1988 demonstrates a simple method of weight displacement.

14 Stature (height) is based upon the osteological data found in Murrill 1968; Robusticity (weight) is extrapolated from Garhammer 1980, Astrand and Rodahl 1970 and Eveleth and Tanner 1990; Owsley (pers. comm. 1992) believes that 58–62 kg is reasonable for our Rapa Nui 'reference man'; Gill (pers. comm.) suggests it may be a conservative figure.

15 The best reference for the calculation of power output and metabolic performance is Astrand and Rodahl 1970: see also Collins and Roberts 1988 on work capacity; Garhammer 1980 and Fleishman *et al.* 1961 for the domains and ramifications of physical strength. Our estimate of 1/3 horsepower is a conservative one and was suggested to us as reasonable by Robert Gregor, Dept. of Physiological Sciences, UCLA.

16 Lay 1959, 69.

17 Firth 1965, 42.

18 Lay 1959 provides a good analysis of dietary variables and requirements on precontact Polynesian high islands; see also Eveleth and Tanner 1990. The role of working women in rural environments when nutrition is marginally adequate is well discussed in the literature but not specifically with regard to Oceania. Rural women have a relatively high expenditure of energy (3–4 times the norm) and their diets are affected greatly by preferential treatment to men. In general, the pattern is that domestic and extra-household work energy requirements are seasonal but that, in those societies where male/female access to food is not the same female diets are inadequate nearly all of the time. There is a wealth of information available on malnutrition, reproduction, work output and energy needs in developing countries. A key outcome of female malnutrition is the birth of small babies, a rise in miscarried pregnancies and inadequate lactation. The relationship of gender to work and food availability thus had population ramifications on prehistoric Rapa Nui.

19 D. Steadman (pers. comm., 1993)

20 Firth 1965, 42.

21 Mulloy and Figueroa G.-H. 1978, 4–5; cal. [14]C dates are from Ayres (pers. comm. 1992, n.d.).

22 ibid., 30 noted the need for a frame to protect the statue when eleven men raised a *moai* during the restoration of Ahu Akivi in eighteen days. In all of the reported cases where statues were reerected using piles of stone in contact with the surface, scarring and other damage was and still is very evident.

23 Heizer 1966, 828.

24 Kirch *et al.* 1992; Rolett 1993 notes long term continuity in some aspects of material culture in both the Marquesas and Cook Islands. Data appear to favour a conservative pattern for some 1,000 years in discrete island societies, with changes in technology, food production systems and sociopolitical organisation ocurring late in prehistory. This continuum is evident in semantic and vernacular architecture and statue style innovation on Rapa Nui. Interisland trade contact, two-way voyaging and geographic isolation were determinant developmental factors throughout Polynesia. Isolation as one shaping force is assumed for Rapa Nui.

EPILOGUE

1 Rappaport 1979b, 5.

2 Gosden 1992

3 Kirch and Yen 1982

4 R.A. Heifetz n.d.

5 Young 1991; Trotta 1985; Bahn and Flenley (1992) call their book 'a message from the past for the future of our planet'.

6 'Apocalyptic fatalism' is a phrase used by Ferris 1992; Bahn and Flenley 1992, 213 use the Club of Rome computer model to interpret Rapa Nui prehistory. They suggest uninhibited growth after settlement until AD 1680, a population peak of 10,000 and then a crash (see also Kirch 1984). Such a model remains to be demonstrated. It is worth noting that this same Club of Rome model also predicted that all gold, silver, mercury and tin resources on the planet would be completely destroyed by the year 1990. The problem, of course, with all such predictive models is that too many purely human variables are not considered (Ferris 1992).

7 Kermode 1990.

8 Van Tilburg 1993b; some of the ideas expressed here were originally explored in a paper I presented at a 1992 Society for American Archaeology symposium entitled 'Who Owns the Past?' and chaired by H. Silverman.

9 A substantial international conflict between Chileans, Japanese, Americans and others concerned about the conduct of the Tongariki project can be traced in various newspapers including the New York *Times*, the London *Times* and Santiago's *El Mercurio* over the course of nearly two years.

Glossary

The Polynesian and other terms given here are written in the manner in which they are encountered in the literature cited, except that occasional hyphens between words are eliminated and repeated words are written as one single word. There is an inconsistency in the use of glottal stops, but this reflects the literature as a whole and no attempt has been made here to correct or to create conformity.

All words in this Glossary are Rapanui unless otherwise indicated. When the name of the island or island group in which the term is found is given it is shown in parentheses following the Polynesian word, and variant forms are noted. The goal is to aid the reader in understanding the material presented in this book.

afu (Tikopia). To heap or pile up, with many cognates throughout Polynesia. Possible linguistic link between the concept of piling or heaping up, procreation and a female deity.

ahu one Heap of sand.

ahu Ceremonial structure as a place of worship, composed of a limited range of architectural attributes creating variant forms. Based upon the Polynesian *marae* concept.

ahu moai As used here, monolithic, male anthropomorphic stone sculpture known to have been erected upon *ahu*. Elsewhere, image *ahu*.

ahu poepoe 'Canoe-shaped' burial cairn.

ana Cave.

ana kionga Refuge cave.

ao (Throughout Polynesia). Day.

'ao Authority, baton or staff of authority, reign of authority, individuals who embody authority.

areauti Lavish, seasonal display of food.

ariki Chief. Believed to have been a term reserved for the dominant kin group called Miru. Variants in Polynesia include *aliki*, *ari'i*, *'eiki*.

ariki mau Paramount chief of the island, drawn from the Honga lineage of the dominant Miru ramage.

ariki paka Aristocracy. Believed to have been a term reserved to the Miru.

atua (variant, *etua*). Widespread Polynesian term meaning god.

avanga Structure within which burials were placed.

eepe Corpulent.

'eho (Hawaii). Stone idol representing the god Lonokaeho.

eo Perfume, fragrance.

eketea (Mangareva). Forked stick image, sometimes with enhanced features in the form of legs.

etmoika Flat bone clappers used in mourning displays or ritual.

haka'iki (Marquesas Islands). Hereditary chief.

'haka paapa A class of *ariki* or high status individuals who cared for the personal needs of the *ariki mau*.

hakatoro repe Ritual elongation of the clitoris.

hami Literally, clothing. Man's loin cloth depicted on ventral side of *ahu moai* at the base.

hanau To be born.

hao Trenches in which *paenga* were placed to construct *hare paenga* foundations.

hare House.

hare moa Rectangular stone structure thought to serve as a chicken coop in late prehistory and protohistory.

hare nui Large *hare paenga* believed to have served special, ceremonial functions.

hare oka Round thatched house used as temporary shelter.

hare paenga Habitation structure of unique 'boat shape' thought to be associated with high social status and spatially related to *ahu*.

haro matatuu Ritual extension of the clitoris, according to Métraux.

hatunga Layer of thatch (of which there were three) in a *hare paenga*.

hau Hat, cord; *Triumfetta semitriloba*. Also *hauhau*.

heiau (Hawaii). Ceremonial site.

heriki Layer of grass on dirt floor of a *hare paenga*.

hiritoke Paved terrace in front of *hare paenga*.

hiva Literally, a foreign place.

hopu Literally, 'bath; to bathe, to cleanse'. See *hopu manu*.

hopu manu Individual who represented a chief during the annual rites of the birdman. See *hopu*.

hua'ai The household unit.

hurumanu Commoner or commoner level of society.

ika Fish. On some islands, sacrificial victim.

ivi atua Literally, 'bone/god'. Priest of the highest social grade.

ivi tika Ridgepoles of a *hare paenga*; also called *hahanga*, *pou*, or *tuu*.

kahi Tuna.

kahi aveave Yellowfin Tuna (*Thunnus albacares*).

kaikai String figures and associated chants.

kainga Traditional Polynesian land division.

kao Flank or side; female genitals; cloth or clothing.

karava Rock shelter.

kaukau Purlins and/or rafters of a *hare paenga*. Also called *kaukau miro*.

kaunga Ceremonial dance and the grounds on which the dance is held.

kava Salt or bitter; plant and drink produced from a plant (*Piper methysticum*) on some islands.

kavakava or **moai kavakava** Name applied to a particular form of Easter Island emaciated male anthropomorphic woodcarving.

keho Thin slabs of basalt used to construct Orongo houses and habitation terraces in Rano Kao.

keke (Tuamotus). Forked stick used as a tightening device for lashings.

kerekere The colour black.

ki'ea Red pigment made from mineralised tuff.

kikino (Marquesas Islands). Landless people, 'refugees.'

kio Social grade equated variously with 'farmer', 'slave'. Someone displaced from the land.

ko rapu Hole drilled in *paenga* to hold poles forming superstructure of *hare paenga*.

kohau rongorongo Inscribed boards or tablets.

komari Vulva or any depiction in art of a vulva. In Mangareva, spawn of certain fish.

kopeka Revenge or vengeance. Also *ati kopeka*.

koro A feast given in honour of an important individual.

koro hakaapo Song sung at feasts.

korohua Learned old ones, with *koroua* meaning old age.

koutu ariki (Cook Islands). Assembly court of ceremonial precinct.

*kupeti (Western Polynesia). Carved wooden design tablet for use in barkcloth manufacture.

kumura Sweet potato (*Ipomoea batatas*)

kura (Mangareva). The colour red; precious.

maea momoa Portable artefacts described as 'phallic stones'. Also called *maea hika*.

mahute Barkcloth. Called *tapa* elsewhere in Polynesia.

maito Favoured, edible herbivorous fish (*Acanthurus leucopareius*).

makohe Frigatebird (*Fregata minor*). Possible emblem of the dominant Miru ramage.

mako'i Tree (*Thespesia populnea*) and wood of the same tree.

malae Communal assembly ground.

mana Power or influence. Throughout Polynesia, supernatural power or efficacy.

manavai Circular stone shelter for banana, paper mulberry, and other plants possibly adapted from the form of Rano Kao in its function as cultigen 'nursery.' The main function was to trap and hold water but it also protected plants from the wind.

mangai kahi Stone fishhook used to catch tuna. Also *mangai ma'ea*.

manu Bird. In some parts of Polynesia, power.

manugutsig (Yap). Canoe figurehead.

manupiri Name applied to a carved motif of two birds or birdmen facing one another.

manutahi (Cook Islands). Y-shaped tattoo placed on man's spine.

manutara Sooty Tern (*Sterna fuscata*). Possible emblem of a god or of a class of priests.

maori Expert in a given profession.

maori hare Expert craftsman in house building.

maori tiki Name said to be given to a master carver.

marae (variants *malae, mala'e*). A sacred ceremonial space throughout Polynesia which is architecturally elaborated in East Polynesia.

marikuru Wood (*Sapindus saponaria*) used in house construction; white pigment.

maro Throughout much of Polynesia, man's loin cloth.

maro kura (Mangareva). Streamers which adorned the forked stick *eketea* images when they were placed on the *marae* in an upright position.

maru Feather garland attached to a staff and carried in procession before the *ariki mau*.

mata The eye, the face or visage, the kin group.

mata'a Flaked obsidian spearpoint.

mata'a rei pure rova Most common form of obsidian *mata'a*. Also called *mata'a arokiri*.

mata'eina'a (Marquesas Islands). Kin unit defined as 'tribe.'

matakeinanga (Mangaia). Group of kinspeople but not necessarily a tribe. In Rakahanga, a tribe.

matakio Inferior or defeated kin groups.

matatoa Warrior of high status.

mata'u Right side of man. Strong or valiant man.

matua hangai Adoptive parents.

mauku Grass. Bundled grass used in thatching *hare paenga*.

mea, meamea The colour red.

me'ae (Marquesas Islands). Sacred site, variation of *marae*.

moai Monolithic stone carvings in human form which constitute a particular class or category of sculpture; thought to derive from '*mo ai*, 'for the progeny, for the descendants'. See also *mo'i*.

moai ma'ea Portable stone anthropomorphic carvings.

moai pa'apa'a Anthropomorphic female wood carving.

moai tangata Anthropomorphic male woodcarving.

moenga Reed mat.

mo'i (Hawaii). A class of individuals which stood at the 'apex of a pyramid and sacred personages were at various steps, depending upon closeness of blood and social rank of their parents'. Also, image of a specific type. See *moai*.

mohai (Hawaii). Temple offering. See *moai*.

moko Carved wood lizard/man hybrid figure; lizard.

momoko Thin.

mono Hairstyle in which the hair is tied on top of the head as a 'topknot'.

nanue Favoured, edible herbivorous fish (*Kiphosus bigibbus*).

naunau Sandalwood (*Santalum*).

neru Specially groomed women displayed during ceremonies involving *kaunga* dancing.

ngongo (Samoa). Name given to a tattoo motif said to represent a tern. The same motif is also called *vae tuli* or 'bent knee'.

ngarua Stone artefact with incised designs called either a 'pillow' or a 'fetish.'

noa Void of *tapu*.

oka End rafters of *hare paenga*.

paenga Cut and dressed basalt blocks; also means family.

paepae Stone pavement attached to a house.

paina Ceremonial feast as well as the image erected as part of the ceremony.

paoa Warrior. Also called *toa*; weapon.

paoa kai tangata Warrior who is a cannibal.

papa (Manihiki, Rapahanga). Terrestrial realm. Elsewhere, earth or stone. In Cook Islands, a horizontal basalt slab associated with basalt pillar on sacred sites.

papare Door to *hare paenga*.

patu (New Zealand). Club or weapon of particular style.

pi'a (Mangaia). Literally, receptacle of the god. Also name of class of inspirational priests.

pini hare paenga Curved end portions of *hare paenga* foundations. Also called *paenga vari pini*.

pipi horeko Property line or *tapu* markers.

pito Navel.

piu Hachlings of the Sooty Tern.

po. Night.

poki manu Bird children. Children who have been secluded and pampered to achieve ritual status. Also called *poki take*.

poko uri' Literally, 'dark abyss'. Said to be the original name of Rano Kau crater.

ponoko Linguistic device which serves to veil or otherwise obscure meaning.

pora Bundled reed float.

poro Naturally round beach cobbles used in paving; also called *tau pea*.

pou (Mangareva). Class of experts.

pou Column, post or pillar. The star Sirius is known as *te pou* or *he pou*, the orientation point.

pou (Tahiti). Props, pillars or posts separating sky from earth.

pou (Tuamotus). Stone upright on ceremonial site.

pouahu (New Zealand). See *tuahu*.

pu Small stone-lined pits in which taro was grown; orifice.

pua Flower, in general; plant (*Curcuma longa*) from which reddish pigment is obtained.

pukao Crown. Name applied to red scoria cylinders on the heads of some *ahu moai*.

puna Reservoirs dug along the coast for water.

punga Coral abrader used to scour the surfaces of *moai*.

rahui Interdiction, prohibition; sacred and prohibited, *tapu*.

rangi (Manihiki, Rapahanga). Celestial realm. Sky.

rano Crater lake.

rapa Name applied to the smaller of two wooden dance paddle types.

rau toa Sugar cane leaves; also called *toa*.

rei miro Carved wood pectoral in crescent form.

renga (variants *lena*, *'olena*). Turmeric (*Curcuma longa*) or the colouring substance produced by the plant throughout much of Polynesia.

retu Tattoo design, in the form of a black triangle, representing women.

rogo To hear, to understand, to comprehend, to believe.

rogorogo (Mangareva). Chanters responsible for assisting in rituals conducted on *marae* and including *eketea* images.

rongorongo Chant and the class of chanters responsible for performance of recitations. Also frequently written *rongo rongo*.

sau (Rotuma). Sacred leader.

taheta Carved or uncarved stone basins.

tahonga Round or egg-shaped wood pendants.

tahuna o'ono (Marquesas). Experts who chanted at ceremonies, tribal bards.

tangata honui Important old men; possibly chiefs of non-*ariki* status.

tangata honui maori Important old men, possibly chiefs of non-*ariki* status, who were experts in a given field, including stone carving.

tangata manu Birdman or carved representation of a birdman.

tangata maori anga moai ma'ea Expert stone carvers.

tangata rongorongo 'Intellectuals'. Chanters, called *taura rongorongo* on Mangareva.

tangata taku Priest of lower grade.

tapu Throughout much of Polynesia, sacred and prohibited.

ta'ua (Cook Islands). Raised stone platform of ceremonial precinct.

tau'a (Marquesas Islands). Ceremonial priests of high status.

taura (Mangareva). Priests who conducted rituals which involved *eketea* forked stick wands and images. Sometimes written *tahura*.

taura Thread, cord, twine, strand.

taura renga The 'belt stained with turmeric' said to have been worn by Hoa Hakananai'a.

taura rongorongo (Mangareva). Experts who chanted at ceremonies; a class of intellectuals.

teatea White, pale; also arrogant, ostentatious.

te kainga The land.

tiki Master of a science or art. Throughout Central and Eastern Polynesia, both a god (Tiki) and a carved anthropomorphic image into which the god may be induced to enter (*tiki*, *ti'i*).

tiki moai According to one source, master sculptor.

timo Mourning, grief, sorrow.

tira (Manihiki, Rapahanga). Celestial realm. Widespread term for mast.

toa Warrior. Also called *paoa*; sugar cane leaves.

toga Post, column, prop. Also winter, and the south as a direction.

tohua (Marquesas Islands). Stone platform on cleared ceremonial grounds.

toki Stone adze.

toko- Throughout much of Polynesia, the human signifier.

toko (Mangaia). Forked stick erected upon *marae*; prop or support; chief who loyally supports the paramount chief.

toko mate (New Zealand). Negative, female power of death represented graphically by a post set in a mound.

toko ora (New Zealand). Male pole of life.

tokotoko Pole, stick, staff.

to'o (Marquesas). Props, pillars or posts separating sky from earth.

toromiro Tree (*Sophoro toromiro*) or wood of the same tree.

tuahu (New Zealand). Sacred site; also called *pouahu* or 'post-mound.'

tufunga Expert. Also *tahunga*, *tohunga*.

tuhuna o'ono (Marquesas). Experts who chanted at ceremonies, ceremonial priests.

tumu Defined exchange relationship between kin groups.

tupa Rectangular stone structure with attached conical 'tower.'

tuu To stand erect; mast, pillar, post. Also written *tu'u*.

tuura A class of *ariki* or high-status individuals who provided for the *ariki mau* by expert skills in farming, fishing, etc.

ua A chiefly stave carved at the apex with two opposing human faces, each the same as the other in attributes and proportions.

umu Traditional earth oven.

umu pae Earth oven delineated by stone patterns.

ura Rapa Nui lobster (*Panulirus pascuencis*).

ure Literally, penis. Lineage.

vaka tangata Expert fishermen.

vaka ure *Hare paenga* foundations. Literally, canoe/lineage.

vaka vaero Canoe owned by *ariki mau*.

whare wananga (New Zealand). Maori schools of learning.

Bibliography

ADAM, J.-P. 1988. *Le passé recomposé: Chroniques d'archéologie fantasque*. Paris, Éditions Du Seuil

ALEXANDER, R. P. 1981a. *Project Orongo*. Bulletin no. 29, 3 August
- 1981b. *Project Orongo*. Bulletin no. 34, 9 November

ALLEN, F. A. 1884. *Polynesian Antiquities*. Congrès International d'Américanistes, Compte Rendu de la Cinquième Session, Copenhagen, 1883, 246–57

ALPERS, A. 1987. *The World of the Polynesians*. London, Oxford University Press

ANON. [1728]. *Tweejaarige Reyze Rondom de Wereld ...* Dordrecht, Johannes Van Braam

ANON. [Powell, W. A.] 1869. 'Easter Island.' London, *The Times*, 21 January

ANON. 1870. 'Die steinbilder auf der Osterinsel.' *Globus*, 17, 248–50

ANON. 1887. 'Prehistoric idols.' *Baltimore American*, 3 May

ANON. 1892. 'Easter Island.' *Nature*, 46, 258–60

ANON. 1910. 'There were GIANTS in the earth in those days.' *The London Magazine*, July, 509–17

Anuario Hidrográfico de la Marina de Chile: 1875 Hasta 1923. Santiago, Biblioteca Nacional

ARCHEY, G. 1971. 'Polynesian stone sculpture.' *Bollettino del Centro Camuno di Studii Preistorici*, 7, 97–115

ARMSTRONG, E. A. 1965. *Bird Display and Behaviour*. New York, Dover Publications

ASHBEE, P. & CORNWALL, I. W. 1961. 'An experiment in field archaeology.' *Antiquity*, XXXV, 129–34

ASTRAND, P.-Ö. & RODAHL, K. 1970. *Textbook of Work Physiology*. New York, McGraw-Hill Book Co.

ATKINSON, R. J. C. 1956. *Stonehenge*. London, Hamish Hamilton

ATTENBOROUGH, D. 1990. 'The first figures to be collected from Easter Island.' In *State and Perspectives of Scientific Research in Easter Island Culture*, H.-M. Esen Baur, ed., Frankfurt a.M., Courier Forsch.-Inst. Senckenberg, 125, 41–50

AYRES, W. S. n.d. 'Calibrated radiocarbon dates from Easter Island.' Unpublished MS on file with the author
- 1973. 'The cultural context of Easter Island religious structures.' Ph.D. dissertation, Tulane University
- 1985. 'Easter Island subsistence.' *Journal de la Société des Océanistes*, XLI(80), 103–24
- 1988. 'The Tahai settlement complex.' In *First International Congress, Easter Island and East Polynesia, 1984*, Vol. 1, *Archaeology*, eds. C. Cristino F. *et al.* Santiago, Universidad de Chile, 95–120

BAHN, P. & FLENLEY, J. 1992. *Easter Island, Earth Island*. London, Thames and Hudson

BAKER, P. E. 1967. 'Preliminary account of recent geological investigations on Easter Island.' *Geological Magazine*, 104(2), 116–22

BALFOUR, H. 1917. 'Some ethnological suggestions in regard to Easter Island, or Rapanui.' *Folklore*, 28, 356–81

BANDY, M. C. 1937. 'Geology and petrology of Easter Island.' *Geological Society of America*, Bulletin 48, 1589–1610

BARBIER, J. P. & NEWTON, D. 1988. *Islands and Ancestors: Indigenous Styles of Southeast Asia*. New York, Metropolitan Museum of Art

BARCLAY, H. V. 1899. 'Easter Island and its colossal statues.' *Royal Geographical Society of Australasia, South Australian Branch, Proceedings*, 3, 127–37

BARCLAY, Capt. 1910. 'The lost land of the Maoris: What we found at Easter Island.' *Life*, 13, 373–6

BARROW, T. 1967. 'Material evidence of the bird-man concept in Polynesia.' In *Polynesian Cultural History*, eds. G. A. Highland, *et al.* Honolulu, Bernice P. Bishop Museum Special Publication 56, 191–213

BARTH, F. 1987. *Cosmologies in the Making: A Generative Approach to Cultural Variation in Inner New Guinea*. Cambridge, Cambridge University Press

BARTHEL, T. S. 1958. 'Female stone figures on Easter Island.' *Journal of the Polynesian Society*, 67(3), 252–5
- 1978. *The Eighth Land: Polynesian Discovery and Settlement of Easter Island*, trans. A. Martin. Honolulu, University of Hawaii Press

BEAGLEHOLE, E. & BEAGLEHOLE, P. 1938. *Ethnology of Pukapuka*. Honolulu, Bernice P. Bishop Museum Bulletin 150, Kraus Reprint Ltd, 1971

BEAGLEHOLE, J. C. (ed.) 1969. *The Journals of Captain James Cook on his Voyages of Discovery: The Voyage of the Resolution and Adventure, 1772–1775*. London, Cambridge University Press for the Hakluyt Society

BEARDSLEY, F. R. 1990. 'Spatial analysis of platform ahu on Easter Island.' Ph.D. dissertation, University of Oregon

BEARDSLEY, F. R., AYRES, W. S. & GOLES, G. G. 1991. 'Characterisation of Easter Island Obsidian Sources.' In *Indo-Pacific Prehistory 1990* ed. P. Bellwood 2(11), 179–87

BEHRENS, C. F. 1908. 'Another narrative of Jacob Roggeveen's visit.' In *The Voyage of Captain Don Felipe González in the Ship of the Line San Lorenzo, with the Frigate Santa Rosalia in Company, to Easter Island in 1770–1: Preceded by an Extract from Mynheer Jacob Roggeveen's Office Log of His Discovery of and Visit to Easter Island, in 1722*, ed. B G Corney. The Hakluyt Society, Ser. II, no. 13, Kraus Reprint Ltd, 1967

BELCHER, E. n.d. [1825–7]. 'Pacific journal and remarks.' PMB, ANU. Microfilm M51

BELLWOOD, P. 1970. 'Dispersal centers in east Polynesia, with special reference to the Society and Marquesas Islands.' In *Studies in Oceanic Culture History*, eds. R.C. Green & M. Kelly. Honolulu, Pacific Anthropological Records, no. 11, 93–104
- 1978. *Archaeological Research in the Cook Islands*. Honolulu, Bernice P. Bishop Museum, Pacific Anthropological Records, no. 27
- 1979. 'The oceanic context.' In *Exploring the Visual Art of Oceania: Australia, Melanesia, Micronesia, and Polynesia*, ed. S M Mead. Honolulu, University of Hawaii Press 6–26
- 1985. *Prehistory of the Indo-Malaysian Archipelago*. Sydney, Academic Press
- 1987. *The Polynesians*. London, Thames and Hudson

BEYER, H. O. 1948. 'Philippine and East Asian archaeology and its relation to the origin of the Pacific Islands population.' *National Research Council of the Philippines*, Bulletin 29, 1–130

BIANCO, J. 1987. 'Un examen critique de la statuaire Pascuane.' *Kadath*, 64, 12–50

BIERBACH, A. & CAIN, H. 1988. 'Tangata Manu and 'Ao, secular power on Rapa Nui.' In *Clava*, no. 4, 37–47, ed. J. M. Ramírez, Viña del Mar, Museo Sociedad Fonck 4, 37–48

BIRD, J. R. 1988. 'Isla de Pascua obsidian.' In *Archaeometry: Australian Studies 1988*, ed. J. R. Prescott. Adelaide, University of Adelaide Press, 115–20

BISHOP, Capt. C. n.d. [1795]. *Journal*. ML, Sydney. Entry beginning 3 March, p. 35. Microfilm FM 3/477

BLACKWOOD, B. 1970. *The Classification of Artefacts in the Pitt Rivers Museum*. Oxford, Oxford University Press

BOROFSKY, R. 1987. *Making History: Pukapukan and Anthropological Construction of Knowledge*. London, Cambridge University Press

BRASSEUR, A. 1870. 'Lettre de M L'Abbé Brasseur de Bourbourg à M V A, Malte-Brun.' *Annales des Voyages*, Paris

BRITISH MUSEUM 1925. *Handbook to the Ethnographic Collections*, 2nd ed. London, Oxford University Press

BRITISH MUSEUM, MUSEUM OF MANKIND. Archives. Ethn. Doc. 974, n.d. Letter to Mr. R. P. Alexander, 28 October 1981

BUCK, P. H. (Te Rangi Hiroa) 1927. *The Material Culture of the Cook Islands (Aitutaki)*. Board of Maori Ethnological Research Memoirs, vol. 1
- 1930. *Samoan Material Culture*. Honolulu, Bernice P. Bishop Museum Bulletin 74
- 1932. *Ethnology of Manihiki and Rakahanga*. Honolulu, Bernice P. Bishop Museum Bulletin 99
- 1934. *Mangaian Society*. Honolulu, Bernice P. Bishop Museum Bulletin 122
- 1935. 'Material representatives of Tongan and Samoan gods.' *Journal of the Polynesian Society*, 44, 48–53
- 1938. *Ethnology of Mangareva*. Honolulu, Bernice P. Bishop Museum Bulletin 157
- 1964. *Arts and Crafts of Hawaii: Religion*. Honolulu, Bernice P. Bishop Museum Special Publication 45

BUTZER, K. W. 1982. *Archaeology as human ecology: Method and theory for a contextual approach.* Cambridge, Cambridge University Press

BYRD, R. 1935. *Discovery: The Second Antarctic Expedition.* New York, G. P. Putnam's Sons

CAMERON, I. 1987. *Lost Paradise: The Exploration of the Pacific.* Topsfield, Mass., Salem House

CAMPBELL, K. S. 1971. 'The stone sculpture of the Pacific Islands: A compilation and stylistic comparison.' MA thesis, University of Hawaii

CAMPBELL, R. 1974. *La Cultura de la Isla de Pascua: Mito y Realidad.* Santiago, Editorial Andres Bello

CAMPOS, L. & PEÑA, L. E. 1973. 'Los insectos de Isla de Pascua.' *Revista Chilena de Entomología.* Santiago, Universidad de Chile, 7, 217–29

CARLQUIST, S. 1967. 'The biota of long-distance dispersal: V: Plant dispersal to the Pacific Islands.' *Bulletin of the Torrey Botanical Club,* 44, 129–62

CARMICHAEL, R. S. (ed.) 1982. *Handbook of Physical Properties of Rocks.* Boca Raton, CRC Press, Inc.

CASTILLA, J. C. & OLIVA, D. (eds.) 1987. *Islas Oceánicas Chilenas: Conocimiento Científico y Necesidades de las Investigaciones.* Valparaiso, Ediciones Universidad Católica de Chile

CERAM, C. W. (ed.) 1975. *Hands on the Past: Pioneer Archaeologists Tell Their Own Stories.* New York, Schocken Books

CHAROLA, A. E. (ed.) 1990. *Lavas and Volcanic Tuffs: Preprints of the Contributions to the International Meeting.* Santiago, Dirección de Bibliotecas, Archivos y Museos

CHICK, J. & CHICK, S. (eds.) 1978. *Grass Roots Art of the Solomons: Images and Islands.* Sydney and New York, Pacific Publications

CHUBB, L. J. 1933. *Geology of Galápagos, Cocos, and Easter Islands.* Honolulu, Bernice P Bishop Museum Bulletin 110

CHURCHILL, W. 1912. *Easter Island. The Rapanui Speech and the Peopling of Southeast Polynesia.* The Carnegie Institution of Washington, no. 174, AMS Press Reprint 1978

CHURCHWARD, C. M. 1959. *Tongan Dictionary.* London, Oxford University Press

CLARK, B. P. 1899. 'Reporting calling at Sala y Gomez and Easter Island.' *Royal Geographical Society of Australasia, South Australian Branch, Proceedings,* 3, 143–6

CLEGHORN, P. L. 1988. *The Settlement & Abandonment of Two Hawaiian Outposts: Nihoa & Necker Islands.* Honolulu, Bernice P. Bishop Museum Occasional Papers 28, 35–49

COLLINS, K. J. & ROBERTS, D. F. (eds.) 1988. *Capacity for Work in the Tropics.* Society for the Study of Human Biology Symposium 26. Cambridge, C.U.P.

COOK, J. 1777. *A Voyage Towards the South Pole, and Around the World. Performed in His Majesty's Ships the Resolution and Adventure, In the Years 1772–1775.* London, W. Strahan and T. Cadel

COOKE, G. H. 1899. *Te Pito Te Henua, Known as Rapa Nui, Commonly Called Easter Island, South Pacific Ocean.* Report of the U S National Museum for 1897. Washington, D.C., Smithsonian Institution

CORNEY, B. G. (ed.) 1908. *The Voyage of Captain Don Felipe González in the Ship of the Line San Lorenzo, with the Frigate Santa Rosalia in Company, to Easter Island in 1770–1: Preceded by an Extract from Mynheer Jacob Roggeveen's Official Log of His Discovery of and Visit to Easter Island, in 1722.* The Hakluyt Society, Ser. II, no. 13, Kraus Reprint Ltd, 1967

– 1917. 'Notes on Easter Island.' *The Geographical Journal,* vol. L, no. 1

COTTERELL, B. & KAMMINGA, J. 1990. *Mechanics of Pre-Industrial Technology.* Cambridge, C.U.P.

COX, J. H. & DAVENPORT, W. H. 1988. *Hawaiian Sculpture.* Honolulu, University of Hawaii Press

CRANSTONE, B. 1976. 'Cultural history of the Pacific.' London, *The Times,* 4 March

CRISTINO, F., C. & VARGAS, C., P. 1980. 'Prospección arqueólogica de Isla de Pascua.' *Anales de la Universidad de Chile.* Santiago, Universidad de Chile, nos. 161–2, 191–215

CRISTINO, F., C. & VARGAS, C., P. & IZAURIETA S., R. 1981. *Atlas Arqueólogica de Isla de Pascua.* Santiago, Facultad de Arquitectura y Urbanismo, Instituto de Estudios, Universidad de Chile

CRISTINO, F. C., VARGAS, P. C., IZAURIETA, S. R. & BUDD, P. R. (eds.) 1988. *First International Congress, Easter Island and East Polynesia, 1984, Vol 1, Archaeology.* Santiago, Universidad de Chile

CROXALL, J. P. (ed.) 1987. *Seabirds: Feeding Ecology and Role in Marine Ecosystems.* Cambridge, Cambridge University Press

CUMING, H. n.d. [1827–8]. 'Journal of a voyage from Valparaiso to the Society and adjacent islands.' ML, Sydney, CY REEL 194, A1336

DANIEL, G. 1981. *A Short History of Archaeology.* London, Thames and Hudson

DARWIN, C. 1859. *On the Origin of Species by Means of Natural Selection or, The Preservation of Favoured Races in the Struggle for Life.* London, J. Murray

DAVENPORT, W. H. 1974. 'Introduction to the revised edition.' (1988). In *Hawaiian Sculpture,* eds. J. H. Cox & W. H. Davenport. Honolulu, University of Hawaii Press

DE BREE, L. W. 1942. *Jacob Roggeveen en zijn reis naar het Zuidland, 1721–1722.* Amsterdam, P. N. Van Kamden & N. V. Zoon

DENNING, G. 1980. *Islands and Beaches: Discourse on a Silent Land: Marquesas 1774–1880,* Honolulu, University of Hawaii Press

DE QUATREFAGES, A. & HAMY, E. T. 1882. *Crania Ethnica.* Paris

DESCANTS, C. 1990. *Symbolic stone structures: Protohistoric and early historic spatial patterns of the 'Opunohu Valley, Mo'orea, French Polynesia.* MA thesis, Auckland University

DI SALVO, L. H., RANDALL, J. E., & CEA, A. 1988. 'Ecological reconnaissance of the Easter Island sublittoral marine environment.' *National Geographic Research,* 4, 451–73

DOMINGUEZ, L. 1968. *Las Esculturas de la Isla de Pascua.* Buenos Aires, Edición del Fondo Nacional de las Artes

DONOVAN, L. J. 1973. 'A study of the decorative system of the Lapita potters in Reef and Santa Cruz Islands.' MA thesis, Auckland University

DRANSFIELD, J., FLENLEY, J. R., KING, S. M., HARKNESS, D. D. & RAPU, S. 1984. 'A recently extinct palm from Easter Island.' *Nature,* 312, 750–2

DUFF, R. 1968. 'Archaeology of the Cook Islands.' In *Prehistoric Culture in Oceania,* eds. I. Yawata & Y. H. Sinoto. Honolulu, Bernice P. Bishop Museum

– 1974. 'Two folk-tales of Rarotonga and Aitutaki.' In *Prehistory of the Southern Cook Islands,* ed. M. M. Trotter, 141–5. Christchurch, Canterbury Museum Bulletin no. 6

DUMONT D'URVILLE, J. S. C. 1833. *Voyage de la Corvette L'Astrolabe. Atlas.* Paris, J. Tastu

DUNDAS, C. 1870. Notice of Easter Island, its inhabitants, antiquities, and colossal statues. *Proceedings of the Society of Antiquaries of Scotland,* 8, 312–20

DUNHAM, D. 1956. 'Building an Egyptian pyramid.' *Archaeology,* 9(3), 156–65

EARLE, T. (ed.) 1991. *Chiefdoms: Power, Economy and Ideology.* Cambridge, Cambridge University Press

EGENTER, N. 1992. 'The present relevance of the primitive in architecture.' *Architectural Anthropology Research Series,* vol. 1. Lausanne, Structura Mundi

ELLIOT, J. & PICKERSGILL, R. 1984. *Captain Cook's Second Voyage: The Journals of Lieutenants Elliott and Pickersgill,* ed. C. Holmes. London, Caliban Books

ELLIS, W. 1969. *Polynesian Researches: Hawaii.* Rutland, VT., and Tokyo, Charles E. Tuttle Co.

EMORY, K. P. 1928. *Archaeology of Nihoa and Necker Islands.* Honolulu, Bernice P. Bishop Museum Bulletin 53

– 1934. *Tuamotuan Stone Structures.* Honolulu, Bernice P. Bishop Museum Bulletin 118

– 1947. *Tuamotuan Religious Structures and Ceremonies.* Honolulu, Bernice P. Bishop Museum Bulletin 191

– 1972. 'Easter Island's position in the prehistory of Polynesia.' *Journal of the Polynesian Society,* 81, 57–69

– 1975. *Material Culture of the Tuamotu Archipelago.* Honolulu, Pacific Anthropological Records, 22

ENGLERT, PÉRE S. 1964. *Primer Siglo Cristiano de la Isla de Pascua.* Imprenta Salesiana

– 1970. *Island at the Center of the World,* trans. W.S. Mulloy. New York, Scribners and Sons

– 1974. *La Tierra de Hotu Matu'a: Historia, Etnología, y Lengua de la Isla de Pascua.* Santiago, Padre de Casas

– 1978. *Idioma Rapanui.* Santiago, Universidad de Chile

ERASMUS, C. J. 1965. 'Monument building: Some field experiments.' *Southwestern Journal of Anthropology,* 21(4), 277–301

ESEN-BAUR, H.-M. 1983. *Untersuchungen Über Den Vogelmannkult Auf Der Osterinsel.* Wiesbaden, Granz Steiner Verlag GMBH

ESTUDIOS SOBRE LA ISLA DE PASCUA. 1980. Monograph. Santiago, Universidad de Chile

ETIENNE, M., MICHEA, G. & DÍAZ, E. 1982. *Flora, Vegetación y Potencial Pastoral de Isla de Pascua.* Facultad de Ciencias Agrarias, Veterinarias y Forestales, Boletin Técnico 47. Santiago, Universidad de Chile

EVELETH, P.-B. & TANNER, J. M. 1990. *Worldwide Variation in Human Growth.* Cambridge, C.U.P.

FERDON, E. N. JR. 1961. 'The ceremonial site of Orongo.' In *Reports of the Norwegian Archaeological Expedition to Easter Island and the East Pacific, Vol. 1, Archaeology of Easter Island*, eds. T. Heyerdahl & E. N. Ferdon, Jr. Santa Fe, Monographs of the School of American Research and the Museum of New Mexico (24), 221–56

– 1981. 'A possible source of origin of the Easter Island boat-shaped house.' *Asian Perspectives*, XXII, 1, 1–8.

– 1987. *Early Tonga as the Explorers Saw It: 1616–1810.* Tucson, University of Arizona Press

– 1988. 'In defence of the Orongo 'Sun Stones'.' *Journal of the Polynesian Society*, 97, 73–7

FERRIS, T. 1992. *The Mind's Sky: Human Intelligence in a Cosmic Context.* New York, Bantam Books

FIGUEROA G.-H. & SANCHEZ G. E. 1965. 'Adzes from certain islands of Eastern Polynesia.' In *Reports of the Norwegian Archaeological Expedition to Easter Island and the East Pacific, Vol. 2, Miscellaneous Papers*, eds T. Heyerdahl and E. N. Ferdon, Jr. Santa Fe, Monographs of the School of American Research and the Museum of New Mexico (24, Part 2), 169–254

FILLIPPI, R. A. [Philippi] 1873. 'Memorias científicas y literarias: La Isla de Pascua y sus habitantes.' *Anales de la Universidad de Chile.* Santiago, Universidad de Chile, XLIII (43), 365–434

FINNEY, B. R. 1979. 'Voyaging.' In *The Prehistory of Polynesia*, ed. J D Jennings. Cambridge, Harvard University Press

FINNEY, B. [in press]. 'Polynesian Voyagers to the New World.' *Man and Culture in Oceania*

– 1993 'Voyaging and Isolation in Rapa Nui prehistory.' *Rapa Nui Journal* 7(1): 1–6

FINNEY, B. R., FROST, P., RHODES, R. & THOMPSON, N. 1989. 'Wait for the west wind.' *Journal of the Polynesian Society*, 98(3), 261–302

FIRTH, R. 1959. *Social Change in Tikopia.* London, Geo. Allen & Unwin

– 1965. *Primitive Polynesian Economy.* New York, The Norton Library

– 1981. 'A commentary.' In *Why Tikopia Has Four Clans*, ed. A. Hopper. Royal Anthropological Institute of Great Britain and Ireland, Occasional Paper 38, 45–64

FISHER, R. L. (ed.) 1958. *Preliminary report on Expedition Downwind.* University of California, Scripps Institution of Oceanography IGY Cruise to the South Pacific. Washington, D.C., IGY General Report Series No. 2

FLEISCHMAN, E. A., KREMER, E. J. & SHOUP, G. W. 1961. *The Dimensions of Physical Fitness: A Factor Analysis of Strength Tests.* New Haven, Yale University Press

FLENLEY, J. R. 1979. 'Stratigraphic evidence of environmental change on Easter Island.' *Asian Perspectives*, 22, 33–40

FLENLEY, J. R. & KING, S. M. 1984. 'Late quaternary pollen records from Easter Island.' *Nature*, 307(5946), 47–50

FLENLEY, J. R., KING, S. M., TELLER, J. T., PRENTICE, M. E., JACKSON, J. & CHEW, C. 1991. 'The late quaternary vegetational and climatic history of Easter Island.' *Journal of Quaternary Science*, 6, 85–115

FORBES, H. O. 1917. 'Easter Island: Discussion.' *The Geographic Journal*, XLIX (5), 346–7

FORMENT, F. 1981. *La Pacifique aux îles Innombrables Île de Pâques.* Brussels, Musées Royaux d'Art et d'Histoire

– 1983. 'Pou hakanononga, God van de tonijnvissers?' *Liber Memorialis Prof. Dr. P J Vandernhoute.* Rijksuniversiteit te Gent. Brussels

– 1991. 'Les figures moai kavakava de l'Île de Pâques.' *Working Papers in Ethnic Art.* Ghent, University of Ghent

FORSTER, G. 1777. *Voyage Around the World in His Britannic Majesty's Sloop, Resolution, Commanded by Captain James Cook, During the Years 1772–1775.* London, B. White

FOWLES, J. 1978. *Islands.* Boston and Toronto, Little, Brown and Company

FRANCIS, CAPT. n.d. [1853]. PMB Microfilm 734, Frames 253–344

FRANK, V. S. 1906. 'A trip to Easter Island [A speck on the ocean].' *Journal Franklin Institute*, September, 179–99

FRAZER, SIR J. G. 1963. *The Golden Bough.* 1 vol. abridged ed. New York, Macmillan

FUENTES, F. 1913. 'Reseña botánica sobre la Isla de Pascua.' *Boletín del Museo Nacional de Chile.* Santiago, 5, 320–37

FUENTES, J. 1960. *Diccionario y Gramática de la Isla de Pascua*, ed. Andrés Bello. Santiago

Gaceta de Lima 1771. Untitled article in no. 44. 27 Enero – 30 Mayo

GANA, I. L. 1870. 'Descripción científica de la Isla de Pascua.' In *Memoria, Que el Ministro de Estado en el Departamento de Marina Presenta al Congreso Nacional de 1870.* Santiago, Departamento de Marina, 90–109

GARANGER, J. 1967. 'Archaeology and the Society Islands.' In *Essays in Honor of Kenneth P. Emory*, eds G. A. Highland *et al.*, Honolulu, Bernice P. Bishop Special Publication no. 56, 377–96

GARHAMMER, J. 1980. 'Evaluation of human power capacity through Olympic weightlifting analysis.' Ph.D. dissertation, Dept. of Kinesiology, UCLA

GASSNER, J. S. trans. 1969. *Voyages and Adventures of La Pérouse.* From the fourteenth ed. of the F. Valentin abridgment, Tours, 1875. Honolulu, University of Hawaii Press

GATHERCOLE, P., KAEPPLER, A. L. & NEWTON, D. 1979. *The Art of the Pacific Islands.* Washington, D.C., National Gallery of Art

GATTY, C. T. 1880. *Catalogue of the Loan Exhibition . . . Held at the Walker Art Gallery, Liverpool, May 1880.* London

GEISELER, KAPITÄNLIEUTENANT 1883. 'Die Oster-Insel: Eine Stätte prähistorischer Kultur in der Südsee. Bericht des Kommandanten S.M. Kbt. "Hyäne", Kapitänlieutenant Geiseler, über die ethnologische Untersuchung der Oster-Insel (Rapanui).' *Beiheft zum Marine-Verordnungsblatt.* Berlin, 44, 1–54

GILL, G. W., OWSLEY, D. W., & BAKER, S. J. n.d. [1983]. 'Craniometric evaluation of prehistoric Easter Island populations.' Paper presented at the 52nd annual meeting of the American Association of Anthropologists, Indianapolis, Indiana. Abstract in the *American Journal of Physical Anthropology*, New York, 60(2), 197

GODWIN, G. (ed.) 1869. Untitled article in *The Builder.* London, 20 November, 930–1

GOLDMAN, I. 1970. *Ancient Polynesian Society.* Chicago, University of Chicago Press

GOLSON, J. 1965. 'Thor Heyerdahl and the prehistory of Easter Island.' *Oceania* 36, 33–8

– 1971. 'Lapita ware and its transformations.' In *Studies in Oceanic Culture History*, eds. R. C. Green & M. Kelly. Honolulu, Pacific Anthropological Records, 12, 67–76

GONZÁLEZ [DE HAEDO], F. 1908. In *The Voyage of Captain Don Felipe González in the Ship of the Line San Lorenzo, with the Frigate Santa Rosalia in Company, to Easter Island in 1770–1: Preceded by an Extract from Mynheer Jacob Roggeveen's Office Log of His Discovery of and Visit to Easter Island, in 1722*, ed. B. G. Corney. The Hakluyt Society, Ser. II, no. 13, Kraus Reprint Ltd, 1967

GONZÁLEZ, M. E. 1984. 'The archaeoastronomy and ethnoastronomy of Easter Island.' MA thesis, California State University of Long Beach

GONZÁLEZ N., L., VAN TILBURG, J. & P VARGAS C. 1988. 'Easter Island statue type, part two: The Moai as socio-political feature.' In *First International Congress, Easter Island and East Polynesia, 1984, Vol. 1, Archaeology*, eds. C. Cristino F. *et al.* Santiago, Universidad de Chile, 150–63

GONZÁLEZ-FERRÁN, O. 1987. 'Evolución geológica de las Islas Chilenas en el Océano Pacífico.' In *Islas Oceánicas Chilenas: Conocimiento Científico y Necesidades de las Investigaciones*, ed. J. C. Castilla. Valparaiso, Ediciones Universidad Católica de Chile, 37–54

GONZÁLEZ-FERRÁN, O. & BAKER, P. E. 1974. *Isla de Pascua – Easter Island: Guide Book – Excursion D-2.* International Symposium on Volcanology: Andean and Antarctic Volcanology Problems. Santiago, Universidad de Chile

GOSDEN, C., ALLEN, J., AMBROSE, W., ANSON, D., GOLSON, J., GREEN, R., KIRCH, P., LILLEY, I., SPECHT, J. & SPRIGGS, M. 1989. 'Lapita sites of the Bismarck Archipelago.' *Antiquity*, 63(240), 561–86

GOSDEN, C. 1992. 'Production systems and the colonization of the Western Pacific.' *World Archaeology*, 24(1), 55–69

GOUGH, G. M. (ed.) 1973. *To the Pacific and Arctic with Beechey: The Journal of Lieutenant George Peard of H.M.S. Blossom', 1825–1828.* Cambridge, University Press for the Hakluyt Society

GRAU, V., J. 1993. *Adventures in Easter Island.* Ediciones 'Oikos' Ltda. Santiago de Chile

GRAVES, M. W. 1993. 'Preface.' *The Evolution and Organisation of Prehistoric Society in Polynesia*, eds M. W. Graves & R. C. Green. New Zealand Archaeological Association Monograph 19, 5

GRAVES, M. W. & SWEENEY, M. 1993. 'Ritual behaviour and ceremonial structures in eastern Polynesia: changing perspectives on archaeological variability.' *The Evolution and Organisation of Prehistoric Society in Polynesia*, eds M. W. Graves & R. C. Green. New Zealand Archaeological Monograph 19, 106–25

GREEN, R. C. 1979a. 'Early Lapita art from Polynesia and Island Melanesia: Continuities in ceramic, barkcloth and tattoo decorations.' In *Exploring the Visual Art of Oceania: Australia, Melanesia, Micronesia, and Polynesia*, ed. S. M. Mead. Honolulu, University of Hawaii Press, 13–31

— 1979b. 'Lapita.' In *The Prehistory of Polynesia*, ed. J.D. Jennings. Cambridge, Harvard University Press, 27–60

— 1982. 'Models for the Lapita cultural complex.' *New Zealand Journal of Archaeology*, 4, 7–19

— 1988. 'Subgrouping of the Rapanui language of Easter Island in Polynesia and its implications for East Polynesia prehistory.' In *First International Congress, Easter Island and East Polynesia, 1984, Vol. 1, Archaeology*, eds. C. Cristino F. *et al*. Santiago, Universidad de Chile, 37–57

— 1989a. 'Lapita people: An introductory context for skeletal materials associated with pottery of this cultural complex.' *Records of the Australian Museum*, 41(3), 207–13

— 1989b. 'Lapita, pottery and Polynesians.' *New Zealand Potter*, 31(3), 4–6

— 1991. 'A reappraisal of the dating of some Lapita sites in the Reef/Santa Cruz group of the southeast Solomons.' *Journal of the Polynesian Society*, 100(2), 197–208

— 1993. 'Tropical Polynesian prehistory: Where are we now?.' In *A Community of Culture: The People and Prehistory of the Pacific*. M. Spriggs *et al*. eds., Canberra, The Australian National University Occasional Papers in Prehistory 21, 219–37.

GREEN, R. C. & ANSON, D. 1991. 'The Reber-Rakival Lapita site on Watom: Implications of the 1985 excavations at the SAC and SDI localities.' In *Report of the Lapita Homeland Project*, eds. J. Allen & C. Gosden. Canberra, Occasional Paper in Prehistory 20

GREEN, R. C., GREEN, K., RAPPAPORT, R. A., RAPPAPORT A. & DAVIDSON, J. 1967. 'Archaeology on the Island of Mo'orea, French Polynesia.' *Anthropological Papers of the American Museum of Natural History* 51(2)

GREINER, R. H. 1927. *Polynesian Decorative Design*. Honolulu, Bernice P. Bishop Museum Bulletin 7

GROVE, D. C. 1981. 'Olmec monuments: Mutilation as a clue to meaning.' In *The Olmec and Their Neighbors: Essays in Memory of Matthew E. Stirling*. Washington, D.C., Dumbarton Oaks Research Library and Collections and the Trustees of Harvard University, 49–68

GUSINDE, M. 1916. 'Prologo.' *Publicaciones del Museo de Etnología y Antropologia*, Santiago, Imprente Cervantes, I(13)

— 1922. 'Bibliographía de la Isla de Pascua.' *Publicaciones del Museo de Etnología y Antropologia de Chile*. Santiago, Imprente Cervantes

— 1933. 'Catálogo de los objetos originarios de la Isla de Pascua conservados en este museo.' *Publicaciones del Museo de Etnología y Antropologia*. Santiago, Imprente Cervantes

GUY, J. B. M. 1988. 'Rjabchikov's decipherments examined.' *Journal of the Polynesian Society* 97(3), 321–4

HADDON, A. C. & HORNELL, J. 1975. *Canoes of Oceania*. Honolulu, Bernice P. Bishop Museum Special Publications 27, 28 & 29

HAMILTON, A. (trans.) 1799. *A Voyage Round the World Performed in the Years 1785, 1787 and 1788 by the Boussole and Astrolabe*. 2 vols and atlas, London, G. G. & J. Robinson

HANDY, E. S. C. 1927. *Polynesian Religion*. Honolulu, Bernice P. Bishop Museum Bulletin 34, Kraus Reprint Ltd, 1971

— 1943. 'Two unique petroglyphs in the Marquesas which point to Easter Island and Malaysia.' *Peabody Museum of American Anthropology and Ethnology Papers*, XX, 22–31

HANSON, F. A. 1982. 'Female pollution in Polynesia?' *Journal of the Polynesian Society*, 91–4, 335–81

HARRISSON, C. S. & SEKI, M. P. 1987. 'Trophic relationships among tropical seabirds at the Hawaiian Islands.' In *Seabirds: Feeding Ecology and Role in Marine Ecosystems*, ed. J. P. Croxall. Cambridge, Cambridge University Press, 305–26

HARRISSON, T. 1962. 'Megaliths of Central Borneo and Western Malaya, compared.' *Sarawak Museum Journal*. Kuching, Sarawak, 10(19–20), 376–82

HARRISSON, T. & LORD MEDWAY 1962. 'A first classification of prehistoric bone and tooth artifacts (based on material from Niah Great Cave).' *Sarawak Museum Journal*. Kuching, Sarawak, 19(19–20), 335–62

HATCHER, E. P. 1974. *Visual Metaphors: A Methodological Study in Visual Communication*. Albuquerque, University of New Mexico Press

HATHER, J. G. 1992. 'The archaeology of subsistence in the Pacific.' *World Archaeology*, 24(1), 70–81

HATHER, J. & KIRCH, P. V. 1991. 'Prehistoric sweet potato [Ipomoea batatas] from Mangaia Island, Central Polynesia.' *Antiquity* 65(249), 887–93

HEIFITZ, R. A. n.d. *To lead or mislead? The challenge of adaptive change*. MS on file with the author

HEINE-GELDERN, R. 1928. 'Die megalithen sudostasiens und ihre bedeutung furdie megalithenfrage in Europa und Polynesien.' *Anthropos*, 23, 276–315

HEISER, C. B. JR. 1974. 'Totoras, taxonomy and Thor.' *Plant Science Bulletin*, 20, 22–5

— 1979. 'The totora (*Scirpus californicus*) in Ecuador and Peru.' *Economic Botany*, 32, 222–36

HEIZER, R. F. 1966. 'Ancient heavy transport, methods and achievement.' *Science* 153, 821–28

HENRY, T. 1928. *Ancient Tahiti*. Honolulu, Bernice P. Bishop Museum Bulletin 48, Kraus Reprint Ltd, 1985

HERFRITZ, H. 1953. *Die Osterinsel*. Zurich, Fretz and Wasmuth

HEYERDAHL, T. 1952. *American Indians in the Pacific: The Theory Behind the Kon-Tiki Expedition*. London, Allen and Unwin Ltd

— 1958. *Aku-Aku*. Chicago, New York, San Francisco, Rand McNally & Company

— 1961a. 'An introduction to Easter Island.' In *Reports of the Norwegian Archaeological Expedition to Easter Island and the East Pacific, Vol. 1, Archaeology of Easter Island*, eds. T. Heyerdahl & E. N. Ferdon, Jr. Santa Fe, Monographs of the School of American Research and the Museum of New Mexico (24), 21–90

— 1961b. 'Surface artifacts.' In *Reports of the Norwegian Archaeological Expedition to Easter Island and the East Pacific, Vol. 1, Archaeology of Easter Island*, eds. T. Heyerdahl & E. N. Ferdon, Jr. Santa Fe, Monographs of the School of American Research and the Museum of New Mexico (24), 397–489

— 1975. *The Art of Easter Island*. Garden City, New York, Doubleday & Co.

— 1981. 'The heterogeneity of small sculptures on Easter Island before 1886.' *Asian Perspectives*, 22(1), 9–32

— 1989. *Easter Island: The Mystery Solved*. New York, Random House

HEYERDAHL, T. & FERDON, E. N. JR. (eds.) 1961. *Reports of the Norwegian Archaeological Expedition to Easter Island and the East Pacific, Vol. 1, Archaeology of Easter Island*. Santa Fe, Monographs of the School of American Research and the Museum of New Mexico (24)

— 1965. *Reports of the Norwegian Archaeological Expedition to Easter Island and the East Pacific, Vol. 2, Miscellaneous Papers*. Santa Fe, Monographs of the School of American Research (24)

HEYERDAHL, T., SKJØLSVOLD, A. & PAVEL, P. 1989. 'The "walking" moai of Easter Island.' In *Kon Tiki Museum Occasional Papers*, ed. A. Skjølsvold. Oslo, Kon Tiki Museum, 1, 7–35

HICKS, D. 1988. 'Art and religion on Timor. In *Islands and Ancestors: Indigenous Styles of Southeast Asia*, eds. J. P. Barbier & D. Newton. New York, Metropolitan Museum of Art, 138–51

HILL, A. V. S. & SERJEANTSON, S. W. (eds.) 1989. *The Colonization of the Pacific: A Genetic Trial*. Oxford, Clarendon Press

HODDER, I. 1984. 'Burials, houses, women and men in the European neolithic.' In *Ideology, Power and Prehistory*, eds. D Miller & C Tilley. Cambridge, Cambridge University Press, 51–68

HOOPER, A. 1981. *Why Tikopia Has Four Clans*. Royal Anthropological Institute of Great Britain and Ireland, Occasional Paper, 38

— 1985. 'Introduction.' In *Transformations of Polynesian Culture*, eds. A. Hooper & J. Huntsman. Auckland, The Polynesian Society, 1–16

HOPPER, A. & HUNTSMAN, J. (eds.) 1985. *Transformations of Polynesian Culture*. Auckland, The Polynesian Society

HOTUS, A. Y otros [El Consejo de Jefes de Rapa Nui] 1988. *Te Mau Hatu'o Rapa Núi*. Editorial Emisión y el Centro de Estudios Políticos Latinoamericanos Simón Bolívar

HOWARD, A. 1985. 'History, myth and Polynesian chieftainship: The case of Rotuman kings.' In *Transformations of Polynesian Culture*, eds. A. Hooper & J. Huntsman. Auckland, The Polynesian Society, 39–78

HUDSON, T., TIMBROOK, J., & REMPE, M. eds. 1978. *Tomol: Chumash Watercraft as Described in the Ethnographic Notes of John P. Harrington*. Santa Barbara, Ballena Press/Santa Barbara Museum of Natural History

HUNT, T. L. 1988. 'Lapita ceramic technological and compositional studies: A critical review.' In *Archaeology of the Lapita Cultural Complex: A Critical Review*, eds. P. V. Kitch & T. L. Hunt. Seattle, Thomas Burke Memorial Washington State Museum Research Report No. 5, 49–60

HUTTON, J. H. 1922. 'Carved monoliths at Dimapur and an Angami Naga ceremony.' *Journal of the Royal Anthropological Institute*, 52(1), 55–70

HYE-KERDAL, K. 1955. '*Tika*, an old mystery game in the Pacific (The dart match as a cultural phenomenon).' *Journal of the Polynesian Society* 64, (2), 197–226

Illustrated London News 1869. 20 March, p. 297

IMBELLONI, J. 1951a. 'La más fina escultura Pascuana.' *Runa*. Buenos Aires, 4(1–2), 289–95

– 1951b. 'Craniología de la Isla de Pascua.' *Runa*. Buenos Aires, 4, 223–81

INSTITUO DE FOMENTO PESQUERO 1988. *Recursos Pesqueros de Isla de Pascua*. Santiago

IRWIN, G. 1989. 'Against, across and down the wind.' *Journal of the Polynesian Society*, 98, 167–206

– 1990. 'Human colonization and change in the remote Pacific.' *Current Anthropology*, 31, 90–4

IRWIN, G., BICKLER, S. & QUIRKE, P. 1990. 'Voyaging by canoe and computer: Experiments in the settlement of the Pacific Ocean.' *Antiquity*, 64, 34–50

ISLER, M. 1976. 'Ancient Egyptian methods of raising weights.' JARCE, XIII, 31–42

– 1987. 'The curious Luxor obelisks.' *The Journal of Egyptian Archaeology*, 73, 138–47

IVENS, W. G. 1927. *Melanesians of the South-East Solomon Islands*. London, Kegan Paul, Trench, Trubner and Co.

JACOBS, J. 1990. *The Nagas*. London, Thames and Hudson

JEFFERSON, C. 1956. *Dendroglyphs of the Chatham Islands*. Wellington, The Polynesian Society

JOHNSON, A. W., MILLIE, W. R. & MOFFETT, G. 1970. 'Birds of Easter Island.' London, *Ibis*. 532–8

JOHNSON, I. & E. 1949. 'The Yankee's wander-world.' *National Geographic Magazine* XCV(1), 1–49

JONES, S. 1991. 'The language of the genes.' London, Reith Lectures, Science Unit, BBC Radio

JOPPIEN, R. & SMITH, B. 1985. *The Art of Captain Cook's Voyages: Volume 2, The Voyage of the Resolution & Adventure*. New Haven and London, Yale University Press in assoc. with the Australian Academy of the Humanities

KAEPPLER, A. L. n.d. [1975]. *Bark cloth images and symbolic continuities in the arts of Easter Island*. Unpublished MS on file with the author

– 1976a. 'Cave caches.' Review of *The Art of Easter Island*. London, *The Times*

– 1976b. 'Dance and interpretation of Pacific traditional literature.' In *Directions in Pacific Traditional Literature: Essays in Honor of Katharine Luomala*, eds. A. L. Kaeppler & A. Nimmo. Honolulu, Bernice P. Bishop Museum, 195–216

– 1978a. '*Artificial Curiosities*': being An Exposition of Native Manufactures Collected on the Three Pacific Voyages of Captain James Cook, R.N. Honolulu, Bernice P. Bishop Museum Special Publication 65

– 1978b (ed.). *Cook Voyage Artifacts in Leningrad, Berne and Florence Museums*. Honolulu, Bernice P. Bishop Museum Special Publication 66

– 1979a. 'Aspects of Polynesian aesthetic traditions.' In *The Art of the Pacific Islands*, eds. P. Gathercole, A. L. Kaeppler & D. Newton. Washington, D.C., National Gallery of Art 77–95

– 1979b. 'A Survey of Polynesia Art.' In *Exploring the Visual Art of Oceania: Australia, Melanesia, Micronesia, and Polynesia*, ed. S. M. Mead. Honolulu, University of Hawaii Press 180–91

– 1980. *Pahu and Puniu: An Exhibition of Hawaiian Drums*. Honolulu, Bernice P. Bishop Museum

– 1982. 'Genealogy and disrespect: A study of symbolism in Hawaiian images.' *Res*, 3, 82–107

– 1989. 'Art and aesthetics.' In *Developments in Polynesian Ethnology*, eds. A. Howard & R. Borofsky. Honolulu, University of Hawaii Press, 211–40

KAEPPLER, A. L., KAUFMANN, C. & NEWTON, D. 1993. *L'Art Océanien*. Paris, Citadelles and Mazenod

KAMAKAU, S. M. 1976. *The works of the people of old (Na Hana a Ka Po'e Kahiko)*. Honolulu, Bernice P. Bishop Museum Special Publication 61

KAUDERN, W. 1938. *Megalithic Finds in Central Celebes*. Goteburg, Elanders

KERMODE, F. (ed.) 1990. *The Arden Edition of the Works of William Shakespeare: The Tempest*. London and New York, Routledge

KIRCH, P. V. 1980a. 'The Archaeological Study of Adaptation: Theoretical and Methodological Issues.' *Advances in Archaeological Method and Theory* 3, 101–6

– 1980b. 'Polynesian Prehistory: Cultural Adaptation.' In *Island Ecosystems*. *American Scientist* 68, 39–48.

– 1984. *The Evolution of the Polynesian Chiefdoms*. Cambridge, Cambridge University Press

– 1985. *Feathered Gods and Fishhooks: An Introduction to Hawaiian Archaeology and Prehistory*. Honolulu, University of Hawaii Press

– 1986. 'Rethinking East Polynesia prehistory.' *Journal of the Polynesian Society*, 95(1), 9–40

– 1987. 'Lapita and Oceanic cultural origins: Excavations in the Mussau Islands, Bismarck Archipelago, 1985.' *Journal of Field Archaeology*, 14, 163–80

– 1990a. 'Monumental architecture and power in Polynesian chiefdoms: A comparison of Tonga and Hawaii.' *World Archaeology*, 22(2), 206–22

– 1990b. 'Regional variation and local style: A neglected dimension in Hawaiian prehistory.' *Pacific Studies*, 13(2), 41–54

– 1990c. 'Specialization and exchange in the Lapita complex of Oceania (1600–500 B.C.).' In *Asian Perspectives*, 29(2), 117–33

– 1991a. 'Polynesian agricultural systems.' In *Islands, Plants, and Polynesians: An Introduction to Polynesian Ethnobotany*, eds. P. A. Cox & S.A. Banack. Portland, Dioscorides Press

– 1991b. 'Chiefship and competitive involution: The Marquesas Islands of Eastern Polynesia.' In *Chiefdoms: Power, Economy, and Ideology*, ed. T. Earle. Cambridge, Cambridge University Press, 119–45

KIRCH, P. V. & HUNT, T. L. (eds.) 1988. *Archaeology of the Lapita Cultural Complex: A Critical Review*. Seattle, Burke Memorial Washington State Museum, Research Report No. 5

KIRCH, P. V., FLENLEY, J. R., STEADMAN, D. W., LAMONT, F. & DAWSON, S. 1992. 'Ancient environmental degradation.' *National Geographic Research and Exploration*, 8(2), 166–79

KIRCH, P. V., CHRISTENSEN, C. C., STEADMAN, D. W. n.d. [in press]. 'Extinct achatinellid land snails from Easter island: biogeographic, ecological and archaeological implications.' *Pacific Science*

KIRCH, P. V. & YEN, D. 1982. *Tikopia: The prehistory and ecology of a Polynesian outlier*. Honolulu, Bernice P. Bishop Museum Bulletin 238

KLEIN, O. 1988. *Iconografía de la Isla de Pascua*. Valparaiso, Universidad Tecnica Federico Santa Maria

KNOCHE, W. 1925. *Die Osterinsel. Eine Zusammenfassung der chilenischen Osterin-selexpedition des Jahres 1911*. Concepción, Verlag des Wissenschaftlichen Archivs von Chile

KOCH, G. 1971. *Materielle Kultur der Santa Cruz-Inseln*. Berlin, Museum für Völkerkunde

KOOIJMAN, S. 1972. *Tapa in Polynesia*. Honolulu, Bernice P. Bishop Museum Bulletin 234

KRAMER, A. 1917–29. 'Palau.' In *Ergenbnisse der Sudsee-Expedition, 1908–1910*, ed. G. Thilenius (Partial translation HRAF). Hamburg

KRUPA, V. 1982. *The Polynesian Languages*. London, Routledge and Kegan Paul

KUSCHEL, G. 1963. 'Composition and relationship of the terrestrial fauna of Easter, Juan Fernández, Desventuradas and Galápagos Islands.' *Occasional Papers of the California Academy of Sciences*. San Francisco, 44, 79–95

KYSELKA, W. 1987. *An Ocean in Mind*. Honolulu, University of Hawaii Press

LA PÉROUSE, J. F. DE, G. COMTE DE 1797. *A Voyage Round the World Performed in the Years 1785–1788*. London, Johnson

LABANG, L. 1962. 'Married megaliths in Upland Kalimantan.' *Sarawak Museum Journal*. Kuching, Sarawak, 19(19–20), 383–5

LANGDON, R. (ed.) 1978. *American Whalers and Traders in the Pacific: A Guide to Records on Microfilm*. Canberra, PMB, Research School of Pacific Studies, Australian National University

– (ed.) 1984. *Where the Whalers Went An Index to the Pacific Ports and Islands Visited by American Whalers (and Some Other Ships) in the 19th Century*. Canberra, PMB, Research School of Pacific Studies, Australian National University

LANGDON, R. & TRYON, D. 1983. *The Language of Easter Island: Its Development and Eastern Polynesian Relationships*. Honolulu, The Institute for Polynesian Studies

LANNING, E. P. 1970. 'South America as a source for aspects of Polynesian cultures.' In *Studies in Oceanic Culture History*, eds. R. C. Green & M. Kelly. Honolulu, Pacific Anthropological Records, 11(2), 175–82

LAROCHE, M-CH. 1990. Alfred Métraux à L'Île de Pâques, de juillet 1934 à janvier 1935.' *Journal de la Société des Océanistes*, 91. 175–87

LAVACHERY, H. 1935. *L'Île de Pâques*. Paris, Editions Bernard Grasset

– 1938. 'Une figure en pierre de L'Île de Pâques.' *Bulletin van de Koninklijke Musea voor Kunst en Geschiedenis*. Brussels, 3, 55–61

– 1939. *Les Pétroglyphes de L'Île de Pâques*. Antwerp, De Sikkel

LAVAL, H. 1938. *Mangareva: L'histoire Ancienne d'un Peuple Polynésien*, eds. A. Métraux and R. P. Maurice Desmedt. Belgium, Maison des Pères des Sacrés-Coeurs

LAY, T. E. 1959. *A study of certain aspects of human ecology in the Polynesian high islands during the pre-contact period.* Ph.D. Dissertation, UCLA Department of Anthropology

LEE, G. 1986. 'Easter Island rock art: Ideological symbols as evidence of socio-political change.' Ph.D. dissertation, UCLA

– 1988. 'Fit for a king: The petroglyphs of Anakena, Rapa Nui.' In *Clava*, ed. J. M. Ramírez. Viña del Mar, Museo Sociedad Fonck 4, 49–62

– 1992. *The Rock Art of Easter Island: Symbols of Power, Prayers to the Gods.* Los Angeles, University of California Los Angeles Institute of Archaeology, Monumenta Archaeological 17

LEE, G. & LILLER, W. 1987. 'Easter Island's "Sun Stones": A critique.' *Journal of the Polynesian Society*, 96, 81–93

– 1988. 'Response to Ferdon.' *Journal of the Polynesian Society*, 97, 77

LEE, V. R. 1986. 'The building of Sacsahuaman.' *Ñawpa Pacha*, 24, 49–55

LILLER, W. 1990. 'The lost observatories on Rapa Nui.' In *State and Perspectives of Scientific Research in Easter Island Cultures*, ed. H.-M. Esen-Baur, Frankfurt a.M., Courier Forschungs institut Senckenberg, 125, 145–59

LINTON, R. 1925. *Archaeology of the Marquesas Islands.* Honolulu, Bernice P. Bishop Museum Bulletin 23

LINTON, R. & WINGERT, P. S. 1946. *Arts of the South Seas.* New York, Museum of Modern Art

LISJANSKIJ, U. 1814. *Voyage Round the World, 1803–1806, in the Ship Neva.* London, Longmans

LOFFS, H. H. E. 1967. *Elements of the Megalithic Complex in Southeast Asia. An Annotated Bibliography.* Oriental Monograph Series, no. 3

LOVE, C. M. 1984. *The Katherine Routledge Lantern Slide Collection of Easter Island and the South Pacific* [in the Museum of Mankind, British Museum]. Western Wyoming College

– 1990. 'How to make and move an Easter Island statue.' In *State and Perspectives of Scientific Research in Easter Island Culture*, ed. H.-M. Esen-Baur, Frankfurt a.M., Courier Forschungsinstitut Senckenberg, 125, 139–40.

LUOMALA, K. 1986. *Voices on the Wind: Polynesian Myths and Chants.* Honolulu, Bernice P. Bishop Museum

– 1971. *Oceanic, American Indian, and African Myths of Snaring the Sun.* Honolulu, Bernice P. Bishop Museum Bulletin 168

LYELL, C. 1990. *Principles of Geology.* Chicago, University of Chicago Press

MAGOFFIN, R. V. D. 1916. 'Mysterious Easter Island.' *Art and Archaeology*, 4(2), 125

MALO, D. 1951. *Hawaiian Antiquities.* Honolulu, Bernice P. Bishop Museum Special Publication 2

MALTE-BRUN, M. V. A. 1870. 'Le mystère de L'Île de Pâques.' In *Annales des Voyages de la Géographie, de L'Histoire et de L'Archéologie.* Paris

MANTER, H. n.d. [1847]. 'Journal of the Virginia', 1847–51. PMB, ANU. Microfilm PMB 677, frames 533–655

MARKS, R. L. 1991. *Three Men of the Beagle.* New York, Alfred A. Knopf

McCALL, G. n.d. *The past in the present on Rapa Nui (Easter Island).* Unpublished MS on file with the author

– 1976. 'Reaction to disaster: Continuity and change in Rapanui social organization.' Ph.D. thesis, Australian National University

– 1980. *Rapanui: Tradition and Survival on Easter Island.* Honolulu, University of Hawaii Press

McCOY, P. C. n.d. [1968]. *Field notes*, Instituto de Estudios, Isla de Pascua

– 1973. 'Excavation of a rectangular house on the east rim of Rano Kau volcano, Easter Island.' *Archaeology and Physical Anthropology in Oceania*, 8, 51–67

– 1976a. 'Easter Island settlement patterns in the late prehistoric and protohistoric periods.' New York, International Fund for Monuments, Bulletin 5, Easter Island Committee

– 1976b. 'A note on Easter Island obsidian cores and blades.' *Journal of the Polynesian Society* 85(3): 327–8

– 1978a. 'Stone-lined earth ovens in Easter Island.' *Antiquity*, LII, 204–16

– 1978b. 'The off near-shore islets in Easter Island prehistory.' *Journal of the Polynesian Society* 83(3): 193–214

– 1979. 'Easter Island.' In *Prehistory of Polynesia*, ed. J. D. Jennings. Cambridge, Harvard University Press, 135–66

McCOY, C. 1979. 'Easter Island.' In *Prehistory of Polynesia*, ed. J.D. Jennings. Cambridge, Harvard University Press

McKERN, W. C. 1929. *Archaeology of Tonga.* Honolulu, Bernice P. Bishop Museum Bulletin 60

McKIE, R. 1991. 'The island hopping gene.' *Geographical.* London, Royal Geographical Society, LXIII(11), 30–4

McKNIGHT, R. K. 1961. 'Mnemonics in preliterate Palau.' *Anthropological Working Papers.* Office of the Staff Anthropologist, Trust Territory of the Pacific Islands

McLENDON, S. AND LOWY, M. J. 1978. 'Eastern Pomo and Southeastern Pomo.' In *Handbook of North American Indians: California*, ed. R.F. Heizer, Washington, D.C., Smithsonian Institution vol. 8, 306–23

MEAD, S. M. n.d. *Stylistic analysis of stone figures from Northern Mo'orea.* Unpublished MS on file, Auckland University

– 1984 (ed.). *Te Maori: Maori Art from New Zealand Collections.* New York, Harry N. Abrams Inc. with the American Federation of Arts

MEAD, S., BIRKS, L., BIRKS, H. & SHAW, E. 1973. *The Lapita Style of Fiji and its Associations.* Wellington, Polynesian Society Memoir 38

MELLÉN-BLANCO, F. 1986. *Manuscritos y Documentos Españoles para la Historia de la Isla de Pascua.* Madrid, Centro de Estudios Historicos de Obras Publicas y Urbanismo (CEHOPU)

MESSAGER DE TAHITI 1867. *Mouvements du Port de Papeete.* Vendredi 31 Mai au Jeudi 27 Juin, inclus.

MÉTRAUX, A. 1940. *Ethnology of Easter Island.* Honolulu, Bernice P. Bishop Museum Bulletin 160

– 1957. *Easter Island.* London, A. Deutsch, Ltd

MILL, H. R. 1930. *The Record of the Royal Geographic Society 1830–1930.* London, The Royal Geographic Society

MILLERSTRÖM, S. 1992. 'Report on the Marquesas Islands rock art project.' In *The Journal of the Pacific Arts Association*, 6, 19–25.

MINNIS, P. E. 1985. *Social Adaptation to Food Stress.* Chicago and London, University of Chicago Press

MORENHOUT, J. A. 1937. *Voyage aux Îles de Grand Océan*, vol 2. Paris

MOORE, H. 1981. *Henry Moore at the British Museum.* London, British Museum Publications

MOOREHEAD, A. 1987. *The Fatal Impact: The Invasion of the South Pacific, 1767–1840.* New York, Harper and Row

MOSKO, M. S. 1992. 'Other messages, other missions; or Sahlins among the Melanesians.' In *Oceania* 63, 97–113

MULERT BARON, F. E. 1911. *Scheepsjournaal, Gehouden op het Schip Tienhoven Tijdens de Ontdekkingsreis van Mr. Jacob Roggeveen, 1721–1722.* Middleburg, Archief van het Zeeuwsch Genootschap

MULLOY, W. n.d. *List of Ahu with alignments.* Unpublished MS

– 1961. 'The ceremonial center of Vinapu.' In *Reports of the Norwegian Archaeological Expedition to Easter Island and the East Pacific, Vol. 1, Archaeology of Easter Island*, eds. T. Heyerdahl & E. N. Ferdon, Jr. Santa Fe, Monographs of the School of American Research and the Museum of New Mexico (24), 93–180

– 1968. *Preliminary Report of Archaeological Field Work February–July, 1968, Easter Island.* New York, International Fund for Monuments, Bulletin 1, Easter Island Committee

– 1970a. *Preliminary Report of the Restoration of Ahu Vai Uri, Easter Island.* New York, International Fund for Monuments, Bulletin 2, Easter Island Committee

– 1970b. 'A speculative reconstruction of techniques of carving, transporting and erecting Easter Island statues.' *Archaeology and Physical Anthropology in Oceania*, 5(1), 1–23

– 1973. *Preliminary Report of the Restoration of Ahu Huri a Urenga and Two Unnamed Ahu of Hanga Kio'e, Easter Island.* New York, International Fund for Monuments, Bulletin 3, Easter Island Committee

– 1975a. 'A solstice oriented ahu on Easter Island.' *Archaeology and Physical Anthropology in Oceania*, 10, 1–39

– 1975b. *Investigation and Restoration of the Ceremonial Center of Orongo, Easter Island.* New York, International Fund for Monuments, Bulletin 4, Easter Island Committee

MULLOY, W. & FIGUEROA, G. 1978. 'The A Kivi-Vai Teka Complex and its relationship to Easter Island architectural prehistory.' *Asian and Pacific Archaeology*, Series 8. University of Hawaii at Manoa

MURRILL, R. I. 1965. 'A study of cranial and postcranial material from Easter Island.' In *Reports of the Norwegian Archaeological Expedition to Easter Island and the East Pacific, Vol. 2: Miscellaneous Papers*, eds. T. Heyerdahl & E. N. Ferdon, Jr. Santa Fe, Monographs of the School of American Research and the Museum of New Mexico, 24(2), 253–327

– 1968. *Cranial and Postcranial Skeletal Remains from Easter Island.* Minneapolis, University of Minnesota Press

MUSÉES ROYAUX D'ART ET D'HISTOIRE 1990. *L'Île de Pâques: Une Énigme?* Brussels

MUSEO SOCIEDAD FONCK 1987. *Catálogo de la Colección Pascuense.* Viña del Mar, Chile

Navy List: *Topaze*, 31 S Frigate Corrected to 20 June 1868, PRO London

Newman, W. A. & Foster, B. A. 1983. 'The Rapanuian faunal district (Easter and Sala y Gomez): In search of ancient archipelagos.' *Bulletin of Marine Science*, 33, 633–44

Newton, D. 1987. 'The Pacific Islands.' In *The Pacific Islands, Africa and the Americas* eds D. Newton *et al*. New York, Metropolitan Museum of Art

– 1988. 'Reflections in bronze: Lapita and Dong-Son art in the Western Pacific.' In *Islands and Ancestors: Indigenous Styles of Southeast Asia*, eds. J. P. Barbier & D. Newton. New York, Metropolitan Museum of Art, 10–23

Newton, D., Jones, J. & Ezra, K. 1987. *The Pacific Islands, Africa and the Americas*. New York, Metropolitan Museum of Art

Nooy-Palm, H. 1979. *The Sa'Dan Toraja: A Study of their Life and Religion, Volume 1, Organization, Symbols and Beliefs*. Verhandelingen van het Koninklijk Institute voor Taal en Volkenkunde. The Hague, Moulton

Odhner, N. H. 1922. 'Mollusca from Juan Fernandez and Easter Island.' In *The Natural History of Juan Fernandez and Easter Island*, Volume 3, ed. C Skottsberg. Uppsala, Almquist and Wiksells, 219–54

Orliac, C. 1984. 'A propos d'un pilier de bois découvert à Papara: Détermination botanique et interprétation palethnologique.' *Bulletin de la Société des Etudes Océaniennes*, xix (228), 1661–6

– 1990a. 'Des arbres et des dieux, choix des matériaux de sculpture en Polynésie.' *Journal de la Société des Océanistes*, 90(1), 35–42

– 1990b. 'Sophora toromiro, one of the raw materials used by Pascuan carvers: Some examples in the collections of Musée de l'Homme.' In *State and Perspectives of Scientific Research in Easter Island Culture*, ed. H.-M. Esen-Baur. Frankfurt a.M., Courier Forschunginstitut Senckenberg 125

Osorio, C. & Cantuarias, V. 1989. 'Vertical distribution of Mollusks on the rocky intertidal of Easter Island.' *Pacific Science*, Honolulu, 43, 302–15

Owsley, D. W., Mires, A. M. & Gill, G. W. 1985. *Caries Frequency in Deciduous Dentitions of Protohistoric Easter Islanders*. Canberra, Australian National University, Bulletin of the Indo-Pacific Prehistory Association 4

– 1985. 'Carious lesions in permanent dentitions of protohistoric Easter Islanders.' *Journal of the Polynesian Society*, 94(4), 415–22

Palmer, J. L. 1869. 'Observations on the inhabitants and the antiquities of Easter Island.' *Journal of the Ethnological Society of London*, 1, 371–7

– 1870a. 'A visit to Easter Island, or Rapa Nui.' *Royal Geographical Society Proceedings*, 14, 108–19

– 1870b. 'A visit to Easter Island, or Rapa Nui, in 1868.' *Royal Geographical Society Journal*, 40, 167–81

– 1875. 'Davis or Easter Island.' In *Literary and Philosophical Society of Liverpool Proceedings*, 275–97

Parsons, C. T. 1978. J. Linton Palmer, Surgeon R.N. Royal Naval Hospital, Haslar, Gosport, Hants, REF. 503/22. Copy on file, RGS Archives, J. Linton Palmer

Paté, T. M. (tagata nu'u papa'i) 1986. *Relatos de la Isla de Pascua ('A'Amu o Rapa Nui)*. Santiago, Editorial Andrés Bello

Pavel, P. 1990. 'Reconstruction of the Transport of Moai.' In *State and Perspectives of Scientific Research in Easter Island Culture*, ed. H.-M. Esen-Baur. Frankfurt a.M., Courier Forschunginstitut Senckenberg 125, 141–4

Peacock, D. J. 1987. *Leo Boo of Belau: A Prince in London*. Honolulu, University of Hawaii Press

Peña, L. E. 1987. 'Consideraciones sobre la fauna de artrodos terrestres de la Islas Oceánicas Chilenas.' In *Islas Oceánicas Chilenas: Conocimiento Científico y Necesidades de las Investigaciones*, ed. J.C.Castilla. Valparaiso, Ediciones Universidad Católica de Chile, 217–23

Pennycuick, C. J. 1987. 'Flight of Seabirds.' In *Seabirds: Feeding Ecology and Role in Marine Ecosystems*, ed. J. P. Croxall. Cambridge, Cambridge University Press

Pereira Salas, E. 1947. *La musica de la Isla de Pascua*. Instituto de Investigaciones Musicales. Santiago, Universidad de Chile

Petrie, W. Flinders 1930. 'The building of a pyramid.' *Ancient Egypt*. British School of Archaeology in Egypt. London and New York, MacMillan and Co., Pt 11, 33–9

Phelps, S. 1975. *Art and Artifacts of the Pacific, Africa and the Americas: The James Hooper Collection*. London, Hutchinson

Pinart, A. L. n.d. [1870–85]. 'Notes and correspondence.' Z-Z 17, 24 vols. Bancroft Library, University of California, Berkeley

Pontius, A. A. 1969. 'Easter Island's stone giants: A neuropsychiatric view.' *Perceptual and Motor Skills* 28, 207–12

Porteous, J. D. 1981. *The Modernization of Easter Island*. Western Geographical Series, vol. 19. British Columbia, University of Victoria

Powell, W. A. 1899. 'Detailed report on Easter Island or Rapa Nui.' *Royal Geographical Society of Australasia, South Australian Branch, Proceedings*, 3, 138–42

Prospection Archéologique de la Vallée de la Papeita. n.d. [1986]. Punaauia, Tahiti, Département d'Archeologie du Centre Polynésien des Sciences Humaines 'Te Anavaharau'

Protzen, J.-P. 1985. 'Inca quarrying and stonecutting.' *Journal of the Society of Architectural Historians*, 44, (2), 161–82

– 1986. 'Inca stone masonry.' *Scientific American*. February, 94–103

Ramírez A., J. M. 1986. *Aproximacion Antropologica al Pasado de la Isla de Pascua. Catálogo de la Colleción Pascuense*. Viña del Mar, Chile, Museo Sociedad Fonck

Randall, J. E. & Cea, A. 1984. *Native names of Easter Island fishes, with comments on the origin of the Rapanui people*. Honolulu, Bernice P. Bishop Museum Occasional Papers, 25(12), 1–16

Rappaport, R. A. 1971. 'The sacred in human evolution.' *Annual Review of Ecology and Systemics*, 2, 23–4.

– 1979a. 'Aspects of man's influence on island ecosystems: Alteration and control.' In *Ecology, Meaning and Religion*. Berkeley, North Atlantic Books, 1–26

– 1979b. 'On cognized models.' In *Ecology, Meaning and Religion*. Berkeley, North Atlantic Books, 97–144

Rapu H., S. n.d. [1986]. 'Anakena.' Slide assisted lecture, UCLA

Rausing, G. 1979. 'Moving large blocks of stone in Pakistan.' *Antiquity*, liii (208), 143–4

Raven, H. C. 1926. 'The stone images and vats of central Celebes.' In *Natural History*, 26, 272–82

Recursos Pesqueros de Isla de Pascua 1988. Santiago, Biblioteca Instituto de Fomento Pesquero Corfo

Rehder, H. 1980. *The Marine Mollusks of Easter Island (Isla de Pascua) and Sala y Gomez*. Smithsonian Contributions to Zoology 289. Washington, Smithsonian Institution

Renfrew, C. 1974. 'Beyond a subsistence economy: the evolution of social organization in prehistoric Europe.' In C.B. Moore, ed., *Restructuring complex societies: an archaeological colloquium*. Supplement to the Bulletin of the American Schools of Oriental Research, Ann Arbor, Michigan, 20, 69–95

Révue Maritime et Coloniale, 1872. 'Untitled' in no. xxxv, 536–8

Riesenfeld, A. 1950. *The Megalithic Culture of Melanesia*. Leiden, E. J. Brill

Rivers, W. H. K. 1920. 'The statues of Easter Island.' *Folk-Lore*, 31, 294–306

Röder, J. von 1944–49. 'Bilder zum megalithentransport.' *Paideuna*, 3, 84–7

Roe, M. (ed.) 1967. *The Journal and Letters of Captain Charles Bishop on the North-West Coast of America, in the Pacific and in New South Wales, 1794–1799*. Cambridge, Cambridge University Press for the Hakluyt Society

Rolett, B. V. 1993. 'Marquesan prehistory and the origins of East Polynesian culture.' *Journal de la Société des Océanistes* 96, (1), 29–47.

Rotberg, R. I. & T. K. Rabb (eds.) 1983. *Hunger and History*. Cambridge, Cambridge University Press.

Roussel, R. P. H. 1926. *Annales de la Congregation Sacrés-Coeurs de la Je'sus et de Marie*. Braine-le-Comte, Belgium, 5(32), 355–499

Routledge, K. S. [Mrs Scoresby] n.d. *Unpublished field notes*. London, Royal Geographical Society

– 1917. 'The bird cult of Easter Island.' *Folk-Lore*, 28(4), 338–55

– 1919. *The Mystery of Easter Island*. London, Sifton, Praed and Co.

– 1920. 'Survey of the village and carved rocks of Orongo, Easter Island, by the Mana Expedition.' *The Journal of the Royal Anthropological Institute of Great Britain and Ireland*, 50, 425–51

– 1921. 'The mystery of Easter Island.' *National Geographic Magazine*, 60(6), 628–48

– n.d. [1925]. Last Will. Office copy without impressed court seal on file, Dept. of Ethnography, British Museum

R. S. [Richard Sainthill] 1870. 'Rapa Nui or Easter Island.' *Macmillan's Magazine*, 21

Sahlins, M. 1958. 'Esoteric Efflorescence in Easter Island.' *American Anthropologist*, 57, 1045–52

– 1985. *Islands of History*. Chicago and London, The University of Chicago Press

Salles, G. 1927. *Une Sculpture de L'Île de Pâques, à Paris*. Paris, Cahiers d'Art

Sanday, P. R. 1986. *Divine Hunger. Cannibalism as a Cultural System*. Cambridge, Cambridge University Press.

Sanjek, R. (ed.) 1990. *Fieldnotes: The Makings of Anthropology*. Ithaca and London, Cornell University Press

SANTELICES, B. & ABBOTT, I. A. 1988. 'Geographic and marine isolation: An assessment of the marine algae of Easter Island.' *Pacific Science*, 41, 1–20

SCHAEFER, C. A. & GORSUCH, R. L. 1993. 'Situational and personal variations in religious coping.' *Journal for the Scientific Study of Religion* 32, (2), 136–47

SCHLATTER, R. P. 1987. 'Conocimiento y situación de la ornitofauna en las Islas Oceánicas Chilenas.' In *Islas Oceánicas Chilenas: Conocimiento Cientifico y Necesidades de las Investigaciones*, eds. J. C. Castilla and D. Oliva. Valparaiso, Ediciones Universidad Catica de Chile, 271–85

SCHMOOKLER, A. B. 1984. *The Parable of the Tribes: The Problem of Power in Social Evolution*. Boston, Houghton Mifflin Co.

SCHUSTER, C. 1952. 'V-shaped chest markings: Distribution of a design-motive in and around the Pacific.' *Anthropos*, 47, (12), 99–118

SEAVER, J. T. 1988. *An ethnology of woodcarving: Continuity in cultural transformations on Easter Island*. Ph.D. dissertation, UCLA

– 1993. '"Traditional" Rapa Nui designs on statues of contemporary Christian saints.' In *Artistic Heritage in a Changing Pacific*, eds P. J. C. Dark and R. G. Rose. Honolulu, University of Hawaii Press, 35–90

SHARP, A. (ed.) 1970. *The Journal of Jacob Roggeveen*. Oxford, Clarendon Press

SHARP, N. 1988. 'Style and substance. A reconsideration of the Lapita decorative system.' In *Archaeology of the Lapita Cultural Complex: A Critical Review*, eds. P. V. Kirch & T. L. Hunt. Seattle, Thomas Burke Memorial Washington State Museum Research Report No. 5, 61–81

SHAW, L. C. n.d. [1986]. *The investigation of nine south coast caves on Easter Island*. MS on file with the author

SHILLER, Z. & GWO, Y.-R. 1991. 'Dynamic motion planning of vehicles.' *IEEE Transactions on Robotics and Automation*, 7(2), 241–9

SHORE, B. 1982. *Sala'ilua, A Samoan Mystery*. New York, Columbia University Press

SIMMONS, D. R. 1984. 'Tribal art styles.' In *Te Maori: Maori Art from New Zealand Collections*, ed. S. M. Mead. New York, Harry Abrams, Inc. with The American Federation of Arts, 76–108

SINOTO, Y. 1966. 'A tentative prehistoric cultural sequence in the northern Marquesas Islands, French Polynesia.' *Journal of the Polynesian Society*, 75, 286–303

– 1970. 'An archaeologically based assessment of the Marquesas Islands as a dispersal center in East Polynesia.' In *Studies of Oceanic Culture History*, eds. R. C. Green & M. Kelly. Honolulu, Pacific Anthropological Records, 11, 105–32

– 1979. 'The Marquesas.' In *Prehistory of Polynesia*, ed. J. D. Jennings. Cambridge, Harvard University Press

SKINNER, H. D. 1922. 'The Easter Island figures.' *Folk-Lore*, 33, 296–9

– 1955. 'Easter Island masonry.' *Journal of the Polynesian Society*, 64, 292–4

– 1958. 'Some recent publications relating to Easter Island culture and its probable history.' *Journal of the Polynesian Society*, 67(3), 248–51

– 1967. *Cylindrical Headdresses in the Pacific Region*. Honolulu, Bernice P. Bishop Museum Special Publication

– 1974. *Comparatively Speaking: Studies in Pacific Material Culture 1921–1972*. Dunedin, University of Otago Press

SKJØLSVOLD, A. 1961a. 'The stone statues and quarries of Rano Raraku.' In *Reports of the Norwegian Archaeological Expedition to Easter Island and the East Pacific, Vol. 1, Archaeology of Easter Island*, eds. T. Heyerdahl & E. N. Ferdon, Jr. Santa Fe, Monographs of the School of American Research and the Museum of New Mexico (24), 339–80

– 1961b. 'House foundations (Hare Paenga) in Rano Raraku.' In *Reports of the Norwegian Archaeological Expedition to Easter Island and the East Pacific, Vol. 1, Archaeology of Easter Island*, eds. T. Heyerdahl & E. N. Ferdon, Jr. Santa Fe, Monographs of the School of American Research and the Museum of New Mexico (24), 291–4

– 1961c. 'Dwellings of Hotu Matu'a.' In *Reports of the Norwegian Archaeological Expedition to Easter Island and the East Pacific, Vol I, Archaeology of Easter Island*, eds. T. Heyerdahl and E.N. Ferdon, Jr., Santa Fe, Monographs of the School of American Research and the Museum of New Mexico (24), 273–6

– 1965. 'The ceremonial enclosure of Te Rae with brief notes on additional marae.' In *Reports of the Norwegian Archaeological Expedition to Easter Island and the East Pacific, Vol. 2, Miscellaneous Papers*, eds. T. Heyerdahl & E. N. Ferdon, Jr. Santa Fe, Monographs of the School of American Research and the Museum of New Mexico (24), 97–107

SKJØLSVOLD, A. & FIGUEROA G.-H., G. 1989. 'An attempt to date a unique, kneeling statue in Rano Raraku, Easter Island.' In *Kon-Tiki Museum Occasional Papers*, ed. A. Skjølsvold. Oslo, Kon-Tiki Museum, 1, 7–35

SKOTTSBERG, C. 1956. *The Natural History of Juan Fernández and Easter Island, Volume 1*. Uppsala, Almquist and Wiksells

SMITH, C. S. 1961a. 'A temporal sequence derived from certain *ahu*.' In *Reports of the Norwegian Archaeological Expedition to Easter Island and the East Pacific, vol 1, Archaeology of Easter Island*, eds T. Heyerdahl and E. N. Ferdon jr. Santa Fe, Monographs of the School of American Research and the Museum of New Mexico (24), 181–218

– 1961b. 'Two habitation canes.' In *Reports* as above, (24), 257–71

– 1961c. 'The Poike Ditch.' In *Reports* as above, (24), 385–92

SMITH, J. A., 1870. 'Commentary.' *Proceedings of the Society of Antiquaries of Scotland*, VIII, 321–3

SMITH, R. J. 1990. 'Hearing voices, joining the chorus: Appropriating someone else's fieldnotes.' In *Fieldnotes: The Making of Anthropology*, ed. R. Sanjek. Ithaca and London, Cornell University Press

SPARRMAN, A. 1953. *A Voyage Around the World*. London, Robert Hale

SPRIGGS, M. 1984. 'The Lapita cultural complex: Origins, distribution, contemporaries, and successors.' In *Journal of Pacific History*, 19, 202–23

– 1990. 'The changing face of Lapita: Transformation of a design.' In *Lapita Design, Form and Composition: Proceedings of the Lapita Design Workshop, Canberra, Australia, Dec. 1988*, ed. M. Spriggs. Canberra, Research School of Pacific Studies, Australian National University, Occasional Papers in Prehistory no. 19

SPRIGGS, M. & ANDERSON, A. 1993. 'Late colonization of East Polynesia.' *Antiquity*. 67, 200–17

SPRIGGS, M. AND CHIPPENDALE, C. (eds). 1989. 'Early settlement of Island Southeast Asia and the Western Pacific.' Special section *Antiquity* 63, 623–6

STEADMAN, D. W. 1989. 'Extinction of birds in Eastern Polynesia: A review of the record, and comparisons with other Pacific island groups.' *Journal of Archaeological Science*, 16, 177–205

– n.d. [in press]. 'Extinction and biogeography of birds from Easter island.' *Proceedings of the National Academy of Sciences USA*

STEADMAN, D. W., CRISTINO F., C. & VARGAS C., P. n.d. [in press]. 'Stratigraphy, chronology, and cultural context of an early faunal assemblage from Easter Island.' *Asian Perspectives*

STEADMAN, D. W. & KIRCH. P. V. 1990. 'Prehistoric extinction of birds on Mangaia, Cook Islands, Polynesia.' *Proceedings of the National Academy of Sciences USA*, 87, 9605–9

STEPHEN-CHAUVET, DR. 1945. *La Isla de Pascua y Sus Misterios*. Santiago de Chile, Zig-Zag

STEVENSON, C. M. 1984. *Corporate descent group structure in Easter Island prehistory*. Ph.D. dissertation, The Pennsylvania State University

– 1986. 'The socio-political structure of the southern coastal area of Easter Island.' In *Island Societies: Archaeological Approaches to Evaluation and Transformation*, ed. P. V. Kirch. Cambridge, Cambridge University Press

STEVENSON, C. M. & CRISTINO F., C. 1986. 'Residential settlement history of Rapa Nui south coastal plain.' *Journal of New World Archaeology*, 7, 29–38

STEVENSON, C. M., SHAW, L. C. & C. CRISTINO F. 1988. 'Obsidian procurement and consumption on Easter Island.' In *First International Congress, Easter Island and East Polynesia, 1984, Vol. 1, Archaeology*, eds. C., Cristino F. *et al.* Santiago, Universidad de Chile, 83–94

STIMSON, J. F. 1933. *Tuamotuan Religion*. Honolulu, Bernice P. Bishop Museum Bulletin 103

STOKES, J. F. G. 1991. *Heiau of the Island of Hawaii*, ed. T. Dye. Honolulu, Bernice P. Bishop Museum

STOLPE, H. 1899. 'Über die Tatowirung der Oster-Insulaner.' In *Abhandlungen und Berichete des Königlisches, Zoologische und Antropologisch-Ethnographisches Museum zu Dresden*, 6, 1–13

SUGGS, R. C. 1960. *The Island Civilizations of Polynesia*. New York, New American Library

SYKES, W. R. & GODLEY, E. J. 1968. 'Transoceanic dispersal of *Sophora* and other genera.' *Nature*, 218, 495

TEILHET, J. H. 1979. 'The equivocal nature of a masking tradition in Polynesia.' In *Exploring the Visual Arts of Oceania: Australia, Melanesia and Polynesia*, ed. S. M. Mead. Honolulu, University of Hawaii Press

TELLEFSEN, O. 1970. 'A new theory of pyramid building.' *Natural History*, 9, 10–23

TERRELL, J. 1986. *Prehistory of the Pacific Islands*. Cambridge, C.U.P.

TERRELL, J. 1989. 'Commentary: What Lapita is and what it isn't.' In *Early settlement of Island Southeast Asia and the Western Pacific*. eds M. Spriggs and C. Chippendale, Special section *Antiquity* 63, 623–6

THOMSON, W. S. 1891. 'Te Pito te Henua, or Easter Island.' In *Report of the U.S. National Museum for the Year Ending 30 June, 1889*. Washington D.C., Smithsonian Institution

– 1980. 'Te Pito te Henua o Isla de Pascua' trans. de H. Fuentes. In *Estudios Sobre la Isla de Pascua*, eds. C. Cristino F. *et al*. Santiago, Anales y Ediciones de la Universidad de Chile, 31–160

THORP, R. S. & O. WILLIAMS 1991. 'The myth of long-distance mega-lithic transport.' *Antiquity* 65, 64–73

TILLEY, C. 1984. 'Ideology and the legitimation of power in the middle neolithic of southern Sweden.' In *Ideology*, eds. D. Miller & C. Tilley. Cambridge, Cambridge University Press, 111–46

Topaze 1868. *Log*. PRO London, ADM 53–9414

TROTTA, G. 1985. 'The ancient mysteries of Easter Island.' In *Travel and Leisure* March, 183–8

TROTTER, M. 1974. 'Prehistory of the southern Cook Islands.' Christchurch, *Canterbury Museum Bulletin* no. 6

TUMARKIN, D. D. & FEDOROVA, I. K. 1990. 'Nikolai Miklouho-Maclay and Easter Island.' *Pacific Studies*, 13(2), 103–17

TUPPER, M. F. 1869. 'The mystery of Easter Island.' *The Builder*, London, 20 November, 930–31

VALERI, V. 1985. *Kinship and Sacrifice: Ritual and Society in Ancient Hawaii*. Chicago, University of Chicago Press

VAN TILBURG, J. n.d. [1984]. 'Three unusual stone figures from Easter Island.' Paper read, 4th Annual Meeting of the So. Ca. Colloquium on the Arts of Africa, Oceania and Native America. UCLA Museum of Cultural History, 5 May 1984

– 1984. 'Easter Island: New pieces in an ancient puzzle.' *Archaeology*, July/August, 58–61

– 1986a. 'Power and symbol: The stylistic analysis of Easter Island monolithic sculpture.' Ph.D. dissertation, UCLA Institute of Archaeology

– 1986b. 'Red scoria on Easter Island: Sculpture, artifacts and architecture.' *Journal of New World Archaeology*, 7(1), 1–28

– 1987a. 'Larger than life: The form and function of Easter Island monolithic sculpture.' *Musées Royaux d'Art et d'Histoire Bulletin*, 58(2), 111–30

– 1987b. 'Symbolic archaeology on Easter Island.' *Archaeology*, 40(2), 26–33

– 1988. 'Stylistic variation of dorsal design on Easter Island statues.' In *Clava* ed. J. M. Ramirez, Viña del Mar, Museo Sociedad Fonct. 4, 95–108

– n.d. [1989]. 'Easter Island statue project: 1989 field season preliminary report.' MS on file, National Geographic Society

– 1990. 'Respect for Rapa Nui: Exhibition and conservation of Easter Island stone statues.' *Antiquity*, 64, 249–58

– n.d. [1991]. 'Easter Island statue project.' Report on file, Consejo de Monumentos, Santiago de Chile

– 1991. *Anthropomorphic Stone Monoliths on the Islands of Oreor and Babeldaob, Republic of Belau (Palau)*, *Micronesia*. Honolulu, Bernice P. Bishop Museum Occasional Papers 31, 3–62

– 1992a. 'HMS *Topaze* on Easter Island: Hoa Hakananai'a and Five Other Museum Sculptures in Archaeological Context.' London, British Museum Press *Occasional Paper* 73.

– 1992b. 'Stone Sentinels.' In *Mysteries of Mankind*. Washington, D.C., National Geographic Society Special Publications, 70–91

– 1993a. 'The use of photogrammetry, laser scan and computer assisted drafting to define relationships between Easter Island statue morphology, transport technology and social organization.' In *The Evolution and Organisation of Prehistoric Society in Polynesia*, eds M. W. Graves and R. C. Green. New Zealand Archaeological Association Monograph, 19, 87–102

– 1993b. 'First Heyerdahl, Now Hollywood.' *Archaeology*, 46 (4), 72

VAN TILBURG, J. & LEE, G. 1987. 'Symbolic stratigraphy: Rock art and the monolithic statues of Easter Island.' *World Archaeology*, 19(2), 133–45

VAN TILBURG, J. & VARGAS C., P. n.d. [1988]. 'Transition and trans formation of Easter Island sculpture: Recent archaeological evidence.' Zagreb, Yugoslavia, Paper presented, 12th International Congress of Anthropological and Ethnological Sciences

VARGAS C., P. 1988. 'Easter Island statue type, part one: The Moai as archaeological artifact.' In *First International Congress, Easter Island and East Polynesia, 1984, Vol. 1, Archaeology*, eds. C. Cristino F. *et al*. Santiago, Universidad de Chile, 133–49

– 1993. 'The Easter Island prehistoric sequence and developments in its settlement patterns.' In *The Evolution and Organisation of Prehistoric Society in Polynesia*, eds M. W. Graves & R. C. Green. Auckland, New Zealand Archaeological Monograph 19, 103–5

VARGAS C., P., GONZALEZ N., L., BUDD P., R. & IZAURIETA S., R. 1990. *Estudios del Asentamiento en Isla de Pascua: Prospección Arqueológica en la Península del Poike y Sector de Mahatua*. Santiago, Universidad de Chile

VÉLAIN, C. 1879. 'Les roches volcaniques de l'île de Pâques (Rapa-Nui).' *Bulletin de la Société Géologique de France*. Paris, 7, 415–25

VITA-FINZI, C. 1978. *Archaeological Sites in their Setting*. London, Thames and Hudson

VON BONIN, G. 1931. 'A contribution to the craniology of the Easter Islanders.' *Biometrica*, London, 23, 249–70

VON FÜRER-HAIMENDORF, C. 1946. *The Naked Nagas: Headhunters of Assam in Peace and War*. Calcutta, Thacker, Spink and Co., Ltd

VON KOTZEBUE, O. 1821. *Voyage of Discovery in the South Seas and to Behring's Straits*. London, Sir Richard Phillips Co.

WAGNER, R. 1981. *The Invention of Culture*. Chicago and London, The University of Chicago Press

WAITE, D. 1993. 'Three images from Mangareva: A reappraisal.' In *Artistic Heritage in a Changing Pacific*, eds P. J. C. Dark & R. G. Rose. Honolulu, University of Hawaii, 106–15

WALLACE, W. J. 1978. 'Southern Valley Yokuts.' In *Handbook of North American Indians: California*, ed. R.F. Heizer, Washington, D.C., Smithsonian Institution vol. 8, 448–61

– 1986. *Symbols that Stand for Themselves*. Chicago and London, University of Chicago Press

WHEELER, SIR M. 1954. *Archaeology From the Earth*. Oxford, Clarendon Press

WILKES, C. 1845. *Narrative of the U.S. Exploring Expedition During the Years 1838–42*. 5 vols. and atlas. Philadelphia, Lea and Blanchard

WILLIAMS, S. L. n.d. [1984]. 'Analysis of Easter Island materials using the Energy Dispersive X-Ray Spectrometer (EDS).' In J. Van Tilburg, *Easter Island statuary: The moai documentation project, 1984 field season*, MS on file, UCLA Rock Art Archive

WILLIAMSON, R. W. 1924. *The Social and Political Systems of Central Polynesia*, 3 vols. Cambridge, Cambridge University Press

– 1933. *Religious and Cosmic Beliefs of Central Polynesia*, 3 vols. Cambridge, Cambridge University Press

YEN, D. E. 1974. *The Sweet Potato and Oceania: An Essay in Ethnobotany*. Honolulu, Bernice P. Bishop Museum Bulletin 236

YOUNG, J. L. 1904. 'Remarks on phallic stones from Rapanui.' Honolulu, Bernice P. Bishop Museum *Occasional Papers* vol. 2, 25, 31

YOUNG, L. B. 1991. 'Easter Island: Scary Parable.' *World Monitor*, August, 40–5

ZUHMBOHM, R. P. G. 1868. Lettre du R. P. Gaspard Zuhmbohm au TRP Rouchouze, Rapa Nui, 10 April 1868. Rome, Archives of the Fathers of the Sacred Hearts (Picpus), 213

– 1879. Lettres du R. P. Gaspard Zuhmbohm au directeur des annales sur la mission de L'Île de Pâques. *Annales de la Congrégation des Sacrés-Cœurs de Jésus et de Marie*, vol. 5. Paris

– 1880. Lettres du R P Gaspard Zuhmbohm au directeur des annales sur la mission de L'Île de Pâques. *Annales de la Congrégation des Sacrés-Cœurs de Jésus et de Marie*, vol. 6. Paris

Index